Eugene O'Neill

A DESCRIPTIVE BIBLIOGRAPHY

Jennifer McCabe Atkinson

UNIVERSITY OF
PITTSBURGH PRESS
1974

Library of Congress Cataloging in Publication Data

Atkinson, Jennifer McCabe, birth date
Eugene O'Neill: a descriptive bibliography.

(Pittsburgh series in bibliography)
1. O'Neill, Eugene Gladstone, 1888–1953–
Bibliography. I. Series.
Z8644.5.A74 016.812'5'2 73-13312
ISBN 0-8229-3279-2

Pittsburgh Series in Bibliography

Pittsburgh Series in Bibliography

HART CRANE: A DESCRIPTIVE BIBLIOGRAPHY
Joseph Schwartz and Robert C. Schweik

F. SCOTT FITZGERALD:
A DESCRIPTIVE BIBLIOGRAPHY
Matthew J. Bruccoli

WALLACE STEVENS: A DESCRIPTIVE BIBLIOGRAPHY
J. M. Edelstein

EUGENE O'NEILL: A DESCRIPTIVE BIBLIOGRAPHY
Jennifer McCabe Atkinson

© Arnold Newman

EUGENE O'NEILL

In memory of Frank M. Durham—

actor, director, teacher, scholar, and friend

Contents

Acknowledgments		xi
Introduction		xiii
List of Abbreviations		xxii
A.	Works by Eugene O'Neill	1
	AA. Supplement: Published Acting Scripts	318
B.	Contributions to Books and Pamphlets	325
C.	First Appearances in Newspapers, Periodicals, or Occasional Publications	341
D.	Blurbs	357
E.	Material Quoted in Catalogues	363
F.	Plays in Collections and Anthologies	369
Appendix. Adaptations of Works by Eugene O'Neill		395
Index		397

Acknowledgments

COMPILING any bibliography requires the work and help of many people; one person can only oversee, organize, and arrange the results of all the labor. I wish to thank the following librarians: Beverly Brooks, Inter-Library Loans Librarian, and John Hostetter, Curator of Rare Books, McKissick Library, University of South Carolina; Mrs. Anne Whelpley of Beinecke Library, Yale University; Dean H. Keller, Curator of Special Collections, Kent State University; Janet B. Keller, Reference Librarian, Public Library of New London, Connecticut. I would also like to thank Rhoda Sirlin of Liveright Publishing Company, Robert K. Spencer of Appleton-Century-Crofts, and Peter L. Wilkie of Yale University Press. For their help in researching certain information, I would like to thank the following students—Amy Boyd, Linda Darby, and I. S. Skelton. For the enormous task of typing this material, my thanks go to Mrs. Marie Willing and especially to Mrs. Janet Abrahamsen.

I particularly wish to express my appreciation for help and advice to the Editorial Board of the Pittsburgh Series in Bibliography—Fredson Bowers, William R. Cagle, and Charles W. Mann.

I have a special debt to Matthew J. Bruccoli, General Editor, for his advice and encouragement throughout my work on this project. He often helped to clear my clouded mind.

An O'Neill scholar cannot do any work without the generous assistance of Donald Gallup, Curator of American Literature, Beinecke Library, Yale University. Dr. Gallup's familiarity with the O'Neill archive at Yale and his special knowledge derived from close acquaintance with the late Carlotta Monterey O'Neill make him an unparalleled source.

I am also grateful to Mrs. Saxe Commins, who kindly allowed me to reprint the notes written by her husband for the Wilderness Edition of the plays of O'Neill. To Betty Hudgens, who gave up vacation time to help with research, who helped in collecting the O'Neill volumes described here, and who shares my respect for Eugene O'Neill, my special thanks.

This book is dedicated to the professor who most opened the doors of research in American drama for me.

Introduction

THERE has not been a descriptive bibliography of the works of Eugene O'Neill since 1931, when Ralph Sanborn and Barrett H. Clark published *A Bibliography of the Works of Eugene O'Neill* (New York: Random House, 1931).[1] At that time, O'Neill had published thirty-one plays. Between 1931 and his death in 1953, O'Neill wrote eight more plays, nearly completed a ninth, and worked on fragments or drafts of eleven others. During this same time, he saw ten more of his plays published. Eight others have been published posthumously. The absence of any bibliographical record of O'Neill's work for more than forty years presents a scholarly void in need of being filled. While biographies and critical interpretations have flowed from the pens of friends, critics, and scholars, no one has attempted to bring together a *descriptive* record of O'Neill's complete published works. This book is a beginning.

In 1943 O'Neill destroyed two incomplete plays and a draft for another play, and in 1953 he and his wife Carlotta destroyed the manuscripts of the drafts or fragments of six more (all unpublished and unproduced). O'Neill's health—he suffered from an unidentified nervous disorder—had been deteriorating since the early 1940s, preventing work during the last years of his life, and he did

---

1. Throughout my bibliography, this work will be referred to as Sanborn and Clark.

not want the unfinished manuscripts completed by another hand.

Limiting this bibliography to Eugene O'Neill's published work, I have not dealt with any of the unpublished early works which he left untouched. Nor have I tried to deal with any of the later manuscript material he chose to destroy.[2] This bibliography aims to provide an inventory of the prodigious amount of material published by O'Neill. Works about him have not been included unless they quote any of his previously unpublished material (see Section B).[3]

A bibliography for a playwright presents special problems. Sometimes a play is published separately; sometimes the author or his publisher collects several plays into a single volume; sometimes a play appears for the first time in an anthology. There are bound volumes of the plays offered for sale to the general reading public and there are editions in wrappers sold to theatre organizations for use in producing the play. Also, scripts are sometimes duplicated through a mimeographing or photocopying process. These scripts are not for sale and usually serve only private purposes (classroom use, cuttings by actors preparing scenes for class or reading performances). These are not *published* scripts, and they are not duplicated in order to be sold. Therefore, such copies of the play have not been given the significance of a published play for sale. The one mimeographed script that has been included is described in a note in Section A (see A 28-I-1.a, *Marco Millions*).

Thus, I was faced with the dilemma of how to

2. For a detailed critical work on every O'Neill play—published, unpublished, and fragmentary—see Travis Bogard, *Contour in Time* (New York: Oxford University Press, 1972).

3. For a useful bibliography of works about O'Neill, see Jordan Y. Miller, *Eugene O'Neill and His Critics* (Hamden, Connecticut: Archon Books, 1962).

arrange this bibliography to aid at the same time both the person looking for information about a particular play and the person interested in the published books. The best solution turned out to be an approach which deals with each individual play but also encompasses the books.

SECTIONS OF THE BOOK

Section A includes all plays, broadsides, or special publications by O'Neill and describes fully all first printings of American first editions of O'Neill's plays. It also includes full descriptions of some important later printings such as limited printings of the plays. First printings of English first editions are described in less detail.

The Code for Section A

I have given each play—one-act plays, full-length plays, as well as two nondramatic items important enough to rank with the plays—an opus number. The opus number is expressed as an arabic numeral. For example: A 4 is "Fog," A 21 is *Anna Christie,* and A 42 is *Long Day's Journey Into Night.* Each book publication of that particular play has a roman numeral; each edition of the book has an arabic number; each printing of a particular edition has a lower-case letter of the alphabet. Thus, A 15-VII-1.c represents: 15 = *The Emperor Jones,* VII = the seventh publication of the play, 1 = the first edition of the particular book, c = the third printing of that edition. To distinguish them from American publications, English publications have an "E" added to the code. Thus, A 30-EI-1.a represents: 30 = *Strange Interlude,* EI = first English publication, 1 = first edition of the particular book, a = first printing of that edition.

In only two instances does the code vary. There was a special publication of excerpts from *Strange*

Interlude used in an attempt to halt performances of the play in Boston. I have given this unique pamphlet an abridged entry in the A section and coded it A 30-S-1. A broadside of O'Neill's inscription to Carlotta O'Neill on the final manuscript of *Mourning Becomes Electra* is the other special publication; it has been coded A 32-S-1.

The code is designed to enable the reader to select any particular O'Neill play and trace its publishing history—except for play scripts for sale, which have been treated in a special section and are not included with books of the plays.

Section AA lists in alphabetical order published acting scripts which have been or are for sale. These are published by the three major acting-script publishing houses (Samuel French, Baker's Plays, and Dramatists Play Service) for purchase by persons interested in mounting a production of a play. Although anyone can order copies of these scripts for individual use, a group wanting to produce the play must purchase scripts and pay royalties through one of these publishing firms. Thus, these acting editions of the plays serve a different purpose than the published book versions. Acting scripts often vary markedly from book editions of a play—texts are sometimes cut and tailored to production requirements; these scripts often include production information or suggestions (for example, prop lists, lighting plots, or set designs) not in book editions. The fact that these scripts are published by French, Baker, or Dramatists Play Service, but with the copyright still held by the original publisher (Boni & Liveright, Random House, etc.), and without any dating by the script-publishing house, causes confusion. Difficulty in determining exactly where these play scripts fit in the chronology of the publication history of a play was one of the reasons for grouping play scripts into a special section. Information on the publication of the play scripts is very limited and unclear.[4] Thus I have looked at plays published in book form for the reading public and play scripts for sale for performing groups as apples and oranges—equal but different.

Occasionally the script-publishing house will use the paperback edition put out by the book publisher for its acting edition. For example, there is no separate acting edition of *Long Day's Journey Into Night* or *A Touch of the Poet;* the Yale paperback editions of these plays are sold as the acting editions. These paperbacks are properly included in the publishing history of the book editions of the play and have not been grouped in Section AA with the acting editions.

Section B contains O'Neill material appearing for the first time in books by other authors—material such as letters, interviews, or conversations quoting O'Neill, or a contribution made by O'Neill to the other author's work. Only books are included in this section, which is arranged chronologically.

Section C lists chronologically material by O'Neill published in newspapers, periodicals, and occasional publications (theatre playbills). Some material either preceded book publication or was never published in book form. Included here are plays, poems, essays, a short story, letters, interviews, and conversations.

Section D includes promotional blurbs by O'Neill on works by other authors which appear either on

---

4. The records of the major acting-script publishing houses have not been searched. Correspondence has not produced sufficient information, and the Library of Congress Copyright Office often does not have any information on these script publications.

dust jackets or in advertisements. Because they are difficult to locate, the blurbs have been quoted in full. They are ordered chronologically.

Section E contains O'Neill material quoted in auction or bookdealer catalogues, a neglected area of first publication of an author's words. The material includes inscriptions and letters by O'Neill. The catalogues are listed chronologically, with undated ones at the end. Title pages appear in condensed quasi-facsimile form. Because of the difficulty in locating these catalogues, the O'Neill material is quoted in full.

Section F catalogues O'Neill's plays in collections and anthologies. It does not include first book appearances for these plays, since such an occurrence would appear in Section A with the history of a play's publication. This section lists those collections or anthologies edited by someone other than O'Neill which include a play by O'Neill either in summary, in part, or in total. The purpose of this section is to give the student or scholar some idea of the vastness of O'Neill's career as well as the relative popularity of the individual plays. The plays are given in alphabetical order; the collections or anthologies are listed chronologically under the individual play title.

The *Appendix* contains adaptations of O'Neill's plays by other writers for other media.

TERMS AND METHODS[5]

Edition. All the copies of a book printed from a single setting of type, including all printings made from standing type, from plates, or by photo offset. When I have been able to get the information, I

5. These terms are used as defined by Matthew J. Bruccoli in his *F. Scott Fitzgerald: A Descriptive Bibliography* (Pittsburgh: University of Pittsburgh Press, 1972).

have stated whether the edition was printed from standing type or plates.

Printing. All the copies of a book printed from one run of the press, without removing the plates from the press. Each time the presses are run, a printing results.

Issue. Issues occur when there is an alteration affecting the conditions of publication or distribution to some copies of a given printing. Issues normally take place after initial publication of the book, and they usually result in alterations to the title page or copyright page.

Although Sanborn and Clark refer to "issues" of *The Moon of the Caribbees and Six Other Plays of the Sea, Beyond the Horizon,* and *The Emperor Jones,* their use of the term is inexact. The differences occurring in these volumes are binding variants, not changes made to the plates during a printing. An instance of a true issue in O'Neill's work occurred in *"Children of the Sea" and Three Other Unpublished Plays by Eugene O'Neill* (A 48) and involved the addition of the colophon and statement of limitation for two hundred copies.

State. States occur when there is an alteration which does not affect the conditions of issue to some copies of a given printing, that is, a stop-press correction or cancellation of leaves. These alterations take place within a printing and normally are prepublication changes. I have discovered no states in O'Neill's work.

Entries for American first printings are described fully—pagination, collation, contents, typography and paper, binding, dust jacket, and/or slipcase. Whenever possible, printing and publishing information has been included.[6] Unnumbered pages

---

6. I have not been able personally to search the records of any of O'Neill's publishers—Frank Shay, Stewart Kidd, Boni & Liveright, Liveright, Random House, and Yale University Press

are bracketed in the pagination rubric, but this distinction is not repeated in the contents rubric.

The form for entries for English first printings is abridged. I have found no instance in which the first printing of an English first edition was the initial publication of a play. An area lacking detailed information is that regarding the printing and publication of English editions. In this shorter form, typeface and size are omitted; printing and publishing rubrics are sometimes omitted. No rubric means no information available.

Binding cloth distinctions are based on a system devised by book-cloth manufacturers. The designations are used by Jacob Blanck, ed., *Bibliography of American Literature* (New Haven, Yale University Press, 1955–). Illustrations of these cloth grains may be seen in any volume of the *BAL*.

Printing on the spines of bindings and dust jackets is horizontal unless otherwise specified.

Ink on title pages and dust jackets is always black unless another color is indicated. The color designation remains until a change is specified. Color descriptions have been kept as simple as possible. Type style is always roman unless noted otherwise.

Dates in brackets do not appear on title pages. They are taken from copyright pages or some other source of publication information.

For location symbols see the list of abbreviations.

The dates for books located in the British Museum are designated as *deposit-stamp* to signify the date

---

in America; Jonathan Cape in England. Some of the records have disappeared; some are inaccessible. Nevertheless, until as many records as possible can be recovered and searched, the printing and publishing information will be slim. When I have been unable to locate printing or publishing information, the rubrics have been omitted. I did receive cooperation from the Liveright Publishing Company and Yale University Press. Both publishers provided helpful information through correspondence.

stamped in the book, not the date appearing in the deposit ledger.

The reader will see that in this volume not enough textual collating has been done, not enough textual notes have been written. During my collecting and researching for this bibliography, I became intensely aware of the prodigious amount of textual work that needed to be done. With manuscript and galley proof material at Yale, Princeton, Harvard, and Dartmouth, with newspaper and periodical publication occasionally preceding book publication of a play, with possible alterations in the American and English editions, and most of all with the problems presented by the published acting scripts, a choice had to be made between embarking on a career of O'Neill textual scholarship or trying to establish a foundation for a record of his published work. The contribution which seemed to have the greatest long-range benefits was the descriptive bibliography. By preparing a record of O'Neill's published work, I could offer the most help to textual scholars. Such a book would enable other scholars (both textual and critical) to see what O'Neill material needed to be investigated, analyzed, and properly interpreted.

The resulting decision was to produce the book you have before you. I repeat, this bibliography is only a beginning. I hope that this volume will stimulate scholars, students, and others interested in dramatic literature to send me information about O'Neill items not included here so that this record may become as complete as possible. Also, perhaps this bibliography will encourage the kind of serious critical and textual attention that America's greatest playwright deserves.

Abbreviations

AC	*Anna Christie*
AGCGW	*All God's Chillun Got Wings*
AMFTM	*A Moon for the Misbegotten*
AW	*Ah, Wilderness!*
BB	*Bread and Butter*
"BB"	"Before Breakfast"
BM	British Museum
BTH	*Beyond the Horizon*
"Cardiff"	"Bound East for Cardiff"
"Caribbees"	"The Moon of the Caribbees"
"Children"	*"Children of the Sea" and Three Other Unpublished Plays by Eugene O'Neill*
"Children"	"Children of the Sea"
CMO	Carlotta Monterey O'Neill
"Cross"	"Where the Cross Is Made"
DUTE	*Desire Under the Elms*
DWE	*Days Without End*
EO	Eugene O'Neill
GGB	*The Great God Brown*
GPB	George Pierce Baker
JMcA	Jennifer McCabe Atkinson
"Kid"	"The Dreamy Kid"
LC	Library of Congress
LDJ	*Long Day's Journey Into Night*
Lilly	Lilly Library, Indiana University
LL	*Lazarus Laughed*
MBE	*Mourning Becomes Electra*

MJB	Matthew J. Bruccoli
MM	*Marco Millions*
MOTC	*The Moon of the Caribbees and Six Other Plays of the Sea*
MSM	*More Stately Mansions*
NIAY	*Now I Ask You*
Poet	*A Touch of the Poet*
PSt	Pennsylvania State Library
ScU	McKissick Library, University of South Carolina
SI	*Strange Interlude*
"SS"	"Shell Shock"
TEJ	*The Emperor Jones*
TFM	*The First Man*
TF	*The Fountain*
THA	*The Hairy Ape*
Thirst	*Thirst and Other One-Act Plays*
TIC	*The Iceman Cometh*
"Voyage"	"The Long Voyage Home"
"Wife"	"A Wife for a Life"
Yale	Beinecke Library, Yale University

A. Works by Eugene O'Neill

All plays, broadsides, or special publications wholly or substantially by EO. The section is arranged chronologically by individual play and includes all printings in English, also arranged chronologically. At the end of Section A there is an AA supplement containing descriptions of published acting scripts.

A 1 "THIRST"
American first book publication (1914)

A 1-I-1
THIRST AND OTHER ONE-ACT PLAYS
American first edition, only printing

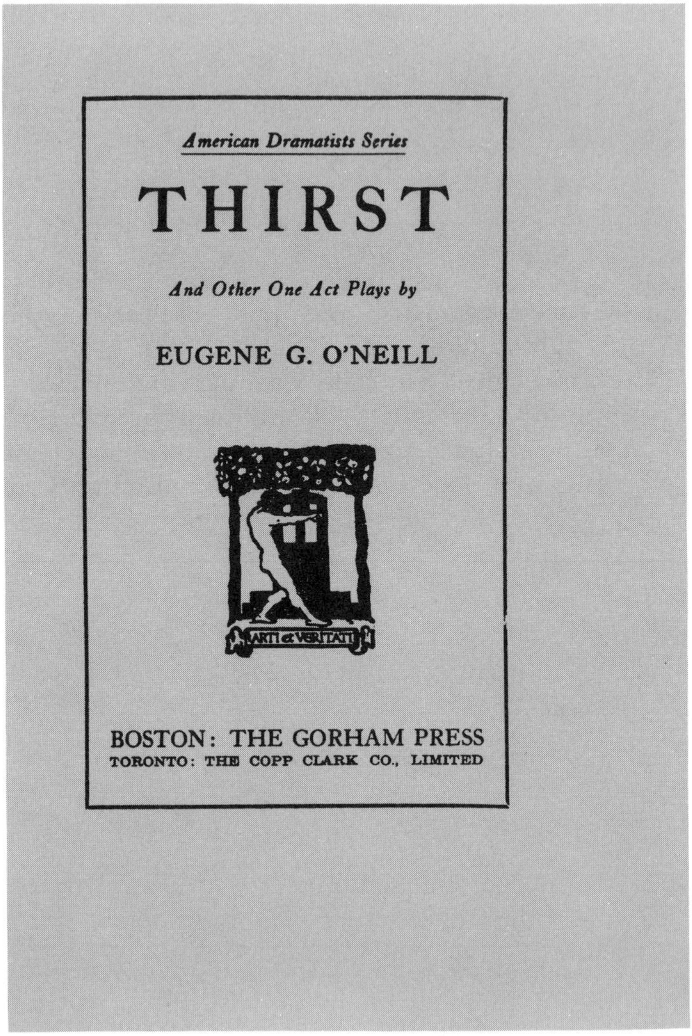
American Dramatists Series

THIRST

And Other One Act Plays by

EUGENE G. O'NEILL

ARTI et VERITATI

BOSTON: THE GORHAM PRESS
TORONTO: THE COPP CLARK CO., LIMITED

A 1-I-1: $7\frac{1}{4}'' \times 4\frac{15}{16}''$

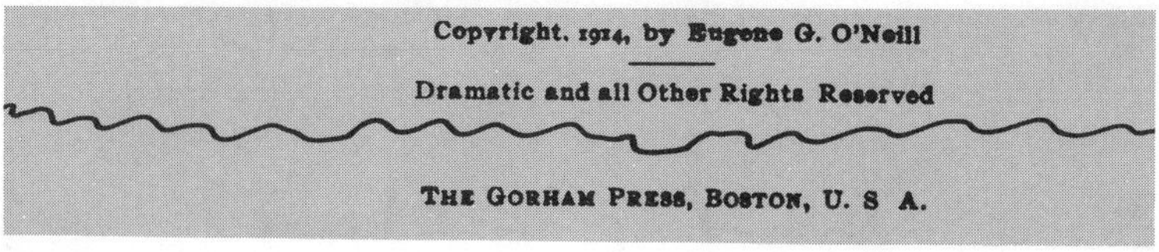
Copyright, 1914, by Eugene G. O'Neill

Dramatic and all Other Rights Reserved

THE GORHAM PRESS, BOSTON, U. S A.

[1–6] 7–43 [44–46] 47–70 [71–72] 73–104 [105–106] 107–134 [135–136] 137–168

[1–10]^{8} [11]^{4}

Contents: p. 1: title; p. 2: copyright; p. 3: 'CONTENTS | [six lines of type]'; p. 4: blank; p. 5: 'THIRST | A PLAY IN ONE ACT | *CHARACTERS* | [three lines of italic type]'; p. 6: blank; pp. 7–43: text, headed 'THIRST | A TRAGEDY IN ONE ACT'; p. 44: blank; p. 45: 'THE WEB | A PLAY IN ONE ACT | *CHARACTERS* | [five lines of italic type]'; p. 46: blank; pp. 47–70: text, headed 'THE WEB | A PLAY IN ONE ACT'; p. 71: 'WARNINGS | A PLAY IN ONE ACT | [five lines of roman and italic type giving scene synopsis] | *CHARACTERS* | [twelve lines of italic type]'; p. 72: blank; pp. 73–104: text, headed 'WARNINGS'; p. 105: 'FOG | A PLAY IN ONE ACT | *CHARACTERS* | [seven lines of italic type]'; p. 106: blank; pp. 107–134: text, headed 'FOG'; p. 135: 'RECKLESSNESS | A PLAY IN ONE ACT | *CHARACTERS* | [five lines of italic type]'; p. 136: blank; pp. 137–168: text, headed 'RECKLESSNESS'.

Typography and paper: $11\frac{1}{2}$ point on 14, Caslon Old Face. 3″ × $4\frac{11}{16}$″ (5″); twenty-eight lines per page. Running heads: rectos and versos, individual play titles. Wove paper.

Binding: Gray paper-covered boards; beige V cloth (fine linen-like grain) shelf back. Front: white paper label ($3\frac{1}{8}$″ × $1\frac{3}{4}$″) '[brown, within double-rule frame] *American Dramatists Series* | [gothic] Thirst | And Other One-Act Plays | [short double rule] | Eugene G. O'Neill'. Spine: white paper label ($3\frac{1}{16}$″ × $\frac{3}{8}$″) '[brown, gothic, vertically, top to bottom] American Dramatists Series—Thirst—O'Neill'. White wove endpapers of different stock from text paper. All edges trimmed.

Dust jacket: Black type on white background. Front: '[double rule] | *THIRST* | *FIVE ONE-ACT PLAYS* | [rule] | *EUGENE G. O'NEILL* | [rule] | [twelve lines of type describing the plays] | [rule] | *American Dramatists Series* | [double rule]'. Spine: '[double rule]| *Thirst* | [rule] | *O'NEILL* | [rule] | \$1.00 | NET [rule] *BADGER* | [double rule]'. Back: list of eight titles (beginning with *The Flower Shop* and ending with *Some People*

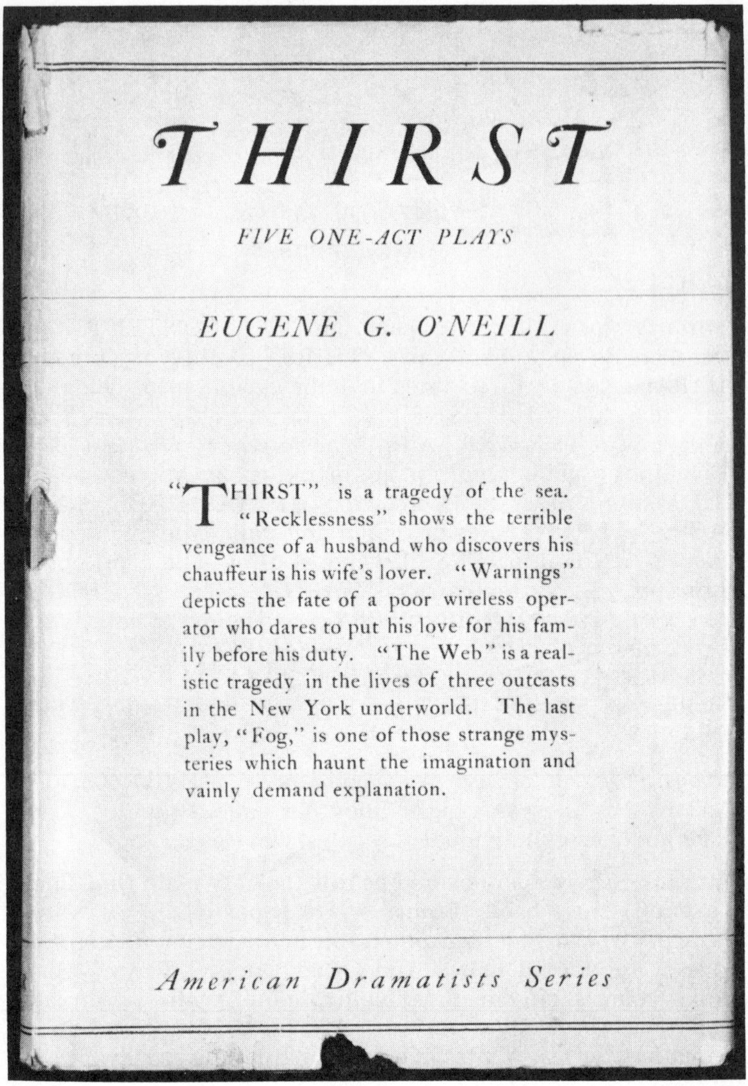
THIRST
FIVE ONE-ACT PLAYS
EUGENE G. O'NEILL
"THIRST" is a tragedy of the sea. "Recklessness" shows the terrible vengeance of a husband who discovers his chauffeur is his wife's lover. "Warnings" depicts the fate of a poor wireless operator who dares to put his love for his family before his duty. "The Web" is a realistic tragedy in the lives of three outcasts in the New York underworld. The last play, "Fog," is one of those strange mysteries which haunt the imagination and vainly demand explanation.
American Dramatists Series

Dust jacket for A 1-I-1

Marry) in the American Dramatists Series and a list of three titles *(Death and the Fool, The Great Galeoto,* and *Advent)* in the Contemporary Dramatists Series, all published by Richard G. Badger of Boston. Front flap blank; back flap: a note 'TO THE | READER'.

Publication: 1,000 copies published 17 August 1914. According to Sanborn and Clark, the type was distributed after one printing. The book was published at James O'Neill's expense for the sum of $450.

Locations: JM[c]A (two, one in dj); LC; Lilly (two, one in dj); MJB; PSt; ScU (two, one in dj); Yale.

A I "THIRST"
American second book publication (1964)

A I-II-I.a
TEN "LOST" PLAYS
American first edition, first printing

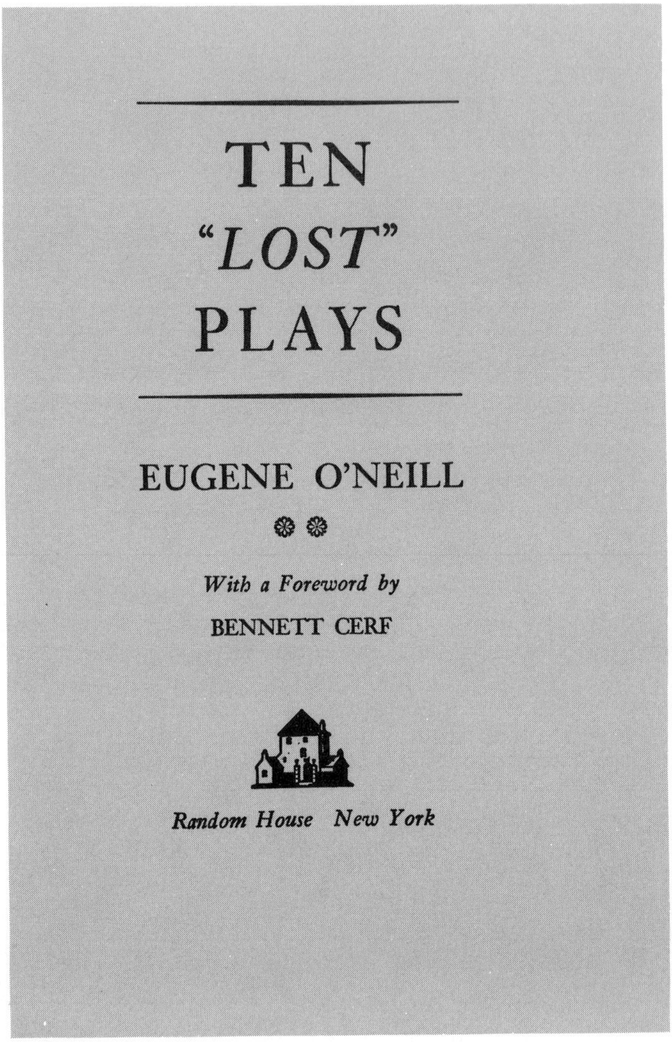

TEN
"*LOST*"
PLAYS

EUGENE O'NEILL

With a Foreword by
BENNETT CERF

Random House New York

A I-II-I.a: $7\frac{15}{16}'' \times 5\frac{3}{8}''$

FIRST PRINTING

Library of Congress catalog card number: 64–17937

MANUFACTURED IN THE UNITED STATES OF AMERICA BY

The H. Wolff Book Manufacturing Co., Inc., New York

[i–xii] [1–3] 4–32 [33–35] 36–54 [55–57] 58–82 [83–85] 86–107 [108–111] 112–137 [138–141] 142–165 [166–169] 170–185 [186–189] 190–207 [208–211] 212–223 [224–227] 228–252 [253] 254–303 [304–308]

$[1–10]^{16}$

Contents: "Thirst," "The Web," "Warnings," "Fog," "Recklessness," "Abortion," "The Movie Man," "The Sniper," *Servitude,* "A Wife for a Life."

"Thirst" appears on pp. 1–32.

Locations: JM^cA (dj); LC (deposit-stamp 13 July 1964).

Note: No first book material by EO. All plays are reprinted from either *Thirst and Other One-Act Plays* (A 1-I-1) or *Lost Plays of Eugene O'Neill* (A 36-I-1.a).

A 1 "THIRST"
English first book publication (1965)

A 1-EI-1.b
TEN "LOST" PLAYS
N.B. This reprinting of the American first edition receives a full description because it is the English first book publication.

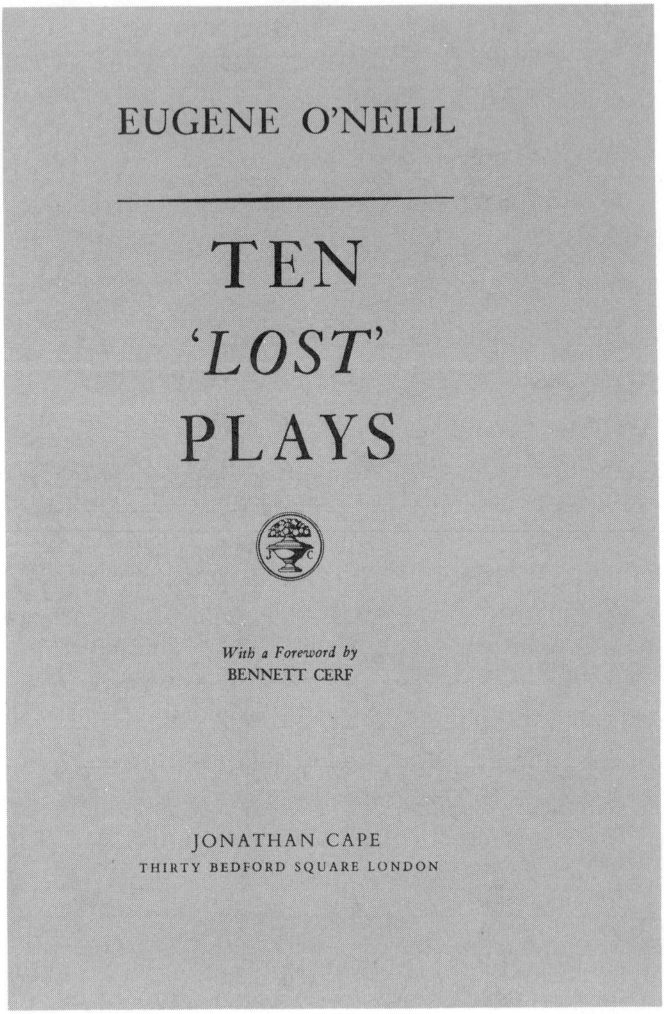
EUGENE O'NEILL

TEN
'*LOST*'
PLAYS

With a Foreword by
BENNETT CERF

JONATHAN CAPE
THIRTY BEDFORD SQUARE LONDON

A 1-EI-1.b: $7\frac{5}{16}'' \times 4\frac{15}{16}''$

FIRST PUBLISHED IN GREAT BRITAIN 1965

PRINTED IN GREAT BRITAIN BY
LOWE AND BRYDONE (PRINTERS) LTD. LONDON
ON PAPER MADE BY JOHN DICKINSON AND CO. LTD
BOUND BY A. W. BAIN AND CO. LTD. LONDON

[A–B] [i–xii] [1–3] 4–32 [33–35] 36–54 [55–57] 58–82 [83–85] 86–107 [108–111] 112–137 [138–141] 142–165 [166–169] 170–185 [186–189] 190–207 [208–211] 212–223 [224–227] 228–252 [253] 254–276 [277] 278–303 [304–308]

$[A]^{16}$ $B\text{–}I^{16}$ K^{16}. A_1 and K_{16} are pastedown endpapers.

Contents: pp. A–B, i–iv: blank; p. v: half title; p. vi: card page; p. vii: title; p. viii: copyright; p. ix: '*A Foreword by* | BENNETT CERF'; p. x: blank; pp. xi–xii: '*Contents*'; p. 1: '[decoration] | THIRST | [rule] | *A Play in One Act* | [decoration]'; p. 2: '[decoration] | CHARACTERS | [three lines of italic type]'; pp. 3–32: text; p. 33: '[decoration] | THE WEB | [rule] | *A Play in One Act* | [decoration]'; p. 34: '[decoration] | CHARACTERS | [five lines of italic type]'; pp. 35–54: text; p. 55: '[decoration] | WARNINGS | [rule] | A Play in One Act | [decoration]'; p. 56: '[decoration] | CHARACTERS | [twelve lines of italic type]'; pp. 57–82: text; p. 83: '[decoration] | FOG | [rule] | *A Play in One Act* | [decoration]'; p. 84: '[decoration] | CHARACTERS | [six lines of italic type]'; pp. 85–107: text; p. 108: blank; p. 109: '[decoration] | RECKLESSNESS | [rule] | *A Play in One Act* | [decoration]'; p. 110: '[decoration] | CHARACTERS | [five lines of italic type]'; pp. 111–137: text; p. 138: blank; p. 139: '[decoration] | ABORTION | [rule] | *A Play in One Act* | [decoration]'; p. 140: '[decoration] | CHARACTERS | [eight lines of italic type]'; pp. 141–165: text; p. 166: blank; p. 167: '[decoration] | THE | MOVIE MAN | [rule] | *A Comedy in One Act';* p. 168: '[decoration] | CHARACTERS | [eight lines of italic type]'; pp. 168–185: text; p. 186: blank; p. 187: '[decoration] | THE SNIPER | [rule] | *A Play in One Act* | [decoration]'; p. 188: '[decoration] | CHARACTERS | [five lines of italic type]'; pp. 189–207: text; p. 208: blank; p. 209: '[decoration] | A WIFE FOR | A LIFE | [rule] | *A Play in One Act* | [decoration]'; p. 210: '[decoration] | CHARACTERS | [three lines of italic type]'; pp. 211–223: text; p. 224: blank; p. 225: '[decoration] | SERVITUDE | [rule] | *A Play in Three Acts* | [decoration]'; p. 226: '[decoration] | CHARACTERS | [eight lines of italic type]'; pp. 227–303: text, headed *'ACT ONE';* pp. 304–308: blank.

Typography and paper: 3⅜" × 5$^{11}/_{16}$" (5$^{15}/_{16}$"); thirty-two lines per page. Running heads: rectos, play titles; versos, 'EUGENE O'NEILL'. Wove paper.

Binding: Blue paper-covered boards of imitation V cloth. Front: '[silverstamped EO signature]'. Spine: '[silverstamped line of decoration] | EUGENE | O'NEILL | [decoration] | TEN | 'LOST' | PLAYS | [publisher's device] | [line of decoration]'. White wove endpapers of same stock as text paper. All edges trimmed.

Dust jacket: White background. Front: '[blue] TEN | 'LOST' | PLAYS | [black] *by* [black on blue patch] EUGENE | O'NEILL'. Spine: '[black] TEN | 'LOST' | PLAYS | [black on blue patch] *by* | [black] EUGENE | O'NEILL | author of | [blue] MOURNING | BECOMES | ELECTRA | etc. | [blue publisher's device]'. Back: list of EO's plays published by Cape, beginning with *TEJ* and ending with *MSM*. Front flap: blurb for *TEN 'LOST' PLAYS;* back flap blank.

Publication: Unknown number of copies published on unknown date in 1965 (as noted on copyright page).

Locations: BM (deposit-stamp 1 March 1966 and 17 October 1966); LC (deposit-stamp 25 August 1966); Lilly (dj); Yale (dj).

A 2 "THE WEB"
American first book publication (1914)

A 2-I-1
Thirst and Other One-Act Plays. Boston: Gorham Press, [1914].

"The Web" appears on pp. 45–70. See A 1-I.1, "Thirst."

A 2 "THE WEB"
American second book publication (1964)

A 2-II-1.a
Ten "Lost" Plays. New York: Random House, [1964].

On copyright page: 'FIRST PRINTING'.

"The Web" appears on pp. 33–54. See A 1-II-1.a, "Thirst."

A 2 "THE WEB"
English first book publication (1965)

A 2-EI-1.b
Ten "Lost" Plays. London: Random House, [1965].

"The Web" appears on pp. 33–54. See A 1-EI-1.b, "Thirst."

A 3 "WARNINGS"
American first book publication (1914)

A 3-I-1
Thirst and Other One-Act Plays. Boston: Gorham Press, [1914].

"Warnings" appears on pp. 71–104. See A 1-I-1, "Thirst."

A 3 "WARNINGS"
American second book publication (1964)

A 3-II-1.a
Ten "Lost" Plays. New York: Random House, [1964].

On copyright page: 'FIRST PRINTING'.

"Warnings" appears on pp. 55–82. See A 1-II-1.a, "Thirst."

A 3 "WARNINGS"
English first book publication (1965)

A 3-EI-1.b
Ten "Lost" Plays. London: Random House, [1965].

"Warnings" appears on pp. 55–82. See A 1-EI-1.b, "Thirst."

A 4 "FOG"
American first book publication (1914)

A 4-I-1
Thirst and Other One-Act Plays. Boston: Gorham Press, [1914].

"Fog" appears on pp. 105–134. See A 1-I-1, "Thirst."

A 4 "FOG"
American second book publication (1964)

A 4-II-1.a
Ten "Lost" Plays. New York: Random House, [1964].

On copyright page: 'FIRST PRINTING'.

"Fog" appears on pp. 83–107. See A 1-II-1.a, "Thirst."

A 4 "FOG"
English first book publication (1965)

A 4-EI-1.b
Ten "Lost" Plays. London: Random House, [1965].

"Fog" appears on pp. 83–107. See A 1-EI-1.b, "Thirst."

A 5 "RECKLESSNESS"
American first book publication (1914)

A 5-I-1
Thirst and Other One-Act Plays. Boston: Gorham Press, [1914].

"Recklessness" appears on pp. 135–168. See A 1-I-1, "Thirst."

A 5 'RECKLESSNESS"
American second book publication (1964)

A 5-II-1.a
Ten "Lost" Plays. New York: Random House, [1964].

On copyright page: 'FIRST PRINTING'.

"Recklessness" appears on pp. 109–137. See A 1-II-1.a, "Thirst."

A 5 "RECKLESSNESS"
English first book publication (1965)

A 5-EI-1.b
Ten "Lost" Plays. London: Random House, [1965].

"Recklessness" appears on pp. 109–137. See A 1-EI-1.b, "Thirst."

A 6 "BOUND EAST FOR CARDIFF"
American first book publication (1916)

A 6-I-1
THE PROVINCETOWN PLAYS: FIRST SERIES
American first edition

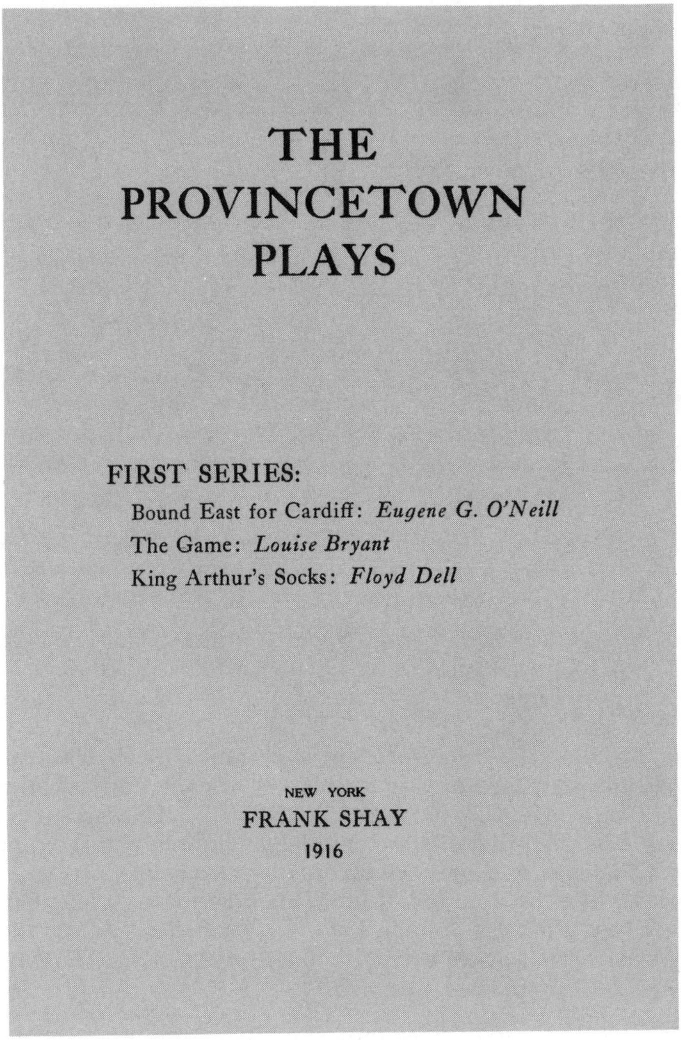

THE
PROVINCETOWN
PLAYS

FIRST SERIES:
Bound East for Cardiff: *Eugene G. O'Neill*
The Game: *Louise Bryant*
King Arthur's Socks: *Floyd Dell*

NEW YORK
FRANK SHAY
1916

A 6-I-1: 8″ × $5^{5}/_{16}$″

[i–ii] [1–5] 6–25 [26–27] 28–42 [43] 44–67 [68–70]

$[1–4]^{8}$ $[5]^{4}$

Contents: pp. i–ii: blank; p. 1: half title; p. 2: blank; p. 3: title; p. 4: copyright; p. 5: 'BOUND EAST FOR CARDIFF | A Sea Play | By Eugene G. O'Neill'; p. 6: list of characters with names of Provincetown Players performers (including EO as The Second Mate); pp. 7–25: text, headed 'Bound East for Cardiff'; p. 26: blank; pp. 27–42: "The Game," by Louise Bryant; pp. 43–67: "King Arthur's Socks," by Floyd Dell; pp. 68–70: blank.

Typography and paper: $11\frac{1}{2}$ point set solid, Caslon Old Face. $3\frac{5}{8}'' \times 5\frac{1}{8}''$ ($5\frac{9}{16}''$); twenty-six to twenty-nine lines per page. Running heads: rectos and versos, 'THE PROVINCETOWN PLAYS'. White wove paper with '◇D | Regal Antique' watermark.

Binding: Blue wrappers. Front: [dark blue] ▲ THE ▲ PR°VINCET°WN ▲ PLAYS ▲ | FIRST SERIES: | Bound East for Cardiff: *Eugene G. O'Neill* | The Game: *Louise Bryant* | King Arthur's Socks: *Floyd Dell* | [stylistic linoleum cut by William Zorach of a scene from "The Game"] | FRANK SHAY, *Publisher* 1916'. Spine: '[dark blue, vertically, top to bottom] THE PROVINCETOWN PLAYS—FIRST SERIES'. Back: 'Plays Worth Reading | [list of six play titles beginning with *Youth*, by Miles Malleson, and ending with *Mariana*, translated by Federico Sarda] | The Washington Square Book Shop | 137 Macdougal Street New York City | *Open Evenings until Ten* | [decoration] | [boxed] "THE DRAMA SHOP" | THE MODERN ART PRINTING CO.'. Bottom edge trimmed.

Publication: 1,200 copies published in November 1916. $.50.

Locations: JM^{c}A; Lilly (two); ScU; Yale.

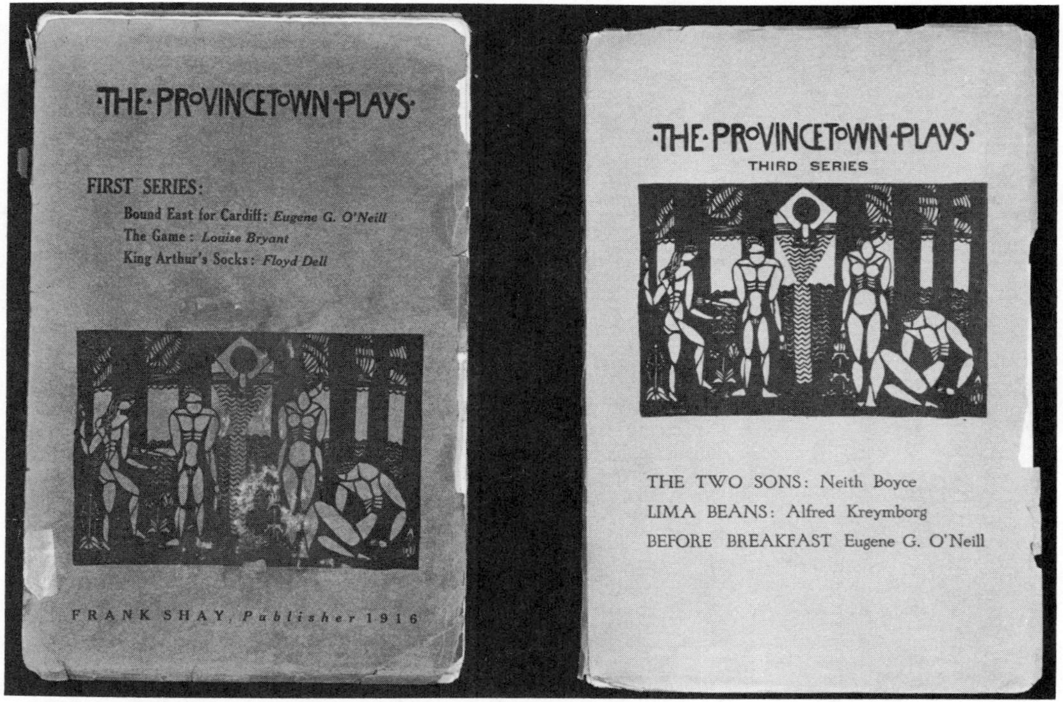

Wrapper covers for A 6-I-1 and A 7-I-1

A 6 "BOUND EAST FOR CARDIFF"
American second book publication (1919)

A 6-II-1.a
The Moon of the Caribbees and Six Other Plays of the Sea. New York: Boni & Liveright, 1919.

"Cardiff" appears on pp. 33–54. See A 8-I-1.a, "Caribbees."

REPRINTINGS

A 6-II-1.b
The Moon of the Caribbees and Six Other Plays of the Sea. New York: Boni & Liveright, [1923], pp. 33–54. Modern Library.

Note: This printing has been seen in three bindings: (a) dark green, leather-like grain; (b) dark blue, leather-like grain; and (c) dark brown, leather-like grain. Priority of binding undetermined.

A 6-II-1.c
The Long Voyage Home. New York: Modern Library, [1940], pp. 33–54.

Note: Same setting of type as A 6-II-1.a, but with changed title.

A 6 "BOUND EAST FOR CARDIFF"
American third book publication (1921)

A 6-III-1
The Provincetown Plays. Edited and selected by George Cram Cook and Frank Shay, with a foreword by Hutchins Hapgood. Cincinnati: Stewart Kidd Company, [1921].

"Cardiff" appears on pp. 157–180.

On page 157: 'BOUND EAST FOR CARDIFF | A PLAY | BY EUGENE G. O'NEILL | [rule] | Copyright, 19 , | BY BONI & LIVERIGHT, *INC.* | *All Rights Reserved* | [rule] | [four lines giving production rights notice] | Reprinted from "Beyond the Horizon," by permission of the | author.'.

Location: Yale.

Note: The copyright date is missing from the copy seen at Yale. The statement that the play is reprinted "from 'Beyond the Horizon' " is inaccurate. At this time, "Cardiff" had appeared only with other EO one-act plays; *Beyond the Horizon* was EO's first full-length play to be published, and it was published alone (see A 14).

A 6 "BOUND EAST FOR CARDIFF"
American fourth book publication (1924)

A 6-IV-1
THE COMPLETE WORKS OF EUGENE O'NEILL. Two volumes

Volume one

Title page: '[within green border with wave motif at top and bottom of border] [black] T H E | COMPLETE WORKS | *of* | EUGENE O'NEILL | *VOLUME ONE* | [green publisher's device] | *NEW YORK* | BONI & LIVERIGHT | *1924*'

Copyright page: 'THE | COMPLETE WORKS | *of* | EUGENE O'NEILL | [rule] | *Copyrighted, 1924, by* | BONI & LIVERIGHT, INC. | [rule] | [twenty-one lines of type listing individual plays]'

[i–x] [1–4] 5–82 [83–88] 89–179 [180–184] 185–252 [253–256] 257–315 [316–320] 321–391 [392–396] 397–416 [417–420] 421–434 [435–438] 439–455 [456–460] 461–480 [481–484] 485–502 [503–504]

$[1–32]^8$

The statement of limitation on p. iv reads: 'THIS EDITION OF THE COMPLETE WORKS OF | EUGENE O'NEILL IS LIMITED TO 1200 NUMBERED | SETS OF TWO VOLUMES EACH, SIGNED BY THE AUTHOR | No . . . .'.

"Cardiff" appears on pp. 417–434.

Note: For volume two, see A 25-I-1. *DUTE.*

Locations: JM^c^A (#856); Yale (#1024).

A 6 "BOUND EAST FOR CARDIFF"
American fifth book publication (1926)

A 6-V-1.a
The Great God Brown, The Fountain, The Moon of the Caribbees, and Other Plays. New York: Boni & Liveright, 1926.

First printing: March 1926

One volume of an unnumbered, ten-volume, uniform series.

"Cardiff" appears on pp. 221–241. See A 26-I-1.a, *GGB*.

REPRINTINGS

A 6-V-1.b
New York: Boni & Liveright, [June 1926].

A 6-V-1.c
New York: Boni & Liveright, [September 1926].

A 6 "BOUND EAST FOR CARDIFF"
American sixth book publication (1935)

A 6-VI-1
THE PLAYS OF EUGENE O'NEILL. Twelve volumes. Wilderness Edition

Volume twelve

Title page: '[within decorated border] [white against gray background] THE | PLAYS | OF | EUGENE | O'NEILL | [wavy rule] | *Nine One-Act Plays* | [wavy rule] | XII | WILDERNESS · EDITION | *NEW YORK* | Charles Scribner's Sons'

Copyright page: 'COPYRIGHT, 1935, BY CHARLES SCRIBNER'S SONS | [twenty-three lines of roman and italic type]'

[A–B] [i–x] xi–xiii [xiv] xv–xvi [1–2] 3–38 [39–40] 41–73 [74–76] 77–112 [113–114] 115–140 [141–142] 143–174 [175–176] 177–212 [213–214] 215–260 [261–262] 263–297 [298–300] 301–314 [315–322]

$[1]^{10}$ $[2\text{–}21]^{8}$

The statement of limitation on p. iv reads: '[decorated rule] [swash *T*'s and *N*'s] *THIS WILDERNESS EDITION* | OF THE

PLAYS OF EUGENE O'NEILL | printed from type now destroyed, is limited | to seven hundred and seventy sets | of which twenty are for presentation | This is number | [decorated rule]'.

The colophon on p. 316 reads: '[decorated rule] | [swash *T* and *K*] *THIS BOOK* | the last of twelve volumes designed by Elmer Adler | set in an eighteenth-century type face | based on the castings made by John Baskerville | is printed on a specially watermarked paper | at the press of the publisher | in the city of New York | in the month of June | MCM XXX V | [publisher's device]'.

Note one: The watermark is: 'CSS | [classical tragedy mask]'.

"Cardiff" appears on pp. 113–140.

On p. xii, in a note written by EO's Random House editor, the following statement is made about "Cardiff": 'BOUND EAST FOR CARDIFF *was the first of my plays to find pro-|duction in a theatre. It was written at New London, Connecticut, in | the spring of 1914, during my first year of play writing. The initial | production was in the summer of 1916 at the Wharf Theatre, Prov-|incetown, Massachusetts. The Provincetown Players inaugurated their | first season in New York with this play on their opening bill.*'.

Note two: In early 1934 (January–February), when negotiations were going on between Scribners and Random House for Scribners' Wilderness Edition, EO was requested to write a preface for each volume. He declined but agreed to Donald Klopfer's suggestion that EO's Random House editor, Saxe Commins, write a foreword for each volume giving facts about the plays and that EO sign these forewords as though they were his own. In a letter of 8 February 1934, Donald Klopfer informed Maxwell Perkins of EO's agreement. On 9 February, Perkins wrote Klopfer confirming the arrangement.

Publication: 770 copies published 28 June 1935.

Locations: JM^c^A (#456); LC (presentation); MJB (#592 boxed); ScU (#749); Yale (presentation).

A 6 "BOUND EAST FOR CARDIFF"
American seventh book publication (1941)

A 6-VII-1.a
THE PLAYS OF EUGENE O'NEILL. Three volumes

Volume one:

Title page: '[within triple-rule frame, black against solid gray beige background] THE PLAYS | OF | EUGENE | O'NEILL | [publisher's device] | RANDOM HOUSE · NEW YORK'

Copyright page: 'FIRST PRINTING | COPYRIGHT, 1920, 1921, 1922, 1926, 1929, 1934, | BY EUGENE O'NEILL | MANUFACTURED IN THE UNITED STATES OF AMERICA'

[i-vi] [1-2] 3-200 [201-202] 203-269 [270-272] 273-371 [372-376] 377-449 [450-454] 455-474 [475-476] 477-490 [491-492] 493-509 [510-512] 513-532 [533-534] 535-552 [553-554] 555-573 [574-576] 577-602 [603-604] 605-622 [623-624] 625-633 [634]

$[1\text{-}20]^{16}$

"Cardiff" appears on pp. 475-490.

Locations: JMcA; ScU; Yale.

REPRINTINGS

A 6-VII-1.b
New York: Random House, [1941].

On copyright page: 'SECOND PRINTING'.

A 6-VII-1.c
New York: Random House, [1951].

A 6-VII-1.d
New York: Random House, [1954-55].

A 6 "BOUND EAST FOR CARDIFF"
American eighth book publication (1944)

A 6-VIII-1
Selected Plays of Eugene O'Neill. New York: Editions for the Armed Services, Inc., [1944]. Published by arrangement with Random House. No. Q-35.

Only in wrappers.

"Cardiff" appears on pp. 305–322.

A 6 "BOUND EAST FOR CARDIFF"
American ninth book publication (1972)

A 6-IX-1
Seven Plays of the Sea. New York: Vintage Books, [1972]. No. V-856.

Only in wrappers.

"Cardiff" appears on pp. 31–51.

A 6 "BOUND EAST FOR CARDIFF"
English first book publication (1923)

A 6-EI-1.a
The Moon of the Caribbees and Six Other Plays of the Sea. London: Jonathan Cape, [1923].

"Cardiff" appears on pp. 1–23. See A 8-EI-1.a, "Caribbees."

REPRINTINGS

A 6-EI-1.b
London: Jonathan Cape, [1926].

A 6-EI-1.c
London: Jonathan Cape, [1929]. The Travellers' Library, No. 116.

A 6-EI-1.d
London: Jonathan Cape, [1931].

A 6-EI-1.e
London: Jonathan Cape, [1942].

A 6-EI-1.f
London: Jonathan Cape, [1951].

A 6-EI-1.g
London: Jonathan Cape, [1955].

A 6-EI-1.h
London: Jonathan Cape, [1960].

A 7 "BEFORE BREAKFAST"
American first book publication (1916)

A 7-I-1
THE PROVINCETOWN PLAYS: THIRD SERIES
American first edition

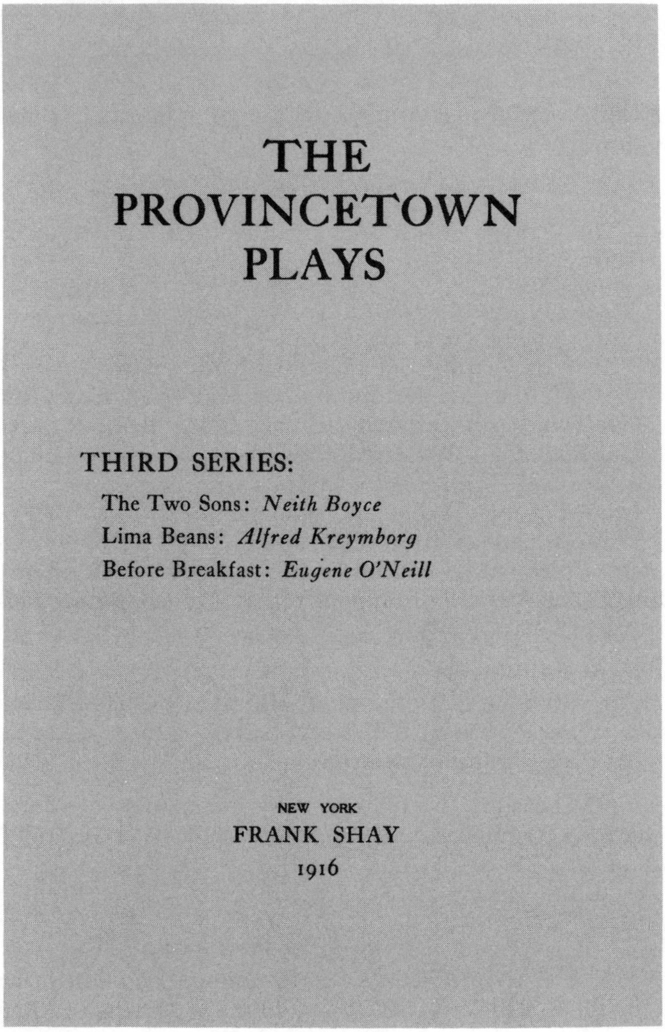
THE
PROVINCETOWN
PLAYS

THIRD SERIES:
The Two Sons: *Neith Boyce*
Lima Beans: *Alfred Kreymborg*
Before Breakfast: *Eugene O'Neill*

NEW YORK
FRANK SHAY
1916

A 7-I-1: $7\frac{15}{16}'' \times 5\frac{5}{16}''$

> Copyright, 1916, by Eugene G. O'Neill.
> Copyright, 1916, by Alfred Kreymborg.
> Copyright, 1916 by Neith Boyce.
>
> Application for permission to perform these plays may be made to the Provincetown Players, 17 West Eighth Street, New York; no performance can take place without arrangement with the owners of the acting rights.

[139–146] 147–169 [170–172] 173–191 [192–194] 195–207 [208–210]

[1–4]^{8} [5]^{4}

Note: The Provincetown Plays series was numbered consecutively.

Contents: pp. 139–140: blank; p. 141: half title; p. 142: blank; p. 143: title; p. 144: copyright; p. 145: 'THE TWO SONS | A Play in One Act | By Neith Boyce'; p. 146: characters with names of Provincetown Players performers; pp. 147–169: text, headed 'The Two Sons'; p. 170: blank; p. 171: 'LIMA BEANS | A Conventional Scherzo | By Alfred Kreymborg'; p. 172: characters with names of Provincetown Players performers; pp. 173–191: text, headed 'Lima Beans'; p. 192: blank; p. 193: 'BEFORE BREAKFAST | A Play in One Act | By Eugene G. O'Neill'; p. 194: characters with names of Provincetown Players performers (including EO as Alfred); pp. 195–207: text, headed *'Before Breakfast';* pp. 208–210: blank.

Typography and paper: 11 point on 13, Ronaldson. $3\frac{5}{8}'' \times 5\frac{1}{8}''$ ($5\frac{9}{16}''$); twenty-nine lines per page. Running heads: rectos and versos, 'THE PROVINCETOWN PLAYS'. White wove paper with '◈| Regal Antique' watermark.

Binding: There are two binding variants for this volume:

Binding A: Orange wrappers. Front: '▲ THE ▲ PR^{o}VINCE-T^{o}WN ▲ PLAYS ▲ | THIRD SERIES: | The Two Sons: *Neith Boyce* | Lima Beans: *Alfred Kreymborg* | Before Breakfast: *Eugene G. O'Neill* | [stylistic linoleum cut by William Zorach of scene from "The Game" (same as First Series, see A 6-I-1)] | FRANK SHAY, *Publisher* 1916'. Spine: '[vertically, top to bottom] THE PROVINCETOWN PLAYS——THIRD SERIES'. Back: ad for ten titles, beginning with *Youth* and ending with *The Provincetown Plays: First Series*, published by Frank Shay,

The Washington Square Book Shop. Bottom edge trimmed.

Binding B: Orange wrappers. Front: '▲ THE ▲ PR°VINCE-T°WN ▲ PLAYS ▲ | THIRD SERIES | [stylistic linoleum cut (see Binding A)] | THE TWO SONS: Neith Boyce | LIMA BEANS: Alfred Kreymborg | BEFORE BREAKFAST Eugene G. O'Neill'. Spine: '[vertically, top to bottom] THE PROVINCETOWN PLAYS——THIRD SERIES'. Back: ad for The Flying Stag Plays, to be published by Egmont H. Arens, Washington Square Book Shop.

According to Sanborn and Clark, "The publisher of this book reports that some copies were later issued but without the imprint 'Frank Shay, Publisher 1916' appearing on the front cover" (p. 12). Thus, the priority of Binding A was established.

Publication: 500 copies published in December 1916. (The compiler found no record of this volume in the copyright office.)

Locations: JM^{c}A (Binding A); Lilly (two, Binding A); ScU (Binding B); Yale.

A 7 "BEFORE BREAKFAST"

American second book publication, first separate book publication (1916)

A 7-II-1

BEFORE BREAKFAST

American first edition, only printing

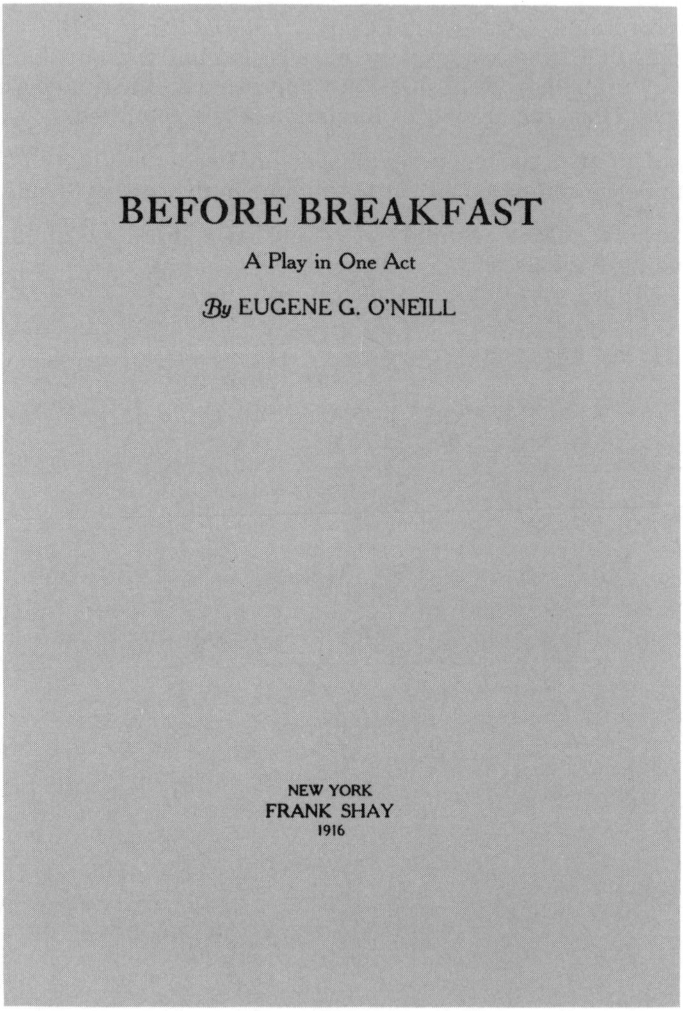

BEFORE BREAKFAST

A Play in One Act

By EUGENE G. O'NEILL

NEW YORK

FRANK SHAY

1916

A 7-II-1: $7^{11}/_{16}'' \times 5^{7}/_{16}''$

Copyright 1916, by Eugene G. O'Neill

All dramatic rights reserved
by the author

[1–6] 7–19 [20–24]

Stapled.

Contents: p. 1: half title; p. 2: blank; p. 3: title; p. 4: copyright; p. 5: second half title; p. 6: 'Before Breakfast | By Eugene G. O'Neill | As Presented by Provincetown Players, | New York City | Mrs. Rowland . . . . Mary Pyne | Alfred, *her husband* (not seen). Eugene G. O'Neill'; pp. 7–19: text, headed '*Before Breakfast*'; pp. 20–24: blank.

Typography and paper: Type face undetermined. $3\frac{5}{8}'' \times 5\frac{1}{16}''$ ($5\frac{9}{16}''$); twenty-nine lines per page. Running heads: rectos, 'EUGENE G. O'NEILL'; versos, 'BEFORE BREAKFAST'. White wove paper with '◈ | Regal Antique' watermark.

Binding: Light, blue gray wrappers. Front: 'BEFORE BREAKFAST *a* | *Play in One Act by Eugene G. O'Neill* | FRANK SHAY, *Publisher* 1916'. Back: ad for ten other titles, beginning with *Youth* and ending with *The Provincetown Plays,* published by Frank Shay. Top and bottom edges trimmed.

Publication: 500 copies published in December 1916. (According to Sanborn and Clark, this edition was set from the *Provincetown Plays: Third Series* and published a few days later. The compiler could find no record of this volume in the copyright office.)

Locations: JMcA; Lilly; PSt; ScU.

A 7 "BEFORE BREAKFAST"
American third book publication (1924)

A 7-III-1
The Complete Works of Eugene O'Neill. New York: Boni & Liveright, 1924. Two volumes.

Limited to 1,200 numbered copies; signed by EO.

"BB" appears in volume two, pp. 447–457. See A 25-I-1, *DUTE.*

A 7 "BEFORE BREAKFAST"
American fourth book publication (1925)

A 7-IV-1.a
Plays, Beyond the Horizon, The Straw, Before Breakfast. New York: Boni & Liveright, 1925.

First printing: July 1925

One volume of an unnumbered, ten-volume, uniform series.

"BB" appears on pp. 243–254.

REPRINTINGS

A 7-IV-1.b
New York: Boni & Liveright, [December 1925].

A 7-IV-1.c
New York: Boni & Liveright, [June 1926].

A 7-IV-1.d
New York: Boni & Liveright, [January 1927].

A 7-IV-1.e
New York: Boni & Liveright, [October 1927].

A 7-IV-1.f
New York: Boni & Liveright, [April 1928].

A 7-IV-1.g
New York: Boni & Liveright, [November 1928].

A 7-IV-1.h
New York: Liveright, [March 1931].

A 7-IV-1.i
New York: Liveright, [September 1932].

A 7 "BEFORE BREAKFAST"
American fifth book publication (1935)

A 7-V-1
The Plays of Eugene O'Neill. New York: Scribners, [1934–35]. Twelve volumes. Wilderness Edition.

Limited to 770 numbered copies.

"BB" appears in volume twelve, pp. 299–314. See A 6-VI-1, "Cardiff."

On p. xiii, in a note written by EO's Random House editor, the following statement is made about "BB": 'BEFORE BREAKFAST *was written at Provincetown in the summer | of 1916. It had its initial performance at the Provincetown Theatre in | New York on December 1, 1916, with Mary Pyne playing the only | part in this monologue play.*'

Publication: 770 copies published 28 June 1935.

A 7 "BEFORE BREAKFAST"
American sixth book publication (1941)

A 7-VI-1.a
The Plays of Eugene O'Neill. New York: Random House, [1941]. Three volumes.

On copyright page: 'FIRST PRINTING'.

"BB" appears in volume one, pp. 623–633. See A 6-VII-1.a, "Cardiff."

REPRINTINGS

A 7-VI-1.b
New York: Random House, [1941].

On copyright page: 'SECOND PRINTING'.

A 7-VI-1.c
New York: Random House, [1951].

A 7-VI-1.d
New York: Random House, [1954–55].

A 7 "BEFORE BREAKFAST"
English first book publication (1926)

A 7-EI-1.a
The Great God Brown, Including The Fountain, The Dreamy Kid and Before Breakfast. London: Jonathan Cape, [1926].

"Before Breakfast" appears on pp. 1–16. See A 26-EI-1.a, *GGB*.

REPRINTING

A 7-EI-1.b
London: Jonathan Cape, [1937]. Nobel Prize Edition. (Not a new edition.)

A 8 "THE MOON OF THE CARIBBEES"
American first book publication (1919)

A 8-I-1.a
THE MOON OF THE CARIBBEES AND SIX OTHER PLAYS OF THE SEA
American first edition, first printing

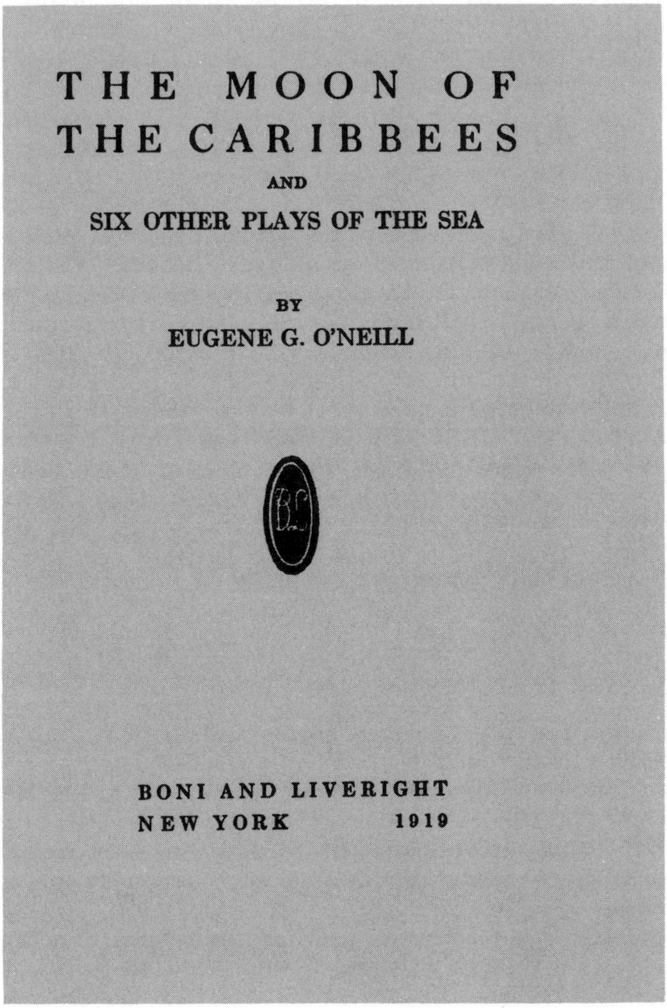
THE MOON OF
THE CARIBBEES
AND
SIX OTHER PLAYS OF THE SEA
BY
EUGENE G. O'NEILL
BONI AND LIVERIGHT
NEW YORK 1919

A 8-1-I.a: 7 3/16" × 5 1/8"

Copyright, 1919,
By BONI & LIVERIGHT, Inc.

[i–iv] 5 [vi] [1–2] 3–32 [33–34] 35–54 [55–56] 57–81 [82–84] 85–114 [115–116] 117–143 [144–146] 147–176 [177–178] 179–217 [218]

[1–14]^8

Contents: p. 1: half title; p. ii: blank; p. iii: title; p. iv: copyright; p. 5: 'CONTENTS [eight lines of type]'; p. vi: blank; p. 1: 'THE MOON OF THE CARIBBEES | A Play In One Act'; p. 2: 'CHARACTERS | [twenty-five lines of roman and italic type]'; pp. 3–32: text, headed 'THE MOON OF THE CARIBBEES'; p. 33: 'BOUND EAST FOR CARDIFF | A Play In One Act'; p. 34: 'CHARACTERS | [eleven lines of type]'; pp. 35–54: text, headed 'BOUND EAST FOR CARDIFF'; p. 55: 'THE LONG VOYAGE HOME | A Play In one Act'; p. 56: 'CHARACTERS | [ten lines of roman and italic type]'; pp. 57–81: text, headed 'THE LONG VOYAGE HOME'; p. 82: blank; p. 83: 'IN THE ZONE | A Play In One Act'; p. 84: 'CHARACTERS | [nine lines of roman and italic type]'; pp. 85–114: text, headed 'IN THE ZONE'; p. 115: 'ILE | A Play In One Act'; p. 116: 'CHARACTERS | [eight lines of roman and italic type]'; pp. 117–143: text, headed 'ILE'; p. 144: blank; p. 145: 'WHERE THE CROSS IS MADE | A Play In One Act'; p. 146: 'CHARACTERS | [seven lines of roman and italic type]'; pp. 147–176: text, headed 'WHERE THE CROSS IS MADE'; p. 177: 'THE ROPE | A Play In One Act'; p. 178: 'CHARACTERS | [five lines of roman and italic type]'; pp. 179–217: text, headed 'THE ROPE'; p. 218: blank.

Typography and paper: 11 point on 13, Scotch. $3\frac{1}{4}'' \times 5\frac{1}{4}''$ ($5\frac{1}{2}''$); twenty-nine lines per page. Running heads: rectos and versos, individual play titles. Wove paper.

Binding: Tan paper-covered boards with buff V cloth (fine linen-like grain) shelf back. Front: '[black] The Moon | of The | Caribbees | Eugene G. O'Neill'. Spine: '[black] The Moon | of The | Caribbees | Eugene G. | O'Neill | BONI AND | LIVERIGHT'. White wove endpapers of different stock from text paper. Top edge only trimmed; other edges originally uncut and unopened.

There are two binding variants for this volume: Binding A: $\frac{7}{8}''$ wide; leaves $7\frac{5}{16}'' \times 5\frac{1}{16}''$; Binding B: $1\frac{3}{16}$: wide; leaves $7\frac{7}{16}'' \times 5\frac{1}{16}''$.

Dust jacket: Front: '[orange background] The Moon of | The Caribbees | and Six Other Plays of the Sea | [seven-line blurb] |—

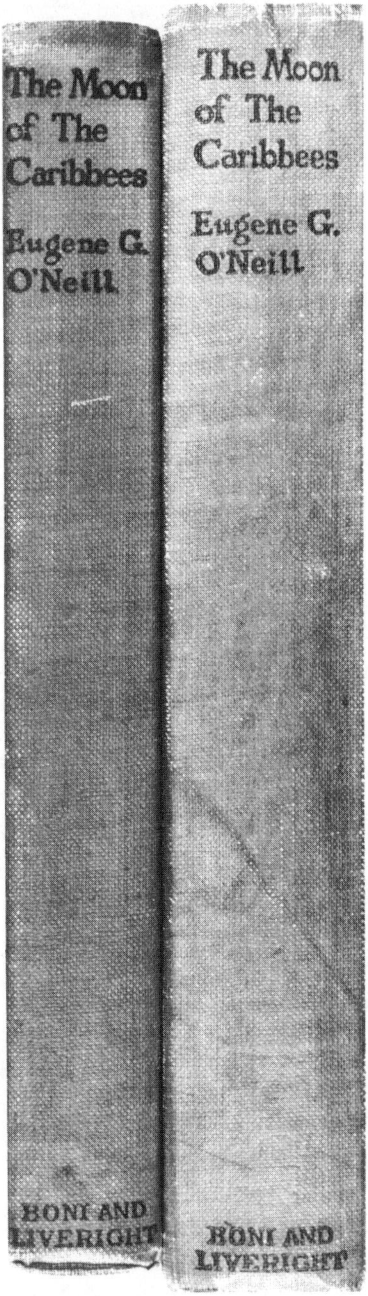

Binding variants of A 8-I-1.a

John Corbin, in the New York Times | [three-line blurb] |–*The Nation* | [three-line blurb] |–*Christian Science Monitor* | By EUGENE O'NEILL'. Spine: '[beige background] [double rule] | THE MOON OF | THE CARIBBEES | [double rule] | EUGENE O'NEILL | [beige against black oval, within beige oval frame and black oval frame] BL | [black] $\$1.^{35}_{\text{NET}}$ | [double rule] | BONI AND | LIVERIGHT | [double rule]'. Back: '[orange background] The Moon of | The Caribbees | and Six Other Plays of the Sea | [three-line blurb] |–*Clayton Hamilton in Vogue* | [eight-line blurb]–*The Theatre Magazine* | [three-line blurb] |–*Current Opinion* | By EUGENE O'NEILL'. Front flap has ad for thirty-two Modern Library titles, beginning with *Dorian Gray* and ending with *Anatol and Other Plays;* back flap has ad for thirty-four more Modern Library titles, beginning with *Dame Care* and ending with *The Belfry.*

Publication: 1,200 copies published 23 April 1919. $1.35.

Printing: Printed 16 April 1919 by J. J. Little & Ives of New York from plates made by J. J. Little & Ives; bound by J. J. Little & Ives.

Locations: JM^{c}A (Binding A); LC; Lilly (Binding A, dj); PSt; ScU; Yale (Bindings A and B).

Note one: Contents page states incorrectly that "The Moon of the Caribbees" begins on p. 1; the text actually begins on p. 3. It states that "Bound East for Cardiff" begins on p. 34; the text begins on p. 35. For all other plays, the page number given in the table of contents is the page on which the text begins.

Note two: "Caribbees" appeared in *The Smart Set,* LV, 4 (August 1918), 73–86. See C 35. Magazine publication preceded book publication.

REPRINTINGS

A 8-I-1.b
The Moon of the Caribbees and Six Other Plays of the Sea. New York: Boni & Liveright, [1923]. Modern Library.

See A 6-II-1.b, "Cardiff," for binding variants.

A 8-I-1.c
The Long Voyage Home. New York: Modern Library. [1940].

Note: Same setting of type as A 8-I-1.a, but with changed title.

A 8 "THE MOON OF THE CARIBBEES"
American second book publication (1924)

A 8-II-1
The Complete Works of Eugene O'Neill. New York: Boni & Liveright, 1924. Two volumes.

Limited to 1,200 numbered copies; signed by EO.

"Caribbees" appears in volume one, pp. 393–416. See A 6-IV-1, "Cardiff."

A 8 "THE MOON OF THE CARIBBEES"
American third book publication (1926)

A 8-III-1.a
The Great God Brown, The Fountain, The Moon of the Caribbees, and Other Plays. New York: Boni & Liveright, 1926.

One volume of an unnumbered, ten-volume, uniform series.

"Caribbees" appears on pp. 193–220. See A 26-I-1.a, *GGB*.

REPRINTINGS

A 8-III-1.b
New York: Boni & Liveright, [June 1926].

A 8-III-1.c
New York: Boni & Liveright, [September 1926].

A 8 "THE MOON OF THE CARIBBEES"
American fourth book publication (1932)

A 8-IV-1
REPRESENTATIVE PLAYS OF EUGENE O'NEILL

Title page: 'REPRESENTATIVE | PLAYS | OF | EUGENE O'NEILL | MARCO MILLIONS | THE EMPEROR JONES | "ANNA CHRISTIE" | WHERE THE CROSS IS MADE | THE MOON OF THE CARIBBEES | [publisher's device without initials] | NEW YORK | LIVERIGHT·INC·PUBLISHERS'

Copyright page: 'REPRESENTATIVE PLAYS OF EUGENE O'NEILL | Marco Millions, Copyright 1927 by Boni and Liveright,

| Inc. | The Emperor Jones, Copyright 1921 by Boni and | Liveright, Inc. | "Anna Christie," Copyright 1922 by Boni and Liveright, | Inc. | Where the Cross Is Made, Copyright 1919, 1923 by | Boni and Liveright, Inc. | The Moon of the Caribbees, Copyright 1919, 1923 by | Boni and Liveright, Inc. | *Printed in the United States of America* | [nine lines of roman and italic type giving translation and production rights notice]'

[A–B] [i–viii] ix [x] xi [12] 13–25 [26–28] 29–81 [82–84] 85–147 [148–150] 151–180 [181–184] 185–226 [227–228] 229–255 [256] 257–275 [276] 277–303 [304] 305–324 [C–D] 325–347 [348–350] 351–374 [375–376]

$[1–23]^8$ $[24]^6$

"Caribbees" appears on pp. 349–374.

A 8 "THE MOON OF THE CARIBBEES"
American fifth book publication (1935)

A 8-V-1
The Plays of Eugene O'Neill. New York: Scribners, [1934–35]. Twelve volumes. Wilderness Edition.

Limited to 770 numbered copies.

"Caribbees" appears in volume twelve, pp. 1–38. See A 6-VI-1, "Cardiff."

On p. xi, in a note written by EO's Random House editor, the following statement is made about "Caribbees"; '[display T]HE MOON OF THE CARIBBEES *has been produced on numerous | occasions. It was written at Provincetown, Massachusetts, in | the winter of 1917, and had its first performance at the Prov-|incetown Theatre in New York on December 20, 1918. In my opinion | this is the most interesting of all my one-act plays.*'

Publication: 770 copies published 28 June 1935.

A 8 "THE MOON OF THE CARIBBEES"
American sixth book publication (1941)

A 8-VI-1.a
The Plays of Eugene O'Neill. New York: Random House, [1941]. Three volumes.

On copyright page: 'FIRST PRINTING'.

"Caribbees" appears in volume one, pp. 453–474. See A 6-VII-1.a, "Cardiff."

REPRINTINGS

A 8-VI-1.b
New York: Random House, [1941].

On copyright page: 'SECOND PRINTING'.

A 8-VI-1.c
New York: Random House, [1951].

A 8-VI-1.d
New York: Random House, [1954–55].

A 8 "THE MOON OF THE CARIBBEES"
American seventh book publication (1944)

A 8-VII-1
Selected Plays of Eugene O'Neill. New York: Editions for the Armed Services, Inc., [1944]. Published by arrangement with Random House. No. Q-35.

Only in wrappers.

"Caribbees" appears on pp. 280–303.

A 8 "THE MOON OF THE CARIBBEES"
American eighth book publication (1972)

A 8-VIII-1
Seven Plays of the Sea. New York: Vintage Books, [1972]. No. V-856.

On copyright page: 'FIRST VINTAGE BOOKS EDITION, NOVEMBER 1972'.

Only in wrappers.

"Caribbees" appears on pp. 1–29.

A 8 "THE MOON OF THE CARIBBEES"
English first book publication (1923)

A 8-EI-1.a
THE MOON OF THE CARIBBEES AND SIX OTHER PLAYS OF THE SEA
English first edition, first printing

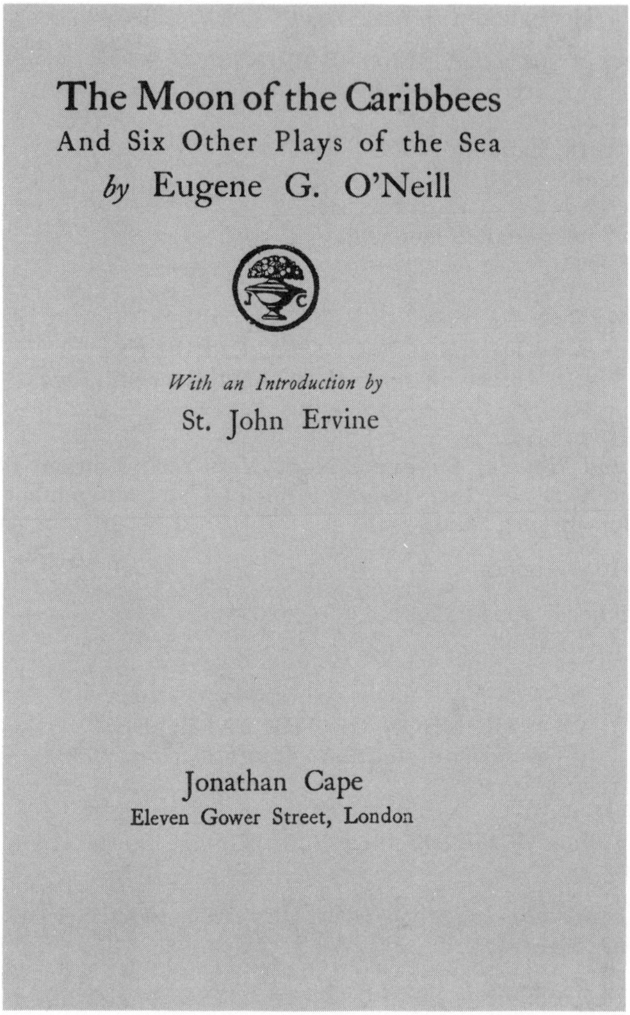

The Moon of the Caribbees
And Six Other Plays of the Sea
by Eugene G. O'Neill

With an Introduction by
St. John Ervine

Jonathan Cape
Eleven Gower Street, London

A 8-EI-1.a: 7⅜″ × 4¾″

Printed in Great Britain by Butler & Tanner, *Frome and London*

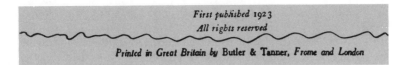

[1–6] 7–17 [18] [1–2] 3–32 [1–2] 3–23 [24] [1–2] 3–28 [1–2] 3–33 [34] [1–2] 3–30 [1–2] 3–32 [1–2] 3–42

[A]^8 B–I^8 K–P^8

Contents: p. 1: half title; p. 2: card page; p. 3: title; p. 4: copyright; p. 5: 'Contents | [eight lines of type]'; p. 6: blank; pp. 7–17: 'Introduction'; p. 18: blank; p. 1: 'The Moon of the Caribbees | A Play in One Act'; p. 2: 'Characters | [twenty-five lines of roman and italic type]'; pp. 3–32: text, headed 'The Moon of the Caribbees'; p. 1: 'Bound East for Cardiff | A Play in One Act'; p. 2: 'Characters | [eleven lines of type]'; pp. 3–23: text, headed 'Bound East for Cardiff'; p. 24: blank; p. 1: 'The Long Voyage Home | A Play in One Act'; p. 2: 'Characters | [ten lines of roman and italic type]'; pp. 3–28: text, headed 'The Long Voyage Home'; p. 1: 'In the Zone | A Play in One Act'; p. 2: 'Characters | [nine lines of roman and italic type]'; pp. 3–33: text, headed 'In the Zone'; p. 34: blank; p. 1: 'Ile | A Play in One Act'; p. 2: 'Characters | [eight lines of roman and italic type]'; pp. 3–30: text, headed 'Ile'; p. 1: 'Where the Cross is Made | A Play in One Act'; p. 2: 'Characters | [seven lines of roman and italic type]'; pp. 3–32: text, headed 'Where the Cross is Made'; p. 1: 'The Rope | A Play in One Act'; p. 2: 'Characters | [five lines of roman and italic type]'; pp. 3–42: text, headed 'The Rope'.

Typography and paper: $3\frac{5}{16}'' \times 5\frac{5}{16}''$ ($5\frac{3}{4}''$); twenty-nine to thirty-one lines per page. Wove paper.

Binding: Coated, sky blue V cloth (fine linen-like grain). Spine: white paper label ($1\frac{3}{16}'' \times 2\frac{5}{16}''$): '[blue line of decorations] | [black] The Moon of | the Caribbees | EUGENE O'NEILL | [blue decoration] | [black] *Jonathan Cape* | [blue line of decorations]'. White wove endpapers of different stock from text paper. All edges trimmed.

Dust jacket: White background. Front: '[black line of decorations] | [blue] The Moon of the Caribbees | [black] and Six Other Plays of the Sea | Eugene O'Neill | [blue publisher's device] | [black] *With Introduction by* St. John Ervine | Jonathan Cape, Eleven Gower Street, London | [line of decorations]'. Spine: '[blue line of decorations] | [black] The Moon of | the Caribbees | [blue decoration] | [black] Eugene O'Neill | *The Moon of the*

Carib-|bees, Bound East for | Cardiff, The Long Voy-|age Home, In the Zone, | Ile, Where the Cross is | Made and The Rope | [blue publisher's device] | [black] Jonathan Cape | [blue line of decorations]'. Back gives list of seven recent Cape titles. Front flap: sixteen-line excerpt from Ervine's introduction, '*7s. 6d. net*'; back flap blank.

Publication: Unknown number of copies published in April 1923. 7s. 6d.

Locations: BM (deposit-stamp 29 March 1923); JM[c]A; ScU; Yale (dj).

Note: This volume contains the first English book publication of "Caribbees," "Cardiff," "Voyage," "In the Zone," "Ile," "Cross," and "The Rope."

REPRINTINGS

A 8-EI-1.b
London: Jonathan Cape, [1926].

A 8-EI-1.c
London: Jonathan Cape, [1929]. The Travellers' Library, No. 116.

A 8-EI-1.d
London: Jonathan Cape, [1931].

A 8-EI-1.e
London: Jonathan Cape, [1942].

A 8-EI-1.f
London: Jonathan Cape, [1951].

A 8-EI-1.g
London: Jonathan Cape, [1955].

A 8-EI-1.h
London: Jonathan Cape, [1960].

A 9 "THE LONG VOYAGE HOME"
American first book publication (1919)

A 9-I-1.a
The Moon of the Caribbees and Six Other Plays of the Sea. New York: Boni & Liveright, 1919.

"Voyage" appears on pp. 55–81. See A 8-I-1.a, "Caribbees."

Note: "Voyage" first appeared in *The Smart Set,* LIII, 2 (October 1917), 83–94. See C 33. Magazine publication preceded book publication.

REPRINTINGS

A 9-I-1.b
The Moon of the Caribbees and Six Other Plays of the Sea. New York: Boni & Liveright, [1923]. Modern Library.

See A 6-II-1.b, "Cardiff," for binding variants.

A 9-I-1.c
The Long Voyage Home. New York: Modern Library, [1940].

Note: Same setting of type as A 9-I-1.a, but with changed title.

A 9 "THE LONG VOYAGE HOME"
American second book publication (1924)

A 9-II-1
The Complete Works of Eugene O'Neill. New York: Boni & Liveright, 1924. Two volumes.

Limited to 1,200 numbered copies; signed by EO.

"Voyage" appears in volume one, pp. 435–455. See A 6-IV-1, "Cardiff."

A 9 "THE LONG VOYAGE HOME"
American third book publication (1926)

A 9-III-1.a
The Great God Brown, The Fountain, The Moon of the Caribbees, and Other Plays. New York: Boni & Liveright, 1926.

One volume of an unnumbered, ten-volume, uniform series.

"Voyage" appears on pp. 243–266. See A 26-I-1.a, *GGB*.

REPRINTINGS

A 9-III-1.b
New York: Boni & Liveright, [June 1926].

A 9-III-1.c
New York: Boni & Liveright, [September 1926].

A 9 "THE LONG VOYAGE HOME"
American fourth book publication (1935)

A 9-IV-1
The Plays of Eugene O'Neill. New York: Scribners, [1934–35]. Twelve volumes. Wilderness Edition.

Limited to 770 numbered copies.

"Voyage" appears in volume twelve, pp. 39–73. See A 6-VI-1, "Cardiff."

On p. xi, in a note written by EO's Random House editor, the following statement is made about "Voyage": 'WRITTEN *at Provincetown in the winter of 1917, "The Long Voyage | Home" was first produced at the Provincetown Theatre in New York | on November 30, 1917. It has since had many revivals throughout the | United States and Great Britain.*'

Publication: 770 copies published 28 June 1935.

A 9 "THE LONG VOYAGE HOME"
American fifth book publication (1941)

A 9-V-1.a
The Plays of Eugene O'Neill. New York: Random House, [1941]. Three volumes.

On copyright page: 'FIRST PRINTING'.

"Voyage" appears in volume one, pp. 491–509. See A 6-VII-1.a, "Cardiff."

REPRINTINGS

A 9-V-1.b
New York: Random House, [1941].

On copyright page: 'SECOND PRINTING'.

A 9-V-1.c
New York: Random House, [1951].

A 9-V-1.d
New York: Random House, [1954–55].

A 9 "THE LONG VOYAGE HOME"
American sixth book publication (1944)

A 9-VI-1
Selected Plays of Eugene O'Neill. New York: Editions for the Armed Services, Inc., [1944]. Published by arrangement with Random House. No. Q-35.

Only in wrappers.

"Voyage" appears on pp. 323–343.

A 9 "THE LONG VOYAGE HOME"
American seventh book publication (1972).

A 9-VII-1
Seven Plays of the Sea. New York: Vintage Books, [1972]. No. V-856.

On copyright page: 'FIRST VINTAGE BOOKS EDITION, NOVEMBER 1972'.

Only in wrappers.

"Voyage" appears on pp. 53–77.

A 9 "THE LONG VOYAGE HOME"
English first book publication (1923)

A 9-EI-1.a
The Moon of the Caribbees and Six Other Plays of the Sea. London: Jonathan Cape, [1923].

"Voyage" appears on pp. 1–28. See A 8-EI-1.a, "Caribbees."

REPRINTINGS

A 9-EI-1.b
London: Jonathan Cape, [1926].

A 9-EI-1.c
London: Jonathan Cape, [1929]. The Travellers' Library, No. 116.

A 9-EI-1.d
London: Jonathan Cape, [1931].

A 9-EI-1.e
London: Jonathan Cape, [1942].

A 9-EI-1.f
London: Jonathan Cape, [1951].

A 9-EI-1.g
London: Jonathan Cape, [1955].

A 9-EI-1.h
London: Jonathan Cape, [1960].

A 10 "IN THE ZONE"
American first book publication (1919)

A 10-I-1.a
The Moon of the Caribbees and Six Other Plays of the Sea. New York: Boni & Liveright, 1919.

"In the Zone" appears on pp. 83–114. See A 8-I-1.a, "Caribbees."

REPRINTINGS

A 10-I-1.b
The Moon of the Caribbees and Six Other Plays of the Sea. New York: Boni & Liveright, [1923]. Modern Library.

See A 6-II-1.b, "Cardiff," for binding variants.

A 10-I-1.c
The Long Voyage Home. New York: Modern Library, [1940].

Note: Same setting of type as A 10-I-1.a, but with changed title.

A 10 "IN THE ZONE"
American second book publication (1924)

A 10-II-1
The Complete Works of Eugene O'Neill. New York: Boni & Liveright, 1924. Two volumes.

Limited to 1,200 numbered copies; signed by EO.

"In the Zone" appears in volume one, pp. 457–480. See A 6-IV-1, "Cardiff."

A 10 "IN THE ZONE"
American third book publication (1926)

A 10-III-1.a
The Great God Brown, The Fountain, The Moon of the Caribbees, and Other Plays. New York: Boni & Liveright, 1926.

One volume of an unnumbered, ten-volume, uniform series.

"In the Zone" appears on pp. 267–294. See A 26-I-1.a, *GGB.*

REPRINTINGS

A 10-III-1.b
New York: Boni & Liveright, [June 1926].

A 10-III-1.c
New York: Boni & Liveright, [September 1926].

A 10 "IN THE ZONE"
American fourth book publication (1935)

A 10-IV-1
The Plays of Eugene O'Neill. New York: Scribners, [1934–35]. Twelve volumes. Wilderness Edition.

Limited to 770 numbered copies.

"In the Zone" appears in volume twelve, pp. 75–112. See A 6-VI-1, "Cardiff."

On p. xi, in a note written by EO's Random House editor, the following statement is made about "In the Zone": 'IN THE ZONE *was written at Provincetown in the winter of 1917. | It had its initial production at the Comedy Theatre in New York by | the Washington Square Players on October 31, 1917. Following this | production it became a headline act in vaudeville in 1918. It has proved | the most popular of all the one-acters, both in this country and abroad.*'

Publication: 770 copies published 28 June 1935.

A 10 "IN THE ZONE"
American fifth book publication (1941)

A 10-V-1.a
The Plays of Eugene O'Neill. New York: Random House, [1941]. Three volumes.

On copyright page: 'FIRST PRINTING'.

"In the Zone" appears in volume one, pp. 511–532. See A 6-VII-1.a, "Cardiff."

REPRINTINGS

A 10-V-1.b
New York: Random House, [1941].

On copyright page: 'SECOND PRINTING'.

A 10-V-1.c
New York: Random House, [1951].

A 10-V-1.d
New York: Random House, [1954–55].

A 10 "IN THE ZONE"
American sixth book publication (1944)

A 10-VI-1
Selected Plays of Eugene O'Neill. New York: Editions for the Armed Services, Inc., [1944]. Published by arrangement with Random House. No. Q-35.

Only in wrappers.

"In the Zone" appears on pp. 345–369.

A 10 "IN THE ZONE"
American seventh book publication (1972)

A 10-VII-1
Seven Plays of the Sea. New York: Vintage Books, [1972]. No. V-856.

On copyright page: 'FIRST VINTAGE BOOKS EDITION, NOVEMBER 1972'.

Only in wrappers.

"In the Zone" appears on pp. 79–107.

A 10 "IN THE ZONE"
English first book publication (1923)

A 10-EI-1.a
The Moon of the Caribbees and Six Other Plays of the Sea. London: Jonathan Cape, [1923].

"In the Zone" appears on pp. 1–33. See A 8-EI-1.a, "Caribbees."

REPRINTINGS

A 10-EI-1.b
London: Jonathan Cape, [1926].

A 10-EI-1.c
London: Jonathan Cape, [1929]. The Travellers' Library, No. 116.

A 10-EI-1.d
London: Jonathan Cape, [1931].

A 10-EI-1.e
London: Jonathan Cape, [1942].

A 10-EI-1.f
London: Jonathan Cape, [1951].

A 10-EI-1.g
London: Jonathan Cape, [1955].

A 10-EI-1.h
London: Jonathan Cape, [1960].

A 11 "ILE"
American first book publication (1919)

A 11-I-1.a
The Moon of the Caribbees and Six Other Plays of the Sea. New York: Boni & Liveright, 1919.

"Ile" appears on pp. 115–143. See A 8-I-1.a, "Caribbees."

Note: "Ile" appeared in *The Smart Set*, LV, 1 (May 1918), 89–100. See C 34. Magazine publication preceded book publication.

REPRINTINGS

A 11-I-1.b
The Moon of the Caribbees and Six Other Plays of the Sea. New York: Boni & Liveright, [1923]. Modern Library.

See A 6-II-1.b, "Cardiff," for binding variants.

A 11-I-1.c
The Long Voyage Home. New York: Modern Library, [1940].

Note: Same setting of type as A 11-I-1.a, but with changed title.

A 11 "ILE"
American second book publication (1924)

A 11-II-1
The Complete Works of Eugene O'Neill. New York: Boni & Liveright, 1924. Two volumes.

Limited to 1,200 numbered copies; signed by EO.

"Ile" appears in volume one, pp. 481–502. See A 6-IV-1, "Cardiff."

A 11 "ILE"
American third book publication (1926)

A 11-III-1.a
The Great God Brown, The Fountain, The Moon of the Caribbees, and Other Plays. New York: Boni & Liveright, 1926.

One volume of an unnumbered, ten-volume, uniform series. "Ile" appears on pp. 295–319. See A 26-I-1.a, *GGB*.

REPRINTINGS

A 11-III-1.b
New York: Boni & Liveright, [June 1926].

A 11-III-1.c
New York: Boni & Liveright, [September 1926].

A 11 "ILE"
American fourth book publication (1935)

A 11-IV-1
The Plays of Eugene O'Neill. New York: Scribners, [1934–35]. Twelve volumes. Wilderness Edition.

Limited to 770 numbered copies.

"Ile" appears in volume twelve, pp. 141–174. See A 6-VI-1, "Cardiff."

On p. xii, in a note written by EO's Random House editor, the following statement is made about "Ile": 'ILE *was written at Provincetown in the winter of 1917. It was first | performed at the Provincetown Theatre in New York on November 30, 1917. It is frequently given by Little Theatre organizations in this | country and Great Britain, and has been reprinted in many anthologies | of plays.'*

Publication: 770 copies published 28 June 1935.

A 11 "ILE"
American fifth book publication (1941)

A 11-V-1.a
The Plays of Eugene O'Neill. New York: Random House, [1941]. Three volumes.

On copyright page: 'FIRST PRINTING'.

"Ile" appears in volume one, pp. 533–552. See A 6-VII-1.a, "Cardiff."

REPRINTINGS

A 11-V-1.b
New York: Random House, [1941].

On copyright page: 'SECOND PRINTING'.

A 11-V-1.c
New York: Random House, [1951].

A 11-V-1.d
New York: Random House, [1954–55].

A 11 "ILE"
American sixth book publication (1944)

A 11-VI-1
Selected Plays of Eugene O'Neill. New York: Editions for the Armed Services, Inc., [1944]. Published by arrangement with Random House. No. Q-35.

Only in wrappers.

"Ile" appears on pp. 371–392.

A 11 "ILE"
American seventh book publication (1972)

A 11-VII-1
Seven Plays of the Sea. New York: Vintage Books, [1972]. No. V-856.

On copyright page: 'FIRST VINTAGE BOOKS EDITION, NOVEMBER 1972'.

Only in wrappers.

"Ile" appears on pp. 109–134.

A 11 "ILE"
English first book publication (1923)

A 11-EI-1.a
The Moon of the Caribbees and Six Other Plays of the Sea. London: Jonathan Cape, [1923].

"Ile" appears on pp. 1–30. See A 8-EI-1.a, "Caribbees."

REPRINTINGS

A 11-EI-1.b
London: Jonathan Cape, [1926].

A 11-EI-1.c
London: Jonathan Cape, [1929]. The Travellers' Library, No. 116.

A 11-EI-1.d
London: Jonathan Cape, [1931].

A 11-EI-1.e
London: Jonathan Cape, [1942].

A 11-EI-1.f
London: Jonathan Cape, [1951].

A 11-EI-1.g
London: Jonathan Cape, [1955].

A 11-EI-1.h
London: Jonathan Cape, [1960].

A 12 "WHERE THE CROSS IS MADE"
American first book publication (1919)

A 12-I-1.a
The Moon of the Caribbees and Six Other Plays of the Sea. New York: Boni & Liveright, 1919.

"Cross" appears on pp. 145–176. See A 8-I-1.a, "Caribbees."

REPRINTINGS

A 12-I-1.b
The Moon of the Caribbees and Six Other Plays of the Sea. New York: Boni & Liveright, [1923]. Modern Library.

See A 6-II-1.b, "Caribbees," for binding variants.

A 12-I-1.c
The Long Voyage Home. New York: Modern Library, [1940].

Note: Same setting ot type as A 12-I-1.a, but with changed title.

A 12 "WHERE THE CROSS IS MADE"
American second book publication (1924)

A 12-II-1
The Complete Works of Eugene O'Neill. New York: Boni & Liveright, 1924. Two volumes.

Limited to 1,200 numbered copies; signed by EO.

"Cross" appears in volume two, pp. 423–446. See A 25-I-1, *DUTE*.

A 12 "WHERE THE CROSS IS MADE"
American third book publication (1926)

A 12-III-1.a
The Great God Brown, The Fountain, The Moon of the Caribbees, and Other Plays. New York: Boni & Liveright, 1926.

One volume of an unnumbered, ten-volume, uniform series.

"Cross" appears on pp. 321–347. See A 26-I-1.a, *GGB*.

REPRINTINGS

A 12-III-1.b
New York: Boni & Liveright, [June 1926].

A 12-III-1.c
New York: Boni & Liveright, [September 1926].

A 12 "WHERE THE CROSS IS MADE"
American fourth book publication

A 12-IV-1
Representative Plays of Eugene O'Neill. New York: Liveright, [1932].

"Cross" appears on pp. [C–D] 325–347. See A 8-IV-1, "Caribbees."

A 12 "WHERE THE CROSS IS MADE"
American fifth book publication (1935)

A 12-V-1
The Plays of Eugene O'Neill. New York: Scribners, [1934–35]. Twelve volumes. Wilderness Edition.

Limited to 770 numbered copies.

"Cross" appears in volume twelve, pp. 175–212. See A 6-VI-1, "Cardiff."

On p. xii, in a note written by EO's Random House editor, the following statement is made about "Cross": 'WHERE THE CROSS IS MADE *is the one-act play which provided the | basis for my later full-length play, "Gold." It was written at Prov-| incetown in the summer of 1918, and was first produced at the Prov-|incetown Theatre in New York on November 22, 1918*'.

Publication: 770 copies published 28 June 1935.

A 12 "WHERE THE CROSS IS MADE"
American sixth book publication (1941)

A 12-VI-1.a
The Plays of Eugene O'Neill. New York: Random House, [1941]. Three volumes.

On copyright page: 'FIRST PRINTING'.

"Cross" appears in volume one, pp. 553–573. See A 6-VII-1.a, "Cardiff."

REPRINTINGS

A 12-VI-1.b
New York: Random House, [1941].

On copyright page: 'SECOND PRINTING'.

A 12-VI-1.c
New York: Random House, [1951].

A 12-VI-1.d
New York: Random House, [1954–55].

A 12 "WHERE THE CROSS IS MADE"
American seventh book publication (1944)

A 12-VII-1
Selected Plays of Eugene O'Neill. New York: Editions for the Armed Services, Inc., [1944]. Published by arrangement with Random House. No. Q-35.

Only in wrappers.

"Cross" appears on pp. 393–416.

A 12 "WHERE THE CROSS IS MADE"
American eighth book publication (1972)

A 12-VIII-1
Seven Plays of the Sea. New York: Vintage Books, [1972]. No. V-856.

On copyright page: 'FIRST VINTAGE BOOKS EDITION, NOVEMBER 1972'.

Only in wrappers.

"Cross" appears on pp. 135–162.

A 12 "WHERE THE CROSS IS MADE"
English first book publication (1923)

A 12-EI-1.a
The Moon of the Caribbees and Six Other Plays of the Sea. London: Jonathan Cape, [1923].

"Cross" appears on pp. 1–32. See A 8-EI-1.a, "Caribbees."

REPRINTINGS

A 12-EI-1.b
London: Jonathan Cape, [1926].

A 12-EI-1.c
London: Jonathan Cape, [1929]. The Travellers' Library, No. 116.

A 12-EI-1.d
London: Jonathan Cape, [1931].

A 12-EI-1.e
London: Jonathan Cape, [1942].

A 12-EI-1.f
London: Jonathan Cape, [1951].

A 12-EI-1.g
London: Jonathan Cape, [1955].

A 12-EI-1.h
London: Jonathan Cape, [1960].

A 13 "THE ROPE"
American first book publication (1919)

A 13-I-1.a
The Moon of the Caribbees and Six Other Plays of the Sea. New York: Boni & Liveright, 1919.

"The Rope" appears on pp. 177–217. See A 8-I-1.a, "Caribbees."

REPRINTINGS

A 13-I-1.b
The Moon of the Caribbees and Six Other Plays of the Sea. New York: Boni & Liveright, [1923], pp. 177–217. Modern Library.

See A 6-II-1.b, "Cardiff," for binding variants.

A 13-I-1.c
The Long Voyage Home. New York: Modern Library, [1940], pp. 177–217.

Note: Same setting of type as A 13-I-1.a, but with changed title.

A 13 "THE ROPE"
American second book publication (1924)

A 13-II-1
The Complete Works of Eugene O'Neill. New York: Boni & Liveright, 1924. Two volumes.

Limited to 1,200 numbered copies; signed by EO.

"The Rope" appears in volume two, pp. 369–398. See A 25-I-1, *DUTE.*

A 13 "THE ROPE"
American third book publication (1926)

A 13-III-1.a
The Great God Brown, The Fountain, The Moon of the Caribbees, and Other Plays. New York: Boni & Liveright, 1926.

One volume of an unnumbered, ten-volume, uniform series.

"The Rope" appears on pp. 349–383. See A 26-I-1.a, *GGB*.

REPRINTINGS

A 13-I-1.b
New York: Boni & Liveright, [June 1926].

A 13-I-1.c
New York: Boni & Liveright, [September 1926].

A 13 "THE ROPE"
American fourth book publication (1935)

A 13-IV-1
The Plays of Eugene O'Neill. New York: Scribners, [1934–35]. Twelve volumes. Wilderness Edition.

Limited to 770 numbered copies.

"The Rope" appears in volume twelve, pp. 213–260. See A 6-VI-1, "Cardiff."

On p. xii, in a note written by EO's Random House editor, the following statement is made about "The Rope": 'THE ROPE *was written at Provincetown in the winter of 1918. It was first performed at the Provincetown Theatre in New York on April 26, 1918.*'

Publication: 770 copies published 28 June 1935.

A 13 "THE ROPE"
American fifth book publication (1941)

A 13-V-1.a
The Plays of Eugene O'Neill. New York: Random House, [1941]. Three volumes.

On copyright page: 'FIRST PRINTING'.

"The Rope" appears in volume one, pp. 575–602. See A 6-VII-1.a, "Cardiff."

REPRINTINGS

A 13-V-1.b
New York: Random House, [1941].

On copyright page: 'SECOND PRINTING'.

A 13-V-1.c
New York: Random House, [1951].

A 13-V-1.d
New York: Random House, [1954–55].

A 13 "THE ROPE"
American sixth book publication (1944)

A 13-VI-1
Selected Plays of Eugene O'Neill. New York: Editions for the Armed Services, Inc., [1944]. Published by arrangement with Random House. No. Q-35.

Only in wrappers.

"The Rope" appears on pp. 417–447.

A 13 "THE ROPE"
American seventh book publication (1972)

A 13-VII-1
Seven Plays of the Sea. New York: Vintage Books, [1972]. No. V-856.

On copyright page: 'FIRST VINTAGE BOOKS EDITION, NOVEMBER 1972'.

Only in wrappers.

"The Rope" appears on pp. 163–199.

A 13 "THE ROPE"
English first book publication (1923)

A 13-EI-1.a
The Moon of the Caribbees and Six Other Plays of the Sea. London: Jonathan Cape, [1923].

"The Rope" appears on pp. 1–42. See A 8-EI-1.a, "Caribbees."

REPRINTINGS

A 13-EI-1.b
London: Jonathan Cape, [1926].

A 13-EI-1.c
London: Jonathan Cape, [1929]. The Travellers' Library, No. 116.

A 13-EI-1.d
London: Jonathan Cape, [1931].

A 13-EI-1.e
London: Jonathan Cape, [1942].

A 13-EI-1.f
London: Jonathan Cape, [1951].

A 13-EI-1.g
London: Jonathan Cape, [1955].

A 13-EI-1.h
London: Jonathan Cape, [1960].

A 14 BEYOND THE HORIZON
American first book publication (1920)

A 14-I-1.a
BEYOND THE HORIZON
American first edition, first printing

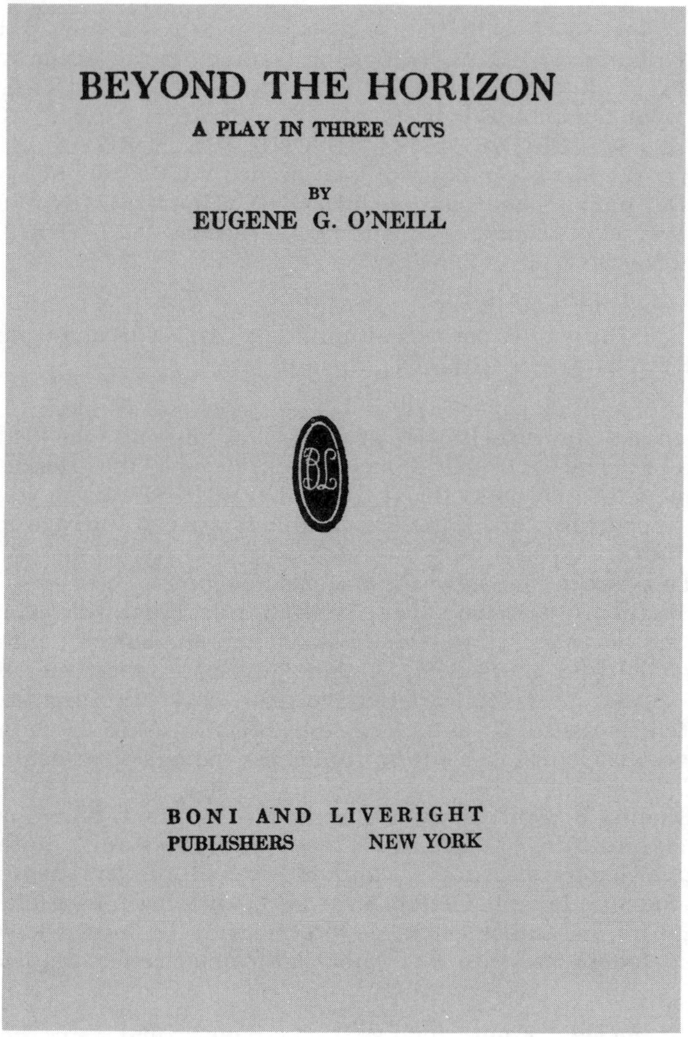
BEYOND THE HORIZON
A PLAY IN THREE ACTS
BY
EUGENE G. O'NEILL
BONI AND LIVERIGHT
PUBLISHERS NEW YORK

A 14-I-1.a: 7 3/8" × 5 1/8"

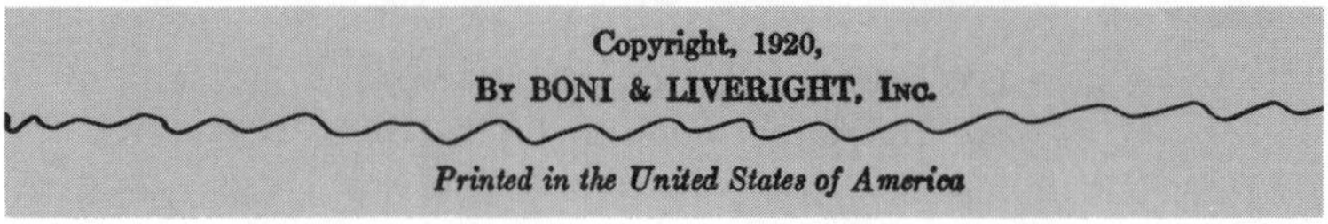
Copyright, 1920,
By BONI & LIVERIGHT, Inc.
Printed in the United States of America

[i–x] 1–62 [63–64] 65–119 [120–122] 123–165 [166]

[1–11]^{8}

Contents: p. i: half title; p. ii: card page; p. iii: title; p. iv: copyright; p. v: 'TO AGNES'; p. vi: blank; p. vii: act-scene synopsis; p. viii: blank; p. ix: 'ACT I'; p. x: 'CHARACTERS | [twelve lines of roman and italic type]'; pp. 1–62: text, headed 'ACT ONE | SCENE ONE'; p. 63: 'BEYOND THE HORIZON | ACT II'; p. 64: blank; pp. 65–119: text, headed 'ACT TWO | SCENE ONE'; p. 120: blank; p. 121: 'BEYOND THE HORIZON | ACT III'; p. 122: blank; pp. 123–165: text, headed 'ACT THREE | SCENE ONE'; p. 166: blank.

Typography and paper: 11 point on 13, Scotch. $3\frac{5}{16}'' \times 5\frac{7}{16}''$ ($5\frac{11}{16}''$); thirty lines per page. Running heads: rectos and versos, 'BEYOND THE HORIZON'. Wove paper.

Binding: Tan paper-covered boards with buff V cloth (fine linen-like grain) shelf back. Front: '[black] Beyond | the | Horizon | Eugene G. O'Neill'. Spine: '[black] Beyond | the | Horizon | Eugene G. | O'Neill | BONI AND | LIVERIGHT'. Sized, white wove endpapers of different stock from text paper. Top edge only trimmed.

There are two binding variants for this volume:

Binding A: dark tan paper-covered boards. Front: title capital letters measure $\frac{9}{16}''$, title lower-case letters measure $\frac{3}{8}''$; author capital letters measure $\frac{3}{8}''$, author lower-case letters measure $\frac{1}{4}''$. Spine: title capital letters measure $\frac{3}{16}''$, title lower-case letters measure $\frac{1}{8}''$; author capital letters measure $\frac{1}{8}''$, author lower-case letters measure $\frac{3}{32}''$; publisher capital letters measure $\frac{3}{32}''$.

Binding B: light tan paper-covered boards. Front: title capital letters measure $\frac{9}{16}''$, title lower-case letters measure $\frac{3}{8}''$; author capital letters measure $\frac{5}{16}''$, author lower-case letters measure $\frac{1}{8}''$. Spine: title capital letters measure $\frac{3}{16}''$, title lower-case letters measure $\frac{1}{8}''$; author capital letters measure $\frac{1}{8}''$, author lower-case letters measure $\frac{1}{16}''$; publisher capital letters measure $\frac{1}{16}''$.

Dust jacket: Front: [orange background] [first three lines to left of center] Beyond | The | Horizon | *Can You Recall More*

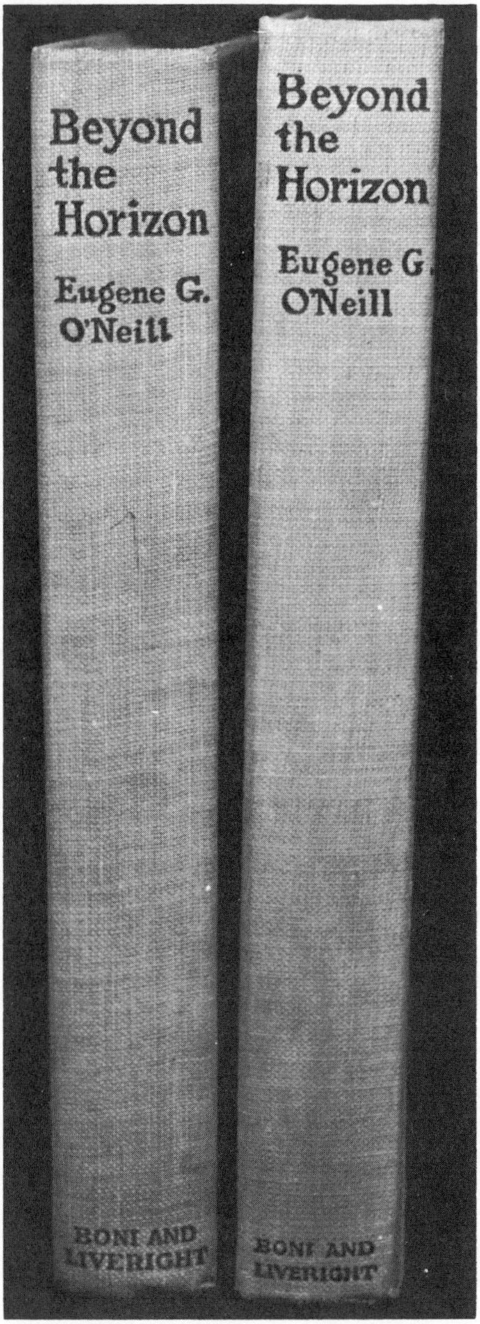

Binding variants of A 14-I-1.a

Enthusiastic | *Comment Than This*: | [ten-line blurb] | *Alexander Woollcott, The New York Times.* | [four-line blurb] | *J. Ranken Towse, New York Evening Post.* | [two-line blurb] | *New York Sun.* | by EUGENE O'NEILL | *Author of* | *"The Moon of the Caribbees"'*. Spine: '[beige background] [double rule] | BEYOND THE | HORIZON | [double rule] | EUGENE O'NEILL | [publisher's device] | $1.50 net | [double rule] | BONI AND | LIVERIGHT | [double rule]'. Back: '[orange background] Beyond | The | Horizon | [three-line blurb] | Heywood Broun, *New York Tribune.* | [eight-line blurb] | *New York World.* | [eight-line blurb] | *The New York Evening Sun.* | By EUGENE O'NEILL | Author of | *"The Moon of the Caribbees"'*. Front and back flaps have quote from Woollcott's review in the *New York Times*, with 'Wollcott' spelling.

Publication: 1,250 copies published 10 March 1920.

Printing: Printed 30 January 1920 by George Held, Albany, New York, and bound by J. J. Little & Ives, New York.

Locations: JM^{c}A (Binding A); LC (deposit-stamp 22 March 1920); Lilly (Binding A); PSt (Binding A); ScU (Binding A); Yale (Bindings A and B).

REPRINTINGS

A 14-I-1.b
New York: Boni & Liveright, [October 1920]

A 14-I-1.c
New York: Boni & Liveright, [February 1921].

A 14-I-1.d
New York: Boni & Liveright, [June 1921].

A 14-I-1.e
New York: Boni & Liveright, [November 1922].

A 14 BEYOND THE HORIZON
American second book publication (1924)

A 14-II-1
The Complete Works of Eugene O'Neill. New York: Boni & Liveright, [1924]. Two volumes.

Limited to 1,200 numbered copies; signed by EO.

BTH appears in volume one, pp. 83–179. See A 6-IV-1, "Cardiff."

A 14 BEYOND THE HORIZON
American third book publication (1925)

A 14-III-1.a
Plays, Beyond the Horizon, The Straw, Before Breakfast.
New York: Boni & Liveright, 1925.

First printing: July 1925.

One volume of an unnumbered, ten-volume, uniform series.

BTH appears on pp. 7–128.

REPRINTINGS

A 14-III-1.b
New York: Boni & Liveright, [December 1925].

A 14-III-1.c
New York: Boni & Liveright, [June 1926].

A 14-III-1.d
New York: Boni & Liveright, [January 1927].

A 14-III-1.e
New York: Boni & Liveright, [October 1927].

A 14-III-1.f
New York: Boni & Liveright, [April 1928].

A 14-III-1.g
New York: Boni & Liveright, [November 1928].

A 14-III-1.h
New York: Liveright, [March 1931].

A 14-III-1.i
New York: Liveright, [September 1932].

A 14 BEYOND THE HORIZON
American fourth book publication (1935)

A 14-IV-1
THE PLAYS OF EUGENE O'NEILL. Twelve volumes. Wilderness Edition

Volume six

Title page: '[within decorated border] [white against gray background] THE | PLAYS | OF | EUGENE | O'NEILL | [wavy rule] | *Beyond the Horizon* | *Welded* | [wavy rule] | VI | WILDERNESS · EDITION | *NEW YORK* | Charles Scribner's Sons'

Copyright page: 'COPYRIGHT, 1935, BY CHARLES SCRIBNER'S SONS | [nineteen lines of roman and italic type]'

[i–x] xi [xii] xiii [xiv] [1–2] 3–115 [116] 117–164 [165–166] 167–260 [261–266]

$[1\text{–}16]^8$ $[17]^4$ $[18]^8$

The statement of limitation on p. iv reads: '[decorated rule] | [swash *T*'s and *N*'s] *THIS WILDERNESS EDITION* | OF THE | PLAYS OF EUGENE O'NEILL | printed from type now destroyed, is limited | to seven hundred and seventy sets | of which twenty are for presentation | This is number | [decorated rule]'.

The colophon on p. 262 reads: '[decorated rule] | [swash *T* and *K*] *THIS BOOK* | the sixth of twelve volumes designed by Elmer Adler | set in an eighteenth-century type face | based on the castings made by John Baskerville | is printed on a specially watermarked paper | at the press of the publisher | in the city of New York | in the month of January | MCM XXX V | [publisher's device]'.

Note: The watermark is: 'CSS | [classical tragedy mask]'.

BTH appears on pp. 1–164.

A facsimile of EO's sketch for the setting for Act I, scene i, his holograph list of characters, and his holograph act-scene synopsis appears on p. x.

On p. xi, in a note written by EO's Random House editor, the following statement is made about *BTH:* '[display B]EYOND THE HORIZON, *written at Provincetown in the winter | of 1918, was the first of my full-length plays to be produced | and published. It had its initial performance at the Morosco Theatre on February 2, 1920, under the Direction of John D. Williams. | Richard Bennett originated the rôle of Robert Mayo, and the late Louise | Closser Hale played Mrs. Atkins. The part of Ruth was performed. on | different occasions, by Helen MacKellar and Aline MacMahon. "Be-|yond the Horizon" was awarded the Pulitzer Prize for 1920.'*

Publication: 770 copies published 30 January 1935.

Locations: JM^cA (#456); LC (presentation); MJB (#592 boxed); ScU (#749); Yale (presentation).

A 14 BEYOND THE HORIZON
American fifth book publication (1936?)

A 14-V-1
Ah, Wilderness! and Two Other Plays. New York: Modern Library, [1936?]. ML #342.

Includes *BTH* and *AGCGW*. *BTH* appears on pp. 197–306.

A 14 BEYOND THE HORIZON
American sixth book publication (1941)

A 14-VI-1.a
THE PLAYS OF EUGENE O'NEILL. Three volumes

Volume three

Title page: '[within triple-rule frame, black against solid gray beige background] THE PLAYS | OF | EUGENE | O'NEILL | [publisher's device] | RANDOM HOUSE · New York'

Copyright page: 'FIRST PRINTING | COPYRIGHT, 1919, 1925, 1926, 1927, 1928, | BY EUGENE O'NEILL | MANUFACTURED IN THE UNITED STATES OF AMERICA'

[i–vi] [1–2] 3–78 [79–80] 81–169 [170–172] 173–204 [205–206] 207–254 [255–256] 257–325 [326–330] 331–416 [417–420] 421–489 [490–492] 493–567 [568–570]

$[1\text{–}18]^{16}$

BTH appears on pp. 79–169.

Locations: JM^cA; ScU; Yale.

REPRINTINGS

A 14-VI-1.b
New York: Random House, [1941].

On copyright page: 'SECOND PRINTING'.

A 14-VI-1.c
New York: Random House, [1951].

A 14-VI-1.d
New York: Random House, [1954–55].

A 14 BEYOND THE HORIZON
English first book publication (1924)

A 14-EI-1.a
BEYOND THE HORIZON AND GOLD
English first edition, first printing

Beyond the Horizon
and Gold *two plays*
by
Eugene O'Neill

Jonathan Cape Ltd
Eleven Gower Street, London

A 14-EI-1.a: $7\frac{3}{8}'' \times 4\frac{3}{4}''$

FIRST PUBLISHED IN MCMXXIV
MADE & PRINTED IN GREAT BRITAIN
BY BUTLER & TANNER LTD.
FROME AND
LONDON

[i–xii] [1–4] 5–69 [70] 71–175 [176] [1–4] 5–33 [34] 35–128 [129–132]

[A]^8 B–I^8 K–U^8. A_1 and U_8 are pastedown endpapers.

Contents: pp. i–iv: blank; p. v: half title; p. vi: card page; p. vii: title; p. viii: copyright; p. ix: 'TO AGNES'; p. x: blank; p. xi: table of contents; p. xii: blank; p. 1: 'Beyond the Horizon | A Play in Three Acts'; p. 2: blank; p. 3: act-scene synopsis; p. 4: 'Characters | [thirteen lines of roman and italic type]'; pp. 5–69: text, headed 'Beyond the Horizon | ACT ONE | SCENE ONE'; p. 70: blank; pp. 71–175: text, headed 'ACT TWO | SCENE ONE'; p. 176: blank; p. 1: 'Gold | A Play in Four Acts'; p. 2: blank; p. 3: act-scene synopsis; p. 4: 'Characters | [twelve lines of roman and italic type]'; pp. 5–33: text, headed 'Gold | ACT ONE'; p. 34: blank; pp. 35–128: text, headed 'ACT TWO'; pp. 129–132: blank.

Typography and paper: $3\frac{5}{16}$″ × 5″ ($5\frac{7}{16}$″); twenty-eight lines per page. Running heads: rectos and versos, individual play titles. Wove paper.

Binding: Coated, sky blue V cloth (fine linen-like grain). Spine: white paper label ($2\frac{1}{16}$″ × $1\frac{3}{8}$″): '[blue line of decorations] | [black] Beyond the | Horizon | EUGENE O'NEILL | [blue decoration] | [black] *Jonathan Cape* | [blue line of decorations]'. White wove endpapers of same stock as text paper. Top and right edges trimmed.

Dust jacket: Not seen.

Publication: Unknown number of copies published in 1924. 7s. 6d.

Locations: BM (deposit-stamp 17 April 1924); JM^{c}A; Yale.

REPRINTING

A 14-EI-1.b
London: Jonathan Cape, [April 1937]. Nobel Prize Edition. (Not a new edition.)

LATER PRINTING

Beyond the Horizon and Marco Millions. London: Jonathan Cape, [1960]. (Not seen by the bibliographer. This volume is the first time these two plays appeared together in England, and it may be a new edition.)

A 15 THE EMPEROR JONES
American first book publication (1921)

A 15-I-1.a
THE EMPEROR JONES, DIFF'RENT, THE STRAW
American first edition, first printing

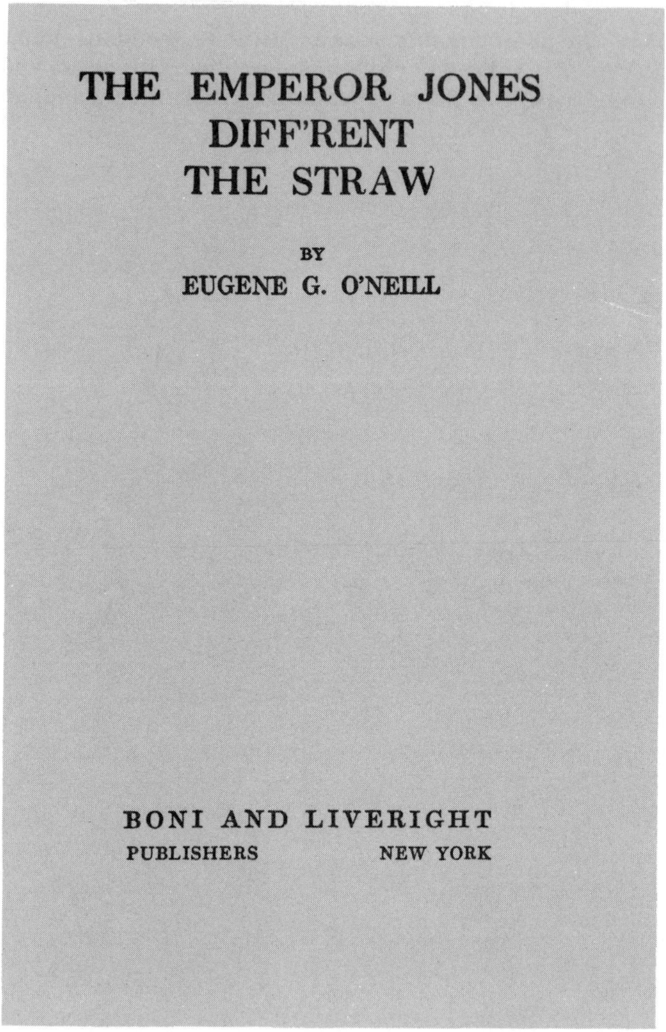

THE EMPEROR JONES
DIFF'RENT
THE STRAW

BY
EUGENE G. O'NEILL

BONI AND LIVERIGHT
PUBLISHERS NEW YORK

A 15-I-1.a: $7\frac{3}{8}'' \times 4\frac{15}{16}''$

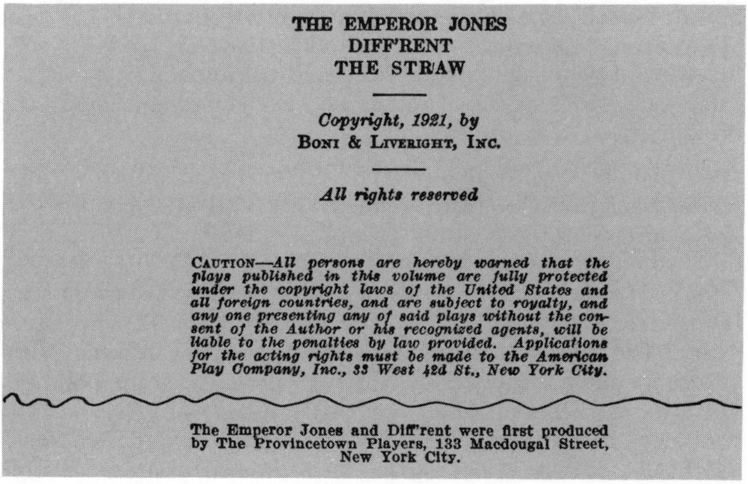
THE EMPEROR JONES
DIFF'RENT
THE STRAW

Copyright, 1921, by
BONI & LIVERIGHT, INC.

All rights reserved

CAUTION—*All persons are hereby warned that the plays published in this volume are fully protected under the copyright laws of the United States and all foreign countries, and are subject to royalty, and any one presenting any of said plays without the consent of the Author or his recognized agents, will be liable to the penalties by law provided. Applications for the acting rights must be made to the American Play Company, Inc., 33 West 42d St., New York City.*

The Emperor Jones and Diff'rent were first produced by The Provincetown Players, 133 Macdougal Street, New York City.

[A–B] [i–viii] ix–x [xi–xii] 1–53 [54–56] 57–101 [102–104] 105–142 [143–146] 147–197 [198–202] 203–285 [286–290]

$[1\text{–}19]^8$

Contents: pp. A–B: blank; p. i: half title; p. ii: card page; p. iii: title; p. iv: copyright; p. v: contents; p. vi: blank; p. vii: 'THE STRAW'; p. viii: blank; p. ix: 'CHARACTERS | [twenty-three lines of roman and italic type]'; p. x: act-scene synopsis; p. xi: 'ACT I'; p. xii: blank; pp. 1–53: text, headed 'ACT I | SCENE ONE'; p. 54: blank; p. 55: 'ACT II'; p. 56: blank; pp. 57–101: text, headed 'ACT II | SCENE ONE'; p. 102: blank; p. 103: 'ACT III'; p. 104: blank; pp. 105–142: text, headed 'ACT III'; p. 143: 'THE EMPEROR JONES'; p. 144: blank; p. 145: 'CHARACTERS | [fifteen lines of roman and italic type]'; p. 146: blank; pp. 147–197: text, headed 'SCENE ONE'; p. 198: blank; p. 199: 'DIFF'RENT | A Play in Two Acts'; p. 200: blank; p. 201: 'CHARACTERS | [eight lines of roman and italic type]'; p. 202: act-scene synopsis; pp. 203–285: text, headed 'ACT ONE'; pp. 286–290: blank.

Typography and paper: 11 point on 13, Scotch. $3\frac{5}{16}'' \times 5\frac{3}{8}''$ $(5\frac{11}{16}'')$; thirty lines per page. Running heads: rectos and versos, individual play titles. Wove paper.

Binding: There are two binding variants for this volume:
Binding A: Tan paper-covered boards with buff B cloth (linen-like grain) shelf back. Front: '[black] The Emperor Jones | Diff'rent [two decorations] | The Straw | Eugene G. O'Neill'.

Spine: '[black] The | Emperor | Jones [one decoration] | Diff'rent | The | Straw | Eugene G. | O'Neill | BONI AND | LIVERIGHT'. Sized white wove endpapers. All edges trimmed.

Binding B: Front cover and spine have 'Eugene O'Neill'; the middle initial '*G*' is omitted.

Dust jacket: Front: photograph of Charles S. Gilpen against white background; '[red] The | EMPEROR JONES | [black] *(In Eight Scenes)* | A study of the psychology of | fear and of race superstition | [at the left of photo] [red] DIFF'RENT | [black] *(In Two Acts)* | The Story of | a Sex-Starved | Woman. | [at the right of photo] [red] The STRAW | [black] *(In Three Acts)* | The first of Mr. O'Neill's | plays to appear in book | form before its stage | production, which is | announced for October | of this year. | [below photo] CHARLES S. | GILPEN | *as* | The Emperor | Jones | Three Plays | In One Volume | *by* EUGENE G. O'NEILL'. Spine: black lettering on white background; '[double rule] | THE | EMPEROR | JONES | [short rule] | DIFF'RENT | [short rule] | The STRAW | [double rule] | BY | EUGENE G. | O'NEILL | $2.00 | [double rule] | BONI AND | LIVERIGHT | [double rule]'. Back: eight blurbs (twenty-nine lines of type) by reviewers of EO plays. Front flap: ad for *BTH*. Back flap: ad for *MOTC*.

Publication: 2,200 copies published 7 April 1921. $2.00.

Printing: Printed 20 March 1921 by J. J. Little & Ives, New York, from plates made by Little & Ives; bound by Little & Ives.

Locations: JM^c^A (Binding A, dj); Lilly (two, Binding A, one in dj): Yale (Binding A, dj).

Note one: *TEJ* appeared in *Theatre Arts Magazine*, V, 1 (January 1921), 29–59. See C 40. Magazine publication preceded book publication. According to Sanborn and Clark, EO edited the magazine text of *TEJ* for book publication.

Note two: The following stage direction and speech by Smithers appear as the ending to both the *Theatre Arts* printing and the first book publication of *TEJ*. They are deleted in most later editions of the play.

Note three: A freak copy of the first printing of *TEJ* has been seen. LC number PS 3529/.N5E5/1921 of *The Emperor Jones, Diff'rent, The Straw* at Rutgers University Library has the following errors. Page 51 (recto) has page 113 superimposed on it; the following verso and recto are blank; the next verso is page

THE EMPEROR JONES 197

limp body. There is a little reddish-purple hole under his left breast. He is dead. They carry him to Lem, *who examines his body with great satisfaction.* Smithers *leans over his shoulder—in a tone of frightened awe.*] Well, they did for yer right enough, Jonsey, me lad! Dead as a 'erring! [*Mockingly.*] Where's yer 'igh an' mighty airs now, yer bloomin' Majesty? [*Then with a grin.*] Silver bullets! Gawd blimey, but yer died in the 'eighth o' style, any'ow! [Lem *makes a motion to the soldiers to carry the body out left.* Smithers *speaks to him sneeringly.*]

Smithers—And I s'pose you think it's yer bleedin' charms and yer silly beatin' the drum that made 'im run in a circle when 'e'd lost 'imself, don't yer? [*But* Lem *makes no reply, does not seem to hear the question, walks out left after his men.* Smithers *looks after him with contemptuous scorn.*] Stupid as 'ogs, the lot of 'em! Blarsted niggers!

[*Curtain Falls.*]

112 (out of proper sequence); the next recto is page 109 (also out of sequence) with ACT II in bold type superimposed on the middle of the page; the following verso and recto are blank. The next verso, page 58, which is in correct sequence, has page 108 superimposed on it; recto page 59 has page 105 superimposed on it; the next verso and recto are blank. The following verso is a clean page 62, but the recto page 63 has page 101 superimposed on it. The following verso and recto are blank. Verso page 66 has page 107 superimposed on it. This completes the series of misprinted pages.

These pages correspond with the fifth gathering or signature in the first edition. The Rutgers Library copy has been rebound by the library.

REPRINTINGS

A 15-I-1.b
New York: Boni & Liveright, [June 1921].

A 15-I-1.c
New York: Boni & Liveright, [August 1921].

A 15-I-1.d
New York: Boni & Liveright, [November 1921].

A 15-I-1.e
New York: Boni & Liveright, [October 1922].

A 15-I-1.f
New York: Boni & Liveright, [March 1924].

A 15 THE EMPEROR JONES
American second book publication, first separate book publication (1921)

A 15-II-1
THE EMPEROR JONES
American first edition, possibly only printing

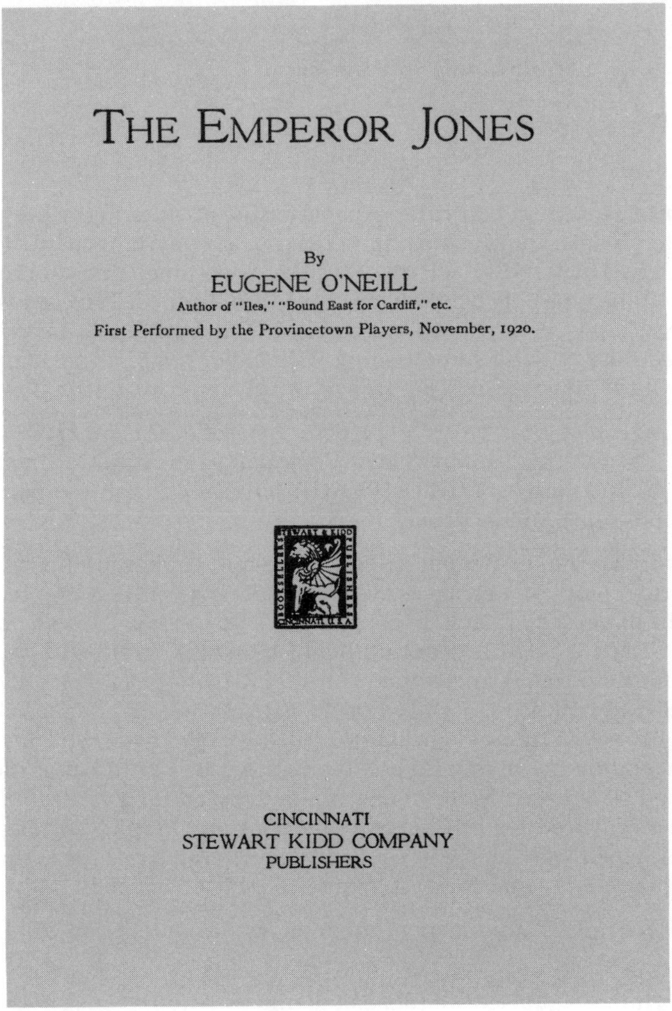

THE EMPEROR JONES

By
EUGENE O'NEILL
Author of "Ile," "Bound East for Cardiff," etc.
First Performed by the Provincetown Players, November, 1920.

CINCINNATI
STEWART KIDD COMPANY
PUBLISHERS

A 15-II-1: $7\frac{1}{2}'' \times 5\frac{1}{16}''$

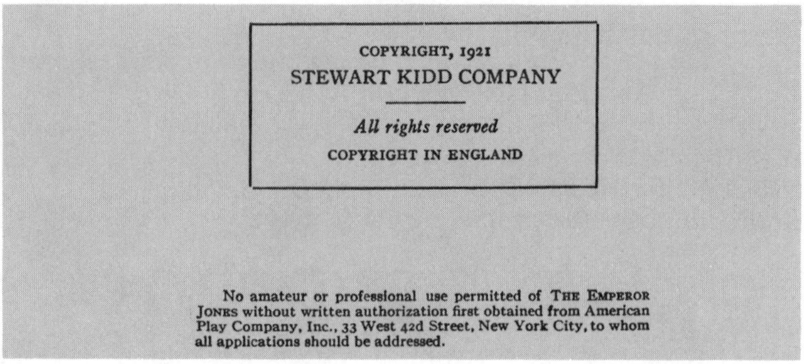
COPYRIGHT, 1921
STEWART KIDD COMPANY

All rights reserved
COPYRIGHT IN ENGLAND

No amateur or professional use permitted of THE EMPEROR JONES without written authorization first obtained from American Play Company, Inc., 33 West 42d Street, New York City, to whom all applications should be addressed.

[1–6] 7–54 [55–56]

Stapled.

Contents: p. 1: half title; p. 2: card page of titles in the Stewart Kidd Modern Plays series; p. 3: title; p. 4: copyright; p. 5: 'THE EMPEROR JONES | CHARACTERS | [seventeen lines of roman and italic type]'; p. 6: blank; pp. 7–54: text, headed 'THE EMPEROR JONES'; p. 55: ad for EO titles published by Boni & Liveright beginning with *TEJ* and ending with *Gold;* p. 56: ad for Barrett H. Clark's *European Theories of the Drama.*

Typography and paper: 12 point set solid, Caslon Old Face. $3\frac{5}{16}'' \times 5\frac{3}{8}''$ ($5\frac{13}{16}''$); thirty-two lines per page. Running heads: rectos and versos, 'THE EMPEROR JONES | [margin-to-margin double rule]'. Wove paper.

Binding: Paper wrappers. Front: '[white background with six vertical blue gray stripes, three to the left of center, three to the right of center] [black, in center] THE | EMPEROR | JONES | BY | EUGENE O'NEILL | [decoration of blue gray circle with white profiles of tragedy and comedy masks] | [black] STEWART KIDD | MODERN PLAYS | EDITED BY | FRANK SHAY'. Back: list of twenty-seven titles, beginning with *The Truth About the Theater* and ending with *Six Who Pass While the Lentils Boil,* published by Stewart Kidd. Inside front cover: ad for *The Provincetown Plays,* edited by George Cram Cook and Frank Shay. Inside back cover: ad for *Fifty Contemporary One-Act Plays,* edited by Frank Shay and Pierre Loving. All edges trimmed.

Publication: Unknown number of copies published 28 July 1921.

Locations: JM^{c}A; LC (deposit-stamp 1 August 1921); Lilly; PSt; Yale.

Note: Original ending appears in this edition. See A 15-I-1.a.

A 15 THE EMPEROR JONES
American third book publication (1924)

A 15-III-1
The Complete Works of Eugene O'Neill. New York: Boni & Liveright, [1924]. Two volumes.

Limited to 1,200 numbered copies; signed by EO.

TEJ appears in volume two, pp. 1–40. See A 25-I-1, *DUTE.*

Note: Original ending deleted from this edition. See A 15-I-1.a.

A 15 THE EMPEROR JONES
American fourth book publication (1925)

A 15-IV-1.a
Plays, The Emperor Jones, Gold, The First Man, The Dreamy Kid. New York: Boni & Liveright, 1925.

First printing: July, 1925.

One volume of an unnumbered, ten-volume, uniform series.

TEJ appears on pp. 7–52.

Note: Original ending deleted from this edition. See A 15-I-1.a.

REPRINTINGS

A 15-IV-1.b
New York: Boni & Liveright, [March 1926].

A 15-IV-1.c
New York: Boni & Liveright, [November 1926].

A 15-IV-1.d
New York: Boni & Liveright, [January 1928].

A 15-IV-1.e
New York: Boni & Liveright, [May 1928].

A 15-IV-1.f
New York: Boni & Liveright, [July 1930].

A 15-IV-1.g
New York: Liveright, [May 1932].

A 15 THE EMPEROR JONES
American fifth book publication (1928)

A 15-V-1
THE EMPEROR JONES
American limited edition, only printing

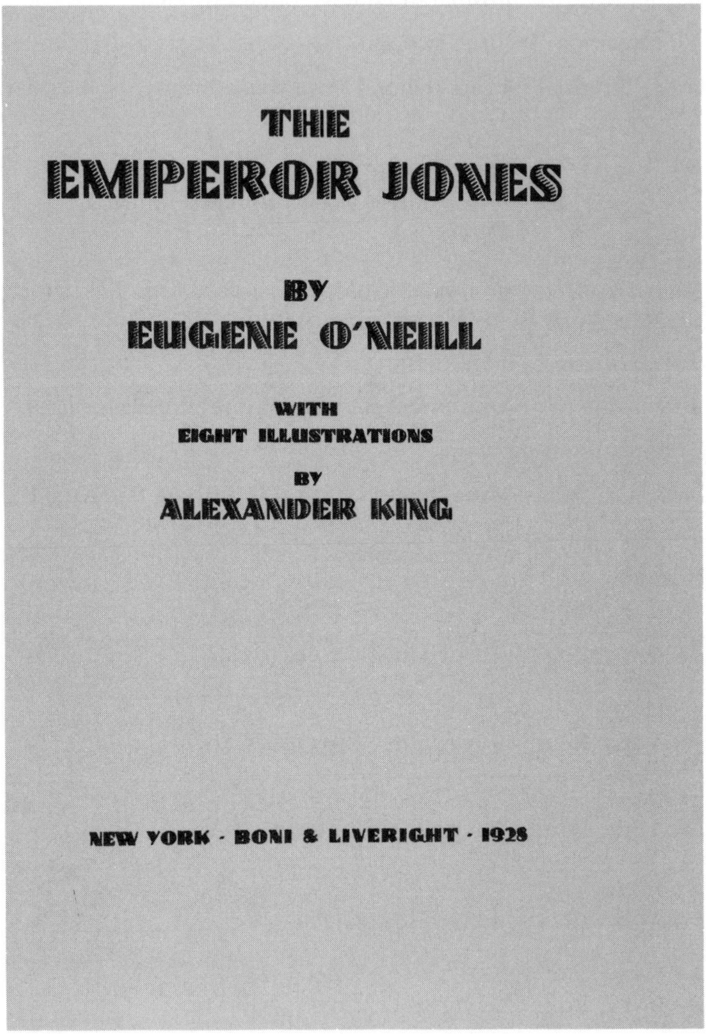
THE
EMPEROR JONES

BY
EUGENE O'NEILL

WITH
EIGHT ILLUSTRATIONS
BY
ALEXANDER KING

NEW YORK · BONI & LIVERIGHT · 1928

A 15-V-1: all in brown; $10\frac{1}{16}'' \times 7\frac{9}{16}''$

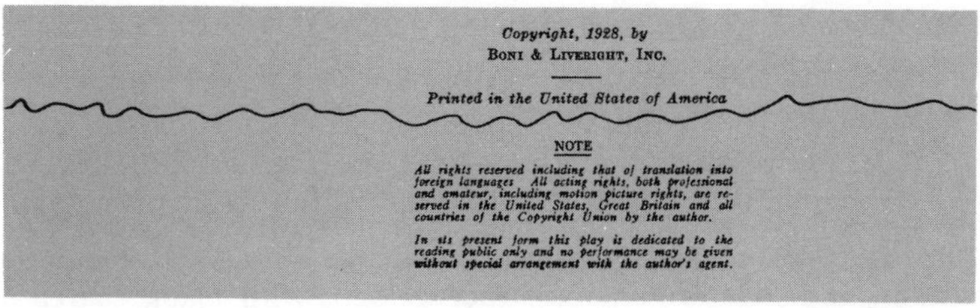

Copyright, 1928, by
BONI & LIVERIGHT, INC.

Printed in the United States of America

NOTE

All rights reserved including that of translation into foreign languages All acting rights, both professional and amateur, including motion picture rights, are reserved in the United States, Great Britain and all countries of the Copyright Union by the author.

In its present form this play is dedicated to the reading public only and no performance may be given without special arrangement with the author's agent.

[i–ii] [1–14] 15–39 [40–42] 43–48 [49–50] 51–54 [55–56] 57–61 [62–64] 65–69 [70–72] 73–75 [76–78] 79–83 [84–86] 87–90 [91–94]

$[1]^4$ $[2\text{–}6]^8$ $[7]^4$; illustrations are tipped in facing pp. 15, 43, 51, 57, 65, 73, 79, and 87.

Contents: pp. i–ii: blank; p. 1: blank; p. 2: statement of limitation: 'This special edition of *The Emperor Jones,* | with eight illustrations by Alexander King, is | limited to 775 numbered copies, of which 750 | are for sale. Each copy is signed by the au-|thor. This copy is no. '; p. 3: half title; p. 4: blank; p. 5: title; p. 6: copyright; p. 7: list of characters; p. 8: blank; p. 9: '[decorated] SCENES | [eighteen lines of type]'; p. 10: blank; p. 11: list of illustrations; p. 12: blank; p. 13: '[decorated] SCENE ONE'; p. 14: blank; pp. 15–39: text, headed '[decorated] SCENE ONE'; p. 40: blank; p. 41: '[decorated] SCENE TWO'; p. 42: blank; pp. 43–48: text, headed '[decorated] SCENE TWO'; p. 49: '[decorated] SCENE THREE'; p. 50: blank; pp. 51–54: text, headed '[decorated] SCENE THREE'; p. 55: '[decorated] SCENE FOUR'; p. 56: blank; pp. 57–61: text, headed '[decorated] SCENE FOUR'; p. 62: blank; p. 63: '[decorated] SCENE FIVE'; p. 64: blank; pp. 65–69: text, headed '[decorated] SCENE FIVE'; p. 70: blank; p. 71: '[decorated] SCENE SIX'; p. 72: blank; pp. 73–75: text, headed '[decorated] SCENE SIX'; p. 76: blank; p. 77: '[decorated] SCENE SEVEN; p. 78: blank; pp. 79–83: text, headed [decorated] SCENE SEVEN'; p. 84: blank; p. 85: '[decorated] SCENE EIGHT'; p. 86: blank; pp. 87–90: text, headed '[decorated] SCENE EIGHT'; p. 91: colophon: '*This edition of* The Emperor Jones *was printed | from Bodoni type, which was distributed after | printing. The typography was designed by* | S. A. JACOBS, *and the book made by* THE | VAN REES ORGANIZATION. *The illustra-|tions were engraved and printed by* THE GRINNELL LITHOGRAPHIC COMPANY, *and | the paper was supplied by* HERMAN SCOTT CHALFANT, INC.; *the entire manufacture | under the direction of* ALBERT H. GROSS | *of* BONI & LIVERIGHT.'; pp. 92–94: blank.

Typography and paper: 12 point on 14, Bodoni. 4 5/16" × 6 13/16" (7 1/4"); thirty to thirty-three lines per page. Laid paper with vertical chain marks 7/8" apart, watermarked with EO signature.

Binding: Black paper-covered boards decorated with red, blue, green, and gold angular abstract design, with black coated V cloth (fine linen-like grain) shelf back. Spine: '[goldstamped in decorated type, vertically from top to bottom] THE EMPEROR JONES · EUGENE O'NEILL'. White wove endpapers, coated black. Edges originally untrimmed and unopened.

Dust jacket: Grayish tan background. Front: '[black] THE | EMPEROR JONES | *by* EUGENE O'NEILL | [pasted-on illustration of Jones in forest, same as the one that appears before p. 43] | *Drawings by* | ALEXANDER KING'. Spine: '[black, two lines, vertically from bottom to top] THE EMPEROR JONES | *by* EUGENE O'NEILL *Drawings by* Alexander King | [horizontally at bottom] [publisher's device] | Boni & | Liveright'. Front flap: ad for this limited edition; back flap blank.

Slipcase: Black paper-covered boards with yellow wraparound label (3 5/8" × 6 1/8"). Front: '[brown] *The* | [two lines of decorated type] EMPEROR | JONES | *by* | [decorated type] EUGENE O'NEILL | *Illustrated by* | [decorated type] ALEXANDER KING | *Limited edition seven* | *hundred and fifty cop-|ies signed by the author*'. Spine: '[brown] *The* | EMPEROR | JONES | *by* | O'NEILL | *Illustrated* | *by* | King | [publisher's device] | Boni & | Liveright'. Back: same as front.

Publication: 775 copies published 21 July 1928. $15.00.

Printing: Printed 14 July 1928 by Van Rees Press, New York, from type set by Van Rees Book Composition; bound by Van Rees Bindery.

Locations: Lilly (#580, dj and boxed); MJB (#146, dj and boxed); PSt (#209, dj); ScU (#381, dj and boxed); Yale (author's copy, dj and boxed, and #302, dj and boxed).

Note: Original ending deleted from this edition. See A 15-I-1.a.

A 15 THE EMPEROR JONES
American sixth book publication (1928)

A 15-VI-1
The Emperor Jones, The Straw. New York: Modern Library, [1928].

On copyright page: '*First* MODERN LIBRARY *Edition* 1928'.

Introduction by Dudley Nichols.

TEJ appears on pp. [xxvii–xxviii], 1–57.

Note: Original ending restored in this edition. See A 15-I-1.a.

A 15 THE EMPEROR JONES
American seventh book publication (1932)

A 15-VII-1.a
NINE PLAYS BY EUGENE O'NEILL

Title page: '[brown double-rule frame] [black decorated-rule frame] [all the following within both frames] [brown, decorated] NINE | PLAYS | [black, roman] BY | *Eugene O'Neill* | SELECTED BY THE AUTHOR | INTRODUCTION BY | JOSEPH WOOD KRUTCH | [decorated rule] | NEW YORK · LIVERIGHT, INC. | 1932'

Copyright page: 'COPYRIGHT, 1932, BY LIVERIGHT, INC. | COPYRIGHT, 1921, 1922, 1924, 1926, 1927, 1928, | BY BONI AND LIVERIGHT, INC. | "MOURNING BECOMES ELECTRA," COPYRIGHT, 1931, | BY HORACE LIVERIGHT, INC. | [eight lines of italic type giving translation and production rights notice] | DESIGNED BY ROBERT S. JOSEPHY | PRINTED IN THE UNITED STATES OF AMERICA | BY QUINN & BODEN CO., INC., RAHWAY, N.J.'

[i–x] xi–xxii [1–2] 3–35 [36–38] 39–88 [89–90] 91–133 [134–136] 137–206 [207–210] 211–304 [305–306] 307–377 [378–380] 381–481 [482–484] 485–682 [683–686] 687–749 [750–752] 753–811 [812–814] 815–867 [868–874]

$[1\text{–}28]^{16}$

TEJ appears on pp. 1–35.

Note one: Original ending deleted from this edition. See A 15-I-1.a.

Note two: This volume has been seen in two bindings:

Binding A: faded green EC cloth (coarse grain) with beveled edges. Front: '[goldstamped EO signature]'. Spine: '[goldstamped against solid black background box] *Eugene O'Neill* | NINE PLAYS'.

Binding B: dark blue BF cloth (coarse, even grain) with beveled edges. Front: '[goldstamped EO signature]'. Spine: '[within decorated double-rule frame, goldstamped] *Eugene O'Neill* | NINE PLAYS | [at bottom] LIVERIGHT'.

Priority undetermined.

Publication: Unknown number of copies published 2 December 1932.

Printing: Printed by Quinn & Boden Co., Inc., Rahway, New Jersey; bound by Quinn & Boden

REPRINTINGS

A 15-VII-1.b
New York: Random House, [1937?]. 'NOBEL PRIZE EDITION'. (Not a new edition.)

A 15-VII-1.c
New York: Random House, [1941].

On copyright page: 'First Modern Library Giant Edition 1941'. (Not a new edition.)

A 15-VII-1.d
New York: Random House, [1954]. ML Giant #G55.

A 15 THE EMPEROR JONES
American eighth book publication (1932)

A 15-VIII-1
Representative Plays of Eugene O'Neill. New York: Liveright, [1932].

TEJ appears on pp. 183–226. See A 8-IV-1, "Caribbees."

Note: Original ending deleted from this edition. See A 15-I-1.a.

A 15 THE EMPEROR JONES
American ninth book publication (1934)

A 15-IX-1
THE PLAYS OF EUGENE O'NEILL. Twelve volumes. Wilderness Edition

Volume three

Title page: '[within decorated border] [white against gray background] THE | PLAYS | OF | EUGENE | O'NEILL | [wavy rule] | *The Emperor Jones* | *Ah, Wilderness!* | [wavy rule] | III | WILDERNESS · EDITION | *NEW YORK* | Charles Scribner's Sons'

Copyright page: 'COPYRIGHT, 1934, BY CHARLES SCRIBNER'S SONS | [nineteen lines of roman and italic type]'

[i–x] xi–xiii [xiv] [1–2] 3–54 [55–60] 61–103 [104] 105–151 [152] 153–201 [202] 203–268 [269–274]

$[1–18]^8$

The statement of limitation on p. iv reads: '[decorated rule] | [swash *T*'s and *N*'s] *THIS WILDERNESS EDITION* | OF THE | PLAYS OF EUGENE O'NEILL | printed from type now destroyed, is limited | to seven hundred and seventy sets | of which twenty are for presentation | This is number | [decorated rule]'.

The colophon on p. 270 reads: '[decorated rule] | [swash *T* and *K*] *THIS BOOK* | the third of twelve volumes designed by Elmer Adler | set in an eighteenth-century type face | based on the castings made by John Baskerville | is printed on a specially watermarked paper | at the press of the publisher | in the city of New York | in the month of December | MCM XXX IV | [publisher's device]'.

Note one: The watermark is: 'CSS | [classical tragedy mask]'.

TEJ appears on pp. 1–54.

On p. xi, in a note written by EO's Random House editor, the following statement is made about *TEJ*: '[display T]HE EMPEROR JONES *was written in Provincetown in the fall | of 1920. It represented an extreme departure, in theme and | treatment, from my earlier one-act and longer plays. I had | been impressed by a story told me by an old circus man concerning Presi-|dent Sam of Haiti. The flamboyant Sam, according to this tale, had | boasted his enemies would never get him—that if he were ever over-|thrown he would kill himself, but not with an ordinary lead bullet; only | a silver one was worthy of that honor. Having read of the uses made of | the drum in religious feasts in the Congo, an experiment suggested itself | to me. What would the effect upon an audience in the theatre be if the | tom-tom, starting at normal heart-beat rhythm, became gradually in-|tensified until it corresponded with the wild pulse of a panic-stricken | Negro as it followed him on his flight through a tropical jungle? My | own experiences while prospecting for gold in Spanish Honduras pro-| vided the effect of the tropical forest on the human imagination. Out of | these elements, "The Emperor Jones" came into being. It was first pro-|duced at the Provincetown Theatre on November 1, 1920, with Charles | Gilpin, the Negro actor, in the title rôle. | Every country in Europe and many cities of the East and Australia | have witnessed performances of "The Emperor Jones."'*

Publication: 770 copies published 28 December 1934.

Locations: JM^cA (#456); LC (presentation); MJB (#592 boxed); ScU (#749); Yale (presentation).

Note two: Original ending deleted from this edition. See A 15-I-1.a.

A 15 THE EMPEROR JONES
American tenth book publication (1937)

A 15-X-1
The Emperor Jones, Anna Christie, The Hairy Ape. New York: Random House, [1937]. ML #146.

On copyright page: '*First Modern Library Edition* | 1937'.

Introduction by Lionel Trilling.

TEJ appears on pp. 1–58.

Publication: Unknown number of copies published 25 February 1937.

Locations: JM^cA (Bindings A and B); Yale (Binding A).

Note one: Original ending restored in this edition. See A 15-I-1.a.

Note two: This volume has been seen in various bindings (brown, red, green) and more than one dust jacket; priorities have not been determined. While a chronology has not been established, there was a printing of the volume as recently as 1964.

A 15 THE EMPEROR JONES
American eleventh book publication (1941)

A 15-XI-1.a
The Plays of Eugene O'Neill. New York: Random House, [1941]. Three volumes.

On copyright page: 'FIRST PRINTING'.

TEJ appears in volume three, pp. 171–204. See A 14-VI-1.a, *BTH.*

Note: Original ending deleted from this edition. See A 15-I-1.a.

REPRINTINGS

A 15-XI-1.b
New York: Random House, [1941].

On copyright page: 'SECOND PRINTING'.

A 15-XI-1.c
New York: Random House, [1951].

A 15-XI-1.d
New York: Random House, [1954–55].

A 15 THE EMPEROR JONES
American twelfth book publication (1944)

A 15-XII-1
Selected Plays of Eugene O'Neill. New York: Editions for the Armed Services, Inc., [1944]. Published by arrangement with Random House. No. Q-35.

Only in wrappers.

TEJ appears on pp. 7–47.

Note: Original ending restored in this edition. See A 15-I-1.a.

A 15 THE EMPEROR JONES
American thirteenth book publication (1967)

A 15-XIII-1
SELECTED PLAYS OF EUGENE O'NEILL

Title page: '[within single-rule frame] Selected | Plays | OF Eugene | O'Neill · [publisher's device] | [within single-rule frame] Random House · *New York*'

Copyright page: 'First Printing| Copyright as an unpublished work, 1940, by Eugene | O'Neill | Copyright 1921, 1922, 1924, 1925, 1928, 1931, 1946 by | Eugene O'Neill | Copyright renewed 1948, 1949, 1952 by Eugene O'Neill | Copyright renewed 1954, © 1955, 1958, 1967 by Carlotta | Monterey O'Neill | [nineteen lines of type giving translation and production rights notice] | Manufactured in the United States of America | by The Book Press, Inc.'

[i–vi] [1–5] 6–16 [17] 18–19 [20] 21 [22] 23–24 [25] 26–27 [28] 29 [30] 31–32 [33] 34 [35–39] 40–57 [58] 59–71 [72] 73–90 [91] 92–104 [105–109] 110–118 [119] 120–123 [124] 125–127 [128] 129–133 [134] 135–139 [140] 141–144 [145] 146–150 [151] 152–154 [155–159] 160–179 [180] 181–196 [197] 198–216 [217–221] 222–230 [231] 232–243 [244] 245–259 [260] 261–269 [270] 271–278 [279] 280 [281–285] 286–373 [374] 375–450 [451–460] 461–478 [479] 480–491 [492] 493–504 [505] 506–510 [511–515] 516–524 [525] 526–536 [537] 538–544 [545] 546–557 [558] 559–564 [565–569] 570–586 [587] 588–593 [594] 595–603 [604] 605–612 [613–616] 617 [618–619] 620–667 [668] 669–699 [700] 701–728 [729] 730–758 [759–762]

$[1\text{–}24]^{16}$

TEJ appears on pp. 1–34.

Locations: LC (deposit-stamp 26 March 1969); ScU.

Note: Original ending deleted from this edition. See A 15-I-1.a.

A 15 THE EMPEROR JONES
American fourteenth book publication (1972)

A 15-XIV-1
The Emperor Jones, Anna Christie, The Hairy Ape. New York: Vintage Books, [1972]. No. V-855.

On copyright page: 'FIRST VINTAGE BOOKS EDITION, NOVEMBER 1972'.

Only in wrappers.

TEJ appears on pp. 1–53.

Note: Original ending restored in this edition. See A 15-I-1.a.

A 15 THE EMPEROR JONES
English first book publication (1922)

A 15-EI-1.a
PLAYS: FIRST SERIES, THE STRAW, THE EMPEROR JONES, AND DIFF'RENT
English first edition, first printing

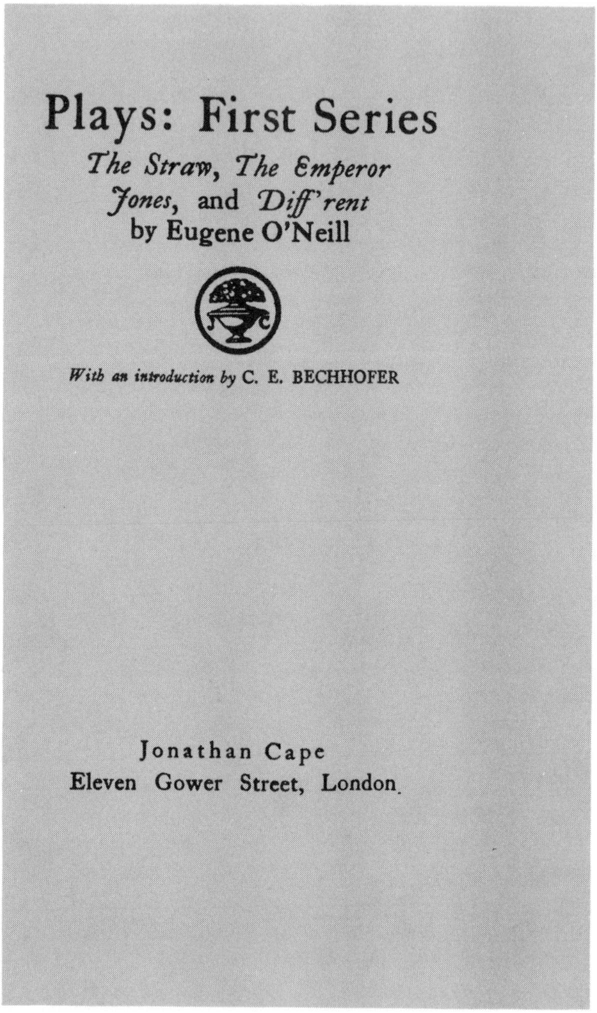

Plays: First Series
The Straw, The Emperor Jones, and *Diff'rent*
by Eugene O'Neill

With an introduction by C. E. BECHHOFER

Jonathan Cape
Eleven Gower Street, London

A 15-EI-1.a: $7\frac{1}{2}'' \times 4\frac{3}{4}''$

First published 1922
All rights reserved

Printed in Great Britain by
THE BOTOLPH PRINTING WORKS
GATE STREET, KINGSWAY, W.C.

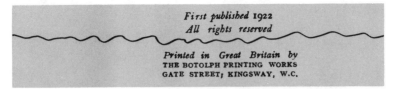

[i–iv] v–viii [ix–x] [1–6] 7–58 [59–60] 61–104 [105–106] 107–142 [143–146] 147–195 [196–202] 203–238 [239–240] 241–282

$[1]^8$ A–I^8 K–R^8 S^2; last gathering glued in.

Contents: p. i: half title; p. ii: blank; p. iii: title; p. iv: copyright; pp. v–viii: 'Introduction'; p. ix: table of contents; p. x: blank; p. 1: 'The Straw'; p. 2: blank; p. 3: 'Characters | [twenty-three lines of roman and italic type]'; p. 4: act-scene synopsis; p. 5: 'The Straw | Act One'; p. 6: blank; pp. 7–58: text, headed 'Act One: Scene One'; p. 59: 'The Straw | Act Two'; p. 60: blank; pp. 61–104: text, headed 'Act Two: Scene One'; p. 105: 'The Straw | Act Three'; p. 106: blank; pp. 107–142: text, headed 'Act Three'; p. 143: 'The Emperor Jones'; p. 144: blank; p. 145: 'Characters | [thirteen lines of type]'; p. 146: blank; pp. 147–195: text, headed 'Scene One'; p. 196: blank; p. 197: 'Diff'rent'; p. 198: blank; p. 199: 'Characters | [eight lines of type]'; p. 200: act synopsis; p. 201: 'Diff'rent | Act One'; p. 202: blank; pp. 203–238: text, headed 'Act One'; p. 239: 'Diff'rent | Act Two'; p. 240: blank; pp. 241–282: text, headed 'Act Two'.

Typography and paper: $3\frac{1}{8}'' \times 5\frac{1}{4}''$ ($5\frac{1}{2}''$); thirty-one lines per page. No running heads. Wove paper.

Binding: Coated sky blue V cloth (fine linen-like grain), with label ($2\frac{1}{4}'' \times 1\frac{1}{4}''$) on spine: '[blue line of decorations] | [black] Plays: | First Series | EUGENE O'NEILL | [blue decoration] | [black] *Jonathan Cape* | [blue line of decorations]'. White wove endpapers of same stock as text paper. Top and right edges trimmed.

Dust jacket: Not seen.

Publication: Unknown number of copies published in 1922. 7s. 6d.

Location: BM (deposit-stamp 18 May 1922); JM^{c}A; Yale.

Note: Original ending restored in this edition. See A 15-I-1.a.

LATER PRINTING

The Emperor Jones, The Straw, and Diff'rent. London: Jonathan Cape, [1953]. (Not seen.)

A 15 THE EMPEROR JONES
English second book publication, first separate book publication (1925)

A 15-EII-1
THE EMPEROR JONES

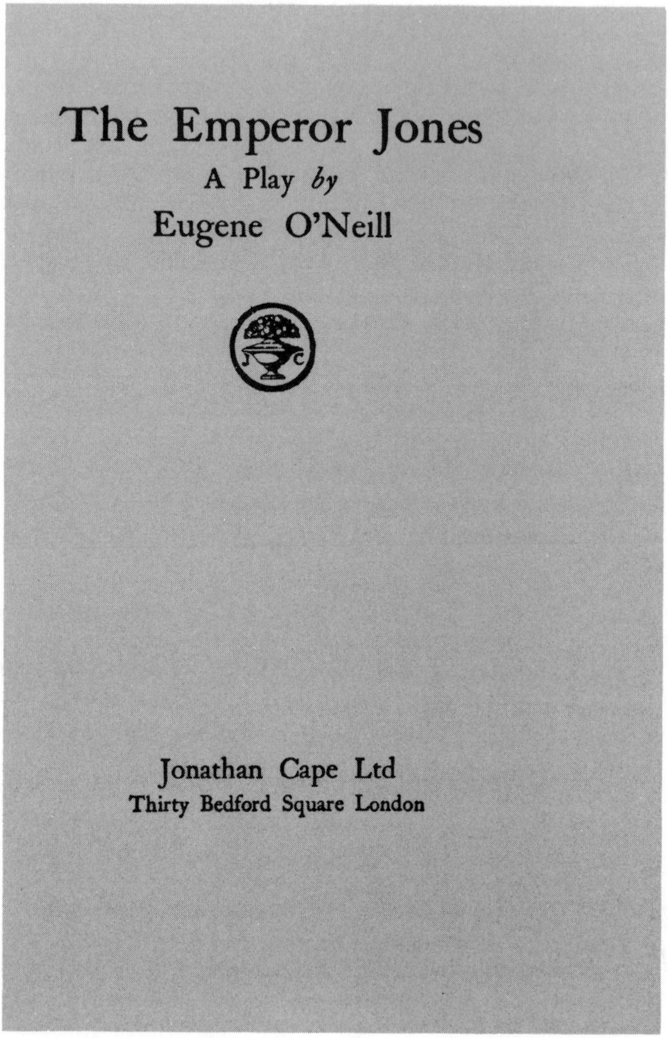

The Emperor Jones
A Play *by*
Eugene O'Neill

Jonathan Cape Ltd
Thirty Bedford Square London

A 15-EII-1: $7\frac{3}{8}'' \times 4\frac{15}{16}''$

FIRST PUBLISHED IN MCMXXV
MADE & PRINTED IN GREAT BRITAIN
BY BUTLER & TANNER LTD
FROME AND
LONDON

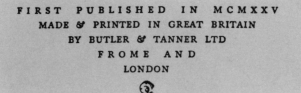

[i–iv] v–viii [1–4] 5–53 [54–56]

$[1–4]^{8}$

Contents: p. i: blank; p. ii: blank; p. iii: title; p. iv: copyright; pp. v–viii: 'Introduction'; p. 1: half title; p. 2: blank; p. 3: 'Characters | [thirteen lines of roman and italic type]'; p. 4: blank; pp. 5–53: text, headed 'Scene One'; pp. 54–56: blank.

Typography and paper: 3⅛″ × 5¼″ (5⅜″); thirty-two lines per page. No running heads. Wove paper.

Binding: Green paper-covered boards, imitation B cloth (linen-like grain). Front: [black] 'The Emperor Jones | Eugene O'Neill'. Spine: '[black, vertically from bottom to top] The Emperor Jones [leaf decoration] Eugene O'Neill'. White endpapers of different stock from text paper. Top edge only trimmed.

Dust jacket: Green imitation B cloth (linen-like grain). Front: '[within black border of decorations] THE | EMPEROR JONES | A PLAY BY | EUGENE O'NEILL | [publisher's device]'. Spine: '[black, vertically from top to bottom] THE EMPEROR JONES [leaf] EUGENE O'NEILL'. Back: ad for eighteen EO titles in five volumes published by Cape, beginning with *TEJ* and ending with *Welded*. Front flap: '[at bottom] *The Emperor Jones*' (corner clipped from copy seen); back flap blank.

Publication: Unknown number of copies published in 1925. 3s.

Locations: BM (deposit-stamp 28 January 1926); JM^{c}A (dj); Yale.

Note one: There was a simultaneous publication of this edition in wrappers for 2s.

Note two: Original ending restored in this edition. See A 15-I-1.a.

A 16 GOLD
American first book publication (1921)

A 16-I-1
GOLD
American first edition, first printing

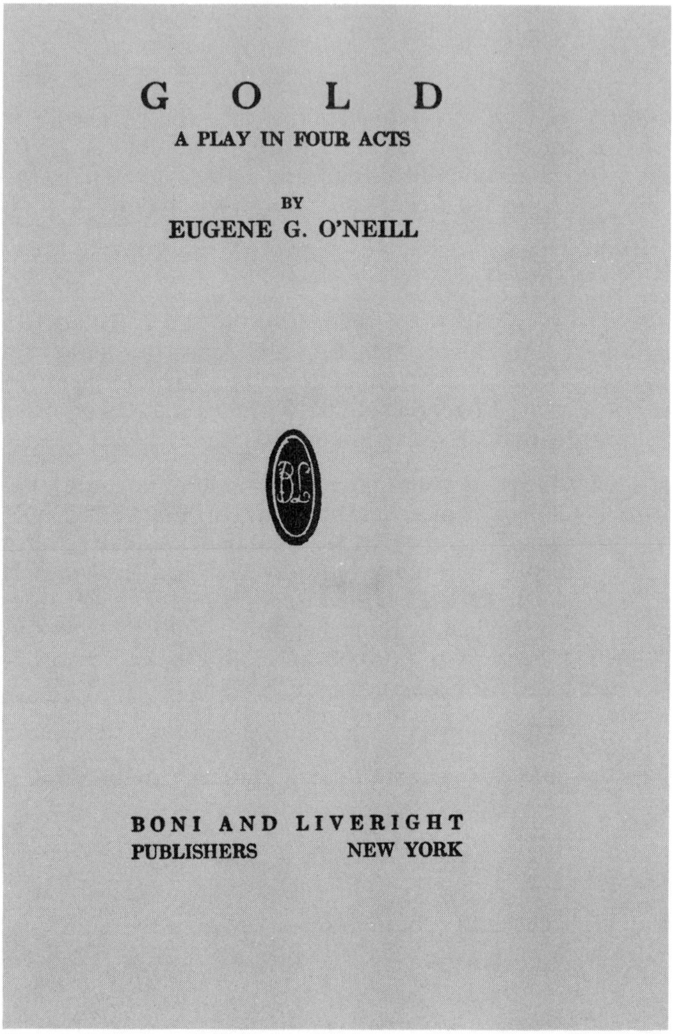
G O L D
A PLAY IN FOUR ACTS
BY
EUGENE G. O'NEILL
BONI AND LIVERIGHT
PUBLISHERS NEW YORK

A 16-I-1: $7\frac{7}{16}'' \times 5\frac{1}{16}''$

GOLD

COPYRIGHT, 1920, BY
BONI & LIVERIGHT, INC.

Printed in the United States of America

[i–viii] 1–120

$[1–8]^{8}$

Contents: p. i: half title; p. ii: card page; p. iii: title; p. iv: copyright page; p. v: act-scene synopsis; p. vi: blank; p. vii: 'ACT I'; p. viii: 'CHARACTERS | [twelve lines of type]'; pp. 1–120: text, headed 'ACT ONE'.

Typography and paper: 11 point on 13, Scotch. $3\frac{5}{16}'' \times 5\frac{3}{16}''$ ($5\frac{1}{2}''$); twenty-nine lines per page. Running heads: rectos and versos, 'GOLD'. Wove paper.

Binding: Dark gray green paper-covered boards with olive green T cloth (fine, lined grain) shelf back. Front: '[black] Gold | Eugene G. O'Neill'. Spine: '[black] Gold | Eugene G. | O'Neill | BONI AND | LIVERIGHT'. Endpapers of different stock from text paper. Top and right edges trimmed.

Dust jacket: Gold background. Front: 'GOLD | *by* | EUGENE O'NEILL | [sixteen lines of type on scroll quoting George Jean Nathan review from *The Smart Set*]'. Spine: 'GOLD | by | EUGENE O'NEILL | $1.50 | [double rule] | BONI AND | LIVERIGHT | [double rule]'. Back: same as front. Front flap has ad for six EO titles; back flap has ad for Ferenc Molnar's *Liliom,* given incorrectly as by 'Franz Molnar'.

Publication: 1,200 copies published 10 September 1921. $1.50.

Locations: JM^{c}A (dj); Lilly (two, djs); PSt; Yale.

Note: "Where the Cross is Made" was expanded into the four-act *Gold.* See EO's notes to the Wilderness Edition, A 12-V-1 and A 16-V-1.

A 16 GOLD
American second book publication (1924)

A 16-II-1
The Complete Works of Eugene O'Neill. New York: Boni & Liveright, 1924. Two volumes.

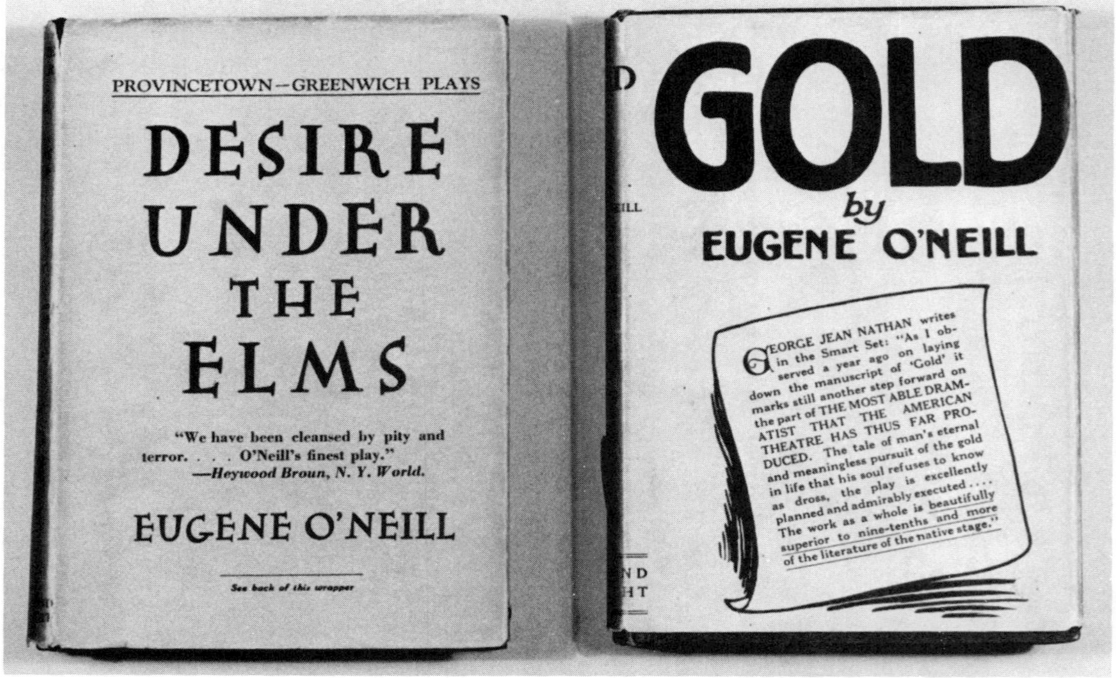

Dust jackets for A 25-II-1 and A 16-I-1

Limited to 1,200 numbered copies; signed by EO.

Gold appears in volume one, pp. 317–391. See A 6-IV-1, "Cardiff."

A 16 GOLD
American third book publication (1925)

A 16-III-1.a
Plays, The Emperor Jones, Gold, The First Man, The Dreamy Kid. New York: Boni & Liveright, 1925.

First printing: July, 1925.

One volume of an unnumbered, ten-volume, uniform series.

Gold appears on pp. 53–142.

REPRINTINGS

A 16-III-1.b
New York: Boni & Liveright, [March 1926].

A 16-III-1.c
New York: Boni & Liveright, [November 1926].

A 16-III-1.d
New York: Boni & Liveright, [January 1928].

A 16-III-1.e
New York: Boni & Liveright, [May 1928].

A 16-III-1.f
New York: Boni & Liveright, [July 1930].

A 16-III-1.g
New York: Liveright, [May 1932].

A 16 GOLD
American fourth book publication (1935)

A 16-IV-1
THE PLAYS OF EUGENE O'NEILL. Twelve volumes. Wilderness Edition

Volume nine

Title Page: '[within decorated border] [white against gray background] THE | PLAYS | OF | EUGENE | O'NEILL | [wavy rule] | *Days Without End* | *Gold* | [wavy rule] | IX | WILDERNESS · EDITION | *NEW YORK* | Charles Scribner's Sons'

Copyright page: 'COPYRIGHT, 1935, BY CHARLES SCRIBNER'S SONS | [nineteen lines of roman and italic type.]'

[i–x] xi [xii] xiii [xiv] [1–2] 3–73 [74] 75–138 [139–140] 141–169 [170] 171–239 [240] 241–272 [273–278]

$[1\text{–}17]^{8}$ $[18]^{10}$

The statement of limitation on p. iv reads: '[decorated rule] [swash *T*'s and *N*'s] *THIS WILDERNESS EDITION* | OF THE | PLAYS OF EUGENE O'NEILL | printed from type now destroyed, is limited | to seven hundred and seventy sets | of which twenty are for presentation | This is number | [decorated rule]'.

The colophon on p. 274 reads: '[decorated rule] | [swash *T* and *K*] *THIS BOOK* | the ninth of twelve volumes designed by Elmer Adler | set in an eighteenth-century type face | based on the castings made by John Baskerville | is printed on a specially watermarked paper | at the press of the publisher | in the city of New York | in the month of March | MCM XXX V | [publisher's device]'.

Note: The watermark is: 'CSS | [classical tragedy mask]'.

Gold appears on pp. 139–272.

On p. xi, in a note written by EO's Random House editor, the following statement is made about *Gold:* 'GOLD, *written at Provincetown in 1920, is an elaboration of an early* | *one-act play, "Where the Cross Is Made." It was produced at the* | *Frazee Theatre on June 1, 1921, by John D. Williams.*'

Publication: 770 copies published 22 March 1935.

Locations: JM^cA (#456); LC (presentation); MJB (#592 boxed); ScU (#749); Yale (presentation).

A 16 GOLD
American fifth book publication (1941)

A 16-V-1.a
THE PLAYS OF EUGENE O'NEILL. Three volumes

Volume two

Title page: '[within triple-rule frame, black against gray beige background] THE PLAYS | OF | EUGENE O'NEILL | [publisher's device] | RANDOM HOUSE · NEW YORK'

Copyright page: 'FIRST PRINTING | COPYRIGHT, 1921, 1922, 1924, 1927, 1931, 1933, | BY EUGENE O'NEILL | MANUFACTURED IN THE UNITED STATES OF AMERICA'

[i–vi] [1–4] 5–64 [65–66] 67–125 [126–128] 129–179 [180–184] 185–298 [299–300] 301–342 [343–346] 347–439 [440–442] 443–489 [490–492] 493–549 [550–552] 553–619 [620–622] 623–692 [693–698]

$[1\text{–}22]^{16}$

Gold appears on pp. 621–692.

Locations: JMcA; ScU.

REPRINTINGS

A 16-V-1.b
New York: Random House, [1941].

On copyright page: 'SECOND PRINTING'.

A 16-V-1.c
New York: Random House, [1951].

A 16-V-1.d
New York: Random House, [1954–55].

A 16 GOLD
English first book publication (1924)

A 16-EI-1.a
Beyond the Horizon and Gold. London: Jonathan Cape, [1924].

Gold appears on pp. 1–128. See A 14-EI-1.a, *BTH*.

REPRINTING

A 16-EI-1.b
London: Jonathan Cape, [April 1937]. Nobel Prize Edition. (Not a new edition.)

A 17 DIFF'RENT
American first book publication (1921)

A 17-I-1.a
The Emperor Jones, Diff'rent, The Straw. New York: Boni & Liveright, [1921].

Diff'rent appears on pp. 199–285. See A 15-I-1.a, *TEJ*.

REPRINTINGS

A 17-I-1.b
New York: Boni & Liveright, [June 1921].

A 17-I-1.c
New York: Boni & Liveright, [August 1921].

A 17-I-1.d
New York: Boni & Liveright, [November 1921].

A 17-I-1.e
New York: Boni & Liveright, [October 1922].

A 17-I-1.f
New York: Boni & Liveright, [March 1924].

A 17 DIFF'RENT
American second book publication (1924)

A 17-II-1
The Complete Works of Eugene O'Neill. New York: Boni & Liveright, 1924. Two volumes.

Limited to 1,200 numbered copies; signed by EO.

Diff'rent appears in volume one, pp. 253–315. See A 6-IV-1 "Cardiff."

A 17 DIFF'RENT
American third book publication (1925)

A 17-III-1.a
Plays, Anna Christie, All God's Chillun Got Wings, Diff'rent. New York: Boni & Liveright, 1925.

First printing: July, 1925

One volume of an unnumbered, ten-volume, uniform series.

Diff'rent appears on pp. 177–254.

REPRINTINGS

A 17-III-1.b
New York: Boni & Liveright, [April 1926].

A 17-III-1.c
New York: Boni & Liveright, [October 1926].

A 17-III-1.d
New York: Boni & Liveright, [April 1927].

A 17-III-1.e
New York: Boni & Liveright, [March 1928].

A 17-III-1.f
New York: Boni & Liveright, [November 1928].

A 17-III-1.g
New York: Boni & Liveright, [August 1929].

A 17 DIFF'RENT
American fourth book publication (1935)

A 17-IV-1
THE PLAYS OF EUGENE O'NEILL. Twelve volumes. Wilderness Edition

Volume seven

Title page: '[within decorated border] [white against gray background] THE | PLAYS | OF | EUGENE | O'NEILL | [wavy rule] | *Dynamo* | *Diff'rent* | [wavy rule] | VII | WILDERNESS · EDITION | *NEW YORK* | Charles Scribner's Sons'

Copyright page: 'COPYRIGHT, 1935, BY CHARLES SCRIBNER'S SONS | [nineteen lines of roman and italic type]'

[i–x] xi [xii] xiii [xiv] [1–4] 5–117 [118–120] 121–167 [168] 169–225 [226–230]

[1–14][8] [15][10]

The statement of limitation on p. iv reads: '[decorated rule] | [swash *T*'s and *N*'s] *THIS WILDERNESS EDITION* | OF THE | PLAYS OF EUGENE O'NEILL | printed from type now destroyed, is limited | to seven hundred and seventy sets | of which twenty are for presentation | This is number | [decorated rule]'.

The colophon on p. 226 reads: '[decorated rule] | [swash *T* and *K*] *THIS BOOK* | the seventh of twelve volumes designed by Elmer Adler | set in an eighteenth-century type face | based on the castings made by John Baskerville | is printed on a specially watermarked paper | at the press of the publisher | in the city of New York | in the month of January | MCM XXX V | [publisher's device]'.

Note: The watermark is: 'CSS | [classical tragedy mask]'.

Diff'rent appears on pp. 119–225.

On p. xi, in a note written by EO's Random House editor, the following statement is made about *Diff'rent:* 'DIFF'RENT *was written at Provincetown, Massachusetts, in the fall | of 1920. It was first produced at the Provincetown Theatre in New | York on December 27, 1920. It was transferred uptown to the Prin-|cess Theatre on February 4, 1921, and ran there with "The Emperor | Jones" ("Diff'rent" being given daily at matinées) until the end of the | season.*'

Publication: 770 copies published 30 January 1935.

Locations: JM^cA (#456); LC (presentation); MJB (#592 boxed); ScU (#749); Yale (presentation).

A 17 DIFF'RENT
American fifth book publication (1941)

A 17-V-1.a
The Plays of Eugene O'Neill. New York: Random House, [1941]. Three volumes.

On copyright page: 'FIRST PRINTING'.

Diff'rent appears in volume two, pp. 491–549. See A 16-V-1.a, *Gold.*

REPRINTINGS

A 17-V-1.b
New York: Random House, [1941].

On copyright page: 'SECOND PRINTING'.

A 17-V-1.c
New York: Random House, [1951].

A 17-V-1.d
New York: Random House, [1954–55].

A 17 DIFF'RENT
English first book publication (1922)

A 17-EI-1.a
Plays: First Series, The Straw, The Emperor Jones, and Diff'-rent. London: Jonathan Cape, [1922].

Diff'rent appears on pp. 197–282. See A 15-EI-1.a, *TEJ*.

REPRINTING

A 17-EI-1.b
The Emperor Jones, The Straw, and Diff'rent. London: Jonathan Cape, [1937]. Nobel Prize Edition. (Not a new edition.)

LATER PRINTING

The Emperor Jones, The Straw, and Diff'rent. London: Jonathan Cape, [1953]. (Not seen.)

A 18 THE STRAW
American first book publication (1921)

A 18-I-1.a
The Emperor Jones, Diff'rent, The Straw. New York: Boni & Liveright, [1921].

The Straw appears on pp. vii–xii, 1–142. See A 15-I-1.a, *TEJ.*

REPRINTINGS

A 18-I-1.b
New York: Boni & Liveright, [June 1921].

A 18-I-1.c
New York: Boni & Liveright, [August 1921].

A 18-I-1.d
New York: Boni & Liveright, [November 1921].

A 18-I-1.e
New York: Boni & Liveright, [October 1922].

A 18-I-1.f
New York: Boni & Liveright, [March 1924].

A 18 THE STRAW
American second book publication (1924)

A 18-II-1
The Complete Works of Eugene O'Neill. New York: Boni & Liveright, 1924. Two volumes.

The Straw appears in volume two, pp. 275–367. See A 25-I-1, *DUTE.*

A 18 THE STRAW
American third book publication (1925)

A 18-III-1.a
Plays, Beyond the Horizon, The Straw, Before Breakfast. New York: Boni & Liveright, 1925.

First printing: July 1925

One volume of an unnumbered, ten-volume, uniform series.

The Straw appears on pp. 129–242.

REPRINTINGS

A 18-III-1.b
New York: Boni & Liveright, [December 1925].

A 18-III-1.c
New York: Boni & Liveright, [June 1926].

A 18-III-1.d
New York: Boni & Liveright, [January 1927].

A 18-III-1.e
New York: Boni & Liveright, [October 1927].

A 18-III-1.f
New York: Boni & Liveright, [April 1928].

A 18-III-1.g
New York: Boni & Liveright, [November 1928].

A 18-III-1.h
New York: Liveright, [March 1931].

A 18-III-1.i
New York: Liveright, [September 1932].

A 18 THE STRAW
American fourth book publication (1928)

A 18-IV-1
The Emperor Jones, The Straw. New York: Modern Library, [1928].

On copyright page: '*First* MODERN LIBRARY *Edition* | 1928'.

Introduction by Dudley Nichols.

The Straw appears on pp. 59–223.

A 18 THE STRAW
American fifth book publication (1935)

A 18-V-1
THE PLAYS OF EUGENE O'NEILL. Twelve volumes. Wilderness Edition

Volume eight

Title page: '[within decorated border] [white against gray background] T H E | PLAYS | O F | E U G E N E | O' N E I L L | [wavy rule] | *The Straw* | *"The First Man"* | [wavy rule] | VIII | WILDERNESS · EDITION | *NEW YORK* | Charles Scribner's Sons'

Copyright page: 'COPYRIGHT, 1935, BY CHARLES SCRIBNER'S SONS | [nineteen lines of roman and italic type]'

[i–x] xi [xii] xiii [xiv] [1–4] 5–161 [162–164] 165–207 [208] 209–259 [260] 261–291 [292–294]

$[1–18]^8$ $[19]^{10}$

The statement of limitation on p. iv reads: '[decorated rule] | [swash *T*'s and *N*'s] *THIS WILDERNESS EDITION* | OF THE PLAYS OF EUGENE O'NEILL | printed from type now destroyed, is limited | to seven hundred and seventy sets | of which twenty are for presentation | This is number | [decorated rule]'.

The colophon on p. 292 reads: '[decorated rule] | [swash *T* and *K*] *THIS BOOK* | the eighth of twelve volumes designed by Elmer Adler | set in an eighteenth-century type face | based on the castings made by John Baskerville | is printed on a specially watermarked paper | at the press of the publisher | in the city of New York | in the month of February | MCM XXX V | [publisher's device]'.

Note: The watermark is: 'CSS | [classical tragedy mask]'.

The Straw appears on pp. 1–161.

On p. xi, in a note written by EO's Random House editor, the following statement is made about *The Straw:* '[display T]HE STRAW *was written at Provincetown, Massachusetts, in 1918 | and 1919. It was produced by George C. Tyler at the Greenwich | Village Theatre in New York on November 10, 1921.'*

Publication: 770 copies published 22 March 1935.

Locations: JM'A (#456); LC (presentation); MJB (#592 boxed); ScU (#749); Yale (presentation).

A 18 THE STRAW
American sixth book publication (1941)

A 18-VI-1.a
The Plays of Eugene O'Neill. New York: Random House, [1941]. Three volumes.

On copyright page: 'FIRST PRINTING'.

The Straw appears in volume three, pp. 327–416. See A 14-VI-1.a, *BTH*.

REPRINTINGS

A 18-VI-1.b
New York: Random House, [1941].

On copyright page: 'SECOND PRINTING'.

A 18-VI-1.c
New York: Random House, [1951].

A 18-VI-1.d
New York: Random House, [1954–55].

A 18 THE STRAW
English first book publication (1922)

A 18-EI-1.a
Plays: First Series, The Straw, The Emperor Jones, and Diff'-rent. London: Jonathan Cape, [1922].

The Straw appears on pp. 1–142. See A 15-EI-1.a, *TEJ*.

REPRINTING

A 18-EI-1.b
The Emperor Jones, The Straw, and Diff'rent. London: Jonathan Cape, [1937]. Nobel Prize Edition. (Not a new edition.)

LATER PRINTING

The Emperor Jones, The Straw, and Diff'rent. London: Jonathan Cape, [1953]. (Not seen.)

A 19 "THE DREAMY KID"
American first book publication (1922)

A 19-I-1
CONTEMPORARY ONE-ACT PLAYS OF 1921
American first edition

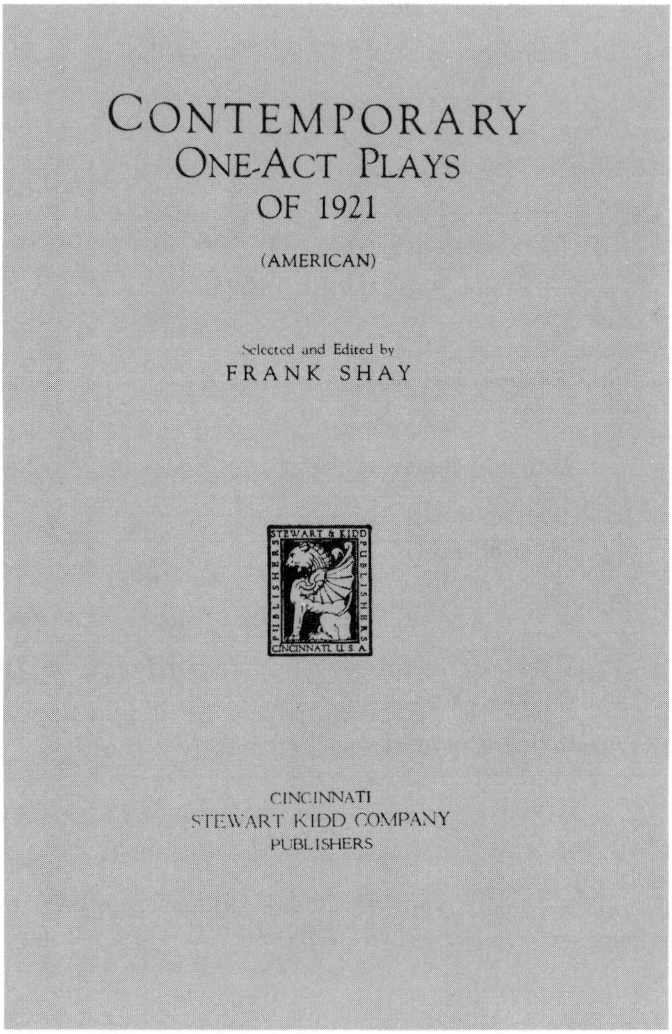
CONTEMPORARY
ONE-ACT PLAYS
OF 1921

(AMERICAN)

Selected and Edited by
FRANK SHAY

STEWART & KIDD PUBLISHERS PUBLISHERS CINCINNATI U.S.A.

CINCINNATI
STEWART KIDD COMPANY
PUBLISHERS

A 19-I-1: 8″ × 5½″

COPYRIGHT, 1922
STEWART KIDD COMPANY

All Rights Reserved

Printed in the United States of America
THE CAXTON PRESS
"*Everybody for Books.*" *This is one of the Interlaken Library*

[i–ii] [1–4] 5–6 [7–10] 11–40 [41–42] 43–62 [63–64] 65–96 [97–98] 99–126 [127–128] 129–162 [163–164] 165–199 [200–202] 203–230 [231–232] 233–250 [251–252] 253–267 [268–270] 271–309 [310–312] 313–352 [353–354] 355–372 [373–374] 375–401 [402–404] 405–442 [443–444] 445–454 [455–456] 457–485 [486–488] 489–517 [518–520] 521–540 [541–542] 543–569 [570–573] 574–613 [614–616] 617–630

$[1\text{–}19]^{16}$ $[20]^{12}$

Contents: p. i: half title; p. ii: blank; p. 1: title; p. 2: copyright; p. 3: 'TO | EUGENE O'NEILL'; p. 4: blank; pp. 5–6: 'FOREWORD'; p. 7: 'CONTENTS | [twenty-six lines of roman and italic type]'; p. 8: blank; p. 9: 'MIRAGE | A PLAY IN ONE ACT | *by* GEORGE M. P. BAIRD'; p. 10: list of characters; pp. 11–40: text, headed 'MIRAGE'; p. 41: 'NAPOLEON'S BARBER | A PLAY | *by* ARTHUR CAESAR'; p. 42: list of characters; pp. 43–62: text, headed 'NAPOLEON'S BARBER'; p. 63: 'GOAT ALLEY | A PLAY IN ONE ACT | *by* ERNEST HOWARD CULBERTSON'; p. 64: list of characters; pp. 65–96: text, headed 'GOAT ALLEY'; p. 97: 'SWEET AND TWENTY | A COMEDY IN ONE ACT | *by* FLOYD DELL'; p. 98: list of characters; pp. 99–126: text, headed 'SWEET AND TWENTY'; p. 127: 'TICKLESS TIME | A COMEDY IN ONE ACT | *by* SUSAN GLASPELL AND GEORGE CRAM COOK'; p. 128: list of characters; pp. 129–162: text, headed 'TICKLESS TIME'; p. 163: 'THE HERO OF SANTA MARIA | A RIDICULOUS TRAGEDY IN ONE ACT | *by* KENNETH SAWYER GOODMAN AND BEN HECHT'; p. 164: list of characters; pp. 165–199: text, headed 'THE HERO | OF SANTA MARIA'; p. 200: blank; p. 201: 'ALL GUMMED UP | A SATIRICAL COMEDY | *by* HARRY WAGSTAFF GRIBBLE'; p. 202: list of characters; pp. 203–230: text, headed 'ALL GUMMED UP'; p. 231: 'THOMPSON'S LUCK | A TRAGEDY IN ONE ACT | *by* HARRY GREENWOOD GROVER'; p. 232: list of characters; pp. 233–250: 'THOMPSON'S LUCK'; p. 251: 'FATA DEORUM | A POETIC PLAY IN TWO SCENES | *by* CARL

W. GUSKE'; p. 252: list of characters; pp. 253–267: text, headed 'FATA DEORUM'; p. 268: blank; p. 269: 'PEARL OF DAWN | A FANTASY IN TEN SCENES | *by* HOLLAND HUDSON'; p. 270: list of characters; pp. 271–309: text, headed 'PEARL OF DAWN'; p. 310: blank; p. 311: 'FINDERS-KEEPERS | A PLAY IN ONE ACT | *by* GEORGE KELLEY'; p. 312: list of characters; pp. 313–352: text, headed 'FINDERS KEEPERS'; p. 353: 'SOLOMON'S SONG | A PASTORAL TRAGI-COMEDY IN ONE ACT | *by* HARRY KEMP'; p. 354: list of characters; pp. 355–372: text, headed 'SOLOMON'S SONG'; p. 373: 'MATINATA | A PLAY IN ONE ACT | *by* LAWRENCE LANGER'; p. 374: list of characters; pp. 375–401: text, headed 'MATINATA'; p. 402: blank; p. 403: 'THE CONFLICT | A DRAMA IN ONE ACT | *by* CLARICE VALLETTE MCCAULEY'; p. 404: list of characters; pp. 405–442: text, headed 'THE CONFLICT'; p. 443: 'TWO SLATTERNS AND A KING | A MORAL INTERLUDE | *by* EDNA ST. VINCENT MILLAY'; p. 444: list of characters; pp. 445–454: text, headed 'TWO SLATTERNS AND A KING'; p. 455: 'THURSDAY EVENING | A COMEDY IN ONE ACT | *by* CHRISTOPHER MORLEY'; p. 456: list of characters; pp. 457–485: text, headed 'THURSDAY EVENING'; p. 486: blank; p. 487: 'THE DREAMY KID | (1918) | A PLAY | *by* EUGENE G. O'NEILL'; p. 488: list of characters; pp. 489–517: text, headed 'THE DREAMY KID'; p. 518: blank; p. 519: 'FORBIDDEN FRUIT | A COMEDY IN ONE ACT | *Based on a Work of Octave Feuillet* | *by* GEORGE JAY SMITH'; p. 520: list of characters; pp. 521–540: text, headed 'FORBIDDEN FRUIT'; p. 541: 'JEZEBEL | A PLAY | *by* DOROTHY STOCKBRIDGE'; p. 542: list of characters; pp. 543–569: text, headed 'JEZEBEL'; p. 570: blank; p. 571: 'SIR DAVID WEARS A CROWN | A PLAY IN ONE ACT | *(A Sequel to "Six Who Pass While the Lentils Boil")* | *by* STUART WALKER'; p. 572: list of characters; p. 573: 'AN OUTLINE OF SIX WHO PASS WHILE THE | LENTILS BOIL'; p. 574: lullaby from "Sir David Wears a Crown"; pp. 575–613: text, headed 'SIR DAVID WEARS A CROWN'; p. 614: blank; p. 615: 'BIBLIOGRAPHIES'; p. 616: blank; pp. 617–630: text, headed 'BOOKS ABOUT THE THEATRE'.

Typography and paper: 12 point set solid, Caslon Old Face. $3\frac{5}{16}'' \times 5\frac{11}{16}''$ ($6\frac{3}{16}''$); thirty-four lines per page. Running heads: rectos and versos, 'THE DREAMY KID | [double rule]'. Wove paper with 'WARREN'S | OLDE STYLE' watermark.

Binding: Green T cloth (fine-lined grain). Front: '[all within blindstamped, single-rule frame] [goldstamped, within double-rule frame] [decorative type] Contemporary | [roman] ONE-

ACT | PLAYS | [short rule] | 1921 | [short rule] | AMERICAN | *Edited By* | FRANK SHAY | [decoration]'. Spine: '[goldstamped] [decorative type] Contemporary | [roman] ONE-ACT | PLAYS | [short rule] | 1921 | [short rule] | AMERICAN | [short rule] | SHAY | [decoration] | STEWART | KIDD'. White wove endpapers of different stock from text paper. All edges trimmed; top edge stained russet.

Dust jacket: Not seen.

Publication: Unknown number of copies published 30 August 1922.

Locations: JM^cA; Lilly.

Note: "The Dreamy Kid" first appeared in *Theatre Arts Magazine*, IV, 1 (January 1920), 41–56. See C 37. Magazine publication preceded book publication.

A 19 "THE DREAMY KID"
American second book publication (1924)

A 19-II-1
The Complete Works of Eugene O'Neill. New York: Boni & Liveright, 1924. Two volumes.

Limited to 1,200 copies; signed by EO.

Kid appears in volume two, pp. 399–421. See A 25-I-1, *DUTE*.

A 19 "THE DREAMY KID"
American third book publication (1925)

A 19-III-1.a
Plays, The Emperor Jones, Gold, The First Man, The Dreamy Kid. New York: Boni & Liveright, 1925.

First printing: July 1925

One volume of an unnumbered, ten-volume, uniform series.

"Kid" appears on pp. 227–252.

REPRINTINGS

A 19-III-1.b
New York: Boni & Liveright, [March 1926].

A 19-III-1.c
New York: Boni & Liveright, [November 1926].

A 19-III-1.d
New York: Boni & Liveright, [January 1928].

A 19-III-1.e
New York: Boni & Liveright, [May 1928].

A 19-III-1.f
New York: Boni & Liveright, [July 1930].

A 19-III-1.g
New York: Liveright, [May 1932].

A 19 "THE DREAMY KID"
American fourth book publication (1935)

A 19-IV-1
The Plays of Eugene O'Neill. New York: Scribners, [1934–35]. Twelve volumes. Wilderness Edition.

Limited to 770 numbered copies.

"Kid" appears in volume twelve, pp. 261–297. See A 6-VI-1, "Cardiff."

On p. xiii, in a note written by EO's Random House editor, the following statement is made about "Kid": 'THE DREAMY KID *was written at Provincetown in the summer of | 1918. It was performed for the first time on October 31, 1919, at the | Provincetown Theatre in New York.*'

Publication: 770 copies published 28 June 1935.

A 19 "THE DREAMY KID"
American fifth book publication (1941)

A 19-V-1.a
The Plays of Eugene O'Neill. New York: Random House, [1941]. Three volumes.

On copyright page: 'FIRST PRINTING'.

"Kid" appears in volume one, pp. 603–622. See A 6-VII-1.a, "Cardiff."

REPRINTINGS

A 19-V-1.b
New York: Random House, [1941].

On copyright page: 'SECOND PRINTING'.

A 19-V-1.c
New York: Random House, [1951].

A 19-V-1.d
New York: Random House, [1954–55].

A 19 "THE DREAMY KID"
English first book publication (1926)

A 19-EI-1.a
The Great God Brown, Including The Fountain, The Dreamy Kid, and Before Breakfast. London: Jonathan Cape, 1926.

"Kid" appears on pp. 1–33. See A 26-EI-1.a, *GGB*.

REPRINTING

A 19-EI-1.b
London: Jonathan Cape, [1937]. Nobel Prize Edition. (Not a new edition.)

A 20 THE HAIRY APE
American first book publication (1922)

A 20-I-1
THE HAIRY APE, ANNA CHRISTIE, THE FIRST MAN
American first edition, possibly only printing

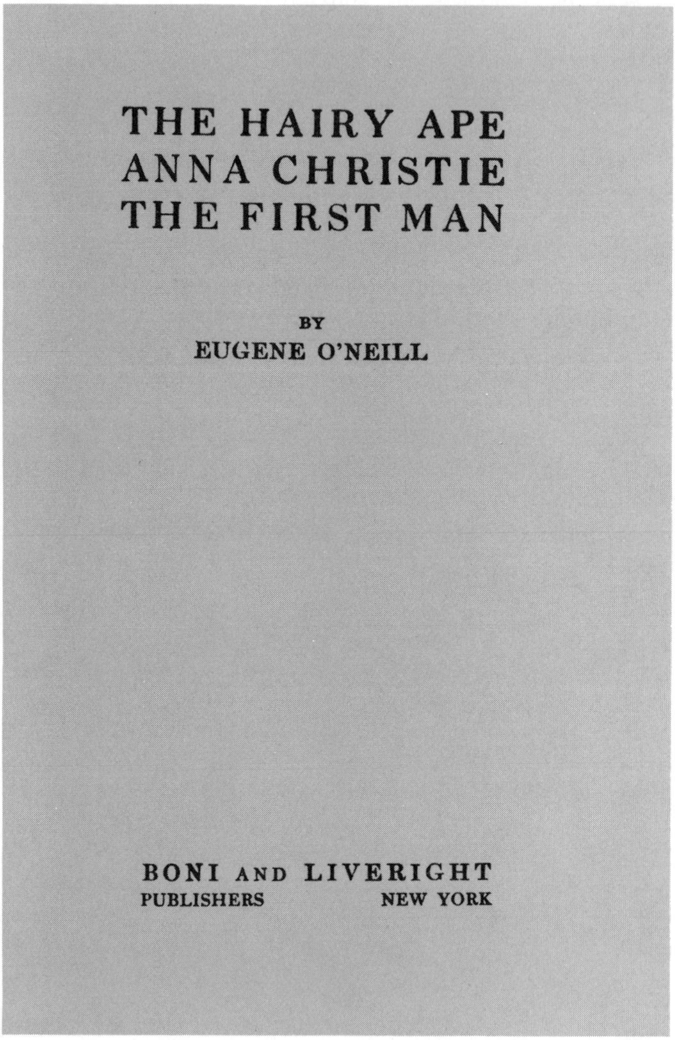
THE HAIRY APE
ANNA CHRISTIE
THE FIRST MAN

BY
EUGENE O'NEILL

BONI AND LIVERIGHT
PUBLISHERS NEW YORK

A 20-I-1: $7\frac{3}{8}'' \times 5''$

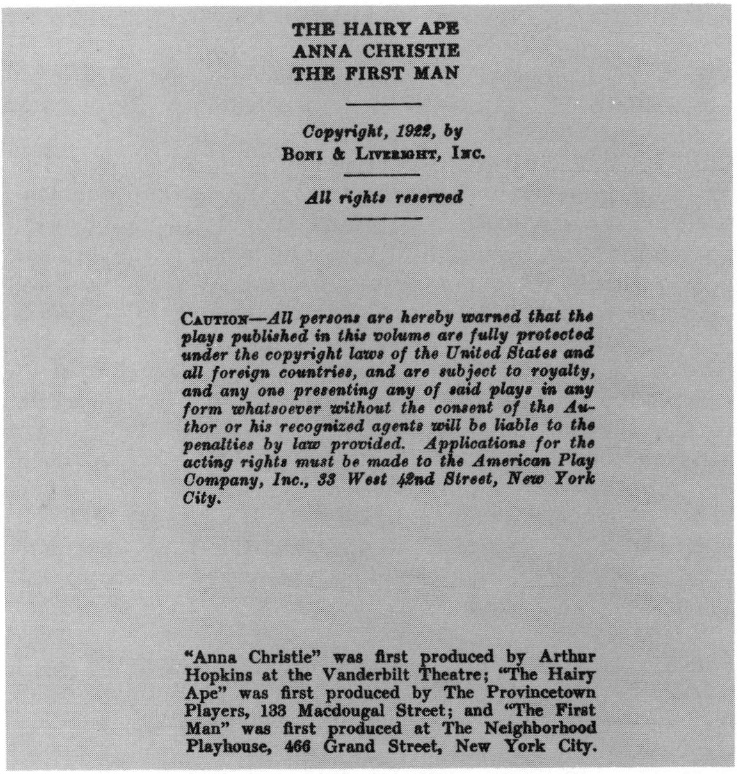

THE HAIRY APE
ANNA CHRISTIE
THE FIRST MAN

Copyright, 1922, by
BONI & LIVERIGHT, INC.

All rights reserved

CAUTION—*All persons are hereby warned that the plays published in this volume are fully protected under the copyright laws of the United States and all foreign countries, and are subject to royalty, and any one presenting any of said plays in any form whatsoever without the consent of the Author or his recognized agents will be liable to the penalties by law provided. Applications for the acting rights must be made to the American Play Company, Inc., 33 West 42nd Street, New York City.*

"Anna Christie" was first produced by Arthur Hopkins at the Vanderbilt Theatre; "The Hairy Ape" was first produced by The Provincetown Players, 133 Macdougal Street; and "The First Man" was first produced at The Neighborhood Playhouse, 466 Grand Street, New York City.

[i–xii] 1–15 [16–18] 19–25 [26–28] 29–34 [35–36] 37–45 [46–48] 49–57 [58–60] 61–68 [69–70] 71–79 [80–82] 83–87 [88–96] 97–127 [128–130] 131–152 [153–154] 155–185 [186–188] 189–211 [212–220] 221–252 [253–254] 255–272 [273–274] 275–295 [296–298] 299–322 [323–324]

[1–21]^{8}

Contents: p. i: half title; p. ii: card page; p. iii: title; p. iv: copyright; p. v: table of contents; p. vi: blank; p. vii: '"THE HAIRY APE" | [four lines of type]'; p. viii: blank; p. ix: 'CHARACTERS | [nine lines of type]'; p. x: act-scene synopsis; p. xi: 'SCENE I'; p. xii: blank; pp. 1–15: text, headed 'SCENE ONE'; p. 16: blank; p. 17: 'SCENE II'; p. 18: blank; pp. 19–25: text, headed 'SCENE TWO'; p. 26: blank; p. 27: 'SCENE III'; p. 28: blank; pp. 29–34: text, headed 'SCENE THREE'; p. 35: 'SCENE IV'; p. 36: blank; pp. 37–45: text, headed 'SCENE FOUR'; p. 46: blank; p. 47: 'SCENE V'; p. 48: blank; pp. 49–57: text, headed 'SCENE FIVE'; p. 58: blank; p. 59: 'SCENE VI'; p. 60: blank; pp. 61–68: text, headed 'SCENE SIX'; p. 69: 'SCENE VII'; p. 70: blank; pp. 71–79: text, headed 'SCENE SEVEN'; p. 80: blank; p. 81: 'SCENE VIII'; p. 82: blank; pp. 83–87: text, headed 'SCENE EIGHT'; p. 88: blank; p. 89: '"A N N A C H R I S T I E" | [three lines of type]'; p. 90: blank; p. 91: 'CHARACTERS' | [eleven lines of roman and italic type]'; p. 92: blank; p. 93: act-scene synopsis; p. 94: blank; p. 95: 'ACT I'; p. 96: blank; pp. 97–127: text, headed 'ACT I'; p. 128: blank; p. 129: 'ACT II'; p. 130: blank; pp. 131–152: text, headed 'ACT TWO'; p. 153: 'ACT III'; p. 154: blank; p. 155–185: text, headed 'ACT THREE'; p. 186: blank; p. 187: 'ACT IV'; p. 188: blank; pp. 189–211: text, headed 'ACT FOUR'; p. 212: blank; p. 213: '"THE FIRST MAN" | [three lines of type]'; p. 214: blank; p. 215: 'CHARACTERS | [fifteen lines of roman and italic type]'; p. 216: blank; p. 217: act-scene synopsis; p. 218: blank; p. 219: 'ACT I'; p. 220: blank; pp. 221–252: text, headed 'ACT I'; p. 253: 'ACT II'; p. 254: blank; p. 255–272: text, headed 'ACT II'; p. 273: 'ACT III'; p. 274: blank; p. 275–295: text, headed 'ACT III'; p. 296: blank; p. 297: 'ACT IV'; p. 298: blank; pp. 299–322: text, headed 'ACT IV'; pp. 323–324: blank.

Typography and paper: 11 point on 13, Scotch. $3^1/_2$″ × $5^3/_8$″ ($5^{11}/_{16}$″); twenty-nine or thirty lines per page. Running heads: rectos and versos, individual play titles. Wove paper.

Binding: Tan paper-covered boards with buff B cloth (linen-like grain) shelf back. Front: '[black] The Hairy Ape | Anna Christie | The First Man | Eugene O'Neill'. Spine: '[black] The | Hairy Ape | Anna | Christie | The | First Man | Eugene | O'Neill | BONI AND | LIVERIGHT'. Endpapers of different stock from text paper. All edges trimmed.

Dust jacket: Front: white background; '[red] THE HAIRY APE | ANNA CHRISTIE | [black] (PULITZER PRIZE WINNER, 1922) | [red] THE FIRST MAN | [black] (THREE LONG PLAYS IN ONE VOLUME) | [red] by Eugene O'Neill | [at left, black, twenty-three lines of type giving blurbs by four reviewers] [at right, photo of Louis Wolheim in "Thinker" position] [black, under the photo] *Louis Wolheim as "The Hairy Ape"*'. Spine: white background, '[red double rule] | [black] THE HAIRY APE | ANNA CHRISTIE | THE FIRST MAN | [red short rule] | Eugene O'Neill | [red publisher's device] | [black] $2.00 | [red double rule] | [black] BONI AND | LIVERIGHT | [red double rule]'. Back: white background, '[red] WHAT THE REVIEWERS

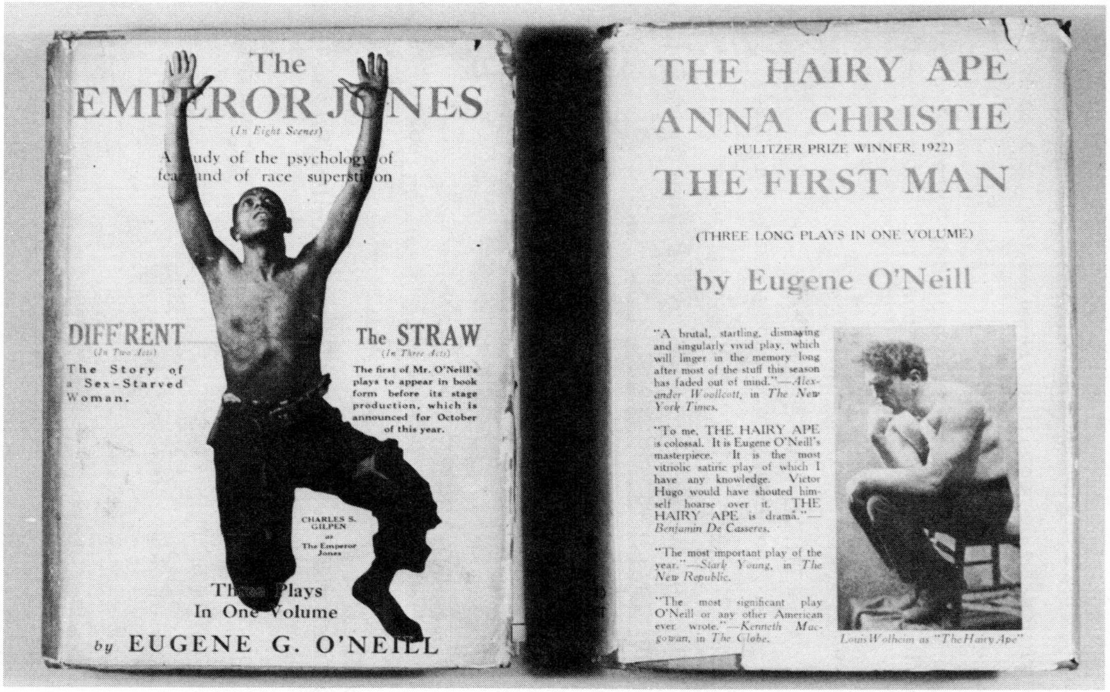

Dust jackets for A 15-I-1.a and A 20-I-1

SAY: | [twenty-six lines of black type about *Anna Christie* with a photo at right of Pauline Lord as Anna Christie] | [red] THE FIRST MAN | [ten lines of black type]'. Front flap: synopsis of each play; back flap: ad for *TEJ*, *BTH*, and *MOTC*.

Publication: 2,620 copies published 24 July 1922. $2.00

Locations: JM^cA (dj); Lilly (two, djs); PSt; Yale.

Note: Excerpts from the play appeared in *Theatre Magazine*, XXXVI (August 1922) following book publication. See C 47.

A 20 THE HAIRY APE
American second book publication (1924)

A 20-II-1
The Complete Works of Eugene O'Neill. New York: Boni & Liveright, 1924. Two volumes.

Limited to 1,200 numbered copies; signed by EO.

THA appears in volume two, pp. 41–95. See A 25-I-1, *DUTE*.

A 20 THE HAIRY APE
American third book publication (1925)

A 20-III-1.a
Plays, Desire Under the Elms, The Hairy Ape, Welded. New York: Boni & Liveright, 1925.

One volume of an unnumbered, ten-volume, uniform series.

First printing: July, 1925

THA appears on pp. 105–169.

REPRINTINGS

A 20-III-1.b
New York: Boni & Liveright, [January 1926].

A 20-III-1.c
New York: Boni & Liveright, [May 1926].

A 20-III-1.d
New York: Boni & Liveright, [November 1926].

A 20-III-1.e
New York: Boni & Liveright, [December 1927].

A 20-III-1.f
New York: Boni & Liveright, [June 1928].

A 20 THE HAIRY APE
American fourth book publication (1929)

A 20-IV-1
THE HAIRY APE
American limited edition, only printing

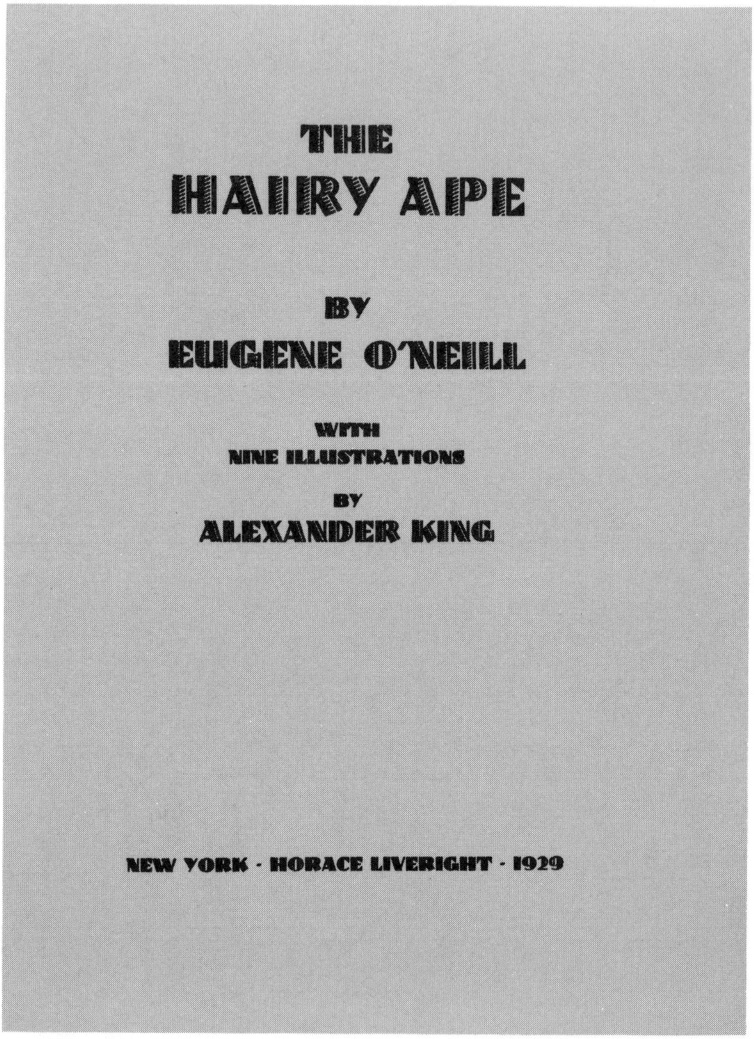
THE
HAIRY APE

BY
EUGENE O'NEILL

WITH
NINE ILLUSTRATIONS
BY
ALEXANDER KING

NEW YORK · HORACE LIVERIGHT · 1929

A 20-IV-1: all in brown; 10″ × 7⅝″

Copyright, 1922, by
BONI AND LIVERIGHT, INC.
Copyright, 1929, by
HORACE LIVERIGHT, INC.

Printed in the U. S. A.

[1–14] 15–30 [31–32] 33–41 [42–44] 45–51 [52–54] 55–65 [66–68] 69–80 [81–82] 83–92 [93–94] 95–105 [106–108] 109–114 [115–116]

$[1]^{2}$ $[2\text{–}8]^{8}$; illustrations are tipped in facing pp. 5 (frontispiece), 15, 33, 45, 55, 69, 83, 95, and 109.

Contents: p. 1: blank; p. 2: statement of limitation: 'This special edition of *The Hairy Ape*, with | nine illustrations by Alexander King, is lim-|ited to 775 numbered copies, of which 750 | are for sale. Each copy is signed by the | author. This copy is no.   '; p. 3: half title; p. 4: blank; p. 5: title; p. 6: copyright; p. 7: list of illustrations; p. 8: blank; p. 9: list of characters; p. 10: blank; p. 11: act-scene synopsis; p. 12: blank; p. 13: '[decorated] SCENE ONE'; p. 14: blank; pp. 15–30: text, headed '[decorated] SCENE ONE'; p. 31: '[decorated] SCENE TWO'; p. 32: blank; pp. 33–41: text, headed '[decorated] SCENE TWO'; p. 42: blank; p. 43: '[decorated] SCENE THREE'; p. 44: blank; pp. 45–51: text, headed '[decorated] SCENE THREE'; p. 52: blank; p. 53: '[decorated] SCENE FOUR'; p. 54: blank; pp. 55–65: text, headed '[decorated] SCENE FOUR'; p. 66: blank; p. 67: '[decorated] SCENE FIVE'; p. 68: blank; pp. 69–80: text, headed '[decorated] SCENE FIVE'; p. 81: '[decorated] SCENE SIX'; p. 82: blank; pp. 83–92: text, headed '[decorated] SCENE SIX'; p. 93: '[decorated] SCENE SEVEN'; p. 94: blank; pp. 95–105: text, headed '[decorated] SCENE SEVEN'; p. 106: blank; p. 107: '[decorated] SCENE EIGHT'; p. 108: blank; pp. 109–114: text, headed '[decorated] SCENE EIGHT'; p. 115: colophon: '*This edition of* The Hairy Ape *was printed* | *from Bodoni type, which was distributed after* | *printing. The book was printed and bound* | *by* THE VAN REES ORGANIZATION. *The illus-*| *trations were engraved and printed by* THE | KNUDSON PROCESS, *and the paper was supplied* | *by* HERMAN SCOTT CHALFANT, INC.; *the entire* | *manufacture under the direction of* | ALBERT H. GROSS *of* HORACE | LIVERIGHT, INC.'; p. 116: blank.

Typography and paper: 12 point on 14, Bodoni. $4\frac{5}{16}'' \times 6\frac{13}{16}''$ ($7\frac{1}{4}''$); thirty-two lines per page. Running heads: rectos, '[number of scene spelled out in decorated capital letters]', versos, '[decorated type] SCENE'. White laid paper with vertical chain marks $^{13}/_{16}''$ apart, with EO's signature as watermark.

Binding: Yellow paper-covered boards, batiked in purple and vermilion swirling design; black, coated V cloth shelf back. Spine: '[goldstamped, decorated type, vertically from top to bottom] THE HAIRY APE · EUGENE O'NEILL'. White wove endpapers, coated black. All edges untrimmed.

Dust jacket: Gray background with black lettering. Front: 'The HAIRY APE | by EUGENE O'NEILL | [reproduction of frontispiece illustration pasted on to jacket] | *Drawings by* | ALEXANDER KING'. Spine: '[two lines vertically from bottom to top at top of spine] The HAIRY APE | by EUGENE O'NEILL | [two lines vertically from bottom to top at middle of spine] *Drawings by* [two decorations] | Alexander King | [horizontally at bottom of spine] [publisher's device] | Horace | Liveright'. Front flap: ad for limited edition of *THA;* back flap blank.

Slipcase: Black paper-covered boards with orange wraparound label ($3^{11}/_{16}'' \times 6^{1}/_{4}''$). Front: '*The* | [two lines of decorated type] HAIRY | APE | *by* | [decorated type] EUGENE O'NEILL | *Illustrated by* | [decorated type] ALEXANDER KING | *Limited edition seven* | *hundred and fifty cop-*|*ies signed by the author*'. Spine: '*The* | HAIRY | APE | *by* | O'NEILL | *Illustrated* | *by* | King | [publisher's device] | Horace | Liveright'. Back: same as front.

Publication: 750 copies published in March 1929. $15.00.

Locations: JM^c^A (#267, dj and boxed); Lilly (#477, dj and boxed); PSt (#610, dj and boxed); Yale (author's copy, dj and boxed).

A 20 THE HAIRY APE
American fifth book publication (1932)

A 20-V-1.a
Nine Plays by Eugene O'Neill. New York: Liveright, 1932. Introduction by Joseph Wood Krutch; plays selected by EO.

THA appears on pp. 37–88. See A 15-VII-1.a, *TEJ*.

REPRINTINGS

A 20-V-1.b
New York: Random House, [1937?]. 'NOBEL PRIZE EDITION'. (Not a new edition.)

A 20-V-1.c
New York: Random House, [1941].

On copyright page: *'First Modern Library Giant Edition* 1941'. (Not a new edition.)

A 20-V-1.d
New York: Random House, [1954?]. ML Giant #G55.

A 20 THE HAIRY APE
American sixth book publication (1935)

A 20-VI-1
THE PLAYS OF EUGENE O'NEILL. Twelve volumes. Wilderness Edition

Volume five

Title page: '[within decorated border] [white against gray background] THE | PLAYS | OF | EUGENE | O'NEILL | [wavy rule] | *"Marco Millions"* | *"The Hairy Ape"* | [wavy rule] | V | WILDERNESS · EDITION | *NEW YORK* | Charles Scribner's Sons'

Copyright page: 'COPYRIGHT, 1935, BY CHARLES SCRIBNER'S SONS | [nineteen lines of roman and italic type]'

[i–x] xi–xiii [xiv] [1–4] 5–71 [72] 73–165 [166] 167–168 [169–170] 171–247 [248–250]

$[1\text{–}15]^8$ $[16]^4$ $[17]^8$

The statement of limitation on p. iv reads: '[decorated rule] | [swash *T*'s and *N*'s] *THIS WILDERNESS EDITION* | OF THE | PLAYS OF EUGENE O'NEILL | printed from type now destroyed, is limited | to seven hundred and seventy sets | of which twenty are for presentation | This is number | [decorated rule]'.

The colophon on p. 248 reads: '[decorated rule] | [swash *T* and *K*] *THIS BOOK* | the fifth of twelve volumes designed by Elmer

Adler | set in an eighteenth-century type face | based on the castings made by John Baskerville | is printed on a specially watermarked paper | at the press of the publisher | in the city of New York | in the month of January | MCM XXX V | [publisher's device]'.

Note: The watermark is: 'CSS | [classical tragedy mask]'.

THA appears on pp. 168–247.

On pp. xi–xii, in a note written by EO's Random House editor, the following statement is made about *THA*: *'It was at Jimmy the Priest's that I knew Driscoll, a Liverpool Irish-|man who was a stoker on a transatlantic liner. Shortly afterwards I | learned that he had committed suicide by jumping overboard in mid-| ocean. Why? The search for an explanation of why Driscoll, proud of | his animal superiority and in complete harmony with his limited concep-|tion of the universe, should kill him-self provided the germ of the idea for | "The Hairy Ape." Whether "The Hairy Ape," written in Province-|town in De-cember 1921 and produced by the Provincetown Players on | March 9, 1922, is to be classified as an Expressionist play or not is of | little consequence. Its manner is inseparable from its matter, and it | found its form as a direct descendant from "The Emperor Jones." | The late Louis Wolheim originated the rôle of Yank when "The | Hairy Ape" opened on March 9, 1922, at the Provincetown Theatre. | He continued in the part under the direction of Arthur Hopkins, when | the play was moved to the Plymouth Theatre and later toured the coun-|try. "The Hairy Ape" has been translated into almost every European | language and has been frequently performed in England and on the | Continent, as well as in the Orient and Australia. Particularly in | Russia have performances of "The Hairy Ape" met with enthusiastic | response.'*

Publication: 770 copies published 30 January 1935.

Locations: JM[c]A (#456); LC (presentation); MJB (#592 boxed); ScU (#749); Yale (presentation).

A 20 THE HAIRY APE
American seventh book publication (1937)

A 20-VII-1
The Emperor Jones, Anna Christie, The Hairy Ape. New York: Random House, [1937]. Introduction by Lionel Trilling. ML #146.

On copyright page: 'First Modern Library Edition | 1937'.

THA appears on pp. 181–260. See A 15-X-1, *TEJ*.

A 20 THE HAIRY APE
American eighth book publication (1941)

A 20-VIII-1.a
The Plays of Eugene O'Neill. New York: Random House, [1941]. Three volumes.

On copyright page: 'FIRST PRINTING'.

THA appears in volume three, pp. 205–254. See A 14-VI-1.a, *BTH*.

REPRINTINGS

A 20-VIII-1.b
New York: Random House, [1941].

On copyright page: 'SECOND PRINTING'.

A 20-VIII-1.c
New York: Random House, [1951].

A 20-VIII-1.d
New York: Random House, [1954–55].

A 20 THE HAIRY APE
American ninth book publication (1967)

A 20-IX-1
Selected Plays of Eugene O'Neill. New York: Random House, [1967].

On copyright page: 'First Printing'.

THA appears on pp. 105–154. See A 15-XIII-1, *TEJ*.

A 20 THE HAIRY APE
American tenth book publication (1972)

A 20-X-1
The Emperor Jones, Anna Christie, The Hairy Ape. New York: Vintage Books, [1972]. No. V-855.

On copyright page: 'FIRST VINTAGE BOOKS EDITION, NOVEMBER 1972'.

Only in wrappers.

THA appears on pp. 161–232.

A 20 THE HAIRY APE
English first book publication (1923)

A 20-EI-1.a
THE HAIRY APE AND OTHER PLAYS
English first edition, first printing

The Hairy Ape
and other Plays *by*
Eugene O'Neill

Jonathan Cape
Eleven Gower Street, London

A 20-EI-1.a: 7¼" × 4¾"

First published 1923
All rights reserved
Printed in Great Britain by Butler & Tanner, Frome and London

[i–vi] [1–2] 3–78 [1–2] 3–122 [1–2] 3–111 [112–114]

$[A]^8$ B–I^8 K–U^8

Contents: p. i: half title; p. ii: card page; p. iii: title; p. iv: copyright; p. v: contents; p. vi: blank; p. 1: 'The Hairy Ape | A Comedy of Ancient and Modern Life'; p. 2: blank; p. 3: 'Characters | [nine lines of type]'; p. 4: scene synopsis; pp. 5–78: text, headed 'The Hairy Ape | Scene I'; p. 1: 'Anna Christie'; p. 2: blank; p. 3: 'Characters | [eleven lines of roman and italic type]'; p. 4: act-scene synopsis; pp. 5–122: text, headed 'Anna Christie | Act I'; p. 1: 'The First Man | A Play in Four Acts'; p. 2: blank; p. 3: 'Characters | [fourteen lines of roman and italic type]'; p. 4: act-scene synopsis; pp. 5–111: text, headed 'The First Man | Act I'; pp. 112–114: blank.

Typography and paper: $3\frac{1}{2}'' \times 5\frac{5}{16}''$ ($5\frac{11}{16}''$); twenty-six to thirty-two lines per page. Running heads: rectos and versos, individual play titles. Wove paper.

Binding: Coated, sky blue V cloth (fine linen-like grain). Spine: white paper label ($2\frac{3}{16}'' \times 1\frac{3}{16}''$): '[blue line of decorations] | [black] The | Hairy Ape | EUGENE O'NEILL | [blue decoration] | [black] *Jonathan Cape* | [blue line of decorations]'. White wove endpapers of different stock from text paper. Top and side edges trimmed.

Dust jacket: Not seen.

Publication: Unknown number of copies published in 1923. 7s. 6d.

Locations: BM (deposit-stamp 4 May 1923); JM^{c}A; ScU; Yale.

REPRINTING

A 20-EI-1.b
London: Jonathan Cape, [1937]. Nobel Prize Edition. (Not a new edition.)

A 21 ANNA CHRISTIE
American first book publication (1922)

A 21-I-1
The Hairy Ape, Anna Christie, The First Man. New York: Boni & Liveright, [1922].

AC appears on pp. 89–211. See A 20-I-1, *THA*.

Note: For a discussion of the relationships among *AC*, "The Ole Davil," and "Chris Christopherson," see Claude R. Flory, "Notes on the Antecedents of *Anna Christie*," *PMLA*, LXXXVI, 1 (January 1971), 77–83.

A 21 ANNA CHRISTIE
American second book publication (1924)

A 21-II-1
The Complete Works of Eugene O'Neill. New York: Boni & Liveright, 1924. Two volumes.

Limited to 1,200 numbered copies; signed by EO.

AC appears in volume one, pp. 1–82. See A 6-IV-1, "Cardiff."

A 21 ANNA CHRISTIE
American third book publication (1925)

A 21-III-1.a
Plays, Anna Christie, All God's Chillun Got Wings, Diff'rent. New York: Boni & Liveright, 1925.

First printing: July, 1925

One volume of an unnumbered, ten-volume, uniform series.

AC appears on pp. 7–114.

REPRINTINGS

A 21-III-1.b
New York: Boni & Liveright, [April 1926].

A 21-III-1.c
New York: Boni & Liveright, [October 1926].

A 21-III-1.d
New York: Boni & Liveright, [April 1927].

A 21-III-1.e
New York: Boni & Liveright, [March 1928].

A 21-III-1.f
New York: Boni & Liveright, [November 1928].

A 21-III-1.g
New York: Boni & Liveright, [August 1929].

A 21 ANNA CHRISTIE
American fourth book publication (1930)

A 21-IV-1
ANNA CHRISTIE
American limited edition, only printing

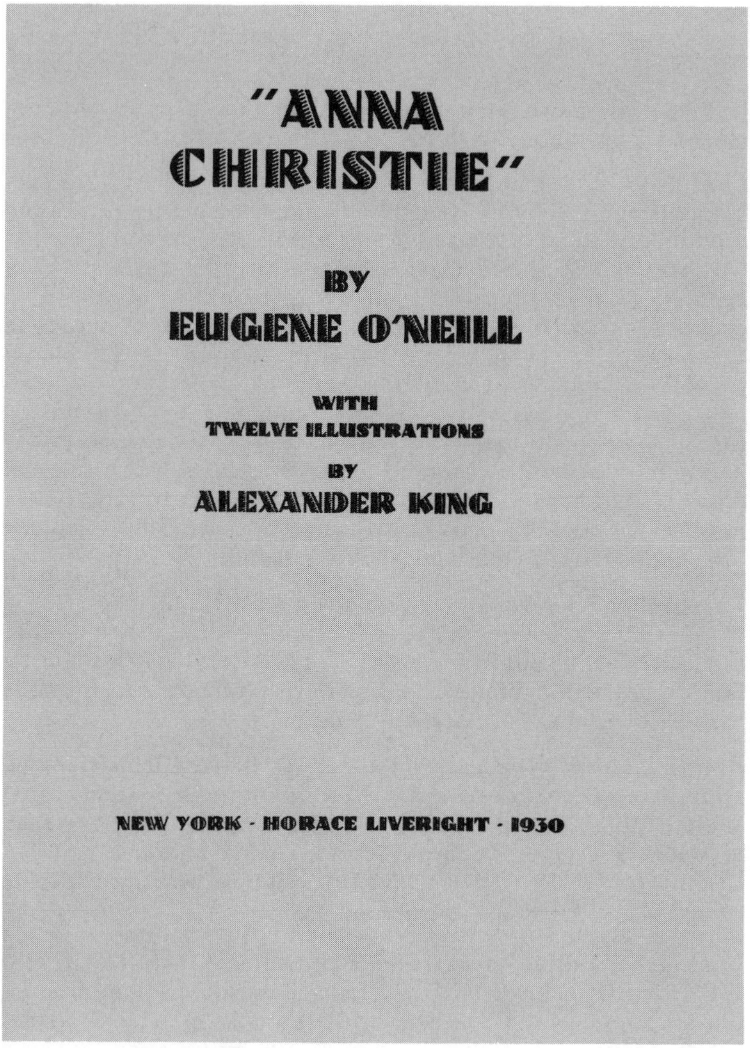
"ANNA
CHRISTIE"

BY
EUGENE O'NEILL

WITH
TWELVE ILLUSTRATIONS
BY
ALEXANDER KING

NEW YORK · HORACE LIVERIGHT · 1930

A 21-IV-1: all in blue green; $10\frac{1}{16}'' \times 7\frac{1}{2}''$

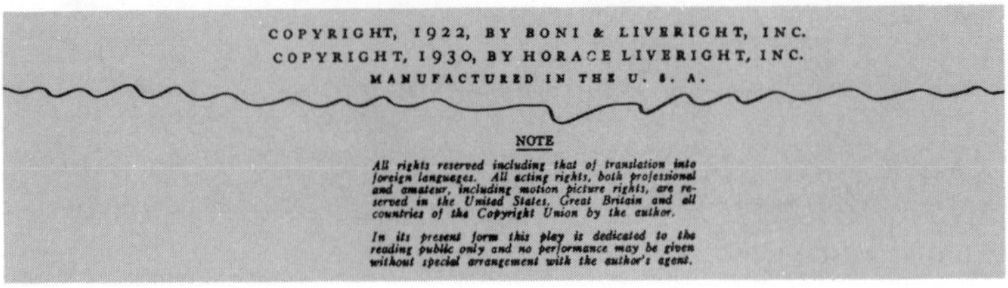
COPYRIGHT, 1922, BY BONI & LIVERIGHT, INC.
COPYRIGHT, 1930, BY HORACE LIVERIGHT, INC.
MANUFACTURED IN THE U. S. A.

NOTE

All rights reserved including that of translation into foreign languages. All acting rights, both professional and amateur, including motion picture rights, are reserved in the United States, Great Britain and all countries of the Copyright Union by the author.

In its present form this play is dedicated to the reading public only and no performance may be given without special arrangement with the author's agent.

[1–14] 15–55 [56–58] 59–86 [87–88] 89–128 [129–130] 131–161 [162–164]

$[1]^{10}$ $[2–10]^{8}$; illustrations are tipped in facing pp. 5 (frontispiece), 15, 35, 59, 71, 81, 89, 97, 109, 131, 147, and 157.

Contents: p. 1: blank; p. 2: statement of limitation: '*This special edition of* ANNA CHRISTIE, | *with twelve illustrations by Alexander King,* | *is limited to* 775 *numbered copies, of which* | 750 *are for sale. Each copy is signed by* | *the author.* | *This copy is No.........*'; p. 3: half title; p. 4: blank; p. 5: title; p. 6: copyright; p. 7: list of characters; p. 8: blank; p. 9: act-scene synopsis; p. 10: blank; p. 11: list of illustrations; p. 12: blank; p. 13: '[decorated] ACT ONE'; p. 14: blank; pp. 15–55: text, headed '[decorated] ACT ONE'; p. 56: blank; p. 57: '[decorated] ACT TWO'; p. 58: blank; pp. 59–86: text, headed '[decorated] ACT TWO'; p. 87: '[decorated] ACT THREE'; p. 88: blank; pp. 89–128: text, headed '[decorated] ACT THREE'; p. 129: '[decorated] ACT FOUR'; p. 130: blank; pp. 131–161: text, headed '[decorated] ACT FOUR'; pp. 162–164: blank.

Typography and paper: 12 point on 14, Bodoni. $4^{5}/_{16}'' \times 6^{13}/_{16}''$ ($7^{5}/_{16}''$); thirty-four lines per page. Running heads: rectos, '[number of act spelled out in decorated capital letters]', versos, '[decorated type] ACT'. White laid paper with vertical chain marks $^{13}/_{16}''$ apart with EO's signature as watermark.

Binding: Yellow paper-covered boards, batiked in purple and vermilion repeated design of circles and triangles; black, coated V cloth (fine linen-like grain) shelf back. Spine: '[goldstamped in decorated type, vertically from top to bottom] "ANNA CHRISTIE" · EUGENE O'NEILL'. White wove endpapers coated black. All edges untrimmed.

Dust jacket: Blue background. Front: '[black] ANNA CHRISTIE | by EUGENE O'NEILL | [pasted-on illustration of Anna Christie, same as the frontispiece] | *Drawings by* | ALEXANDER KING'. Spine: '[black, two lines vertically from bottom to top at

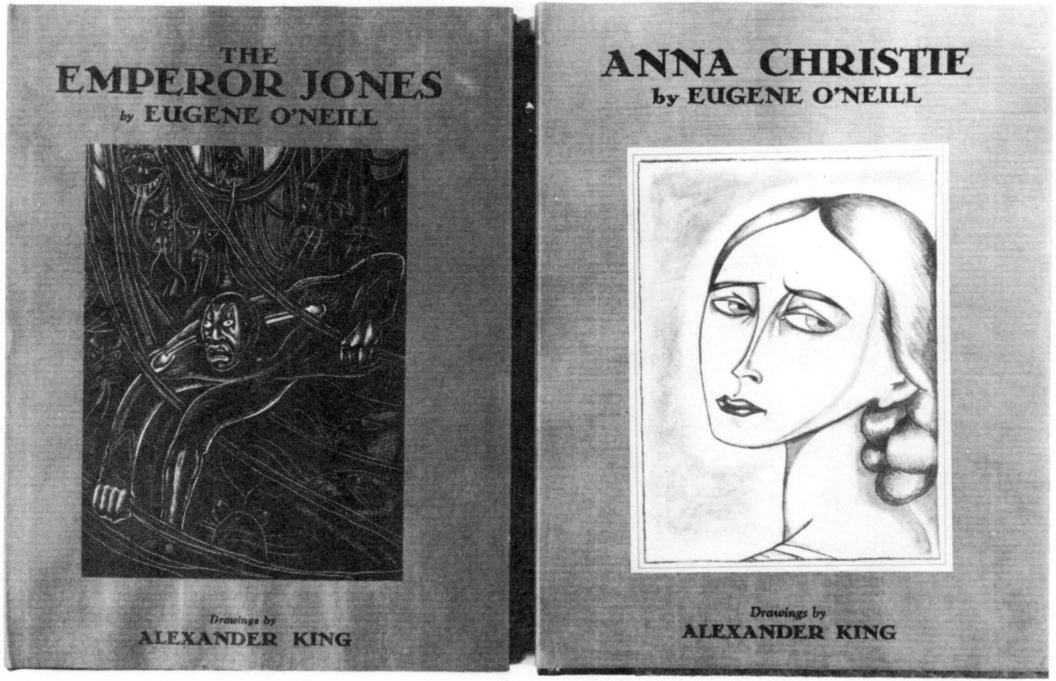

Dust jackets for A 15-V-1 and A 21-IV-1

top of spine] ANNA CHRISTIE | by EUGENE O'NEILL | [two lines vertically from bottom to top in center of spine] *Drawings by* [two decorations] | Alexander King | [horizontally at bottom of spine] [publisher's device] | Horace | Liveright'. Front flap: ad for *Anna Christie, The Emperor Jones*, and *The Hairy Ape* limited editions. The front flap includes the following announcement: *'There will also be twelve copies, | specially bound in leather, with an | autographed original illustration by Alexander King, the price one hun-|dred and twenty-five dollars.'* Back flap: blank.

Slipcase: Black paper-covered boards with blue wraparound label (3 13/16" × 6 1/4"). Front: '[black, two lines of decorated type] ANNA | CHRISTIE | *by* | [decorated type] EUGENE O'NEILL | *Illustrated by* | [decorated type] ALEXANDER KING | *Limited edition seven | hundred and fifty cop-|ies signed by the author*'. Spine: '[black] ANNA | CHRISTIE | *by* | O'NEILL | *Illustrated | by* | KING | [publisher's device] | Horace | Liveright'. Back: same as front.

Publication: 775 copies published in 1930. $15.00.

Locations: JMcA (#421); Lilly (#121, dj and boxed); PSt (#265, dj and boxed); ScU (#83, dj and boxed); Yale (#20, dj and boxed).

A 21 ANNA CHRISTIE
American fifth book publication (1932)

A 21-V-1
Representative Plays of Eugene O'Neill. New York: Liveright, [1932].

AC appears on pp. 227–324. See A 8-IV-1, "Caribbees."

A 21 ANNA CHRISTIE
American sixth book publication (1935)

A 21-VI-1
THE PLAYS OF EUGENE O'NEILL. Twelve volumes. Wilderness Edition

Volume ten

Title page: '[within decorated border] [white against gray background] THE PLAYS OF EUGENE O'NEILL [wavy rule] | *The Great God Brown* | *"Anna Christie"* | [wavy rule] | X | WILDERNESS · EDITION | *NEW YORK* | Charles Scribner's Sons'

Copyright page: 'COPYRIGHT, 1935, BY CHARLES SCRIBNER'S SONS | [nineteen lines of roman and italic type]'

[i–x] xi–xiii [xiv] [1–4] 5–128 [129–130] 131–271 [272–274]

[1–18]^{8}

The statement of limitation on p. iv reads: '[decorated rule] | [swash *T*'s and *N*'s] *THIS WILDERNESS EDITION* | OF THE | PLAYS OF EUGENE O'NEILL | printed from type now destroyed, is limited | to seven hundred and seventy sets | of which twenty are for presentation | This is number | [decorated rule]'.

The colophon on p. 272 reads: '[decorated rule] | [swash *T* and *K*] *THIS BOOK* | the tenth of twelve volumes designed by Elmer Adler | set in an eighteenth-century type face | based on the castings made by John Baskerville | is printed on a specially watermarked paper | at the press of the publisher | in the city of New York | in the month of April | MCM XXX V | [publisher's device]'.

Note: The watermark is: 'CSS | [classical tragedy mask]'.

AC appears on pp. 129–271.

On p. xi, in a note written by EO's Random House editor, the following statement is made about *AC*: *'The final version of "Anna Christie," written at Provincetown in | the summer of 1920, was the outgrowth of an earlier play, named | "Chris." In this earlier work the emphasis was placed upon the father, | Chris Christopherson, but "Anna Christie" became the play of his | daughter, Anna. When it was produced it provoked a great deal of | controversy over its so-called happy ending. The fact that at the last | curtain Anna and Burke are to be married led, by the convention of the | theatre, to the conclusion that all must continue happily ever after. But | in their conflicts there is the question implicit in Chris's last speech— | the closing lines of the play. The ultimate decision remains with the | sea—fate—the symbol of life. | "Anna Christie" was produced by Arthur Hopkins at the Vander-|bilt Theatre on November 2, 1921, with Pauline Lord starred in the | rôle of Anna. It ran for seven months and the next year toured the coun-|try. In 1924 a silent moving picture version was made, with Blanche | Sweet playing Anna, and in 1929 Greta Garbo was featured in a talk-|ing picture of "Anna Christie." It was awarded the Pulitzer Prize for | 1922. | In Europe, in the East, in South America and Australia productions | of "Anna Christie" have found favor with audiences of the most diverse character.'*

Publication: 770 copies published 28 May 1935.

Locations: JM^cA (#456); LC (presentation); MJB (#592 boxed); ScU (#749); Yale (presentation).

A 21 ANNA CHRISTIE
American seventh book publication (1937)

A 21-VII-1
The Emperor Jones, Anna Christie, The Hairy Ape. New York: Random House, [1937]. Introduction by Lionel Trilling. ML #146.

On copyright page: '*First Modern Library Edition* | 1937'.

AC appears on pp. 59–179.

A 21 ANNA CHRISTIE
American eighth book publication (1941)

A 21-VIII-1.a
The Plays of Eugene O'Neill. New York: Random House, [1941]. Three volumes.

On copyright page: 'FIRST PRINTING'.

AC appears in volume three, pp. 1–78. See A 14-VI-1.a, *BTH*.

REPRINTINGS

A 21-VIII-1.b
New York: Random House, [1941].

On copyright page: 'SECOND PRINTING'.

A 21-VIII-1.c
New York: Random House, [1951].

A 21-VIII-1.d
New York: Random House, [1954–55].

A 21 ANNA CHRISTIE
American ninth book publication (1944)

A 21-IX-1
Selected Plays of Eugene O'Neill. New York: Editions for the Armed Services, Inc., [1941]. Published by arrangement with Random House. No. Q-35.

Only in wrappers.

AC appears on pp. 49–139.

A 21 ANNA CHRISTIE
American tenth book publication (1967)

A 21-X-1
Selected Plays of Eugene O'Neill. New York: Random House, [1967].

On copyright page: 'First Printing'.

AC appears on pp. 35–104. See A 15-XIII-1, *TEJ*.

A 21 ANNA CHRISTIE
American eleventh book publication (1972)

A 21-XI-1
The Emperor Jones, Anna Christie, The Hairy Ape. New York: Vintage Books, [1972]. No. V-855.

On copyright page: 'FIRST VINTAGE BOOKS EDITION, NOVEMBER 1972'.

Only in wrappers.

AC appears on pp. 55–160.

A 21 ANNA CHRISTIE
English first book publication (1923)

A 21-EI-1.a
The Hairy Ape and Other Plays. London: Jonathan Cape, [1923].

AC appears on pp. 1–122. See A 20-EI-1.a, *THA*.

REPRINTING

A 21-EI-1.b
London: Jonathan Cape, [1937]. Nobel Prize Edition. (Not a new edition.)

A 21 ANNA CHRISTIE
English second book publication, first separate book publication (1923)

A 21-EII-1.a
ANNA CHRISTIE
English first edition

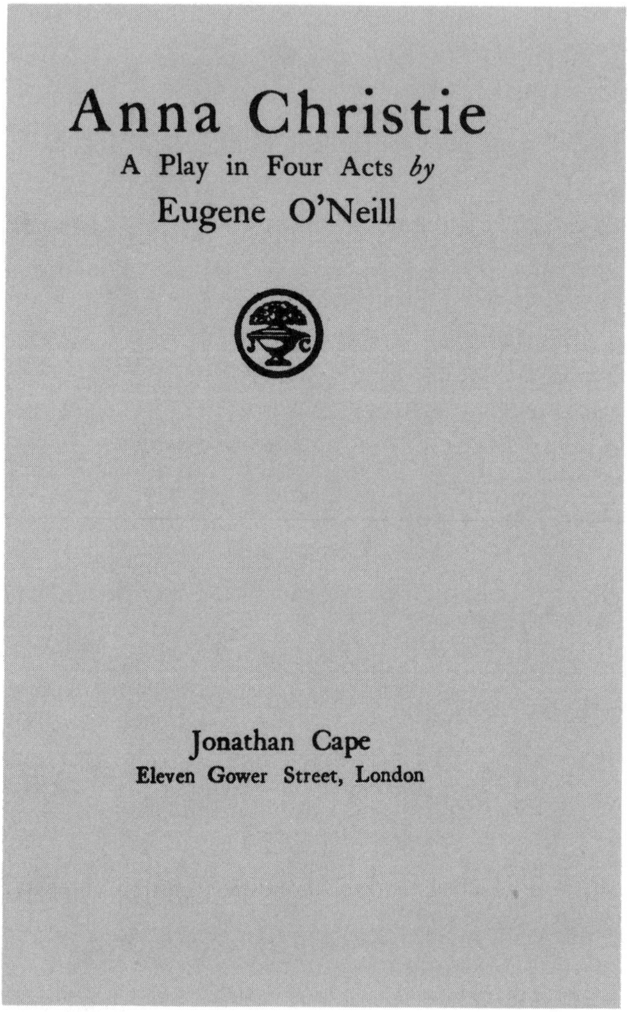

Anna Christie
A Play in Four Acts *by*
Eugene O'Neill

Jonathan Cape
Eleven Gower Street, London

A 21-EII-1.a: $7\frac{7}{16}'' \times 5''$

First published 1923
All rights reserved

[i–iv] [1–2] 3–122 [123–128]

$[a]^2$ $[A]^8$ B–H^8. $H_{7,8}$ are pastedown endpapers.

Contents: p. i: half title; p. ii: card page; p. iii: title; p. iv: copyright; p. 1: second half title; p. 2: colophon: *'Printed in Great Britain by* Butler & Tanner, *Frome and London.';* p. 3: 'Characters | [eleven lines of roman and italic type]'; p. 4: act-scene synopsis; pp. 5–122: text, headed 'Anna Christie | Act I'; pp. 123–124: blank; pp. 125–128: pastedown endpaper.

Typography and paper: 3½" × 5⁵⁄₁₆" (5¹¹⁄₁₆"); twenty-nine lines per page. Running heads: rectos and versos, 'ANNA CHRISTIE'. Wove paper.

Binding: Published simultaneously in boards and wrappers.
Boards: buff paper-covered boards. Front: '[black] Anna Christie | Eugene O'Neill'. Spine: '[black] Anna | Christie | [decoration] | Eugene | O'Neill | JONATHAN | CAPE'. Top edge only trimmed.
Wrappers: Dust jacket of heavier stock than text paper. Buff background. Front: '[within decorated frame] ANNA CHRISTIE | A PLAY IN FOUR ACTS BY | EUGENE O'NEILL | [publisher's device]'. Spine: '[vertically from top to bottom] ANNA CHRISTIE [decoration] EUGENE O'NEILL'. (Specimen seen was torn.) Back has list of three EO collections by Cape. Front flap: '[swash *A* and *C*] *Anna Christie* 2*s.* 6*d. net*'. Back flap blank.

Dust jacket: Not seen.

Publication: Unknown number of copies published in April 1923. 3s. 6d. Wrappers 2s. 6d.

Locations: JM[c]A (boards and wrappers); Yale (wrappers).

REPRINTING

A 21-EII-1.b
London: Jonathan Cape, [1923].

On copyright page: *'First published* 1923 | *Second Impression* 1923'.

Seen only in boards.

A 22 THE FIRST MAN
American first book publication (1922)

A 22-I-1
The Hairy Ape, Anna Christie, The First Man. New York: Boni & Liveright, [1922].

TFM appears on pp. 213–322. See A 20-I-1, *THA*.

A 22 THE FIRST MAN
American second book publication (1924)

A 22-II-1
The Complete Works of Eugene O'Neill. New York: Boni & Liveright, 1924. Two volumes.

Limited to 1,200 numbered copies; signed by EO.

TFM appears in volume one, pp. 181–252. See A 6-IV-1, "Cardiff."

A 22 THE FIRST MAN
American third book publication (1925)

A 22-III-1.a
Plays, The Emperor Jones, Gold, The First Man, The Dreamy Kid. New York: Boni & Liveright, 1925.

First printing: July, 1925

One volume of an unnumbered, ten-volume, uniform series.

TFM appears on pp. 143–225.

REPRINTINGS

A 22-III-1.b
New York: Boni & Liveright, [March 1926].

A 22-III-1.c
New York: Boni & Liveright, [November 1926].

A 22-III-1.d
New York: Boni & Liveright, [January 1928].

A 22-III-1.e
New York: Boni & Liveright, [May 1928].

A 22-III-1.f
New York: Boni & Liveright, [July 1930].

A 22-III-1.g
New York: Liveright, [May 1932].

A 22 THE FIRST MAN
American fourth book publication (1935)

A 22-IV-1
The Plays of Eugene O'Neill. New York: Scribners, [1934–35]. Twelve volumes. Wilderness Edition

Limited to 770 numbered copies.

TFM appears in volume eight, pp. 163–291. See A 18-V-1, *The Straw.*

On p. xi, in a note written by EO's Random House editor, the following statement is made about *TFM:* '"THE FIRST MAN" *was written at Provincetown in the winter of | 1921. It had its initial performance at the Neighborhood Playhouse in | New York on March 4, 1922.*'

Publication: 770 copies published 22 March 1935.

A 22 THE FIRST MAN
American fifth book publication (1941)

A 22-V-1.a
The Plays of Eugene O'Neill. New York: Random House, [1941]. Three volumes.

On copyright page: 'FIRST PRINTING'.

TFM appears in volume two, pp. 551–619. See A 16-V-1.a, *Gold.*

REPRINTINGS

A 22-V-1.b
New York: Random House, [1941].

On copyright page: 'SECOND PRINTING'.

A 22-V-1.c
New York: Random House, [1951].

A 22-V-1.d
New York: Random House, [1954–55].

A 22 THE FIRST MAN
English first book publication (1923)

A 22-EI-1.a
The Hairy Ape and Other Plays. London: Jonathan Cape, [1923].

TFM appears on pp. 1–111. See A 20-EI-1.a, *THA*.

REPRINTING

A 22-EI-1.b
London: Jonathan Cape, [1937]. Nobel Prize Edition. (Not a new edition.)

A 23 ALL GOD'S CHILLUN GOT WINGS
American first book publication (1924)

A 23-I-1
ALL GOD'S CHILLUN GOT WINGS AND WELDED
American first edition

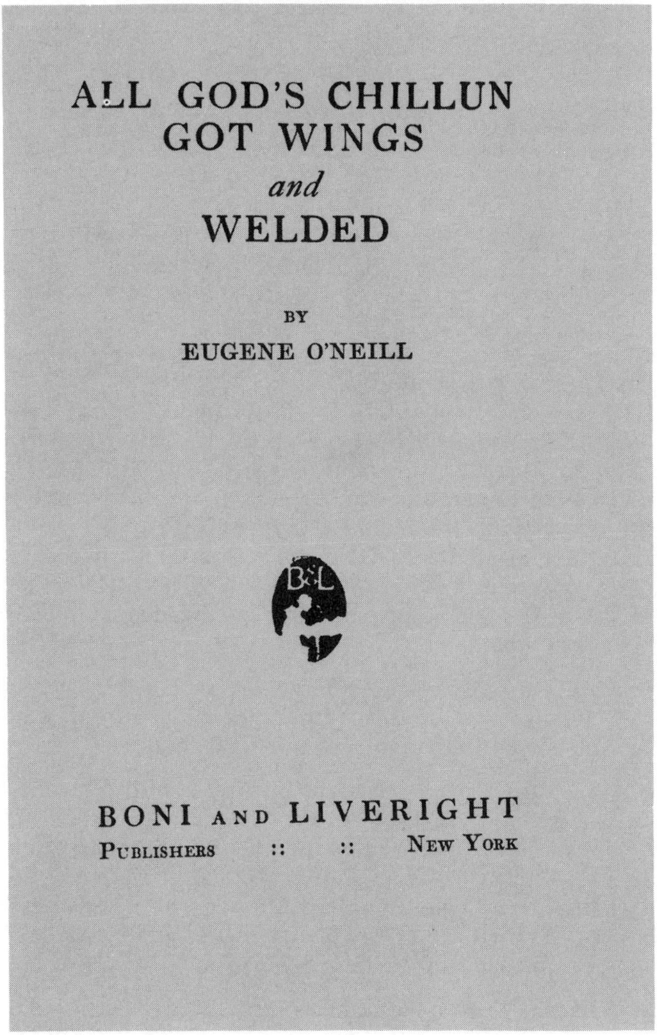
ALL GOD'S CHILLUN
GOT WINGS
and
WELDED

BY
EUGENE O'NEILL

BONI AND LIVERIGHT
PUBLISHERS :: :: NEW YORK

A 23-I-1: 7$\frac{1}{2}$″ × 5$\frac{1}{4}$″

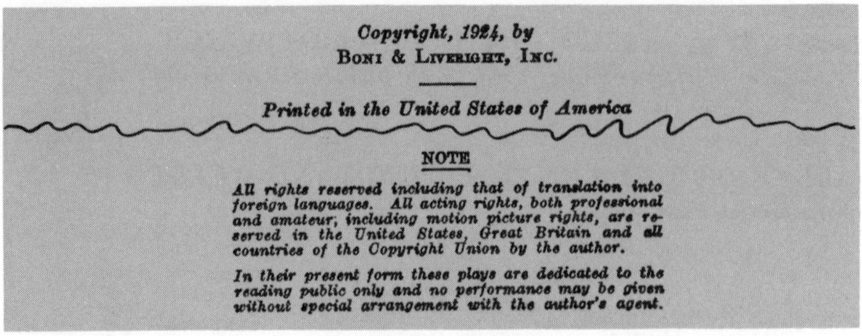

Copyright, 1924, by
BONI & LIVERIGHT, INC.

Printed in the United States of America

NOTE

All rights reserved including that of translation into foreign languages. All acting rights, both professional and amateur, including motion picture rights, are reserved in the United States, Great Britain and all countries of the Copyright Union by the author.

In their present form these plays are dedicated to the reading public only and no performance may be given without special arrangement with the author's agent.

[i–ii] [1–14] 15–44 [45–46] 47–79 [80–88] 89–120 [121–122] 123–152 [153–154] 155–170 [171–174]

$[1\text{–}11]^8$

Contents: pp. i–ii: blank; p. 1: half title; p. 2: card page; p. 3: title; p. 4: copyright; p. 5: 'CONTENTS | [three lines of type]'; p. 6: blank; p. 7: 'ALL GOD'S CHILLUN | GOT WINGS'; p. 8: blank; p. 9: 'CHARACTERS | [eight lines of roman and italic type]'; p. 10: blank; p. 11: act-scene synopsis; p. 12: blank; p. 13: 'ACT I'; p. 14: blank; pp. 15–44: text, headed 'ACT ONE | SCENE ONE'; p. 45: 'ACT II'; p. 46: blank; pp. 47–79: text, headed 'ACT TWO | SCENE ONE'; p. 80: blank; p. 81: 'WELDED | A Play in Three Acts'; p. 82: blank; p. 83: 'CHARACTERS | [four lines of roman and italic type]'; p. 84: blank; p. 85: act-scene synopsis; p. 86: blank; p. 87: 'ACT I'; p. 88: blank; pp. 89–120: text, headed 'ACT ONE'; p. 121: 'ACT II'; p. 122: blank; pp. 123–152: text, headed 'ACT TWO | SCENE ONE'; p. 153: 'ACT III'; p. 154: blank; pp. 155–170: text, headed 'ACT THREE'; pp. 171–174: blank.

Typography and paper: 11 point on 13, Scotch. $3\frac{5}{16}'' \times 5\frac{3}{8}''$ ($5\frac{11}{16}''$); twenty-nine or thirty lines per page. Running heads: rectos and versos, individual play titles. Wove paper.

Binding: Tan paper-covered boards with buff V cloth (fine linen-like grain) shelf back. Front: '[black] All God's Chillun | Got Wings and | Welded | Eugene O'Neill'. Spine: '[black] All God's | Chillun | Got Wings | and | Welded | [triangular decoration] | Eugene | O'Neill | [blindstamped publisher's device] | BONI & | LIVERIGHT'. White endpapers of different stock from text paper. Top edge only trimmed.

Dust jacket: Tan background. Front: '[black] ALL GOD'S | CHILLUN | GOT WINGS | and WELDED | *TWO NEW FULL* | *LENGTH PLAYS BY* | EUGENE | O'NEILL'. Spine: '[black]

ALL | GOD'S | CHILLUN | GOT | WINGS | *and* | WELDED | *Two new full* | *length plays by* | EUGENE | O'NEILL | [publisher's device] | $2.00 | Boni & | Liveright'. Back: Hugo Gellert's charcoal sketch of EO and a list of five volumes by EO, beginning with *TEJ, Diff'rent and The Straw* and ending with *MOTC* (in the Modern Library). Front flap: blurb for *AGCGW*. Back flap: blurb for *Welded.*

Publication: 3,200 copies published 17 April 1924. $2.00.

Printing: Printed 9 April 1924 by Van Rees Press, New York, from plates made by Van Rees Composition; bound by Van Rees Bindery.

Locations: JM^cA (dj); Lilly (two, djs); MJB; ScU; Yale.

Note: *AGCGW* first appeared in *The American Mercury,* V, 2 (February 1924), 129–148. See C 53. Magazine publication preceded book publication.

A 23 ALL GOD'S CHILLUN GOT WINGS
American second book publication (1924)

A 23-II-1
The Complete Works of Eugene O'Neill. New York: Boni & Liveright, 1924. Two volumes.

Limited to 1,200 numbered copies; signed by EO.

AGCGW appears in volume two, pp. 97–144. See A 25-I-1, *DUTE.*

A 23 ALL GOD'S CHILLUN GOT WINGS
American third book publication (1925)

A 23-III-1.a
Plays, Anna Christie, All God's Chillun Got Wings, Diff'rent. New York: Boni & Liveright, 1925.

First printing: July, 1925

One volume of an unnumbered, ten-volume, uniform series.

AGCGW appears on pp. 115–175.

REPRINTINGS

A 23-III-1.b
New York: Boni & Liveright, [April 1926].

A 23-III-1.c
New York: Boni & Liveright, [October 1926].

A 23-III-1.d
New York: Boni & Liveright, [April 1927].

A 23-III-1.e
New York: Boni & Liveright, [March 1928].

A 23-III-1.f
New York: Boni & Liveright, [November 1928].

A 23-III-1.g
New York: Boni & Liveright, [August 1929].

A 23 ALL GOD'S CHILLUN GOT WINGS
American fourth book publication (1932)

A 23-IV-1.a
Nine Plays by Eugene O'Neill. New York: Liveright, 1932. Introduction by Joseph Wood Krutch; plays selected by EO.

AGCGW appears on pp. 89–133. See A 15-VII-1.a, *TEJ*.

REPRINTINGS

A 23-IV-1.b
New York: Random House, [1937?]. 'NOBEL PRIZE EDITION'. (Not a new edition.)

A 23.IV-1.c
New York: Random House, [1941].

On copyright page: 'First Modern Library Giant Edition | 1941'. (Not a new edition.)

A 23-IV-1.d
New York: Random House, [1954?]. ML Giant #G55.

A 23 ALL GOD'S CHILLUN GOT WINGS
American fifth book publication (1934)

A 23-V-1
THE PLAYS OF EUGENE O'NEILL. Twelve volumes. Wilderness Edition

Volume four

Title page: '[within decorated border] [white against gray background] THE | PLAYS | OF | EUGENE | O'NEILL | [wavy rule] | IV | WILDERNESS · EDITION | *NEW YORK* | Charles Scribner's Sons'

Copyright page: 'COPYRIGHT, 1934, BY CHARLES SCRIBNER'S SONS | [nineteen lines of roman and italic type]'

[i–x] xi–xiii [xiv] [1–2] 3–44 [45–46] 47–85 [86–90] 91–129 [130] 131–215 [216] 217–252 [253–258]

$[1\text{–}17]^8$

The statement of limitation on p. iv reads: '[decorated rule] | [swash *T*'s and *N*'s] *THIS WILDERNESS EDITION* | OF THE | PLAYS OF EUGENE O'NEILL | printed from type now destroyed, is limited | to seven hundred and seventy sets | of which twenty are for presentation | This is number | [decorated rule]'.

The colophon on p. 254 reads: '[decorated rule] | [swash *T* and *K*] *THIS BOOK* | the fourth of twelve volumes designed by Elmer Adler | set in an eighteenth-century type face | based on the castings made by John Baskerville | is printed on a specially watermarked paper | at the press of the publisher | in the city of New York | in the month of December | MCM XXX IV | [publisher's device]'.

Note: The watermark is: 'CSS | [classical tragedy mask]'.

AGCGW appears on pp. 1–85.

On p. xi, in a note written by EO's Random House editor, the following statement is made about *AGCGW:* '[display E]VEN BEFORE *"All God's Chillun Got Wings" was written at | Provincetown in the summer and fall of 1923 and produced at | the Provincetown Theatre on May 15, 1924, the preliminary | furor over the suggestion that miscegenation would be treated in the | theatre obscured the real intention of the play. In the eyes of those who | had not yet seen it, or even read the manuscript, it became an incendiary | drama threatening to stir up race riots. The actual production must have | disappointed the howlers. Nothing happened. Paul Robeson, playing | the part of Jim Harris made his début to a New York audience in "All | God's Chillun Got Wings." | Of all my plays produced in Europe, none has had so widespread a | success as "All God's Chillun Got Wings." It has been played in nearly | all countries of Europe and South America. Especially in Russia, where | it celebrated its 200th performance at the Kamerny Theatre, Moscow, a | year ago under the direction of Alexander Tairov, has it had phenomenal | success. And the Kamerny is a repertory theatre at that!'*

Publication: 770 copies published 28 December 1934.

Locations: JM^cA (#456); LC (presentation); MJB (#592 boxed); ScU (#749); Yale (presentation).

A 23 ALL GOD'S CHILLUN GOT WINGS
American sixth book publication (1936?)

A 23-VI-1
Ah, Wilderness! and Two Other Plays. New York: Modern Library, [1936?].

Includes *AGCGW* and *BTH*. *AGCGW* appears on pp. 143–196.

A 23 ALL GOD'S CHILLUN GOT WINGS
American seventh book publication (1941)

A 23-VII-1.a
The Plays of Eugene O'Neill. New York: Random House, [1941]. Three volumes.

On copyright page: 'FIRST PRINTING'.

AGCGW appears in volume two, pp. 299–342. See A 16-V-1.a, *Gold*.

REPRINTINGS

A 23-VII-1.b
New York: Random House, [1941].

On copyright page: 'SECOND PRINTING'.

A 23-VII-1.c
New York: Random House, [1951].

A 23-VII-1.d
New York: Random House, [1954–55].

A 23 ALL GOD'S CHILLUN GOT WINGS
English first book publication (1925)

A 23-EI-1.a
ALL GOD'S CHILLUN GOT WINGS. DESIRE UNDER THE ELMS, AND WELDED
English first edition, first printing

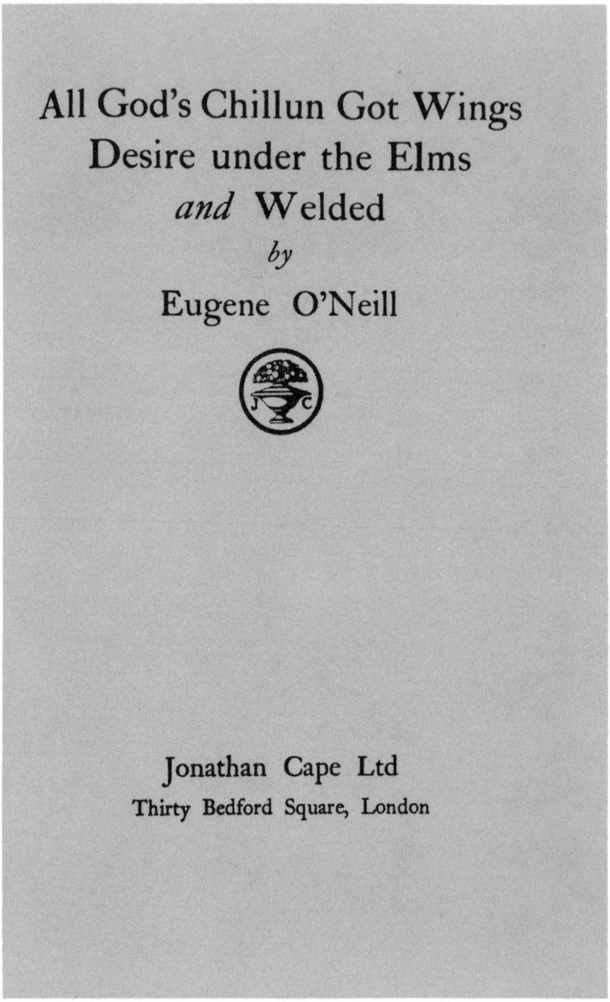
All God's Chillun Got Wings
Desire under the Elms
and Welded
by
Eugene O'Neill

Jonathan Cape Ltd
Thirty Bedford Square, London

A 23-EI-1.a: $7^{7}/_{16}'' \times 4^{11}/_{16}''$

FIRST PUBLISHED IN MXMXXV
MADE & PRINTED IN GREAT BRITAIN
BY BUTLER & TANNER LTD
FROME AND
LONDON

[i–vi] [1–6] 7–74 [1–6] 7–115 [116] [1–6] 7–91 [92]

[A]^8 B–I^8 K–S^8

Contents: p. i: half title; p. ii: card page; p. iii: title; p. iv: copyright; p. v: 'Contents'; p. vi: blank; p. 1: 'All God's Chillun Got Wings'; p. 2: blank; p. 3: 'Characters | [eight lines of roman and italic type]'; p. 4: blank; p. 5: act-scene synopsis; p. 6: blank; pp. 7–74: text, headed 'ACT I | Scene I'; p. 1: 'Desire Under the Elms | A Play in Three Parts | (1924)'; p. 2: blank; p. 3: 'Characters | [eight lines of roman and italic type]'; p. 4: blank; p. 5: description of setting; p. 6: blank; pp. 7–115: text, headed 'Desire Under the Elms | PART I | Scene I'; p. 116: blank; p. 1: 'Welded | A Play in Three Acts'; p. 2: blank; p. 3: 'Characters | [four lines of roman and italic type]'; p. 4: blank; p. 5: act-scene synopsis; p. 6: blank; pp. 7–91: text, headed 'ACT I'; p. 92: blank.

Typography and paper: $3\frac{5}{16}'' \times 5\frac{1}{8}''$ ($5\frac{9}{16}''$); twenty-seven to thirty-one lines per page. Running heads: rectos and versos, individual play titles. Wove paper.

Binding: Coated, sky blue V cloth (fine linen-like grain). Spine: white paper label ($2\frac{3}{16}'' \times 1\frac{3}{16}''$)–'[blue line of decorations] | [black] All | God's Chillun | Got Wings | EUGENE O'NEILL | [blue decoration] | [black] *Jonathan Cape* | [blue line of decorations]'. White endpapers of different stock from text paper. Top and right edges trimmed.

Dust jacket: White background. Front: '[black line of decorations | [blue] All God's Chillun Got Wings | [black] Desire Under the Elms *and* Welded | Eugene O'Neill | [blue publisher's device] | [black] Jonathan Cape Ltd., Thirty Bedford Square, London | [line of decorations]'. Spine: '[blue line of decorations] | [black] All God's | Chillun Got | Wings | Desire Under | the Elms | *and* | Welded | [blue decoration] | [black] Eugene O'Neill | [blue publisher's device] | [black] JONATHAN CAPE | [blue line of decorations]'. Back: list of six EO titles, beginning and ending with *TEJ*, published by Jonathan Cape. Front flap: seventeen-line blurb for *AGCGW* by St. John Ervine; at bottom, '*All God's Chillun | Got Wings 7s.6d. net*'. Back flap blank.

Publication: Unknown number of copies published in 1925. 7s. 6d.

Locations: BM (deposit-stamp 16 October 1925); JM[c]A; Lilly (dj); ScU (dj).

REPRINTING

A 23-EI-1.b
London: Jonathan Cape, [1958].

A 24 WELDED
American first book publication (1924)

A 24-I-1
All God's Chillun Got Wings and Welded. New York: Boni & Liveright, [1924].

Welded appears on pp. 81–170. See A 23-I-1, *AGCGW*.

A 24 WELDED
American second book publication (1924)

A 24-II-1
The Complete Works of Eugene O'Neill. New York: Boni & Liveright, 1924. Two volumes.

Limited to 1,200 numbered copies; signed by EO.

Welded appears in volume two, pp. 223–274. See A 25-I-1, *DUTE*.

A 24 WELDED
American third book publication (1925)

A 24-III-1.a
Plays, Desire Under the Elms, The Hairy Ape, Welded. New York: Boni & Liveright, 1925.

First printing: July, 1925

One volume of an unnumbered, ten-volume, uniform series.

Welded appears on pp. 171–238.

REPRINTINGS

A 24-III-1.b
New York: Boni & Liveright, [January 1926].

A 24-III-1.c
New York: Boni & Liveright, [May 1926].

A 24-III-1.d
New York: Boni & Liveright, [November 1926].

A 24-III-1.e
New York: Boni & Liveright, [December 1927].

A 24-III-1.f
New York: Boni & Liveright, [June 1928].

A 24 WELDED
American fourth book publication (1935)

A 24-IV-1
The Plays of Eugene O'Neill. New York: Scribners, [1934–35]. Twelve volumes. Wilderness Edition.

Limited to 770 numbered copies.

Welded appears in volume six, pp. 165–260. See A 14-IV-1, *BTH.*

On p. xi, in a note written by EO's Random House editor, the following statement is made about *Welded:* 'WELDED *was written at Ridgefield, Conn., in 1923 and was pro-|duced by Kenneth MacGowan, Robert Edmund Jones and myself, in | association with the Selwyns, at the Thirty-ninth Street Theatre on | March 17, 1924. Doris Keene appeared as Eleanor and Jacob Ben-|Ami as Michael.*'

Publication: 770 copies published 30 January 1935.

A 24 WELDED
American fifth book publication (1941)

A 24-V-1.a
The Plays of Eugene O'Neill. New York: Random House, [1941]. Three volumes.

On copyright page: 'FIRST PRINTING'.

Welded appears in volume two, pp. 441–489. See A 16-V-1.a, *Gold.*

REPRINTINGS

A 24-V-1.b
New York: Random House, [1941].

On copyright page: 'SECOND PRINTING'.

A 24-V-1.c
New York: Random House, [1951].

A 24-V-1.d
New York: Random House, [1954–55].

A 24 WELDED
English first book publication (1925)

A 24-EI-1.a
All God's Chillun Got Wings, Desire Under The Elms, and Welded. London: Jonathan Cape, [1925].

Welded appears on pp. 1–91. See A 23-EI-1.a, *AGCGW.*

REPRINTING

A 24-EI-1.b
London: Jonathan Cape, [1958].

A 25 DESIRE UNDER THE ELMS
American first book publication (1924)

A 25-I-1
THE COMPLETE WORKS OF EUGENE O'NEILL. Two volumes. American first edition, only printing

Volume two

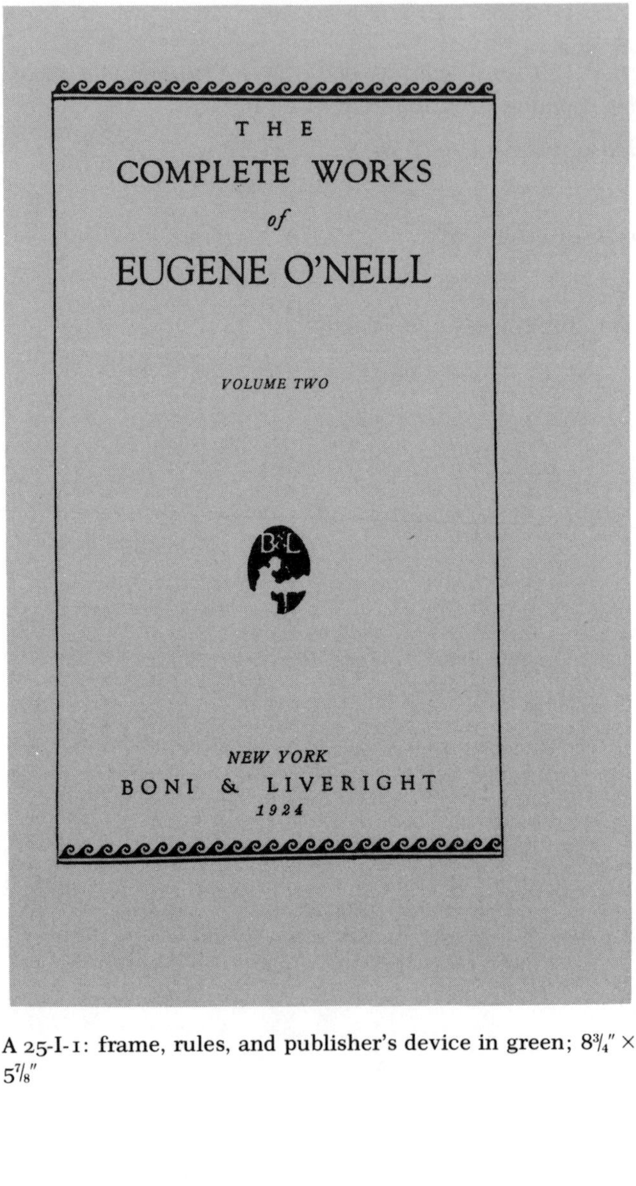
THE
COMPLETE WORKS
of
EUGENE O'NEILL

VOLUME TWO

NEW YORK
BONI & LIVERIGHT
1924

A 25-I-1: frame, rules, and publisher's device in green; $8\frac{3}{4}'' \times 5\frac{7}{8}''$

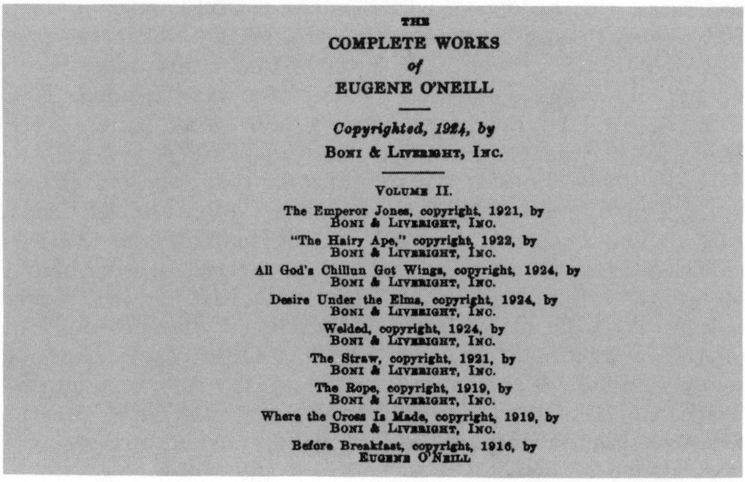

THE
COMPLETE WORKS
of
EUGENE O'NEILL

Copyrighted, 1924, by
Boni & Liveright, Inc.

Volume II.
The Emperor Jones, copyright, 1921, by
Boni & Liveright, Inc.
"The Hairy Ape," copyright, 1922, by
Boni & Liveright, Inc.
All God's Chillun Got Wings, copyright, 1924, by
Boni & Liveright, Inc.
Desire Under the Elms, copyright, 1924, by
Boni & Liveright, Inc.
Welded, copyright, 1924, by
Boni & Liveright, Inc.
The Straw, copyright, 1921, by
Boni & Liveright, Inc.
The Rope, copyright, 1919, by
Boni & Liveright, Inc.
Where the Cross Is Made, copyright, 1919, by
Boni & Liveright, Inc.
Before Breakfast, copyright, 1916, by
Eugene O'Neill

[i–vi] [1–4] 5–40 [41–44] 45–95 [96–100] 101–144 [145–148] 149–221 [222–226] 227–274 [275–278] 279–367 [368–372] 373–398 [399–402] 403–421 [422–426] 427–446 [447–448] 449–457 [458]

$[1\text{–}29]^8$

Contents: p. i: half title; p. ii: blank; p. iii: title; p. iv: copyright; p. v: '*CONTENTS* | of | VOLUME TWO | [twelve lines of roman and italic type]'; p. vi: blank; p. 1: 'THE EMPEROR JONES | (1920)'; p. 2: blank; p. 3: 'CHARACTERS | [twelve lines of roman and italic type]'; p. 4: 'SCENES | [nine lines of type]'; pp. 5–40: text, headed 'THE EMPEROR JONES | SCENE ONE'; p. 41: ' "THE HAIRY APE" | A Comedy of Ancient and Modern Life | in Eight Scenes | (1922)'; p. 42: blank; p. 43: 'CHARACTERS | [nine lines of type]'; p. 44: 'SCENES | [ten lines of type]'; pp. 45–95: text, headed ' "THE HAIRY APE" | SCENE ONE'; p. 96: blank; p. 97: 'ALL GOD'S CHILLUN GOT WINGS | (1923)'; p. 98: blank; p. 99: 'CHARACTERS | [eight lines of roman and italic type]'; p. 100: act-scene synopsis; pp. 101–144: text, headed 'ALL GOD'S CHILLUN GOT WINGS | ACT ONE | Scene One'; p. 145: 'DESIRE UNDER THE ELMS | A Play in Three Parts | (1924)'; p. 146: blank; p. 147: 'CHARACTERS | [seven lines of roman and italic type]'; p. 148: scene description; pp. 149–221: text, headed 'DESIRE UNDER THE ELMS | PART I | SCENE ONE'; p. 222: blank; p. 223: 'WELDED | A Play in Three Acts | (1923)'; p. 224: blank; p. 225: 'CHARACTERS | [four lines of type]'; p. 226: act-scene synopsis; pp.

227–274: text, headed 'WELDED | ACT ONE'; p. 275: 'THE STRAW | A Play in Three Acts | (1919)'; p. 276: blank; p. 277: 'CHARACTERS | [twenty-one lines of roman and italic type]'; p. 278: act-scene synopsis; pp. 279–367: text, headed 'THE STRAW | ACT ONE | Scene One'; p. 368: blank; p. 369: 'THE ROPE | A Play in One Act | (1918)'; p. 370: blank; p. 371: 'CHARACTERS | [five lines of roman and italic type]'; p. 372: blank; pp. 373–398: text, headed 'THE ROPE'; p. 399: 'THE DREAMY KID | A Play in One Act | (1918)'; p. 400: blank; p. 401: 'CHARACTERS | [four lines of roman and italic type]'; p. 402: blank; pp. 403–421: text, headed 'THE DREAMY KID'; p. 422: blank; p. 423: 'WHERE THE CROSS IS MADE | A Play in One Act | (1918)'; p. 424: blank; p. 425: 'CHARACTERS | [seven lines of roman and italic type]'; p. 426: blank; pp. 427–446: text, headed 'WHERE THE CROSS IS MADE'; p. 447: 'BEFORE BREAKFAST | A Play in One Act | (1916)'; p. 448: blank; pp. 449–457: text, headed 'BEFORE BREAKFAST'; p. 458: blank.

Typography and paper: 10 point on 12, Scotch. $3^{13}/_{16}'' \times 6^{1}/_{16}''$ ($6^{7}/_{16}''$); thirty-six lines per page. Running heads: rectos, 'DESIRE UNDER THE ELMS | [double rule]'; versos, 'PLAYS OF EUGENE O'NEILL | [double rule]'. White laid paper with vertical chains $1^{1}/_{16}''$ apart. No watermark.

Binding: Blue paper-covered boards with laid paper effect (horizontal chains $1^{1}/_{2}''$ apart). Front: '[goldstamped EO signature]'. Spine (royal blue shelf back of V cloth, fine linen-like grain): '[gold, within gold frame of wave motif] COLLECTED | PLAYS | OF | EUGENE | O'NEILL | [below frame in gold]⋆⋆ | [blindstamped publisher's device] | [goldstamped] BONI AND | LIVERIGHT | [border of goldstamped wave motif]'. White endpapers of different stock from text paper. All edges untrimmed.

Dust jacket: Not seen.

Slipcase: For two-volume set, not seen.

Publication: 1,200 numbered sets, signed by EO in volume one, published 27 December 1924. [Sanborn and Clark give January 1925 as publication date.]

Printing: Printed 17 December 1924 by Van Rees Press, New York, from type set by Van Rees Composition; bound by Van Rees Bindery.

Locations: JM^{c}A (#856); PSt (#602); Yale (#1024).

Note: Excerpts from the play appeared in *Theatre,* XXXIX (June 1924), preceding book publication. See C 55.

A 25 DESIRE UNDER THE ELMS
American second book publication, first separate book publication (1925)

A 25-II-1
DESIRE UNDER THE ELMS
American first edition

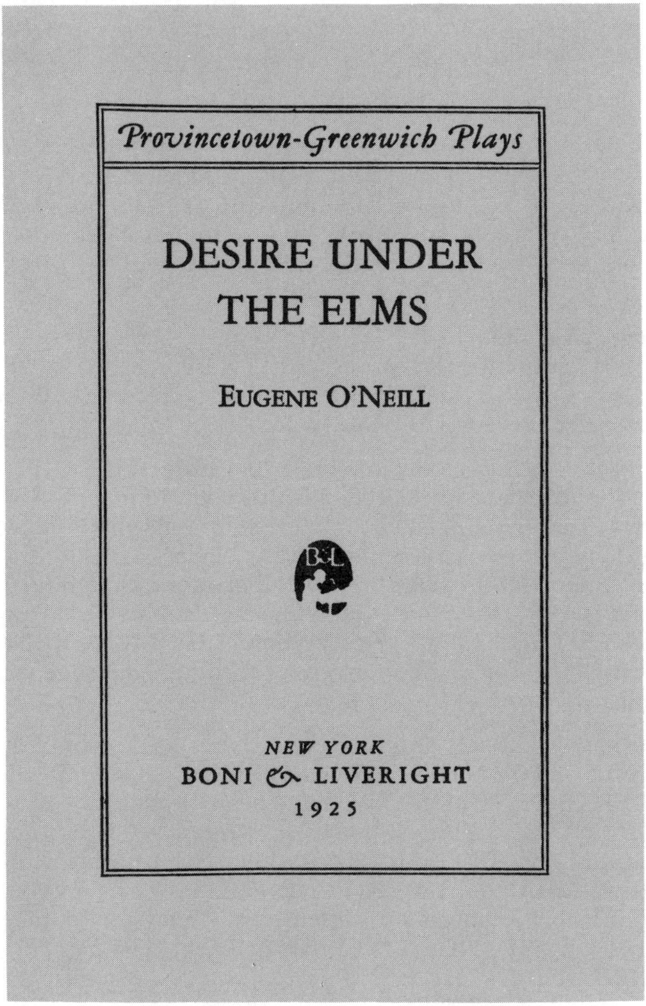
Provincetown-Greenwich Plays

DESIRE UNDER THE ELMS

EUGENE O'NEILL

NEW YORK
BONI & LIVERIGHT
1925

A 25-II-1: $7\frac{7}{16}'' \times 5\frac{3}{16}''$

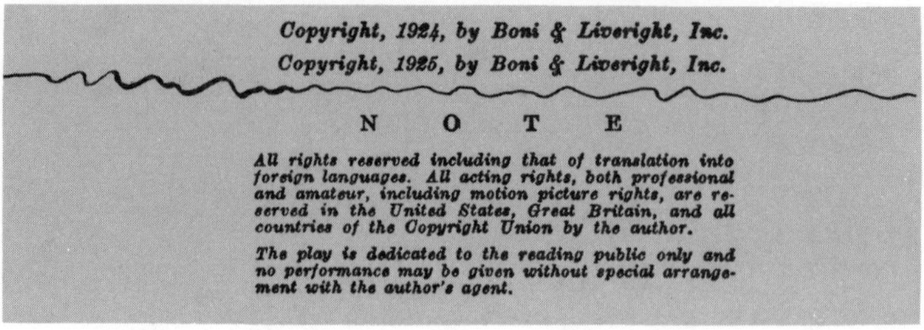
Copyright, 1924, by Boni & Liveright, Inc.
Copyright, 1925, by Boni & Liveright, Inc.

N O T E

All rights reserved including that of translation into foreign languages. All acting rights, both professional and amateur, including motion picture rights, are reserved in the United States, Great Britain, and all countries of the Copyright Union by the author.

The play is dedicated to the reading public only and no performance may be given without special arrangement with the author's agent.

[3–10] 11–166 [167–170]

$[1\text{–}10]^8$ $[11]^4$

Contents: p. 3: half title; p. 4: blank; p. 5: title; p. 6: copyright; p. 7: 'DESIRE UNDER THE ELMS | A Play in Three Parts'; p. 8: blank; p. 9: 'CHARACTERS [seven lines of roman and italic type]'; p. 10: blank; pp. 11–12: set description; pp. 13–166: text, headed: 'DESIRE UNDER THE ELMS | PART I | SCENE ONE'; pp. 167–170: blank.

Typography and paper: 11 point on 13, Scotch. $3\frac{5}{16}'' \times 5\frac{1}{4}''$ ($5\frac{9}{16}''$); twenty-nine lines per page. Running heads: rectos, 'DESIRE UNDER THE ELMS | [rule]'; versos, 'PROVINCETOWN-GREENWICH PLAYS | [rule]'. Wove paper.

Binding: Black V cloth (fine linen-like grain). Front: '[illustration of sailing vessel in harbor seen through four-pane window, window frame stamped in orange, ship and wharf pilings in white] [in black against orange below window panes] Provincetown|-Greenwich | Plays'. Spine: '[all stamped in orange] PROVINCETOWN|-GREENWICH | PLAYS | [double rule] | DESIRE | UNDER THE | ELMS | [decoration] | O'NEILL | BONI & | LIVERIGHT'. Top and bottom edges trimmed; top edge stained orange.

Dust jacket: Black lettering against tan background. Front: 'PROVINCETOWN-GREENWICH PLAYS | [rule] | DESIRE | UNDER | THE | ELMS | "We have been cleansed by pity and | terror. . . . O'Neill's finest play." | —*Heywood Broun, N. Y. World.* | EUGENE O'NEILL | [rule] | see back of this wrapper'. Spine: 'DESIRE | UNDER | THE | ELMS | *by* | EUGENE | O'NEILL | Provincetown-|Greenwich | Plays | [publisher's device] | BONI AND | LIVERIGHT'. Back: *'The attack upon DESIRE UNDER THE | ELMS which has been vindicated by the | citizen play jury, has aroused the public. | Here are some expressions of opinion.* | [thirty-eight lines of type quoting support for the play from Augustus Thomas, Norman Hapgood, Sidney E. Mezes, Rev. John Haynes Holmes, Mary Nash, Don Marquis, Herbert Bayard Swope, Doris Keane, Clare Briggs, and Ring W. Lardner] | [in the right-hand bottom corner, there is a sketch of the house and elm trees with the following lines set against the house] *Eugene O'Neill's* | *greatest play* | DESIRE | UNDER the ELMS'. Front flap: blurb for *DUTE;* back flap: blurb for six other EO titles, and an announcement that the two-volume Collected Plays limited edition (1924) has sold out.

Publication: 2,000 copies published 11 April 1925. $2.00.

Printing: Printed 2 April 1925 by Van Rees Press, New York, from plates made by Van Rees Composition; bound by Van Rees Bindery.

Locations: JM^cA (dj); LC (deposit-stamp 21 April 1925); Lilly; PSt; Yale.

A 25 DESIRE UNDER THE ELMS
American third book publication (1925)

A 25-III-1.a
Plays, Desire Under the Elms, The Hairy Ape, Welded. New York: Boni & Liveright, 1925.

First printing: July, 1925

One volume of an unnumbered, ten-volume, uniform series.

DUTE appears on pp. 7–103.

REPRINTINGS

A 25-III-1.b
New York: Boni & Liveright, [January 1926].

A 25-III-1.c
New York: Boni & Liveright, [May 1926].

A 25-III-1.d
New York: Boni & Liveright, [November 1926].

A 25-III-1.e
New York: Boni & Liveright, [December 1927].

A 25-III-1.f
New York: Boni & Liveright, [June 1928].

A 25 DESIRE UNDER THE ELMS
American fourth book publication (1932)

A 25-IV-1.a
Nine Plays by Eugene O'Neill. New York: Liveright, 1932. Introduction by Joseph Wood Krutch; plays selected by EO.

DUTE appears on pp. 135–206. See A 15-VII-1.a, *TEJ*.

REPRINTINGS

A 25-IV-1.b
New York: Random House, [1937?]. 'Nobel Prize Edition'. (Not a new edition.)

A 25-IV-1.c
New York: Random House, [1941].

On copyright page: 'First Modern Library Giant Edition | 1941'. (Not a new edition.)

A 25-IV-1.d
New York: Random House, [1954?]. ML Giant #G55.

A 25 DESIRE UNDER THE ELMS
American fifth book publication (1935)

A 25-V-1
THE PLAYS OF EUGENE O'NEILL. Twelve volumes. Wilderness Edition.

Volume eleven

Title page: '[within decorated border] [white against gray background] THE | PLAYS | OF | EUGENE O'NEILL | [wavy rule] | *Desire Under the Elms* | *The Fountain* | [wavy rule] | XI | WILDERNESS · EDITION | *NEW YORK* | Charles Scribner's Sons'

Copyright page: 'COPYRIGHT, 1935, BY CHARLES SCRIBNER'S SONS | [nineteen lines of roman and italic type]' [i–x] xi–xiii [xiv] [1–4] 5–132 [133–136] 137–227 [228] 229–266 [267–270]

$[1\text{–}17]^8$ $[18]^6$

The statement of limitation on p. iv reads: '[decorated rule] | [swash *T*'s and *N*'s] *THIS WILDERNESS EDITION* | OF THE | P L A Y S O F E U G E N E O' N E I L L | printed from type now destroyed, is limited | to seven hundred and seventy sets | of which twenty are for presentation | This is number | [decorated rule]'.

The colophon on p. 268 reads: '[decorated rule] [swash *T* and *K*] *THIS BOOK* | the eleventh of twelve volumes designed by Elmer Adler | set in an eighteenth-century type face | based on the castings made by John Baskerville | is printed on a specially watermarked paper | at the press of the publisher | in the city of New York | in the month of May | MCM XXX V | [publisher's device]'.

Note: The watermark is: 'CSS | [classical tragedy mask]'.

DUTE appears on pp. 1–132.

On p. xi, in a note written by EO's Random House editor, the following statement is made about *DUTE:* '[display D]ESIRE UNDER THE ELMS *was written at Ridgefield, Conn.,* | *in the winter and spring of 1924. It was first produced at the* | *Greenwich Village Theatre on November 11, 1924, by Ken-*|*neth MacGowan, Robert Edmund Jones and myself, allied at that time* | *for the staging of my own and other plays. The leading rôles were acted* | *by Walter Huston, as Ephraim Cabot, and Mary Morris, as Abbie* | *Putnam. "Desire Under the Elms" was later brought uptown to the* | *Earl Carroll Theatre, where it became the object of an attack by some* | *self-appointed purifiers of the stage. It withstood this onslaught and had* | *a run of nearly a year. It has since been translated into many languages* | *and has been produced in almost every European country. In Russia par-*|*ticularly, "Desire Under the Elms" is played frequently to enthusiastic* | *audiences.*'

Publication: 770 copies published 28 May 1935.

Locations: JM^c^A (#456); LC (presentation); MJB (#592 boxed); ScU (#749); Yale (presentation).

A 25 DESIRE UNDER THE ELMS
American sixth book publication (1941)

A 25-VI-1.a
The Plays of Eugene O'Neill. New York: Random House, [1941]. Three volumes.

On copyright page: 'FIRST PRINTING'.

DUTE appears in volume one, pp. 201–269. See A 6-VII-1.a, "Cardiff."

REPRINTINGS

A 25-VI-1.b
New York: Random House, [1941].

On copyright page: 'SECOND PRINTING'.

A 25-VI-1.c
New York: Random House, [1951].

A 25-VI-1.d
New York: Random House, [1954–55].

A 25 DESIRE UNDER THE ELMS
American seventh book publication (1958)

A 25-VII-1
Desire Under the Elms. New York: The New American Library, [1958]. Signet Book #1502.

On copyright page: 'FIRST PRINTING, MARCH 1958'.

A 25 DESIRE UNDER THE ELMS
American eighth book publication (1967)

A 25-VIII-1
Selected Plays of Eugene O'Neill. New York: Random House, [1967].

On copyright page: 'First Printing'.

DUTE appears on pp. 155–216. See A 15-XIII-1, *TEJ*.

A 25 DESIRE UNDER THE ELMS
English first book publication (1925)

A 25-EI-1.a
All God's Chillun Got Wings, Desire Under the Elms, and Welded. London: Jonathan Cape, [1925].

DUTE appears on pp. 1–115. See A 23-EI-1.a, *AGCGW*.

REPRINTING

A 25-EI-1.b
London: Jonathan Cape, [1958].

A 26 THE GREAT GOD BROWN
American first book publication (1926)

A 26-I-1.a
THE GREAT GOD BROWN, THE FOUNTAIN, THE MOON OF THE CARIBBEES, AND OTHER PLAYS
American first edition, first printing

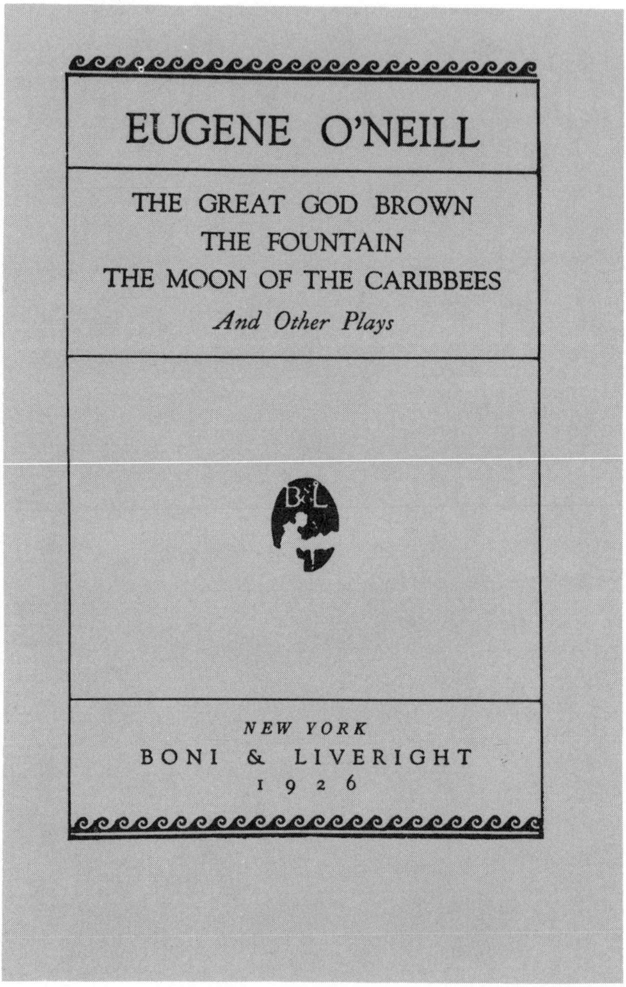

EUGENE O'NEILL

THE GREAT GOD BROWN
THE FOUNTAIN
THE MOON OF THE CARIBBEES
And Other Plays

NEW YORK
BONI & LIVERIGHT
1926

A 26-I-1.a: frame, rules, and publisher's device in green; $8\frac{1}{16}'' \times 5\frac{1}{2}''$

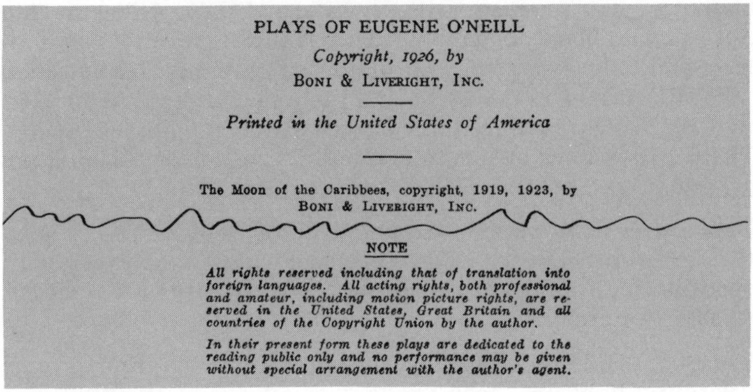

PLAYS OF EUGENE O'NEILL

Copyright, 1926, by

BONI & LIVERIGHT, INC.

Printed in the United States of America

The Moon of the Caribbees, copyright, 1919, 1923, by

BONI & LIVERIGHT, INC.

NOTE

All rights reserved including that of translation into foreign languages. All acting rights, both professional and amateur, including motion picture rights, are reserved in the United States, Great Britain and all countries of the Copyright Union by the author.

In their present form these plays are dedicated to the reading public only and no performance may be given without special arrangement with the author's agent.

[1–10] 11–98 [99–102] 103–192 [193–196] 197–220 [221–224] 225–241 [242–246] 247–266 [267–270] 271–294 [295–298] 299–319 [320–324] 325–347 [348–352] 353–383 [384]

$[1–24]^{8}$

Contents: p. 1: half title; p. 2: card page; p. 3: title; p. 4: copyright; p. 5: 'CONTENTS | [ten lines of type]'; p. 6: blank; p. 7: 'THE GREAT GOD BROWN | (1920)'; p. 8: blank; p. 9: 'CHARACTERS | [eleven lines of roman and italic type]'; p. 10: act-scene synopsis; pp. 11–98: text, headed 'THE GREAT GOD BROWN | PROLOGUE'; p. 99: 'THE FOUNTAIN | A Play in Eleven Scenes | (1921–22)'; p. 100: blank; p. 101: 'CHARACTERS | [twenty-six lines of roman and italic type]'; p. 102: scene synopsis; pp. 103–192: text, headed 'THE FOUNTAIN | SCENE ONE'; p. 193: 'THE MOON OF THE CARIBBEES | A Play in One Act'; p. 194: blank; p. 195: 'CHARACTERS | [twenty-one lines of roman and italic type]'; p. 196: note on time of these plays; pp. 197–220: text, headed 'THE MOON OF THE CARIBBEES'; p. 221: 'BOUND EAST FOR CARDIFF | A Play in One Act'; p. 222: blank; p. 223: 'CHARACTERS | [eleven lines of type]'; p. 224: blank; pp. 225–241: text, headed 'BOUND EAST FOR CARDIFF'; p. 242: blank; p. 243: 'THE LONG VOYAGE HOME | A Play in One Act'; p. 244: blank; p. 245: 'CHARACTERS | [ten lines of roman and italic type]'; p. 246: blank; pp. 247–266: text, headed 'THE LONG VOYAGE HOME'; p. 267: 'IN THE ZONE | A Play in One Act'; p. 268: blank; p. 269: 'CHARACTERS | [nine lines of roman and italic type]'; p. 270: blank; pp. 271–294: text, headed 'IN THE ZONE'; p. 295: 'ILE | A Play in One Act'; p. 296: blank; p. 297: 'CHARACTERS | [seven lines of roman and italic type]'; p. 298: blank; pp. 299–319: text, headed 'ILE'; p. 320:

blank; p. 321: 'WHERE THE CROSS IS MADE | A Play in One Act'; p. 322: blank; p. 323: 'CHARACTERS | [seven lines of roman and italic type]'; p. 324: blank; pp. 325–347: text, headed 'WHERE THE CROSS IS MADE'; p. 348: blank; p. 349: 'THE ROPE | A Play in One Act'; p. 350: blank; p. 351: 'CHARACTERS | [five lines of roman and italic type]'; p. 352: blank; pp. 353–383: text, headed 'THE ROPE'; p. 384: blank.

Typography and paper: 10 point on 14, Scotch. $3^{13}/_{16}''$ × $5^{13}/_{16}''$ ($6^{3}/_{16}''$); twenty-nine or thirty lines per page. Laid paper with vertical chain marks $^{11}/_{16}''$ apart and with 'WARREN'S | OLDE STYLE' watermark.

Binding: Blue green, sized V cloth (fine linen-like grain). Front: '[within a light sea green frame with a wave motif at bottom] [goldstamped EO signature]'. Spine: '[goldstamped border of wave motif] | [goldstamped] EUGENE | O'NEILL | [single wave motif] | The Great | God Brown | The | Fountain | The Moon | of the | Caribbees | [blindstamped publisher's device] | [goldstamped] BONI AND | LIVERIGHT | [goldstamped border of wave motif]'. Illustrated endpapers front and rear: [aqua and buff] steamship on rolling sea silhouetted against setting sun and with the word 'O'NEILL' above. Top edge only trimmed and stained dark blue.

Dust jacket: Front: '[light blue green background] [black] THE GREAT GOD BROWN | THE FOUNTAIN | THE MOON OF THE CARIBBEES | *And Six Other Plays of the Sea* | [orange shell decoration] [black] *by* Eugene O'Neill [orange shell decoration] | [black drawing of William A. Brown with Dion Anthony's mask] | [orange] COURTESY OF THE GREENWICH VILLAGE PLAYBILL'. Spine: '[dark blue] THE GREAT | GOD BROWN | [orange short rule] | [dark blue] THE FOUNTAIN | [orange short rule] | [dark blue] THE MOON OF THE | CARIBBEES | [orange short rule] | [dark blue] *And Six Other* | *Plays of the Sea* | [same illustration as front] | *by* | EUGENE | O'NEILL | [orange publisher's device] | [dark blue] BONI & | LIVERIGHT'. Back: '[dark blue border of sea motif with porpoises riding crest of waves, framing drawing of EO] | [below border in dark blue against light blue green background] The Works of | EUGENE | O'NEILL | [eighteen lines of italic type listing sixteen EO titles, interrupted by five orange decorations] | [to left of title list in orange] *Each volume* | *large 12mo. End* | *Papers. Per vol-*|*ume $2.50.* | *Five volumes,* | *boxed, $12.50.* | [to right of title list in orange] *Uniform Bind-*|*ing. Comprising* | *the Collected* | *Works of* | *Eugene O'Neill.*' Front flap: blurbs for *GGB* by J. Brooks

Atkinson, Gilbert W. Gabriel, and George Jean Nathan. Back flap: blurbs for *TF* by Alexander Woollcott, John Anderson, Percy Hammond, and Barrett H. Clark; blurb for plays included in *MOTC*.

Publication: Unknown number of copies published 15 March 1926. $2.50.

Printing: Printed 8 March 1926 by Van Rees Press, New York, from plates made by Van Rees Composition; bound by Van Rees Bindery.

Locations: JM[c]A (dj); Lilly (dj); Yale (dj).

Note: Excerpts of the play appeared in *Theatre*, XLIV (November 1926), following book publication. See C 67.

REPRINTINGS

A 26-I-1.b
New York: Boni & Liveright, [June 1926].

A 26-I-1.c
New York: Boni & Liveright, [September 1926].

A 26 THE GREAT GOD BROWN
American second book publication (1932)

A 26-II-1.a
Nine Plays by Eugene O'Neill. New York: Liveright, 1932. Introduction by Joseph Wood Krutch; plays selected by EO.

GGB appears on pp. 305–377. See A 15-VII-1.a, *TEJ*.

REPRINTINGS

A 26-II-1.b
New York: Random House, [1937]. 'NOBEL PRIZE EDITION'. (Not a new edition.)

A 26-II-1.c
New York: Random House, [1941].

On copyright page: 'First Modern Library Giant Edition 1941'. (Not a new edition.)

A 26-II-1.d
New York: Random House, [1954?]. ML Giant #G55.

A 26 THE GREAT GOD BROWN
American third book publication (1935)

A 26-III-1
The Plays of Eugene O'Neill. New York: Scribners, [1934–35]. Twelve volumes. Wilderness Edition.

Limited to 770 numbered copies.

GGB appears in volume ten, pp. 1–128. See A 21-VI-1, *AC*.

On p. xi, in a note written by EO's Random House editor, the following statement is made about *GGB*: '[display T]HE GREAT GOD BROWN, *written in Bermuda in the winter | of 1925, attempts to foreshadow the mystical patterns created by | the duality of human character and the search for what lies hid-|den behind and beyond the words and actions of men and women. More | by the use of overtones than by explicit speech, I sought to convey the | dramatic conflicts in the lives and within the souls of the characters. | The use of masks seemed indispensable for the accomplishment of this | purpose. The masks enabled me to dramatize the transfer of personality | and express symbolically the mystery inherent in all human lives. | "The Great God Brown" was produced at the Greenwich Village | Theatre on January 23, 1926, by Kenneth MacGowan, Robert Edmund | Jones and myself. Later it was moved to the Garrick Theatre and ran | in New York for nine months. "The Great God Brown" has since | been done with success in many European countries.*'

Publication: 770 copies published 28 May 1935.

A 26 THE GREAT GOD BROWN
American fourth book publication (1941)

A 26-IV-1.a
The Plays of Eugene O'Neill. New York: Random House, [1941]. Three volumes.

On copyright page: 'FIRST PRINTING'.

GGB appears in volume three, pp. 255–325. See A 14-VI-1.a, *BTH*.

REPRINTINGS

A 26-IV-1.b
New York: Random House, [1941].

On copyright page: 'SECOND PRINTING'.

A 26-IV-1.c
New York: Random House, [1951].

A 26-IV-1.d
New York: Random House, [1954–55].

A 26 THE GREAT GOD BROWN
American fifth book publication (1967)

A 26-V-1
Selected Plays of Eugene O'Neill. New York: Random House, [1967].

On copyright page: 'First Printing'.

GGB appears on pp. 217–280. See A 15-XIII-1, *TEJ*.

A 26 THE GREAT GOD BROWN
English first book publication (1926)

A 26-EI-1.a
THE GREAT GOD BROWN, INCLUDING THE FOUNTAIN, THE DREAMY KID, AND BEFORE BREAKFAST
English first edition, first printing

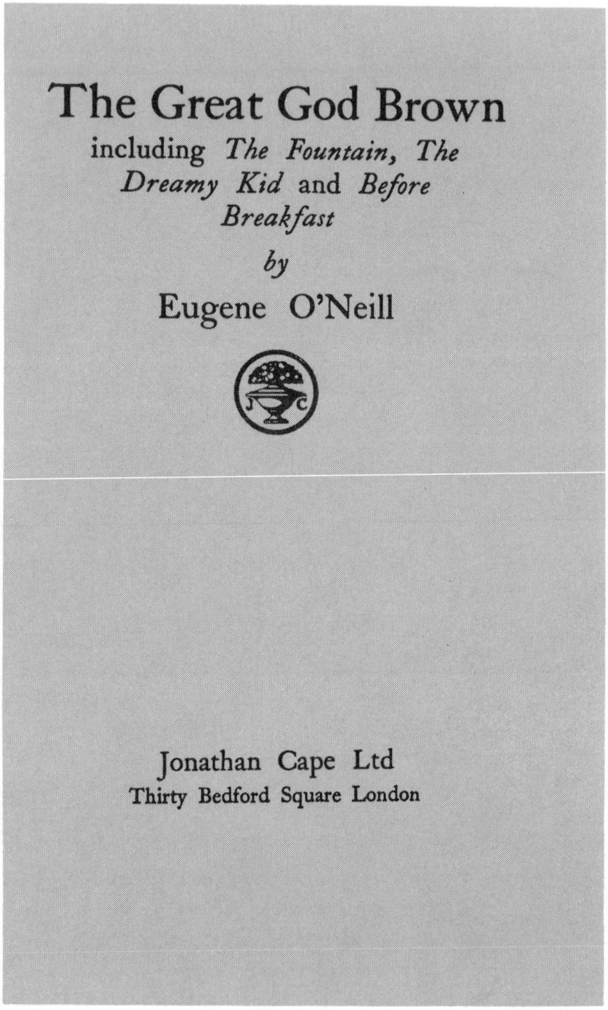
The Great God Brown
including *The Fountain, The Dreamy Kid* and *Before Breakfast*
by
Eugene O'Neill

Jonathan Cape Ltd
Thirty Bedford Square London

A 26-EI-1.a: $7\frac{1}{2}'' \times 4\frac{11}{16}''$

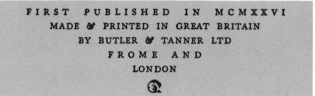

FIRST PUBLISHED IN MCMXXVI
MADE & PRINTED IN GREAT BRITAIN
BY BUTLER & TANNER LTD
FROME AND
LONDON

[i–vi] [1–4] 5–112 [1–2] 3 [4] 5 [6] 7–118 [1–4] 5–33 [34] [1–2] 3–16 [17–18]

$[A]^8$ $B–I^8$ $K–S^8$

Contents: p. i: half title; p. ii: card page; p. iii: title; p. iv: copyright; p. v: 'Contents | [four lines of type]'; p. vi: blank; p. 1: 'The Great God Brown'; p. 2: blank; p. 3: 'Characters | [eleven lines of roman and italic type]'; p. 4: blank; pp. 5–6: act-scene synopsis; pp. 7–112: text, headed 'The Great God Brown'; p. 1: 'The Fountain'; p. 2: blank; p. 3: 'Characters | [twenty-eight lines of roman and italic type]'; p. 4: blank; p. 5: act-scene synopsis; p. 6: blank; pp. 7–118: text, headed 'The Fountain'; p. 1: 'The Dreamy Kid | A Play in One Act'; p. 2: blank; p. 3: 'Characters | [four lines of roman and italic type]'; p. 4: blank; pp. 5–33: text, headed 'The Dreamy Kid'; p. 34: blank; p. 1: 'Before Breakfast | A Play in One Act'; p. 2: blank; pp. 3–16: text, headed 'Before Breakfast'; pp. 17–18: blank.

Typography and paper: $6\frac{5}{16}'' \times 7\frac{3}{16}''$ ($7\frac{9}{16}''$); thirty lines per page. Running heads: rectos and versos, individual play titles. Wove paper.

Binding: Coated sky blue V cloth (fine linen-like grain). Spine: white paper label ($1\frac{3}{16}'' \times 2\frac{1}{4}''$): '[blue line of decorations] | [black] The Great | God Brown | EUGENE O'NEILL | [blue decoration] | [black] *Jonathan Cape* | [blue line of decoration]'. Wove endpapers of same stock as text paper. Top and right edges trimmed.

Dust jacket: Not seen.

Publication: Unknown number of copies published in 1926. 7s. 6d. (Later 5s.)

Locations: BM (deposit-stamp 3 September 1926); JM^{c}A: Yale (Nobel Prize dj).

REPRINTING

A 26-EI-1.b
London: Jonathan Cape, [1937]. Nobel Prize Edition. (Not a new edition.)

LATER PRINTING

The Great God Brown and Lazarus Laughed. London: Jonathan Cape, [1960]. (Not seen.)

A 27 THE FOUNTAIN
American first book publication (1926)

A 27-I-1.a
The Great God Brown, The Fountain, The Moon of the Caribbees and Other Plays. New York: Boni & Liveright, 1926.

First printing: 15 March 1926

One volume of an unnumbered, ten-volume, uniform series.

The Fountain appears on pp. 99–192. See A 26-I-1.a, *GGB.*

REPRINTINGS

A 27-I-1.b
New York: Boni & Liveright, [June 1926].

A 27-I-1.c
New York: Boni & Liveright, [September 1926].

A 27 THE FOUNTAIN
American second book publication (1935)

A 27-II-1
The Plays of Eugene O'Neill. New York: Scribners, [1934–35]. Twelve volumes. Wilderness Edition.

Limited to 770 numbered copies.

The Fountain appears in volume eleven, pp. 133–266. See A 25-V-1, *DUTE.*

On pp. xi–xii, in a note written by EO's Random House editor, the following statement is made about *The Fountain*: '*The idea of writing "The Fountain" came from my interest in the | recurrence in folklore of the beautiful legend of a healing spring of | eternal youth. The play is only incidentally concerned with the Era of | Discovery in America. It has sought merely to express the urging spirit | of that period without pretending to any too rigid accuracy in the matter | of dates and facts in general. The characters, with the exception of | Columbus, are fictitious. Juan Ponce de Leon, in so far as I have been | able to make him a human being, is wholly imaginary. I have simply | filled in the bare outline of his career, as briefly reported in the Who's | Who of the histories, with a conception of what could have been the | truth behind his "life-sketch" if he had been the man it was romanti-|cally—and religiously—moving to me to believe he might have been. | "The Fountain" was written in 1921 and 1922 at Provincetown, | Mass., and produced on December 10, 1925, at the Greenwich Village | Theatre by Kenneth MacGowan, Robert Edmund Jones and myself. | Walter Huston appeared in the rôle of Juan Ponce de Leon.'*

Publication: 770 copies published 28 May 1935.

A 27 THE FOUNTAIN
American third book publication (1941)

A 27-III-1.a
The Plays of Eugene O'Neill. New York: Random House, [1941]. Three volumes.

On copyright page: 'FIRST PRINTING'.

The Fountain appears in volume one, pp. 373–449. See A 6-VII-1.a, "Cardiff."

REPRINTINGS

A 27-III-1.b
New York: Random House, [1941].

On copyright page: 'SECOND PRINTING'.

A 27-III-1.c
New York: Random House, [1951].

A 27-III-1.d
New York: Random House, [1954–55].

A 27 THE FOUNTAIN
English first book publication (1926)

A 27-EI-1.a
The Great God Brown, Including The Fountain, The Dreamy Kid, and Before Breakfast. London: Jonathan Cape, 1926.

The Fountain appears on pp. 1–118. See A 26-EI-1.a, *GGB*.

REPRINTING

A 27-EI-1.b
London: Jonathan Cape, [1937]. Nobel Prize Edition. (Not a new edition.)

A 28 MARCO MILLIONS
American first book publication (1927)

A 28-I-1.a
MARCO MILLIONS
American first edition, trade printing

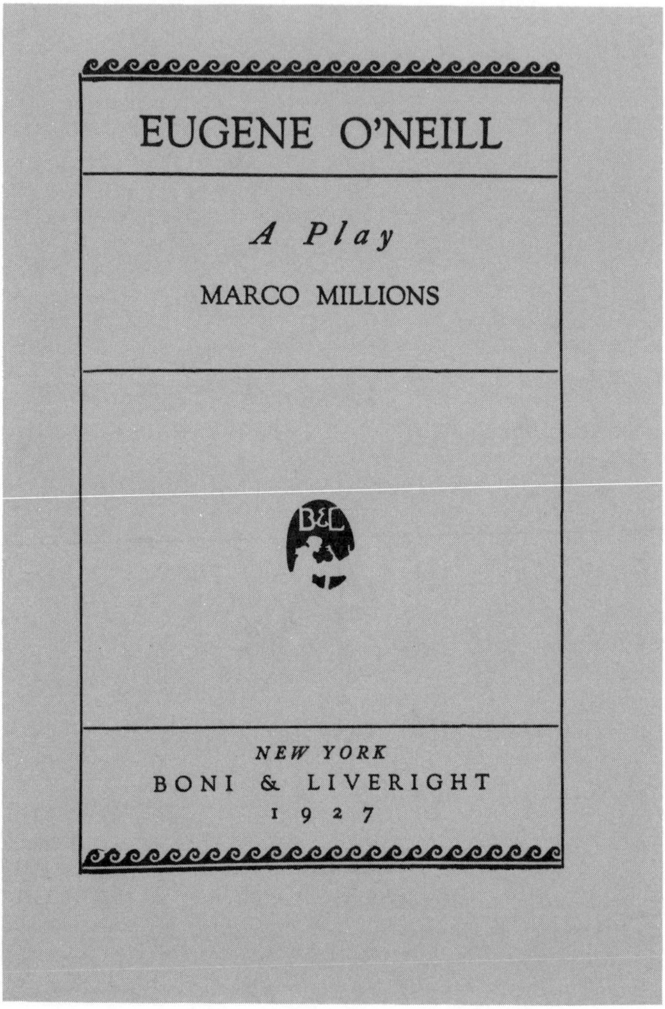

EUGENE O'NEILL

A Play

MARCO MILLIONS

NEW YORK
BONI & LIVERIGHT
1 9 2 7

A 28-I-1.a: frame, rules, and publisher's device in green; 8″ × 5½″

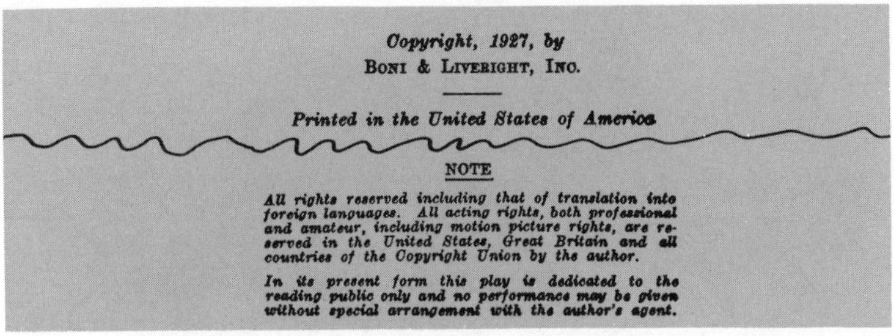
Copyright, 1927, by
BONI & LIVERIGHT, INC.

Printed in the United States of America

NOTE

All rights reserved including that of translation into foreign languages. All acting rights, both professional and amateur, including motion picture rights, are reserved in the United States, Great Britain and all countries of the Copyright Union by the author.

In its present form this play is dedicated to the reading public only and no performance may be given without special arrangement with the author's agent.

[i–iv] v [vi] vii [viii] ix [x–xii] 13–25 [26–28] 29–81 [82–84] 85–147 [148–150] 151–180 [181–184]

$[1\text{–}11]^8$ $[12]^4$

Contents: p. i: half title; p. ii: blank; p. iii: title; p. iv: copyright; p. v: 'FOREWORD'; p. vi: blank; pp. vii–viii: 'CHARACTERS'; p. ix: act-scene synopsis; p. x: blank; p. xi: 'PROLOGUE'; p. xii: blank; pp. 13–25: text, headed '"MARCO MILLIONS" | PROLOGUE'; p. 26: blank; p. 27: 'ACT ONE'; p. 28: blank; pp. 29–81: text, headed 'ACT ONE | SCENE ONE'; p. 82: blank; p. 83: 'ACT TWO'; p. 84: blank; pp. 85–147: text, headed 'ACT TWO | SCENE ONE'; p. 148: blank; p. 149: 'ACT THREE'; p. 150: blank; pp. 151–180: text, headed 'ACT THREE | SCENE ONE'; p. 181: 'EPILOGUE'; p. 182: blank; p. 183: text, headed 'EPILOGUE'; p. 184: blank.

Typography and paper: 10 point on 14, Scotch. $3^{13}/_{16}'' \times 5^{13}/_{16}''$ ($6^{3}/_{16}''$); thirty lines per page. Running heads: rectos and versos, "MARCO MILLIONS" | [double rule]'. White laid paper with vertical chains $1^{3}/_{4}''$ apart and with the Boni & Liveright publisher's device as watermark.

Binding: Blue green sized V cloth (fine linen-like grain). Front: '[within a light sea green frame with a wave motif at bottom] [goldstamped EO signature]'. Spine: '[goldstamped border of wave motif] | [goldstamped] EUGENE | O'NEILL | [single wave motif] | Marco | Millions | [blindstamped publisher's device] | [goldstamped] BONI AND | LIVERIGHT | [border of wave motif]'. Illustrated endpapers front and rear: [aqua and buff] steamship on rolling sea silhouetted against setting sun with the word 'O'NEILL' above. Top edge only trimmed and stained dark blue green.

Dust jacket: Front: '[light blue green background; dark blue border of sea motif with porpoises riding crest of waves]; [in light blue green in center of border] THE WORKS OF | Eugene

Dust jackets for A 28-I-1.a, A 31-I-1.a, and A 29-I-1.a

O'Neill | [seven lines within double rule, dark blue shield] *his New Play is* | [dark blue and orange square Serif type] MARCO | MILLIONS [dark blue] *The* first long Play | by O'Neill to be | published *before* | Production [orange coins and dollar symbols strewn diagonally left to right in lower left-hand corner]'. Spine: '[dark blue border of sea motif with porpoises riding crest of waves]; [stenciled in light blue green in center of border] THE WORKS OF | Eugene | O'Neill | [dark blue below border] Marco | Millions | [orange coins and dollar signs strewn diagonally left to right] | [publisher's device] | [dark blue] BONI & LIVERIGHT | [rule] | [orange decorative border]'. Back: '[dark blue border of sea motif with porpoises riding crest of waves, framing a drawing of EO] | [below border in dark blue against light blue green background] The Works of | EUGENE | O'NEILL | [twenty lines of italic type listing seventeen EO titles with prices, interrupted by six orange decorations] | [to left of title list, in orange] *Each volume* | *Large 12mo. End* | *Papers.* | *Six volumes,* | *boxed, $15.00* | [to right of title list, in orange] *Uniform Bind-|ing. Comprising* | *the Collected* | *Works of* | *Eugene O'Neill.*' Front flap: blurb for *MM;* back flap: blurb for *GGB, TF, MOTC.*

Publication: 7,500 copies published 23 April 1927, $2.50. Sixth volume of an unnumbered, ten-volume, uniform series.

Printing: Printed 15 April 1927 by Van Rees Press, New York, from plates made by Van Rees Book Composition; bound by Van Rees Bindery. (Not distinguished from limited printing, A 28-I-1.b.)

Locations: JM^c^A (dj); LC (deposit-stamp 6 May 1927); Lilly (three, djs); Yale.

Note: The compiler has acquired an undated, mimeographed acting script of *Marco Millions.* The pagination is by act-scene-page. The script has a blue green, paper cover, and wing clips hold it together. The front cover contains the following: '[five lines goldstamped in upper left-hand corner] ANNE MEYERSON INC. | TYPING & MIMEOGRAPHING | 101 PARK AVENUE–ROOM 514 | NEW YORK 17, N.Y. | LEXINGTON 2-5318 | [goldstamped in center] "MARCO MILLIONS"'.

So far, I have been unable to determine the theatre (amateur or professional) which may have used the script or the date of the script.

A 28 MARCO MILLIONS
American limited printing (1927)

A 28-I-1.b
MARCO MILLIONS
American first edition, limited printing

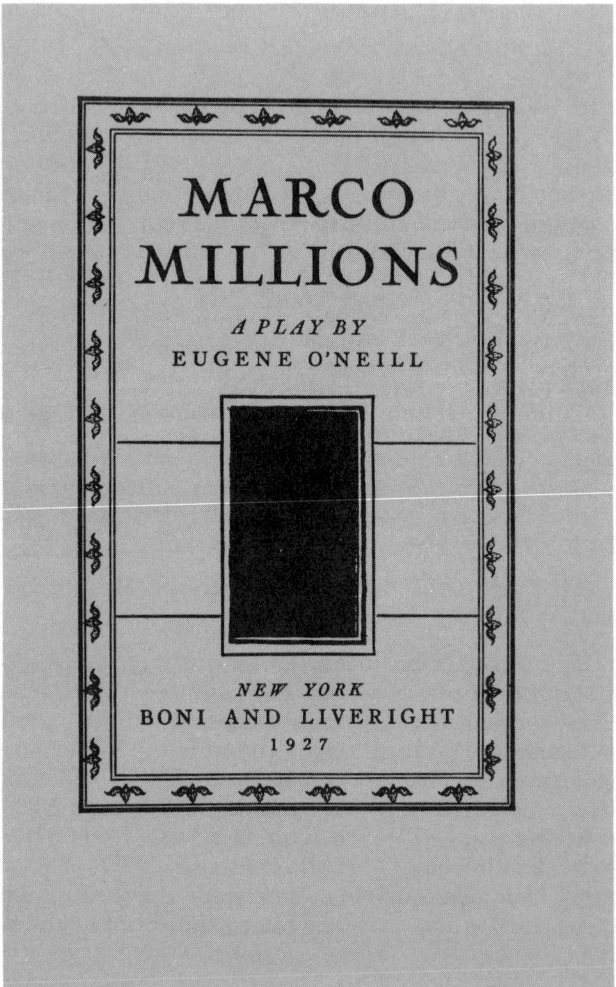

A 28-I-1.b: border decoration and illustration in orange; 8¾" × 5¾". Illustration: black line drawing of Marco Polo's travels.

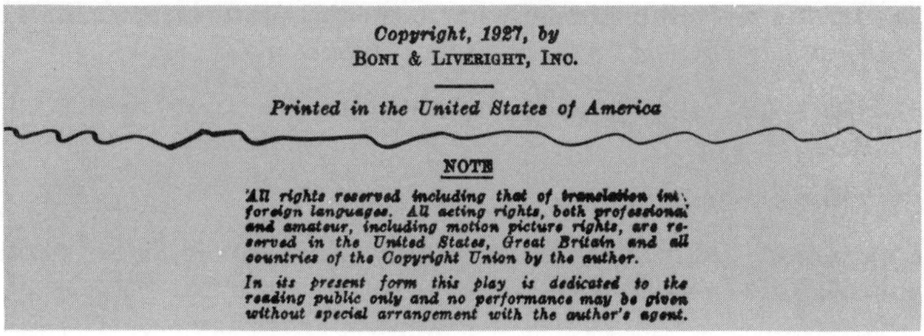

Copyright, 1927, by
Boni & Liveright, Inc.

Printed in the United States of America

NOTE

All rights reserved including that of translation into foreign languages. All acting rights, both professional and amateur, including motion picture rights, are reserved in the United States, Great Britain and all countries of the Copyright Union by the author.

In its present form this play is dedicated to the reading public only and no performance may be given without special arrangement with the author's agent.

[i–iv] v [vi] vii [viii] ix [x–xii] 13–25 [26–28] 29–81 [82–84] 85–147 [148–150] 151–180 [181–184]

$[1]^4$ $[2\text{–}10]^8$ $[11\text{–}12]^4$

Contents: p. i: half title; p. ii: statement of limitation: 'THIS EDITION OF MARCO | MILLIONS IS LIMITED TO | 450 NUMBERED COPIES, OF | WHICH 440 ARE FOR SALE. | EACH COPY IS SIGNED BY | THE AUTHOR. | THIS COPY IS NO. . . . .'; p. iii: title; p. iv: copyright; p. v: 'FOREWORD'; p. vi: blank; pp. vii–viii: list of characters; p. ix: act-scene synopsis; p. x: blank; p. xi: 'PROLOGUE'; p. xii: blank; pp. 13–25: text, headed '"MARCO MILLIONS" | PROLOGUE'; p. 26: blank; p. 27: 'ACT ONE'; p. 28: blank; pp. 29–81: text, headed 'ACT ONE | Scene One'; p. 82: blank; p. 83: 'ACT TWO'; p. 84: blank; pp. 85–147: text, headed 'ACT TWO | Scene One'; p. 148: blank; p. 149: 'ACT THREE'; p. 150: blank; pp. 151–180: text, headed 'ACT THREE | Scene One'; p. 181: 'EPILOGUE'; p. 182: blank; p. 183: text, headed 'EPILOGUE'; p. 184: blank.

Typography and paper: 10 point on 14, Scotch. $3^{13}/_{16}'' \times 5^{13}/_{16}''$ ($6^{3}/_{16}''$); thirty lines per page. Running heads: rectos and versos, '"MARCO MILLIONS" | [double rule]'. White laid paper with vertical chains $1^{3}/_{4}''$ apart and with the Boni & Liveright publisher's device as watermark.

Binding: Reddish brown paper-covered boards with gold and white filigree-like pattern; ivory paper shelf back. Spine: '[brown paper label ($1^{5}/_{16}'' \times {}^{15}/_{16}''$) with black type] MARCO | MILLIONS | *A Play* | *by* | Eugene | O'NEILL'. White coated endpapers of different stock from text paper. All edges untrimmed.

Slipcase: Blue paper-covered boards with gold, green, and brown plant-like decoration. Front: '[pale green paper label ($4^{1}/_{4}'' \times 2^{3}/_{4}''$) with brown type] [decorative N]*umbered* | [rule] | [decorative A]*utographed* | [rule] | [decorative C]*opy of* | MARCO | MILLIONS | *by* Eugene O'Neill | *Edition Limited To*

| *440 Copies* | [publisher's device to the left of the last two lines] BONI & LIVERIGHT | *Publishers* NEW YORK'.

Publication: 450 copies published 23 April 1927? See A 28-I-1.a.

Printing: See A 28-I-1.a.

Locations: JM[c]A (#286 boxed); Lilly (#258 boxed); PSt (#109 boxed); Yale (#83 boxed).

REPRINTINGS
First edition, trade printing

A 28-I-1.c
New York: Boni & Liveright, [September 1927].

A 28-I-1.d
New York: Boni & Liveright, [January 1928].

A 28-I-1.e
New York: Boni & Liveright, [April 1928].

A 28-I-1.f
New York: Boni & Liveright, [October 1928].

A 28 MARCO MILLIONS
American second book publication (1932)

A 28-II-1
Representative Plays of Eugene O'Neill. New York: Liveright, [1932].

MM appears on pp. vii–xii, 13–181. See A 8-IV-1, "Caribbees."

A 28 MARCO MILLIONS
American third book publication (1932)

A 28-III-1.a
Nine Plays by Eugene O'Neill. New York: Liveright, 1932. Introduction by Joseph Wood Krutch; plays selected by EO.

MM appears on pp. 207–304. See A 15-VII-1.a, *TEJ.*

REPRINTINGS

A 28-III-1.b
New York: Random House, [1937?]. 'NOBEL PRIZE EDITION'. (Not a new edition.)

A 28-III-1.c
New York: Random House, [1941].

On copyright page: 'First Modern Library Giant Edition | 1941'. (Not a new edition.)

A 28-III-1.d
New York: Random House, [1954?]. ML Giant #G55.

A 28 MARCO MILLIONS
American fourth book publication (1935)

A 28-IV-1
The Plays of Eugene O'Neill. New York: Scribners, [1934–35]. Twelve volumes. Wilderness Edition.

Limited to 770 numbered copies.

MM appears in volume five, pp. 1–168. See A 20-VI-1, *THA*.

On p. xi, in a note written by EO's Random House editor, the following statement is made about *MM*: '[display W]RITTEN *during the years 1923–25, "Marco Millions" | was produced at the Guild Theatre on January 9, 1928, | with Alfred Lunt and Margalo Gilmore in the leading | rôles. In 1925 "Marco Millions" was bought by David Belasco, who | later relinquished his rights to the Theatre Guild. From time to time | this play has been produced successfully in several European countries.*'

Publication: 770 copies published 30 January 1935.

A 28 MARCO MILLIONS
American fifth book publication (1941)

A 28-V-1.a
The Plays of Eugene O'Neill. New York: Random House, [1941]. Three volumes.

On copyright page: 'FIRST PRINTING'.

MM appears in volume two, pp. 343–439. See A 16-V-1.a, *Gold*.

REPRINTINGS

A 28-V-1.b
New York: Random House, [1941].

On copyright page: 'SECOND PRINTING'.

A 28-V-1.c
New York: Random House, [1951].

A 28-V-1.d
New York: Random House, [1954–55].

A 28 MARCO MILLIONS
English first book publication (1927)

A 28-EI-1
MARCO MILLIONS
English first edition

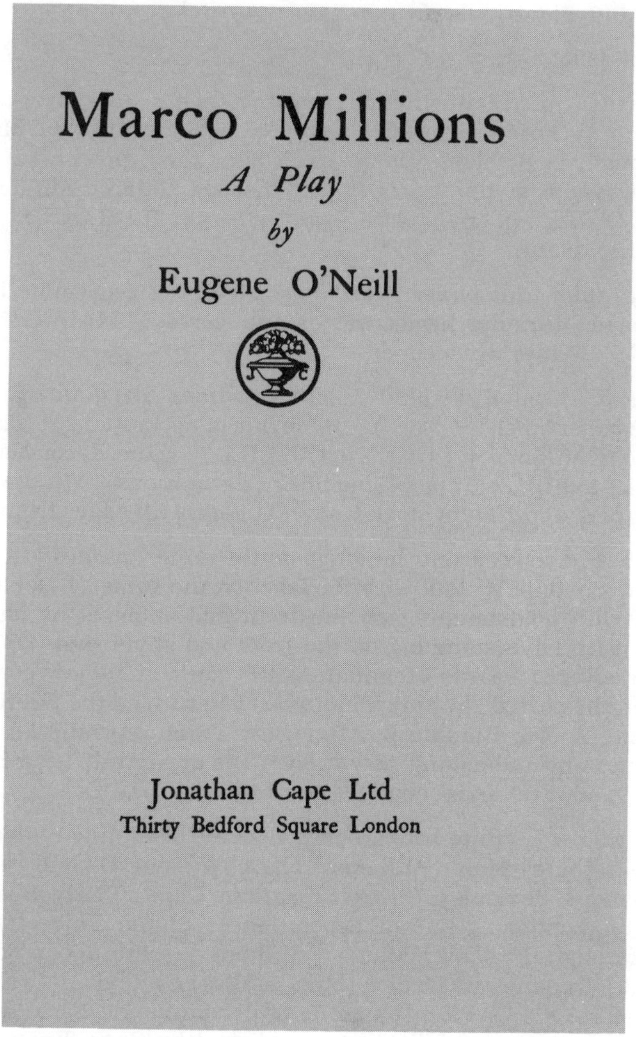
Marco Millions
A Play
by
Eugene O'Neill

Jonathan Cape Ltd
Thirty Bedford Square London

A 28-EI-1: $7\frac{1}{2}'' \times 4\frac{13}{16}''$

FIRST PUBLISHED IN MCMXXVII
MADE & PRINTED IN GREAT BRITAIN
BY BUTLER & TANNER LTD
FROME AND
LONDON

[1–4] 5 [6–8] 9–155 [156] 157–158 [159–160]

[A]^8 B–I^8 K^8

Contents: p. 1: half title; p. 2: card page; p. 3: title; p. 4: copyright; p. 5: 'Foreword'; p. 6: blank; p. 7: second half title: "Marco Millions"; p. 8: blank; pp. 9–10: 'Characters'; pp. 11–12: act-scene synopsis; pp. 13–155: text, headed "Marco Millions' | PROLOGUE'; p. 156: blank; pp. 157–158: 'EPILOGUE'; pp. 159–160: blank.

Typography and paper: 3$^5/_{16}$″ × 5¼″ (5$^9/_{16}$″); twenty-nine lines per page. Running heads: rectos and versos, "MARCO MILLIONS". White wove paper.

Binding: Coated sky blue V cloth (fine linen-like grain). Spine: white paper label (2$^3/_{16}$″ × ⅞″)–'[blue line of decorations] | [black] Marco | Millions | EUGENE O'NEILL | [blue decoration] | [black] *Jonathan Cape* | [blue line of decorations]'. White wove endpapers of different stock from text paper. All edges trimmed.

Note: I have seen four bindings on the Cape volumes–(A) the coated sky blue V cloth with the label on the spine, (B) a blue V cloth with goldstamping on the front and spine, (C) a blue B cloth with silverstamping on the front and spine, and (D) blue paper-covered boards of imitation BF cloth. A review copy of *MM* in the coated sky blue V cloth has determined the priority of Binding A over Binding B. After 1927, when reprinting earlier volumes and publishing new titles, Cape apparently used Binding B, and after 1940, changed to Bindings C and D.

Dust jacket: White background. Front: '[black line of decorations] | [blue] Marco Millions |[black] Eugene O'Neill | [blue publisher's device] | [black] Jonathan Cape, Thirty Bedford Square, London | [line of decorations]'. Spine: '[blue line of decorations] | [black] Marco | Millions | [blue decoration] | [black] Eugene | O'Neill | [blue publisher's device] | [black] JONATHAN | CAPE | [blue line of decorations]'. Back: list of six other volumes of EO plays published by Cape. Front flap: blurb for *MM;* back flap blank.

Publication: Unknown number of copies published in 1927. 5s.

Locations: BM (deposit-stamp 28 September 1927); JM[c]A; Yale.

LATER PRINTING

Beyond the Horizon and Marco Millions. London: Jonathan Cape, [1960]. (Not seen. This may be a new edition.)

A 29 LAZARUS LAUGHED
American first book publication (1927)

A 29-I-1.a
LAZARUS LAUGHED
American first edition, trade printing

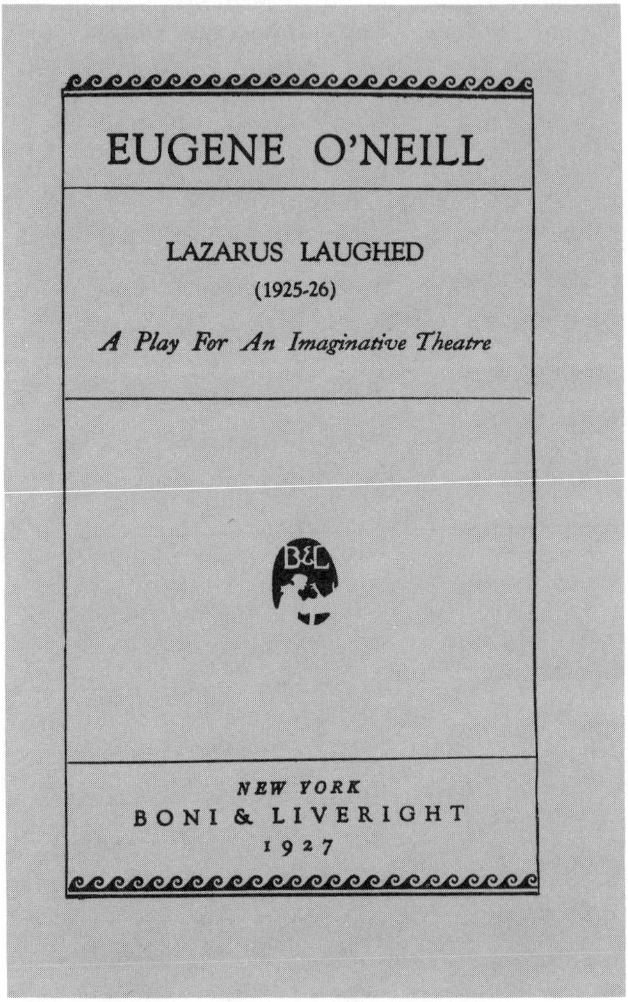

EUGENE O'NEILL

LAZARUS LAUGHED

(1925-26)

A Play For An Imaginative Theatre

NEW YORK
BONI & LIVERIGHT
1927

A 29-I-1.a: frame, waves, rules, and publisher's device in green; $8\frac{1}{8}'' \times 5\frac{1}{2}''$

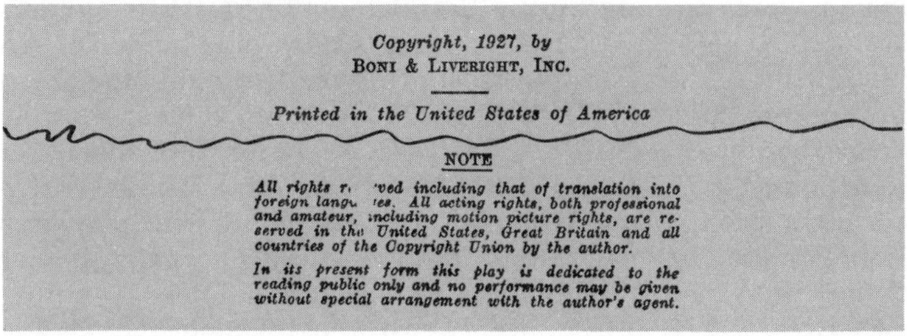
Copyright, 1927, by
Boni & Liveright, Inc.

Printed in the United States of America

NOTE

All rights r. ·ved including that of translation into foreign langu. ·es. All acting rights, both professional and amateur, including motion picture rights, are reserved in the United States, Great Britain and all countries of the Copyright Union by the author.

In its present form this play is dedicated to the reading public only and no performance may be given without special arrangement with the author's agent.

[i–ii] [1–10] 11–49 [50–52] 53–95 [96–98] 99–139 [140–142] 143–179 [180–182]

$[1\text{–}11]^8$ $[12]^4$

Contents: pp. i–ii: blank; p. 1: half title; p. 2: blank; p. 3: title; p. 4: copyright; p. 5: act-scene synopsis; p. 6: blank; p. 7: 'CHARACTERS | [twenty-six lines of type]'; p. 8: blank; p. 9: 'ACT ONE'; p. 10: blank; pp. 11–49: text, headed 'LAZARUS LAUGHED | ACT ONE | Scene One'; p. 50: blank; p. 51: 'ACT TWO'; p. 52: blank; pp. 53–95: text, headed 'ACT TWO | Scene One'; p. 96: blank; p. 97: 'ACT THREE'; p. 98: blank; pp. 99–139: text, headed 'ACT THREE | Scene One'; p. 140: blank; p. 141: 'ACT FOUR'; p. 142: blank; pp. 143–179: text, headed 'ACT FOUR | Scene One'; pp. 180–182: blank.

Typography and paper: 10 point on 14, Scotch. $3\frac{13}{16}'' \times 5\frac{13}{16}''$ ($6\frac{3}{16}''$); thirty lines per page. Running heads: rectos and versos, 'LAZARUS LAUGHED | [double rule]'. White laid paper with vertical chains $1\frac{3}{4}''$ apart and with the Boni & Liveright publisher's device as watermark. Top edge only trimmed and stained dark blue green.

Binding: Blue green sized V cloth (fine linen-like grain). Front: '[within a light sea green frame with a wave motif at bottom] [goldstamped EO signature]'. Spine: '[goldstamped border of wave motif] | [goldstamped] EUGENE | O'NEILL | [single wave motif] | Lazarus | Laughed | [blindstamped publisher's device] | [goldstamped] BONI AND | LIVERIGHT | [border of wave motif]'. Illustrated endpapers front and rear: [aqua and buff] steamship on rolling sea silhouetted against setting sun with the word 'O'NEILL' above.

Dust jacket: Front: '[charcoal sketch of the skyline of a Middle East city in biblical times with desert in the foreground, clouds above, all against light blue green background] [in center between clouds and city, purple] *LAZARUS* | *LAUGHED* | *by* [decoration] EUGENE O'NEILL'. Spine: [dark blue border of sea motif with porpoises riding crest of waves] [in light blue green in center of border] THE WORKS OF | Eugene | O'Neill | [purple below border] *LAZARUS* | *LAUGHED* | [publisher's device] | [dark blue] BONI & | LIVERIGHT | [rule] | [purple decorative border]'. Back: '[dark blue border of sea motif with porpoises riding crest of waves, framing a drawing of EO] | [below border in dark blue against light blue green background] The Works of | EUGENE | O'NEILL | [twenty-two lines of italic type listing eighteen EO titles with prices, interrupted by seven purple decorations] | [to left of title list, in purple] *Each volume* | *large 12mo. End* | *Papers.* | *Six volumes,* | *boxed. $15.00* | [to right of title list, in purple] *Uniform Bind-*|*ing. Comprising* | *the Collected* | *Works of* | *Eugene O'Neill.*' Front flap: blurb for *LL;* back flap: blurb for *MM.*

Publication: 7,500 copies published 11 November 1927. Seventh volume of an unnumbered, ten-volume uniform series.

Printing: Printed 2 November 1927 by Van Rees Press, New York, from plates made by Van Rees Book Composition; bound by Van Rees Bindery. (Not distinguished from limited printing, A 29-I-1.b.)

Locations: JM[c]A (dj); LC (deposit-stamp 28 November 1927); Lilly (three, djs); Yale.

Note: The first act only of *LL* appeared in *The American Caravan,* edited by Van Wyck Brooks et al. (New York: The Macaulay Company, [1927]), pp. 807–833.

According to Sanborn and Clark (pp. 67 and 71) EO contributed Act I to *American Caravan* "in response to a personal request from the editors. . . ." EO made considerable substantive textual changes in Act I for book publication of the entire play. See B 7.

A 29 LAZARUS LAUGHED
American limited book publication (1927)

A 29-I-1.b
LAZARUS LAUGHED
American first edition, limited printing

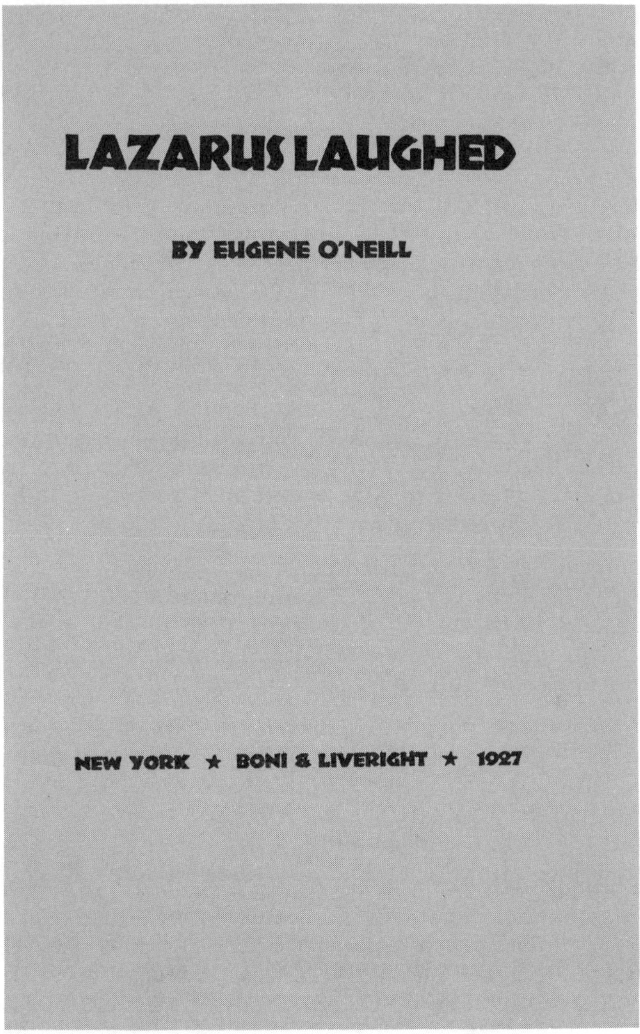
LAZARUS LAUGHED

BY EUGENE O'NEILL

NEW YORK ★ BONI & LIVERIGHT ★ 1927

A 29-I-1.b: all in purple; 8¾″ × 4⅞″

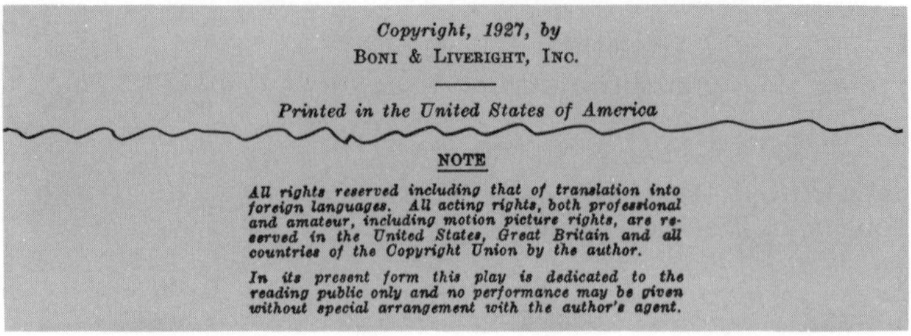

Copyright, 1927, by
BONI & LIVERIGHT, INC.

Printed in the United States of America

NOTE

All rights reserved including that of translation into foreign languages. All acting rights, both professional and amateur, including motion picture rights, are reserved in the United States, Great Britain and all countries of the Copyright Union by the author.

In its present form this play is dedicated to the reading public only and no performance may be given without special arrangement with the author's agent.

[1–10] 11–49 [50–52] 53–95 [96–98] 99–139 [140–142] 143–179 [180]

$[1]^4$ $[2–11]^8$ $[12]^6$

Contents: p. 1: half title; p. 2: statement of limitation: 'This edition of *Lazarus Laughed* | is limited to 775 numbered and | signed copies, of which 750 are | for sale. | No. ....'; p. 3: title; p. 4: copyright; p. 5: 'CHARACTERS' | [twenty-six lines of type]; p. 6: blank; p. 7: act-scene synopsis; p. 8: blank; p. 9: 'ACT ONE'; p. 10: blank; pp. 11–49: text, headed 'LAZARUS LAUGHED | ACT ONE | SCENE ONE'; p. 50: blank; p. 51: 'ACT TWO'; p. 52: blank; pp. 53–95: text, headed 'ACT TWO | SCENE ONE'; p. 96: blank; p. 97: 'ACT THREE'; p. 98: blank; pp. 99–139: text, headed 'ACT THREE | SCENE ONE'; p. 140: blank; p. 141: 'ACT FOUR'; p. 142: blank; pp. 143–179: text, headed 'ACT FOUR | SCENE ONE'; p. 180: blank.

Typography and paper: 10 point on 14, Scotch. 3 13/16″ × 5 13/16″ (6 3/16″); thirty lines per page. Running heads: rectos and versos, 'LAZARUS LAUGHED | [double rule]'. White laid paper with vertical chains 1 3/4″ apart and with the Boni & Liveright publisher's device as watermark.

Binding: Black paper-covered boards batiked in vermilion, yellow, and green stylistic smile design; ivory paper shelf back. Spine: '[light purple paper label (1 13/16″ × 13/16″)] [black decoration] | [rule] | LAZARUS | LAUGHED | [rule] | EUGENE | O'NEILL | [rule] | [decoration]'. White coated endpapers of different stock from text paper. All edges untrimmed.

Slipcase: Black paper-covered boards. Front: '[gold paper label (4 1/16″ × 2 1/2″) with purple type] [inside three frames] LAZARUS | LAUGHED | *by* | EUGENE O'NEILL | [decoration] | [rule] | LIMITED AUTOGRAPHED | EDITION SEVEN HUNDRED | & FIFTY NUMBERED COPIES | [rule] | [decoration] | *Boni & Liveright* | 61 West 48th St. New York'.

Publication: 775 copies published 11 November 1927?

Printing: See A 29-I-1.a.

Locations: JM[c]A (#1 boxed); Lilly (#741 boxed); PSt (#601); Yale (author's copy boxed and #82 boxed).

REPRINTINGS
First edition, trade printing

A 29-I-1.c
New York: Horace Liveright, [January 1928].

A 29-I-1.d
New York: Horace Liveright, [February 1928].

A 29-I-1.e
New York: Horace Liveright, [May 1928].

A 29-I-1.f
New York: Horace Liveright, [February 1929].

A 29 LAZARUS LAUGHED
American second book publication (1932)

A 29-II-1.a
Nine Plays by Eugene O'Neill. New York: Liveright, 1932. Introduction by Joseph Wood Krutch; plays selected by EO.

LL appears on pp. 379–481. See A 15-VII-1.a, *TEJ*.

REPRINTINGS

A 29-II-1.b
New York: Random House, [1937?]. 'NOBEL PRIZE EDITION'. (Not a new edition.)

A 29-II-1.c
New York: Random House, [1941].

On copyright page: 'First Modern Library Giant Edition 1941'. (Not a new edition.)

A 29-II-1.d
New York: Random House, [1954?]. ML Giant #G55.

A 29 LAZARUS LAUGHED
American third book publication (1934)

A 29-III-1
The Plays of Eugene O'Neill. New York: Scribners, [1934–35]. Twelve volumes. Wilderness Edition.

Limited to 770 numbered copies.

LL appears in volume four, pp. 87–252. See A 23-V-1, *AGCGW.*

On pp. xi–xii, in a note written by EO's Random House editor, the following statement is made about *LL:* '*"Lazarus Laughed" was written at Ridgefield, Connecticut, and | Bermuda in 1925–1926. Under the direction of Gilmore Brown, and | with Irving Pichel in the rôle of Lazarus, it was very successfully | and imaginatively produced by the Pasadena Community players at the | Pasadena Theatre in 1927. Subsequently it was moved to the Music | Box in Hollywood. These were the only performances of "Lazarus | Laughed" in America. The cost of mounting such an elaborate play has | deterred the New York commercial theatre from risking the gamble.*'

Publication: 770 copies published 28 December 1934.

A 29 LAZARUS LAUGHED
American fourth book publication (1941)

A 29-IV-1.a
The Plays of Eugene O'Neill. New York: Random House, [1941]. Three volumes.

On copyright page: 'FIRST PRINTING'.

LL appears in volume one, pp. 271–371. See A 6-VII-1.a, "Cardiff."

REPRINTINGS

A 29-IV-1.b
New York: Random House, [1941].

On copyright page: 'SECOND PRINTING'.

A 29-IV-1.c
New York: Random House, [1951].

A 29-IV-1.d
New York: Random House, [1954–55].

A 29 LAZARUS LAUGHED
English first book publication (1929)

A 29-EI-1.a
LAZARUS LAUGHED
English first edition, first printing.

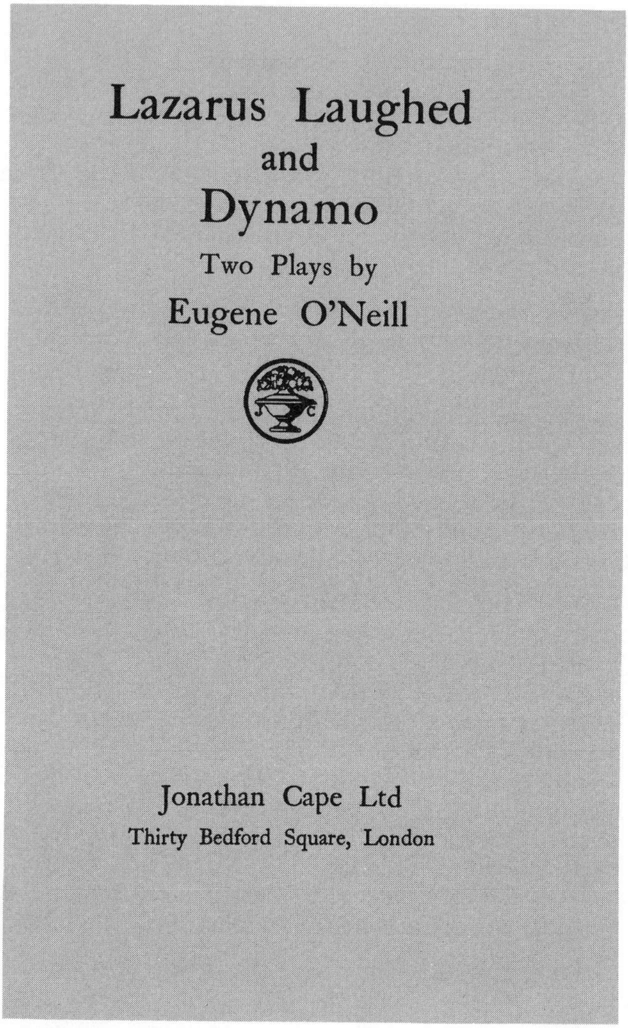
Lazarus Laughed
and
Dynamo
Two Plays by
Eugene O'Neill

Jonathan Cape Ltd
Thirty Bedford Square, London

A 29-EI-1.a: $7\frac{1}{2}'' \times 4\frac{3}{4}''$

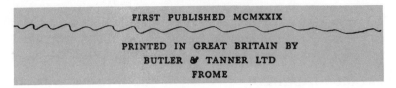

FIRST PUBLISHED MCMXXIX

PRINTED IN GREAT BRITAIN BY
BUTLER & TANNER LTD
FROME

[1–6] 7–150 [1–2] 3–102 [103–106]

$[A]^8$ B–I^8 K–Q^8

Contents: p. 1: half title; p. 2: card page; p. 3: title; p. 4: copyright; p. 5: 'Lazarus Laughed | (1925–1926) | A Play for an Imaginative Theatre'; p. 6: blank; p. 7: act-scene synopsis; p. 8: 'Characters | [twenty-six lines of roman and italic type]'; pp. 9–150: text, headed 'ACT ONE | SCENE ONE'; p. 1: 'Dynamo'; p. 2: 'Characters | [eight lines of roman and italic type]'; pp. 3–4: act-scene synopsis; pp. 5–102: text, headed 'ACT ONE | SCENE ONE'; pp. 103–106: blank.

Typography and paper: $3\frac{5}{16}'' \times 5\frac{5}{16}''$ ($5\frac{3}{4}''$); thirty to thirty-two lines per page. Running heads: rectos and versos, individual play titles. Wove paper.

Binding: Blue V cloth (fine linen-like grain). Front: '[goldstamped EO signature]'. Spine: '[goldstamped line of decorations] | EUGENE | O'NEILL | [decoration] | LAZARUS | LAUGHED | JONATHAN CAPE | [line of decorations]'. Back: '[blindstamped publisher's device]'. White endpapers of different stock from text paper. All edges trimmed.

Dust jacket: Off-white background. Front: '[green border of sea motif with porpoises riding crest of waves] | [black woodcut of EO profile by SLH] | EUGENE O'NEILL | [green star] | [black] LAZARUS LAUGHED | *and Dynamo* | [green star] | [border of wave motif]'. Spine: '[green border of sea motif with porpoises riding crest of waves] | [black] EUGENE | O'NEILL | [green star] | [black] LAZARUS | LAUGHED | [green star] | [publisher's device] | [black] JONATHAN CAPE | [green border of wave motif]'. Back: ad for nine titles, beginning with *TEJ: and Other Plays* and ending with *LL and Dynamo,* published by Jonathan Cape. Front flap: blurb for *LL and Dynamo,* notice of ad on back, and at bottom: '7s. 6d. net'. Back flap blank.

Publication: Unknown number of copies published in 1929. 7s. 6d.

Locations: BM (deposit-stamp 6 November 1929); ScU (dj); Yale.

LATER PRINTING

The Great God Brown and Lazarus Laughed. London: Jonathan Cape, [1960]. (Not seen.)

A 30 STRANGE INTERLUDE
American first book publication (1928)

A 30-I-1.a
STRANGE INTERLUDE
American first edition, first printing

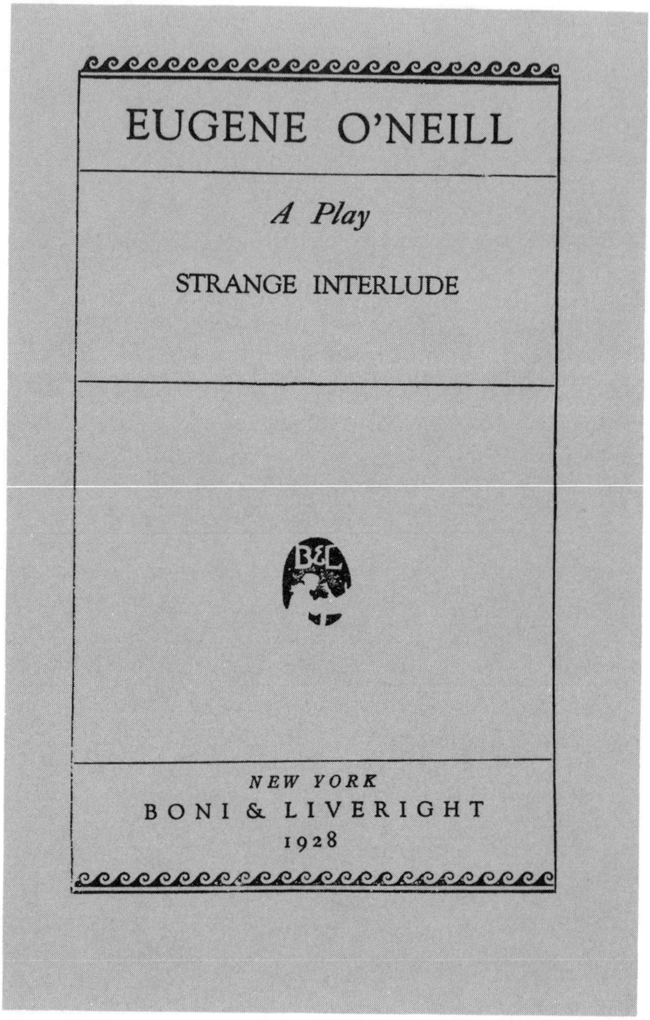

EUGENE O'NEILL

A Play

STRANGE INTERLUDE

NEW YORK
BONI & LIVERIGHT
1928

A 30-I-1.a: frame, waves, rules, and publisher's device in green; $8\frac{1}{16}'' \times 5\frac{1}{2}''$

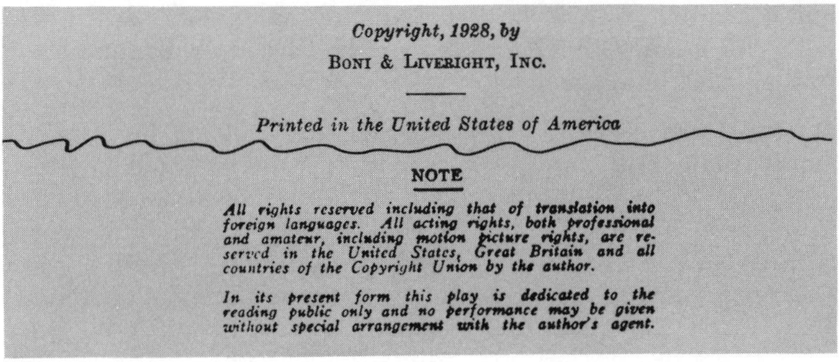
Copyright, 1928, by
BONI & LIVERIGHT, INC.

Printed in the United States of America

NOTE

All rights reserved including that of translation into foreign languages. All acting rights, both professional and amateur, including motion picture rights, are reserved in the United States, Great Britain and all countries of the Copyright Union by the author.

In its present form this play is dedicated to the reading public only and no performance may be given without special arrangement with the author's agent.

[1–10] 11–43 [44–46] 47–85 [86–88] 89–116 [117–118] 119–156 [157–158] 159–192 [193–194] 195–236 [237–238] 239–274 [275–276] 277–322 [323–324] 325–352

[1–22]^{8}

Contents: p. 1: half title; p. 2: blank; p. 3: title; p. 4: copyright; p. 5: 'CHARACTERS | [eight lines of type]'; p. 6: blank; p. 7: act-scene synopsis; p. 8: blank; p. 9: 'FIRST PART | ACT ONE'; p. 10: blank; pp. 11–43: text, headed 'STRANGE INTERLUDE | ACT ONE'; p. 44: blank; p. 45: 'ACT TWO'; p. 46: blank; pp. 47–85: text, headed 'ACT TWO'; p. 86: blank; p. 87: 'ACT THREE'; p. 88: blank; pp. 89–116: text, headed 'ACT THREE'; p. 117: 'ACT FOUR'; p. 118: blank; pp. 119–156: text, headed 'ACT FOUR'; p. 157: 'ACT FIVE'; p. 158: blank; pp. 159–192: text, headed 'ACT FIVE'; p. 193: 'SECOND PART | ACT SIX'; p. 194: blank; pp. 195–236: text, headed 'ACT SIX'; p. 237: 'ACT SEVEN'; p. 238: blank; pp. 239–274: text, headed 'ACT SEVEN'; p. 275: 'ACT EIGHT'; p. 276: blank; pp. 277–322: text, headed 'ACT EIGHT'; p. 323: 'ACT NINE'; p. 324: blank; pp. 325–352: text, headed 'ACT NINE'.

Typography and paper: 10 point on 14, Scotch. $3\frac{13}{16}'' \times 5\frac{7}{8}''$ ($6\frac{3}{16}''$); twenty-nine to thirty-three lines per page. Running heads: rectos and versos, 'STRANGE INTERLUDE | [double rule]'. White laid paper with vertical chains $1\frac{11}{16}''$ apart and with the Boni & Liveright publisher's device as watermark.

Binding: Blue green sized V cloth (fine linen-like grain). Front: '[within a light sea green frame with a wave motif at bottom] [goldstamped EO signature]'. Spine: '[goldstamped border of wave motif] | [goldstamped] EUGENE | O'NEILL | [single wave motif] | Strange | Interlude | [blindstamped publisher's device] | [goldstamped] BONI AND | LIVERIGHT | [border of wave motif]'. Illustrated endpapers front and rear: [aqua and buff] steamship on rolling sea silhouetted against setting sun with the word 'O'NEILL' above. Top edge only trimmed and stained dark blue green.

Dust jacket: Front: expressionistic drawing of four figures (three male and one female) with their elongated shadows against gold background framed by purple curtains; above the illustration against dark blue background, '[light blue green] STRANGE | INTERLUDE | [gold] by | Eugene | O'Neill'. Spine: '[against dark blue background] [light blue green] STRANGE | INTERLUDE | [gold] by | Eugene | O'Neill | [light blue green publisher's device] | [dark blue type against light blue green background] BONI & | LIVERIGHT'. Back: across the top, a dark blue border of the sea motif with porpoises riding the crest of waves, framing a purple drawing of EO's profile. Below the border, in dark blue and purple against a light blue green background, are blurbs for *SI* and listing of all the titles in the uniform edition of The Collected Works of Eugene O'Neill. Front flap: blurb for *SI;* back flap continues blurbs for *SI*.

Publication: 20,000 copies published 3 March 1928. $2.50. Eighth volume of an unnumbered, ten-volume, uniform series.

Printing: Printed 24 February 1928 by Van Rees Press, New York, from plates made by Van Rees Book Composition; bound by Van Rees Bindery.

Locations: JM^c^A (dj); LC (deposit-stamp 5 March 1928); Lilly (three, djs); Yale.

REPRINTINGS

A 30-I-1.b
New York: Horace Liveright, [March 1928].

A 30-I-1.c
New York: Horace Liveright, [March 1928].

A 30-I-1.d
New York: Horace Liveright, [May 1928].

A 30-I-1.e
New York: Horace Liveright, [June 1928].

A 30-I-1.f
New York: Horace Liveright, [August 1928].

A 30-I-1.g
New York: Horace Liveright, [October 1928].

A 30-I-1.h
New York: Horace Liveright, [January 1929].

A 30-I-1.i
New York: Horace Liveright, [September 1929].

A 30-I-1.j
New York: Horace Liveright, [September 1929].

A 30-I-1.k
New York: Horace Liveright, [October 1929].

A 30-I-1.l
New York: Horace Liveright, [December 1929].

A 30-I-1.m
New York: Horace Liveright, [July 1930].

A 30-I-1.n
New York: Horace Liveright, [February 1932].

A 30-I-1.o
New York: Horace Liveright, [n.d.] Black and Gold Library.

A 30 STRANGE INTERLUDE
American second book publication (1928)

A 30-II-1
STRANGE INTERLUDE
American limited edition

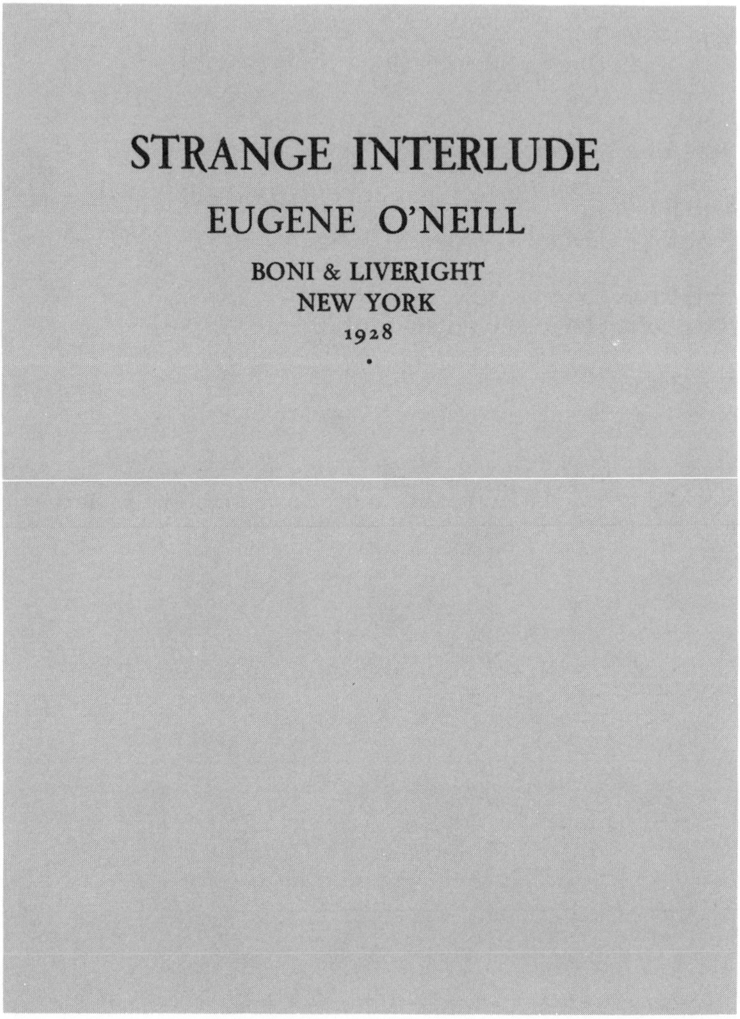
STRANGE INTERLUDE

EUGENE O'NEILL

BONI & LIVERIGHT
NEW YORK
1928

A 30-II-1: all in blue; $10'' \times 7\frac{11}{16}''$

All rights reserved including that of translation into foreign languages. All acting rights, both professional and amateur, including motion picture rights, are reserved in the United States, Great Britain and all countries of the Copyright Union by the author. In its present form this play is dedicated to the reading public only and no performance may be given without special arrangement with the author's agent.

COPYRIGHT, 1928, BY BONI & LIVERIGHT

PRINTED IN THE UNITED STATES OF AMERICA

[i–x] [1–2] 3–30 [31–32] 33–65 [66–68] 69–91 [92–94] 95–126 [127–128] 129–157 [158–160] 161–196 [197–198] 199–229 [230–232] 233–271 [272–274] 275–297 [298–302]

$[1]^{2}$ $[2\text{–}19]^{8}$ $[20]^{10}$

Contents: pp. i–ii: blank; p. iii: half title; p. iv: statement of limitation: 'Of this first edition of | STRANGE INTERLUDE | Boni & Liveright have printed in February, 1928 | 775 copies on all-rag watermarked paper. | 750 copies only are for sale | Each copy is numbered and signed by the author | This copy is number | [rule]'; p. v: title; p. vi: copyright; p. vii: '[blue] CHARACTERS | [eight lines of type in black ink]'; p. viii: blank; p. ix: act-scene synopsis; p. x: blank; p. 1: '[blue] *FIRST PLAY*'; p. 2: blank; pp. 3–30: text, headed '[blue] ACT ONE'; p. 31: '[blue] *ACT TWO*'; p. 32: blank; pp. 33–65: text, headed '[blue] ACT TWO'; p. 66: blank; p. 67: '[blue] *ACT THREE*'; p. 68: blank; pp. 69–91: text, headed '[blue] ACT THREE'; p. 92: blank; p. 93: '[blue] *ACT FOUR*'; p. 94: blank; pp. 95–126: text, headed '[blue] ACT FOUR'; p. 127: '[blue] *ACT FIVE*'; p. 128: blank; pp. 129–157: text, headed '[blue] ACT FIVE'; p. 158: blank; p. 159: '[blue] *SECOND PLAY*'; p. 160: blank; pp. 161–196: text, headed '[blue] ACT SIX'; p. 197: '[blue] *ACT SEVEN*'; p. 198: blank; pp. 199–229: text, headed '[blue] ACT SEVEN'; p. 230: blank; p. 231: '[blue] *ACT EIGHT*'; p. 232: blank; pp. 233–271: text, headed '[blue] ACT EIGHT'; p. 272: blank; p. 273: '[blue] *ACT NINE*'; p. 274: blank; pp. 275–298: text, headed '[blue] ACT NINE'; pp. 299–300: blank; p. 301: colophon: '*This edition of* Strange Interlude *was printed from | Caslon Old Face type which was distributed after print-|ing. The printing in two colors was done to achieve the | author's intention to distinguish, in his dialogue, the | spoken words from the actual thoughts of his characters. | The typography was designed by* S. A. JACOBS, *and the | book made by* THE VAN REES PRESS. *The paper was | supplied by* EDWIN D. PECK; *the entire manufacture | under the direction of* ALBERT H. GROSS, *of* BONI & | LIVE-

RIGHT. *The work was completed in February, 1928.'*; p. 302: blank.

Typography and paper: 10 point on 13, Caslon Old Face. $4\frac{5}{16}'' \times 6\frac{9}{16}''$ ($7\frac{1}{4}''$); thirty to thirty-five lines per page in blue ink and black ink. Running heads: rectos, act number; versos, play number. White laid paper with vertical chain marks $\frac{13}{16}''$ apart and EO's signature as watermark.

Binding: Antique white paper-covered boards with beveled edges. Front: [goldstamped EO signature within blue, single-rule frame]'. Spine: '[black label ($1\frac{5}{16}'' \times 1\frac{13}{16}''$) with gold frame] [goldstamped] STRANGE | INTERLUDE | EUGENE | O'NEILL'. Back has blue, single-rule frame. All edges untrimmed.

Slipcase: Orange paper-covered boards. Spine: '[buff label ($1\frac{9}{16}'' \times 3''$)] [brown] Strange | Interlude | [decoration] | Eugene | O'Neill.'

Publication: 775 copies published on unknown date in 1928. $25.00.

Locations: JM^cA (#300); Lilly (author's copy, #3 boxed, and #661 boxed); MJB (presentation boxed); PSt (#761 boxed); ScU (#299 boxed); Yale (author's copy, #5 boxed, and author's copy, #6 in parchment dj, boxed).

A 30 STRANGE INTERLUDE
American third book publication (1932)

A 30-III-1.a
Nine Plays by Eugene O'Neill. New York: Liveright, 1932. Introduction by Joseph Wood Krutch; plays selected by EO.

SI appears on pp. 483–682. See A 15-VII-1.a, *TEJ*.

REPRINTINGS

A 30-III-1.b
New York: Random House, [1937?].

A 30-III-1.c
New York: Random House, [1941].

On copyright page: '*First Modern Library Giant Edition* 1941'. (Not a new edition.)

A 30-III-1.d
New York: Random House, [1954?]. ML Giant #G55.

A 30 STRANGE INTERLUDE
American fourth book publication (1934)

A 30-IV-1
THE PLAYS OF EUGENE O'NEILL. Twelve volumes. Wilderness Edition

Volume one

Title page: '[within decorated border] [white against gray background] | THE | PLAYS | OF | EUGENE | O'NEILL | [wavy rule] | *Strange Interlude* | [wavy rule] | I | WILDERNESS · EDITION | *NEW YORK* | Charles Scribner's Sons'

Copyright page: 'COPYRIGHT, 1934, BY CHARLES SCRIBNER'S SONS | [eleven lines of roman and italic type]'

[i–x] xi [xii] xiii [xiv] [1–2] 3–35 [36] 37–75 [76] 77–180 [181–182] 183–263 [264] 265–311 [312] 313–341 [342–346]

$[1–21]^8$ $[22]^4$ $[23]^8$

The statement of limitation on p. iv reads: '[decorated rule] | [swash *T*'s and *N*'s] *THIS WILDERNESS EDITION* | OF THE | PLAYS OF EUGENE O'NEILL | printed from type now destroyed, is limited | to seven hundred and seventy sets | of which twenty are for presentation | This is number | [decorated rule]'.

Note one: Volume one is the only volume of the twelve signed by EO.

The colophon on p. 342 reads: '[decorated rule] | [swash *T* and *K*] *THIS BOOK* | the first of twelve volumes designed by Elmer Adler | set in an eighteenth-century type face | based on the castings made by John Baskerville | is printed on a specially watermarked paper | at the press of the publisher | in the city of New York | in the month of December | MCM XXX IV | [publisher's device]'.

Note two: The watermark is: 'CSS | [classical tragedy mask]'.

SI appears on pp. 1–341.

On p. xi, in a note written by EO's Random House editor, the following statement is made about *SI*: '[display S]TRANGE INTERLUDE *was written in Bermuda and Maine during | the years 1926 and 1927. It was produced at the John Golden | Theatre by the Theatre Guild on January 30, 1928, with a cast | that included Lynn Fontanne, Glen Anders, Earle Larimore, Tom | Powers and Helen Westley. It was awarded the Pulitzer Prize for | drama for 1928, marking the third time a play of mine had received this | award. My own hopes, and those of the Guild, were exceeded by the as-|tonishing popular success of this play. I had expected that it might run | three months or so, and the Theatre Guild directors foresaw the usual | subscription period of only six or seven weeks. However, "Strange In-|terlude" played in New York for seventeen months and there were two | companies on the road in 1929. Productions in nearly all European | countries have met with the same extraordinary success. "Strange Inter-|lude" was adapted into a talking picture in which Norma Shearer | played the role of Nina Leeds.*'

Publication: 770 copies published 30 November 1934.

Locations: JM[c]A (#456); LC (presentation); MJB (#592 boxed); ScU (#749); Yale (presentation).

A 30 STRANGE INTERLUDE
American fifth book publication (1941)

A 30-V-1.a
The Plays of Eugene O'Neill. New York: Random House, [1941]. Three volumes.

On copyright page: 'FIRST PRINTING'.

SI appears in volume one, pp. 1–200. See A 6-VII-1.a, "Cardiff."

REPRINTINGS

A 30-V-1.b
New York: Random House, [1941].

On copyright page: 'SECOND PRINTING'.

A 30-V-1.c
New York: Random House, [1951].

A 30-V-1.d
New York: Random House, [1954–55].

A 30 STRANGE INTERLUDE
American sixth book publication (1967)

A 30-VI-1
Selected Plays of Eugene O'Neill. New York: Random House, [1967].

On copyright page: 'First Printing'.

SI appears on pp. 281–450. See A 15-XIII-1, *TEJ*.

A 30 STRANGE INTERLUDE
English first book publication (1928)

A 30-EI-1.a
STRANGE INTERLUDE
English first edition, first printing

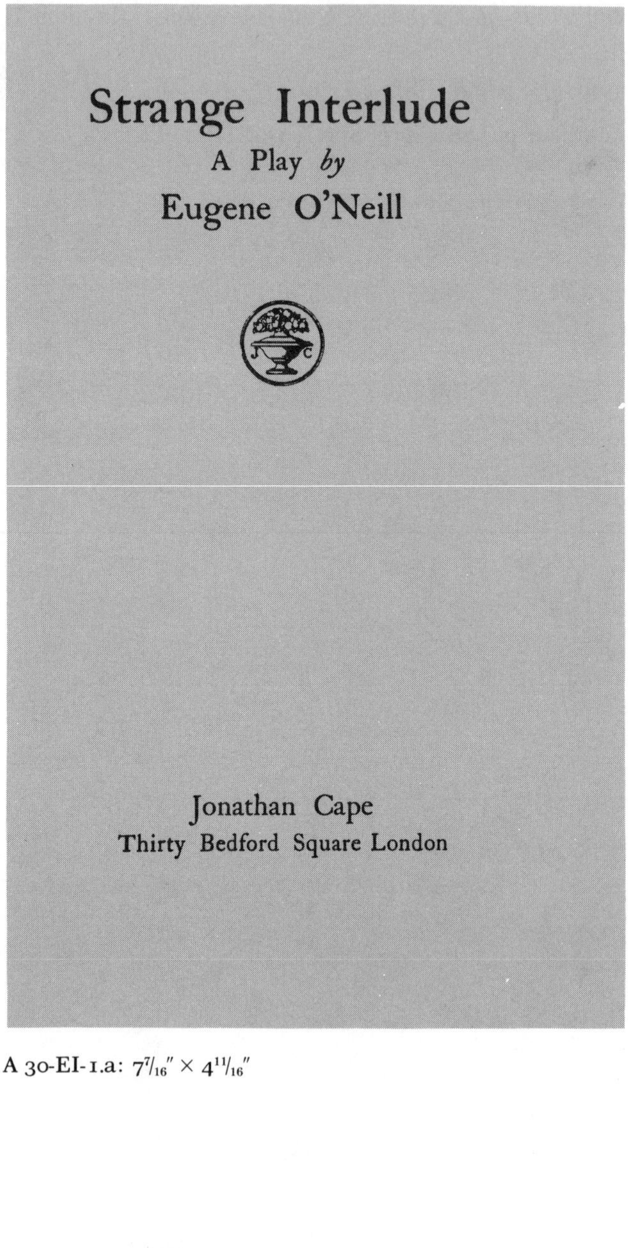
Strange Interlude
A Play *by*
Eugene O'Neill

Jonathan Cape
Thirty Bedford Square London

A 30-EI-1.a: $7\frac{7}{16}'' \times 4\frac{11}{16}''$

FIRST PUBLISHED MCMXXVIII

PRINTED IN GREAT BRITAIN BY
BUTLER & TANNER LTD
FROME

[1–4] 5 [6] 7 [8–10] 11–188 [189–190] 191–348 [349–352]

$[A]^{16}$ $[B–I]^{16}$ $[K–L]^{16}$

Contents: p. 1: half title; p. 2: card page; p. 3: title; p. 4: copyright; p. 5: 'Characters | [eight lines of roman and italic type]'; p. 6: blank; p. 7: act-scene synopsis; p. 8: blank; p. 9: 'FIRST PART'; p. 10: blank; pp. 11–188: text, headed 'ACT ONE'; p. 189: 'SECOND PART'; p. 190: blank; pp. 191–348: text, headed 'ACT SIX'; pp. 349–352: blank.

Typography and paper: $3\frac{1}{4}'' \times 5\frac{1}{4}''$ ($5\frac{11}{16}''$); thirty-eight lines per page. Running heads: rectos and versos, 'STRANGE INTERLUDE'. Wove paper.

Binding: Blue V cloth (fine linen-like grain). Front: '[goldstamped EO signature]'. Spine: '[goldstamped line of decorations] | EUGENE | O'NEILL | [decoration] | STRANGE | INTERLUDE | JONATHAN CAPE | [line of decorations]'. Back has blindstamped publisher's device. White wove endpapers of different stock from text paper. All edges trimmed.

Dust jacket: Off-white background. Front: '[green border of sea motif with porpoises riding crest of waves] | [black woodcut of EO profile by SLH] | EUGENE O'NEILL | [green star] | [black] STRANGE INTERLUDE | A Play in Nine Acts | [green star] | [border of wave motif]'. Spine: '[green border of sea motif with porpoises riding crest of waves] | [black] EUGENE | O'NEILL | [green star] | [black] STRANGE | INTERLUDE | [green star] | [publisher's device] | [black] JONATHAN CAPE | [green border of wave motif]'. Back lists seven volumes of EO's plays published by Cape. Front flap has blurb for *SI;* back flap blank.

Note: In 1937, when Cape published a new printing of the volume, a new dust jacket advertising the book as the "Nobel Prize Edition" was also printed.

Publication: Unknown number of copies published in 1928. 7s. 6d.

Locations: JM^{c}A (dj); ScU; Yale (Nobel Prize dj).

REPRINTINGS

A 30-EI-1.b
London: Jonathan Cape, [1937]. Nobel Prize Edition. (Not a new edition.)

A 30-EI-1.c
London: Jonathan Cape, [1953].

A 30 STRANGE INTERLUDE
Special publication (1929)

A 30-S-1
EXTRACTS FROM "STRANGE INTERLUDE"

[1] 2–6 [7–8]

Stapled.

No cover. No title. No copyright.

Text (excerpts from all six acts) appears on pp. 1–6, headed by 'EXTRACTS FROM "THE STRANGE INTERLUDE." | [rule]'. This was an unauthorized collection of scenes, and the publisher has never been identified.

Printing: Unknown number of copies printed in Boston, Mass., September 1929.

Location: Yale (with letter).

Note: A letter (TL, 1 p.) accompanied the pamphlet. The heading and date read: 'Boston, Mass., September 21, 1929'; no salutation; the body of the letter urges clergymen to read the pamphlet and support Mayor Nichols of Boston in prohibiting production of the play upon the Boston stage; seven clergymen of the Boston area are listed; no signature. One page (8½" × 11"), typed on recto only.

EXTRACTS FROM "THE STRANGE INTERLUDE."

By Eugene G. O'Neill
1927

FIRST ACT.

Page 14. "To the devil with sex—— our impotent pose of today to be beat on the loud drum of fornication—— eunuchs parading with the phallus."

Page 15. "prep school. ——Easter vacation—— Fatty Boggs and Jack Frazer—— that house of cheap vice—— one dollar—— why did I go—— Jack the dead game sport—— how I admired him—— afraid of the taunts—— he pointed to the Italian girl—— take her—— daring me—— I went—— miserably frightened—— what a pig she was—— pretty vicious face under caked powder and rouge—— surly and contemptuous—— Lumpy body—— short legs and thick ankles—— slums of Naples——" What are you gawking about—— git a move on kid—— kid—— I was only a kid—— sixteen—— test of manhood—— ashamed to face Jack again, unless—— fool I might have lied to him."

Page 36. (Nina.) "But Gordon never possessed me—— I am—— still Gordon's silly virgin—— and Gordon is muddy ashes—— and I've lost my happiness forever. All that last night I knew Gordon wanted me. I knew it was only the honorable code bound Gordon who kept commanding from his brain, no you mustn't, you must respect her, you must wait until you have a marriage license."

Page 37. Gordon wanted me—— I wanted Gordon—— I should have made him take me. I didn't make him take me—— I lost him forever——. And now I am lonely, not pregnant with anything at all but—— loathing."

ACT TWO.

Page 73. (Marsden.) "She's hard—— like a whore—— tearing your heart out with dirty finger nails—— cruel bitch—— no kinder at heart than dollar tarts——

Page 75. (Nina.) "How could that God care about our trifling misery of death or of death. I couldn't believe in him and I wouldn't if I could. I'd rather imitate His indifference and prove that I had that one trait at least in common."

Page 80.
(Marsden.) "What do you want to be punished for Nina."
(Nina.) "For playing the silly slut, Charlie, or giving my cool clean body to men with hot hands and greedy eyes which they call love, ugh.

Page 81.
(Marsden) thinking. "Then she did—— the little filth."
(Marsden to Nina.) "Then you did—— but no Darrel."
(Nina.) No, how could I, ——the war hadn't maimed him—— there would have been no point in that. But I did with others, oh, four or five or six or seven men Charlie, ——I forget—— and it doesn't matter. They were all the same. Count them all as one and that one a ghost of nothing, that is, to me. They were important to themselves if I remember rightly. But I forget.

Page 83. (Nina.) I want children—— I must become a mother so I can give myself.

A 30-S-1: $9\frac{5}{8}'' \times 6\frac{1}{2}''$

A 31 DYNAMO
American first book publication (1929)

A 31-I-1.a
DYNAMO
American first edition, first printing

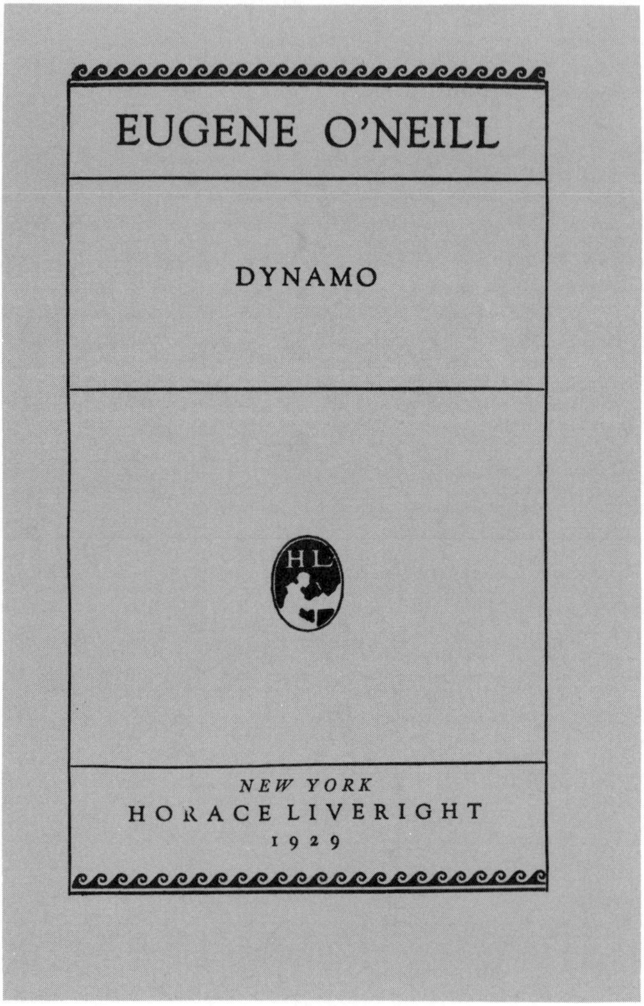
EUGENE O'NEILL

DYNAMO

NEW YORK
HORACE LIVERIGHT
1929

A 31-I-1.a: frame, waves, rules, and publisher's device in green; $8\frac{1}{16}'' \times 5\frac{7}{16}''$

Copyright, 1929, by
HORACE LIVERIGHT, INC.

Printed in the United States of America

NOTE

All rights reserved including that of translation into foreign languages. All acting rights, both professional and amateur, including motion picture rights, are reserved in the United States, Great Britain and all countries of the Copyright Union by the author.
In their present form these plays are dedicated to the reading public only and no performance may be given without special arrangement with the author's agent.

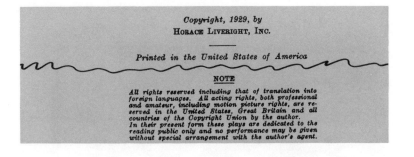

[i–vi] vii–viii [9–10] 11–80 [81–82] 83–128 [129–130] 131–159 [160]

$[1\text{–}10]^8$

Contents: p. i: half title; p. ii: blank; p. iii: title; p. iv: copyright; p. v: 'CHARACTERS [eight lines of type]'; p. vi: blank; pp. vii–viii: act-scene synopsis and set description; p. 9: 'ACT ONE'; p. 10: blank; pp. 11–80: text, headed 'ACT ONE'; p. 81: 'ACT TWO'; p. 82: blank; pp. 83–128: text, headed 'ACT TWO'; p. 129: 'ACT THREE'; p. 130: blank; pp. 131–159: text, headed 'ACT THREE'; p. 160: blank.

Typography and paper: 12 point on 14, Scotch. $3^{13}/_{16}'' \times 5^{3}/_{16}''$ ($5^{13}/_{16}''$); twenty-five to twenty-seven lines per page. Running heads: rectos and versos, 'DYNAMO | [double rule]'. White laid paper with vertical chains $1^{11}/_{16}''$ apart, with the Horace Liveright publisher's device as watermark.

Binding: Blue green sized V cloth (fine linen-like grain). Front: '[within a light sea green frame with a wave motif at bottom] [goldstamped EO signature]'. Spine: '[goldstamped border of wave motif] | [goldstamped] EUGENE | O'NEILL | [single wave motif] | DYNAMO | [blindstamped publisher's device] | [goldstamped] HORACE | LIVERIGHT | [border of wave motif]'. Illustrated endpapers front and rear: [aqua and buff] steamship on rolling sea silhouetted against setting sun with the word 'O'NEILL' above. Top edge only trimmed and stained dark blue green.

Dust jacket: Front: '[dark blue wave motif running vertically against light blue green background] [at top in dark blue] EUGENE | O'NEILL'S | [vertically at right in dark blue] DYNAMO | [at bottom in light blue green script] by the author of | [light blue green roman] STRANGE INTERLUDE | · · [script] The [roman] HAIRY APE · · | [roman] MARCO MILLIONS'.

Dust jackets for A 32-I-1.a and A 30-I-1.a

Spine: '[dark blue against light blue green background] [horizontally] EUGENE | O'NEILL'S | [vertically, top to bottom] DYNAMO | [horizontally] [publisher's device] | HORACE | LIVERIGHT'. Back: across the top, a dark blue border of the sea motif with porpoises riding the crest of waves, framing a drawing of EO's portrait against a light blue green background. Below the border, in dark blue against light blue green, are blurbs for *SI* and a list of volumes in the uniform edition of The Collected Works of Eugene O'Neill (now includes nine volumes). Front flap: blurb for *Dynamo;* back flap: blurb for *MM.*

Publication: 10,000 copies published 5 October 1929. $2.50. Ninth volume of an unnumbered, ten-volume, uniform series.

Printing: Printed 20 September 1929 by Van Rees Press, New York, from plates made by Van Rees Book Composition; bound by Van Rees Bindery.

Locations: JM^cA (dj); Lilly (three, djs); Yale.

Note: EO prepared three versions of the play for publication. Version one, according to Sanborn and Clark (p. 79), was set in galleys "from approximately the same manuscript as that used in the production of the play by the New York Theatre Guild. It never went beyond this stage." Version two was set in galleys by Liveright and sent to Jonathan Cape in London. Before version two was released by Cape, EO submitted version three to Liveright. The American first edition, then, was set from the third, and EO's final, version of the play. The English first edition is EO's second version of the play. There are substantial variances between the final third version (American first edition) and the second version (English first edition).

REPRINTINGS

A 31-I-1.b
New York: Horace Liveright, [October 1929].

A 31-I-1.c
New York: Horace Liveright, [October 1929].

A 31-I-1.d
New York: Horace Liveright, [October 1929].

A 31 DYNAMO
American second book publication (1929)

A 31-II-1
DYNAMO
American limited edition

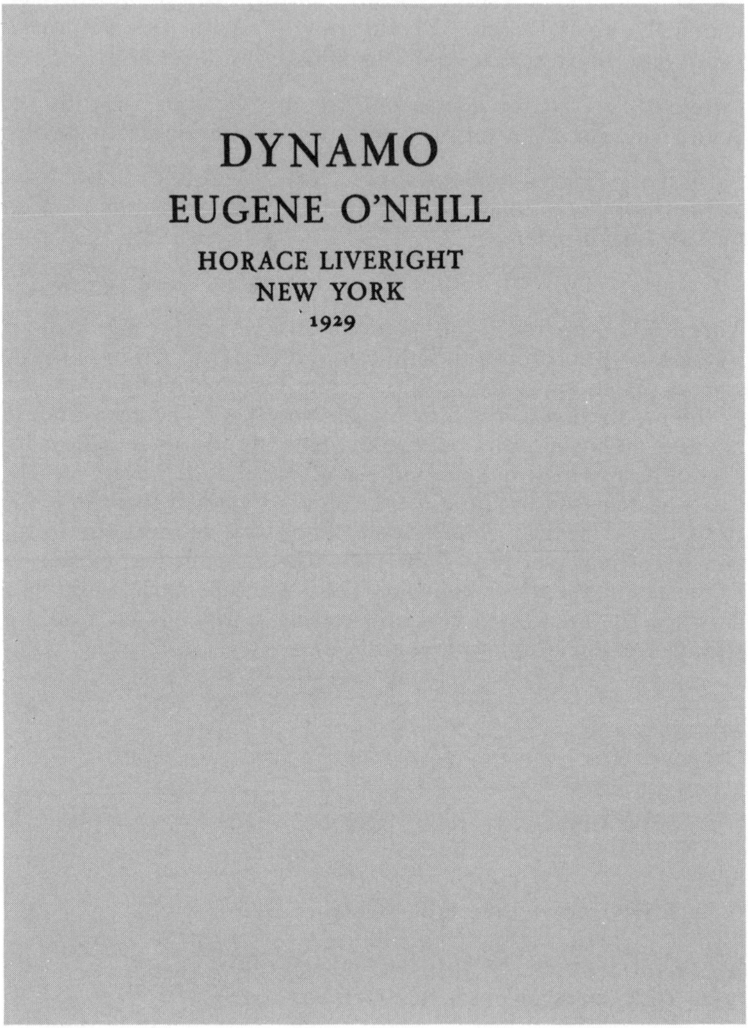

DYNAMO
EUGENE O'NEILL
HORACE LIVERIGHT
NEW YORK
1929

A 31-II-1: all in blue; 10″ × 7⅝″

All rights reserved including that of translation into foreign languages. All acting rights, both professional and amateur, including motion picture rights, are reserved in the United States, Great Britain and all countries of the Copyright Union by the author. In its present form this play is dedicated to the reading public only and no performance may be given without special arrangement with the author's agent.

COPYRIGHT, 1929, BY HORACE LIVERIGHT, INC.

PRINTED IN THE UNITED STATES OF AMERICA

[A–D] [i–vi] vii–viii [1–2] 3–72 [73–74] 75–120 [121–122] 123–151 [152]

[1]^{2} [2–11]^{8}

Contents: pp. A–B: blank; p. C: statement of limitation: 'Of this edition of | D Y N A M O | Horace Liveright has printed in October, 1929 | 775 copies on all-rag watermarked paper. | 750 copies only are for sale | Each copy is numbered and signed by the author | This copy is number | [short rule]'; p. D: blank; p. i: half title; p. ii: blank; p. iii: title; p. iv: copyright; p. v: list of characters; p. vi: blank; pp. vii–viii: act-scene synopsis; p. 1: '[swash *T* and *N*] *ACT ONE*'; p. 2: blank; pp. 3–72: text, headed 'SCENE ONE'; p. 73: '[swash *T*'s] *ACT TWO*'; p. 74: blank; pp. 75–120: text, headed: 'SCENE ONE'; p. 121: '[swash *T*'s] *ACT THREE*'; p. 122: blank; pp. 123–151: text, headed 'SCENE ONE'; p. 152: colophon: '*This edition of* Dynamo *was printed from Caslon Old | Face type which was distributed after printing. The | printing in two colors was done to achieve the author's | intention to distinguish his dialogue, the spoken | words from the actual thoughts of his characters. The | book was made by the* VAN REES PRESS; *the paper sup-|plied by* Edwin D. PECK; *the entire manufacture | under the direction of* ALBERT H. GROSS *of* | HORACE LIVERIGHT, INC. *The work was com-|pleted in November, 1929.*'

Typography and paper: 14 point on 16, Caslon Old Face. $3\frac{13}{16}'' \times 5\frac{9}{16}''$ ($6\frac{3}{16}''$); twenty-five lines per page in blue and black ink. Running heads: rectos, scenes in decorated type; versos, acts in decorated type. Laid paper with vertical chain marks $\frac{13}{16}''$ apart with EO's signature as watermark.

Binding: Blue paper-covered boards with mottled effect. Front: '[goldstamped EO signature]'. Spine: '[white label $1\frac{3}{4}'' \times \frac{13}{16}''$] [goldstamped within single-rule goldstamped frame] DYNAMO | EUGENE | O'NEILL'. White wove endpapers of different stock from text paper. All edges untrimmed.

Slipcase: Purple paper-covered boards with raised silver spider-web design. Front: '[white paper label 1¾″ × 1 13/16″] [goldstamped within single-rule goldstamped frame] DYNAMO | EUGENE | O'NEILL'.

Publication: 775 copies published October–November 1929. $25.00.

Locations: JMcA (#189 boxed); Lilly (#539 boxed); PSt (#581 boxed); Yale (#18 boxed and #39 boxed).

A 31 DYNAMO
American third book publication (1935)

A 31-III-1
The Plays of Eugene O'Neill. New York: Scribners, [1934–35]. Twelve volumes. Wilderness Edition.

Limited to 770 numbered copies.

Dynamo appears in volume seven, pp. 1–117. See A 17-IV-1, *Diff'rent.*

On p. xi, in a note written by EO's Random House editor, the following statement is made about *Dynamo:* 'DYNAMO *was written in France in 1928 and was produced by the | Theatre Guild at the Martin Beck Theatre on February 11, 1929.*'

Publication: 770 copies published 30 January 1935.

A 31 DYNAMO
American fourth book publication (1941)

A 31-IV-1.a
The Plays of Eugene O'Neill. New York: Random House, [1941]. Three volumes.

On copyright page: 'FIRST PRINTING'.

Dynamo appears in volume three, pp. 417–489. See A 14-VI-1.a, *BTH.*

REPRINTINGS

A 31-IV-1.b
New York: Random House, [1941].

On copyright page: 'SECOND PRINTING'.

A 31-IV-1.c
New York: Random House, [1951].

A 31-IV-1.d
New York: Random House, [1954–55].

A 31 DYNAMO
English first book publication (1929)

A 31-EI-1
Lazarus Laughed. London: Jonathan Cape, 1929.

Dynamo appears on pp. 1–102. See A 29-EI-1.a, *LL*.

Note: see A 31-I-1.a for note on three versions of the play. American book publication was 5 October 1929; English publication was in November 1929.

A 32 MOURNING BECOMES ELECTRA
American first book publication (1931)

A 32-I-1.a
MOURNING BECOMES ELECTRA
American first edition, trade printing

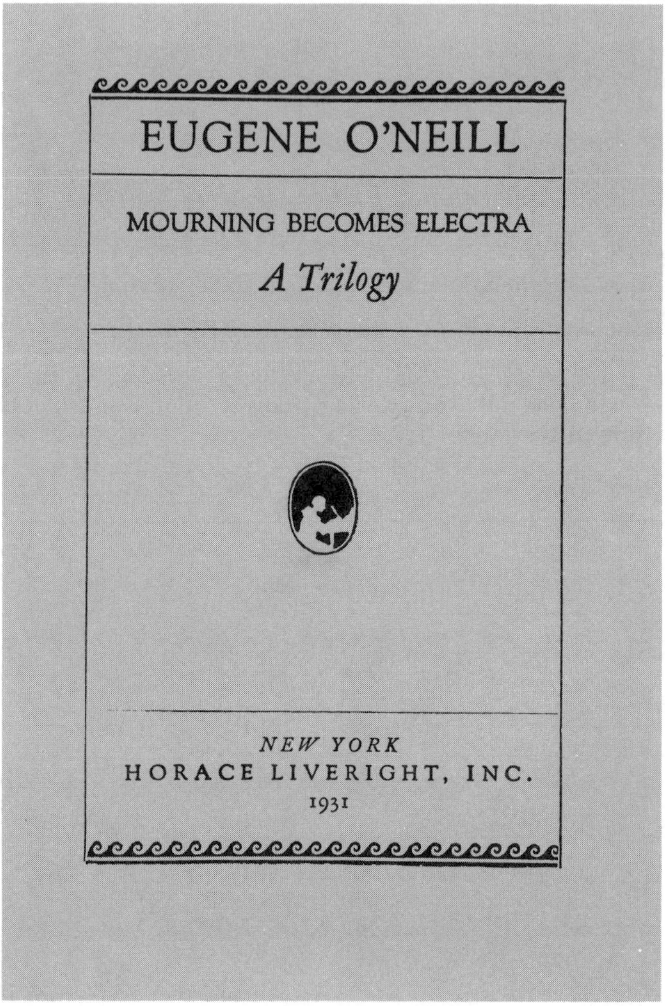
EUGENE O'NEILL

MOURNING BECOMES ELECTRA

A Trilogy

NEW YORK
HORACE LIVERIGHT, INC.
1931

A 32-I-1.a: frame, waves, rules, and publisher's device in green; $8\frac{1}{16}'' \times 5\frac{7}{16}''$

PRINTED IN THE UNITED STATES OF AMERICA

MANUFACTURED BY VAN REES PRESS, NEW YORK CITY

[1–8] 9–10 [11–16] 17–44 [45–46] 47–65 [66–68] 69–86 [87–88] 89–96 [97–102] 103–116 [117–118] 119–135 [136–138] 139–150 [151–152] 153–170 [171–172] 173–182 [183–188] 189–214 [215–216] 217–226 [227–228] 229–242 [243–244] 245–256

[1–16]^{8}

Contents: p. 1: half title; p. 2: blank; p. 3: title; p. 4: copyright; p. 5: 'To | Carlotta | my wife'; p. 6: blank; p. 7: 'CONTENTS'; p. 8: blank; pp. 9–10: 'GENERAL SCENE OF THE TRILOGY'; p. 11: 'HOMECOMING | A Play in Four Acts | Part One of the Trilogy | MOURNING BECOMES ELECTRA'; p. 12: blank; p. 13: 'HOMECOMING | CHARACTERS | [ten lines of roman and italic type]'; p. 14: act-scene synopsis; p. 15: 'PART ONE | HOMECOMING'; p. 16: blank; pp. 17–44: text, headed 'HOMECOMING | ACT ONE'; p. 45: 'HOMECOMING | ACT TWO'; p. 46: blank; pp. 47–65: text, headed 'ACT TWO'; p. 66: blank; p. 67: 'HOMECOMING | ACT THREE'; p. 68: blank; pp. 69–86: text, headed 'ACT THREE'; p. 87: 'HOMECOMING | ACT FOUR'; p. 88: blank; pp. 89–96: text, headed 'ACT FOUR'; p. 97: 'THE HUNTED | A Play in Five Acts | Part Two of the Trilogy | MOURNING BECOMES ELECTRA'; p. 98: blank; p. 99: 'THE HUNTED | CHARACTERS | [twelve lines of roman and italic type]'; p. 100: act-scene synopsis; p. 101: 'PART TWO | THE HUNTED'; p. 102: blank; pp. 103–116: text, headed 'THE HUNTED | ACT ONE'; p. 117: 'THE HUNTED | ACT TWO'; p. 118: blank; pp. 119–135: text, headed 'ACT TWO'; p. 136: blank; p. 137: 'THE HUNTED | ACT THREE'; p. 138: blank; pp. 139–150: text, headed 'ACT THREE'; p. 151: 'THE HUNTED | ACT FOUR'; p. 152: blank; pp. 153–170: text, headed 'ACT FOUR'; p. 171: 'THE HUNTED | ACT FIVE'; p. 172: blank; pp. 173–182: text, headed 'ACT FIVE'; p. 183: 'THE HAUNTED | A Play in Four Acts | Part Three of the Trilogy | MOURNING BECOMES ELECTRA'; p. 184: blank; p. 185: 'THE HAUNTED

| CHARACTERS | [nine lines of roman and italic type]'; p. 186: act-scene synopsis; p. 187: 'PART THREE | THE HAUNTED'; p. 188: blank; pp. 189–214: text, headed 'THE HAUNTED | ACT ONE | SCENE ONE'; p. 215: 'THE HAUNTED | ACT TWO'; p. 216: blank; pp. 217–226: text, headed 'ACT TWO'; p. 227: 'THE HAUNTED | ACT THREE'; p. 228: blank; pp. 229–242: text, headed 'ACT THREE'; p. 243: 'THE HAUNTED | ACT FOUR'; p. 244: blank; pp. 245–256: text, headed 'ACT FOUR'.

Typography and paper: 10 point on 14, Scotch. 3 13/16" × 5 13/16" (6 3/16"); thirty lines per page. Running heads: rectos, individual play titles with double rule; versos, 'MOURNING BECOMES ELECTRA | [double rule]'. White laid paper with vertical chains 1 11/16" apart, with Horace Liveright publisher's device as watermark.

Binding: Blue green sized V cloth (fine linen-like grain). Front: '[within a light sea green frame with a wave motif at bottom] [goldstamped EO signature]'. Spine: [goldstamped border of wave motif] | [goldstamped] EUGENE | O'NEILL | [single wave motif] | Mourning | Becomes | Electra | [blindstamped publisher's device] | [goldstamped] LIVERIGHT | [border of wave motif]'. Illustrated endpapers front and rear: [aqua and buff] steamship on rolling sea silhouetted against setting sun with the word 'O'NEILL' above. Top edge only trimmed and stained dark blue green.

Dust jacket: Front: illustration of female figure in mid-nineteenth-century dress standing on porch of Georgian mansion, signed 'Robert Edmond Jones | 1931'; above the illustration against light blue green background, '[dark blue green] EUGENE O'NEILL | [below the illustration] MOURNING | BECOMES | ELECTRA | *A Trilogy* | [in semicircle] HOMECOMING · THE HUNTED · THE HAUNTED'. Spine: '[dark blue green against light blue green background] MOURNING | BECOMES | ELECTRA | by | EUGENE | O'NEILL | [publisher's device] | LIVERIGHT'. Back: advertising copy for previous nine volumes in the unnumbered, ten-volume, uniform series of EO plays. Front and back flaps: blurb for *MBE* which quotes from EO's working Diary. Back flap also gives jacket design credit to Robert Edmond Jones and has ad for Liveright publications.

Publication: Unknown number of copies published 2 November 1931. $2.50. Tenth volume of an unnumbered, ten-volume, uniform series.

Printing: Printed 23 October 1931 by Van Rees Press, New York; composed by Van Rees Book Composition Company; bound by Van Rees Bindery.

Locations: JM^{c}A (dj); LC (third printing, deposit-stamp 1 December 1931); Lilly (three, djs); PSt; ScU (dj); Yale.

A 32 MOURNING BECOMES ELECTRA
American limited publication (1931)

A 32-I-1.b
MOURNING BECOMES ELECTRA
American first edition, limited printing

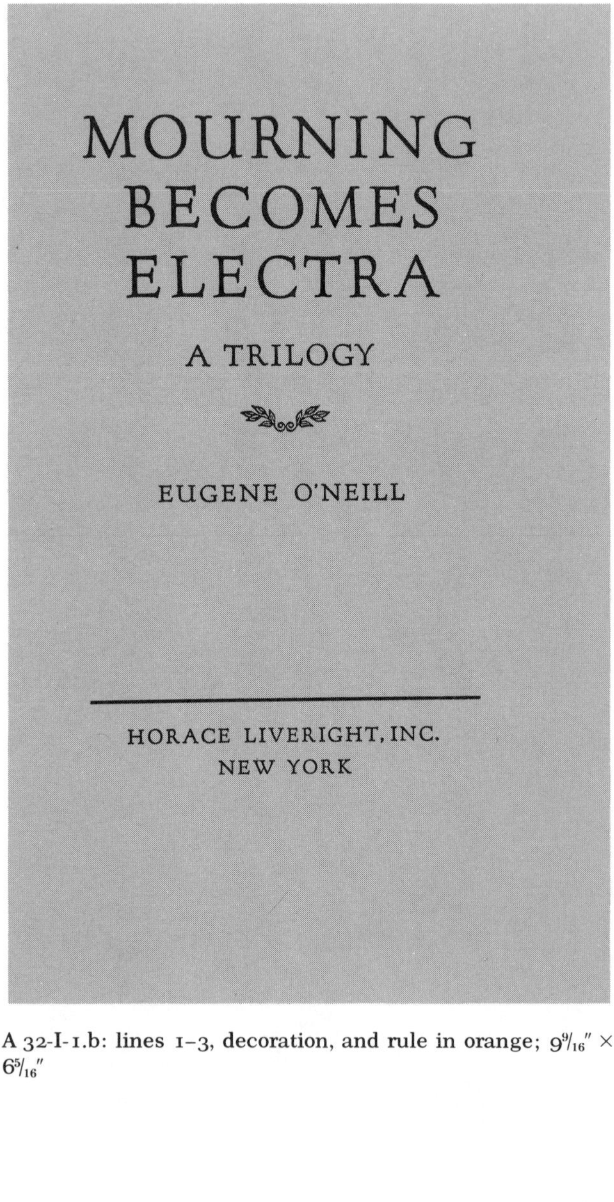
MOURNING
BECOMES
ELECTRA

A TRILOGY

EUGENE O'NEILL

HORACE LIVERIGHT, INC.
NEW YORK

A 32-I-1.b: lines 1–3, decoration, and rule in orange; $9\frac{9}{16}'' \times 6\frac{5}{16}''$

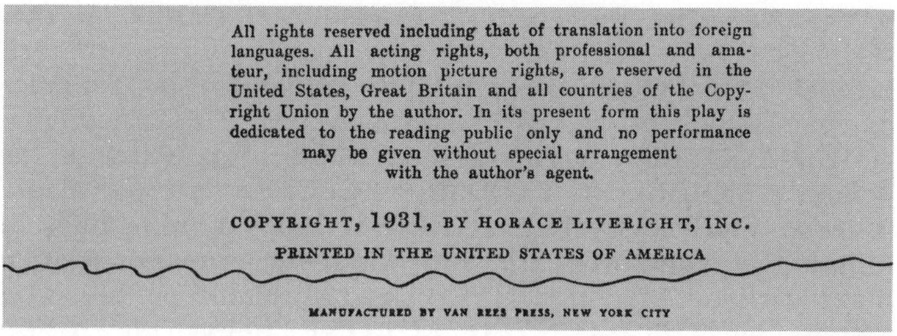
All rights reserved including that of translation into foreign languages. All acting rights, both professional and amateur, including motion picture rights, are reserved in the United States, Great Britain and all countries of the Copyright Union by the author. In its present form this play is dedicated to the reading public only and no performance may be given without special arrangement with the author's agent.

COPYRIGHT, 1931, BY HORACE LIVERIGHT, INC.

PRINTED IN THE UNITED STATES OF AMERICA

MANUFACTURED BY VAN REES PRESS, NEW YORK CITY

[1–8] 9–10 [11–16] 17–44 [45–46] 47–65 [66–68] 69–86 [87–88] 89–96 [97–102] 103–116 [117–118] 119–135 [136–138] 139–150 [151–152] 153–170 [171–172] 173–182 [183–188] 189–214 [215–216] 217–226 [227–228] 229–242 [243–244] 245–256 [257–276]

$[1]^{10}$ $[2\text{–}17]^{8}$

Contents: p. 1: half title; p. 2: statement of limitation: 'THIS SPECIAL EDITION OF | MOURNING BECOMES ELECTRA | CONSISTS OF | FIVE HUNDRED AND FIFTY COPIES, | OF WHICH FIVE HUNDRED COPIES | (NUMBERED 1 to 500) | ARE FOR SALE, AND FIFTY COPIES | (NUMBERED 501 to 550) ARE FOR PRESENTATION. | *THIS COPY IS NUMBER* | [four rules]'; p. 3: title; p. 4: copyright; p. 5: 'To | Carlotta | my wife'; p. 6: blank; p. 7: 'CONTENTS | [three lines of type]'; p. 8: blank; pp. 9–10: 'GENERAL SCENE OF THE TRILOGY'; p. 11: 'HOMECOMING | A Play in Four Acts | Part One of the Trilogy | MOURNING BECOMES ELECTRA'; p. 12: blank; p. 13: 'HOMECOMING | CHARACTERS | [ten lines of roman and italic type]'; p. 14: act-scene synopsis; p. 15: 'PART ONE | HOMECOMING'; p. 16: blank; pp. 17–44: text, headed 'HOMECOMING | ACT ONE'; p. 45: 'HOMECOMING | ACT TWO'; p. 46: blank; pp. 47–65: text, headed 'ACT TWO'; p. 66: blank; p. 67: 'HOMECOMING | ACT THREE'; p. 68: blank; pp. 69–86: text, headed 'ACT THREE'; p. 87: 'HOMECOMING | ACT FOUR'; p. 88: blank; pp. 89–96: text, headed 'ACT FOUR'; p. 97: 'THE HUNTED | A Play in Five Acts | Part Two of the Trilogy | MOURNING BECOMES ELECTRA'; p. 98: blank; p. 99: 'THE HUNTED | CHARACTERS | [twelve lines of roman and italic type]'; p. 100: act-scene synopsis; p. 101: 'PART TWO | THE HUNTED'; p. 102: blank; pp. 103–116: text, headed 'THE HUNTED | ACT ONE'; p. 117: 'THE HUNTED | ACT TWO'; p. 118: blank; pp. 119–135: text, headed 'ACT TWO'; p. 136: blank; p. 137: 'THE HUNTED | ACT THREE';

p. 138: blank; pp. 139–150: text, headed 'ACT THREE'; p. 151: 'THE HUNTED | ACT FOUR'; p. 152: blank; pp. 153–170: text, headed 'ACT FOUR'; p. 171: 'THE HUNTED | ACT FIVE'; p. 172: blank; pp. 173–182: text, headed 'ACT FIVE'; p. 183: 'THE HAUNTED | A Play in Four Acts | Part Three of the Trilogy | MOURNING BECOMES ELECTRA'; p. 184: blank; p. 185: 'THE HAUNTED | CHARACTERS | [nine lines of roman and italic type]'; p. 186: act-scene synopsis; p. 187: 'PART THREE | THE HAUNTED'; p. 188: blank; pp. 189–214: text, headed 'THE HAUNTED | ACT ONE | SCENE ONE'; p. 215: 'THE HAUNTED | ACT TWO'; p. 216: blank; pp. 217–226: text, headed 'ACT TWO'; p. 227: 'THE HAUNTED | ACT THREE'; p. 228: blank; pp. 229–242: text, headed 'ACT THREE'; p. 243: 'THE HAUNTED | ACT FOUR'; p. 244: blank; pp. 245–256: text, headed 'ACT FOUR'; p. 257: 'WORKING NOTES | AND | EXTRACTS | FROM A FRAGMENTARY | WORK DIARY'; p. 258: blank; pp. 259–271: text, headed 'MOURNING BECOMES ELECTRA | *Working notes and extracts from a fragmentary work diary';* pp. 272–276: blank.

Typography and paper: 10 point on 14, Scotch. 3 13/16" × 5 13/16" (6 3/16"); thirty lines per page. Running heads: rectos, individual play titles with double rule; versos, 'MOURNING BECOMES ELECTRA | [double rule]'. White laid paper with vertical chains 1 11/16" apart, with Horace Liveright publisher's device as watermark.

Binding: Antique white paper-covered boards with beveled edges. Front: '[goldstamped EO signature]'. Spine: goldstamped '[all within a single-rule border] [double rule] | [rule] | [rule] | [triple rule] | [black label (1" × 2 1/4")] MOURNING | BECOMES | ELECTRA | [leaf decoration] | *A TRILOGY* | [rule] | EUGENE | O'NEILL | [below the label, triple rule] | [rule] | [rule] | [rule] | [triple rule] | [double rule]'. White wove endpapers. Inside back cover has pocket containing eight sheets (8 1/2" × 11") which facsimile EO's holograph working notes on *MBE*. The notes have been reproduced in edited form on pp. 259–271. All edges untrimmed.

Slipcase: Black paper-covered boards. Spine: goldstamped '[all within a single-rule border] [double rule] | [rule] | [rule] | [triple rule] | MOURNING | BECOMES | ELECTRA | [leaf decoration] | *A TRILOGY* | [rule] | EUGENE | O'NEILL | [triple rule] | [rule] | [rule] | [rule] | [triple rule] | [double rule]'.

Publication: 550 copies published in November 1931.

Locations: JM[c]A (#445 boxed); Lilly (#169 boxed); MJB (#391 boxed); ScU (#404 boxed); Yale (#55 boxed and presentation).

Note: The last section (pp. 257–271), notes and fragments from EO's diary, contains previously unpublished material. In a pocket inside the back cover, the publisher included eight sheets of 8½″ × 11″ paper bearing a facsimile of EO's pencil holograph notes and diary fragments. The facsimiled pages are printed on one side only. The holograph notes are not transcribed exactly on pp. 252–271, however; deletions and strikeovers have been edited out.

REPRINTINGS
First edition, trade printing

A 32-I-1.c
New York: Liveright, [November 1931].

A 32-I-1.d
New York: Liveright, [November 1931].

A 32-I-1.e
New York: Liveright, [November 1931].

A 32-I-1.f
New York: Liveright, [November 1931].

A 32-I-1.g
New York: Liveright, [November 1931].

Note: EO had fifteen copies of the seventh printing of *MBE* specially bound. A discrepancy exists between dates on copyright pages. On copyright page: '[sixteen lines of type] | Seventh Printing, December, 1931 | [one line of type]'. Binding: Batiked green paper-covered boards with brown design. Black coated V cloth (fine linen-like grain) shelf back. Spine: '[goldstamped line of wave motif] | EUGENE | O'NEILL | [single wave motif] | Mourning | Becomes | Electra | [blindstamped publisher's device] | [goldstamped] LIVERIGHT | [line of wave motif] | [rule]'.

A 32-I-1.h
New York: Liveright, [December 1931].

A 32-I-1.i
New York: Liveright, [December 1931].

A 32-I-1.j
New York: Liveright, [February 1932].

A 32 MOURNING BECOMES ELECTRA
American second book publication (1932)

A 32-II-1.a
Nine Plays by Eugene O'Neill. New York: Liveright, 1932. Introduction by Joseph Wood Krutch; plays selected by EO.

MBE appears on pp. 683–867. See A 15-VII-1.a, *TEJ*.

REPRINTINGS

A 32-II-1.b
New York: Random House, [1937?]. 'NOBEL PRIZE EDITION'. (Not a new edition.)

A 32-II-1.c
New York: Random House, [1941].

On copyright page: 'First Modern Library Giant Edition | 1941'. (Not a new edition.)

A 32-II-1.d
New York: Random House, [1954?]. ML Giant #G55.

A 32 MOURNING BECOMES ELECTRA
American third book publication (1934)

A 32-III-1
THE PLAYS OF EUGENE O'NEILL. Twelve volumes. Wilderness Edition

Volume two

Title page: '[within decorated border] [white against gray background] THE | PLAYS | OF | EUGENE | O'NEILL | [wavy rule] | *Mourning* | *Becomes Electra* | [wavy rule] | II | WILDERNESS · EDITION | *NEW YORK* | Charles Scribner's Sons'

Copyright page: 'COPYRIGHT, 1934, BY CHARLES SCRIBNER'S SONS | [eleven lines of roman and italic type]'

[i–xii] xiii [xiv] xv [xvi] xvii [xviii] [1–2] 3–69 [70] 71–97 [98] 99–111 [112–114] 115–135 [136] 137–161 [162] 163–205 [206] 207–220 [221–222] 223–275 [276] 277–315 [316–322]

$[1]^{10}$ $[2–21]^{8}$

The statement of limitation on p. vi reads: '[decorated rule] | [swash *T*'s and *N*'s] *THIS WILDERNESS EDITION* | OF THE | PLAYS OF EUGENE O'NEILL | printed from type now destroyed, is limited | to seven hundred and seventy sets | of which twenty are for presentation | This is number | [decorated rule]'.

The colophon on p. 218 reads: '[decorated rule] | [swash *T* and K] *THIS BOOK* | the second of twelve volumes designed by Elmer Adler | set in an eighteenth-century type face | based on the castings made by John Baskerville | is printed on a specially watermarked paper | at the press of the publisher | in the city of New York | in the month of November | MCM XXX IV | [publisher's device]'.

Note: The watermark is: 'CSS | [classical tragedy mask]'.

MBE appears on pp. 1–316.

On p. xiii, in a note written by EO's Random House editor, the following statement is made about *MBE:* '[display F]OR MANY YEARS *the idea of using one of the old legend plots | of Greek tragedy as a basis for a modern psychological drama | had occurred to me. Would it be possible to achieve a modern | psychological approximation of the Greek sense of fate which would | seem credible to a present-day audience and at the same time prove | emotionally affecting? The Electra story, with its complex human in-|terrelationships and its chain of fated crime and retribution, seemed | best suited in its scope and in its implications to this purpose. Certain | departures from the old Greek plots were made to add to its modern | imaginative possibilities. For example, I wanted an ending for Electra | worthy of her character. The choice of the Civil War as the background | for this drama of murderous family love and hate was made because it | lent distance and perspective to what is really an essentially modern | psychological drama. By the title, "Mourning Becomes Electra," I | sought to convey that mourning befits Electra; it becomes Electra to | mourn; it is her fate; black is becoming to her and it is the color that | becomes her destiny. The actual writing of "Mourning Becomes Elec-|tra" was begun in France in 1929 and was completed in the Canary | Islands in 1931. It was produced by the Theatre Guild on October 26, | 1931, with Alice Brady, Alla Nazimova and Earle Larimore in the | leading rôles. | "Mourning Becomes Electra" has been produced in several Euro-|pean countries.'*

Publication: 770 copies published 30 November 1934.

Locations: JM^c^A (#456); LC (presentation); MJB (#592 boxed); ScU (#749); Yale (presentation).

A 32 MOURNING BECOMES ELECTRA
American fourth book publication (1941)

A 32-IV-1.a
The Plays of Eugene O'Neill. New York: Random House, [1941]. Three volumes.

On copyright page: 'FIRST PRINTING'.

MBE appears in volume two, pp. 1–179. See A 16-V-1.a, *Gold.*

REPRINTINGS

A 32-IV-1.b
New York: Random House, [1941].

On copyright page: 'SECOND PRINTING'.

A 32-IV-1.c
New York: Random House, [1951].

A 32-IV-1.d
New York: Random House, [1954–55].

A 32 MOURNING BECOMES ELECTRA
American fifth book publication (1967)

A 32-V-1
Selected Plays of Eugene O'Neill. New York: Random House, [1967].

On copyright page: 'First Printing'.

MBE appears on pp. 451–612. See A 15-XIII-1, *TEJ.*

A 32 MOURNING BECOMES ELECTRA
English first book publication (1932)

A 32-EI-1.a
MOURNING BECOMES ELECTRA
English first edition, first printing

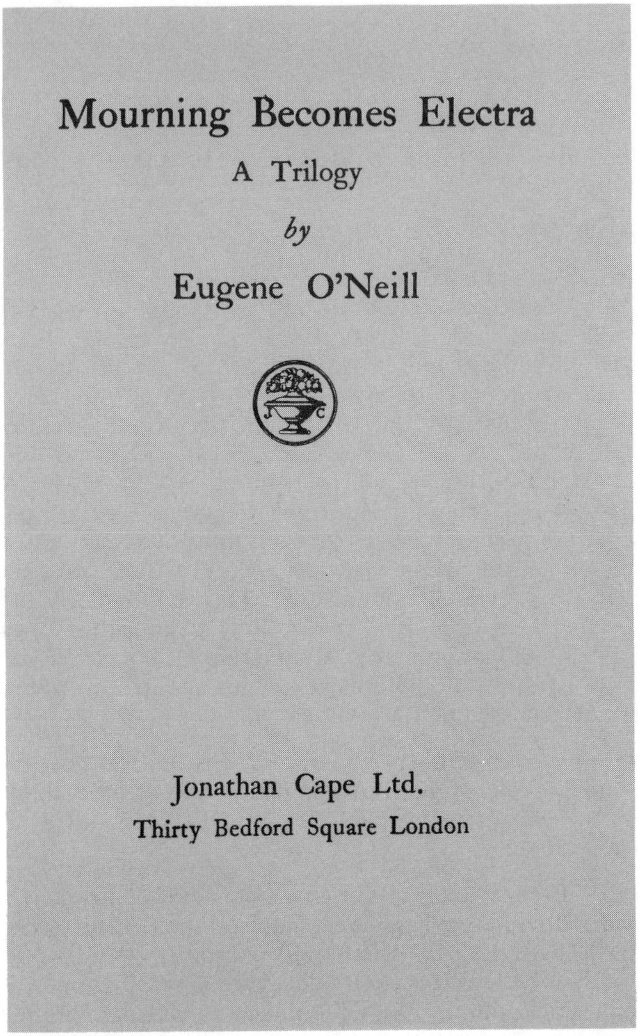
Mourning Becomes Electra
A Trilogy
by
Eugene O'Neill
Jonathan Cape Ltd.
Thirty Bedford Square London

A 32-EI-1.a: $7\frac{1}{2}'' \times 4\frac{13}{16}''$

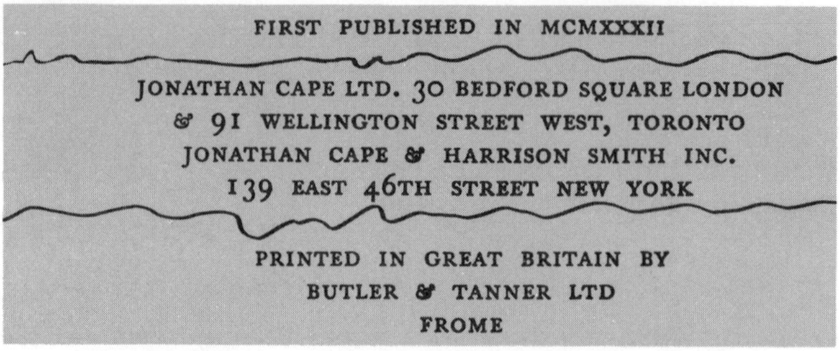
FIRST PUBLISHED IN MCMXXXII

JONATHAN CAPE LTD. 30 BEDFORD SQUARE LONDON
& 91 WELLINGTON STREET WEST, TORONTO
JONATHAN CAPE & HARRISON SMITH INC.
139 EAST 46TH STREET NEW YORK

PRINTED IN GREAT BRITAIN BY
BUTLER & TANNER LTD
FROME

[1–5] 6–7 [8] 9–10 [11–12] 13–108 [109–110] 111–203 [204–206] 207–288

$[A]^8$ B–I^8 K–S^8

Contents: p. 1: half title; p. 2: card page; p. 3: title; p. 4: copyright; p. 5: dedication; p. 6: twelve-line statement giving translation and production rights notice; p. 7: 'Contents'; p. 8: blank; pp. 9–10: 'General Scene of the Trilogy'; p. 11: 'Homecoming | A Play in Four Acts | Part One of the Trilogy | Mourning Becomes Electra'; p. 12: blank; p. 13: 'Characters | [eleven lines of roman and italic type]'; p. 14: act-scene synopsis; pp. 15–108: text, headed 'ACT ONE'; p. 109: 'The Hunted | A Play in Five Acts | Part Two of the Trilogy | Mourning Becomes Electra'; p. 110: blank; p. 111: 'Characters | [thirteen lines of roman and italic type]'; p. 112: act-scene synopsis; pp. 113–203: text, headed 'ACT ONE'; p. 204: blank; p. 205: 'The Haunted | A Play in Four Acts | Part Three of the Trilogy | Mourning Becomes Electra'; p. 206: blank; p. 207: 'Characters | [nine lines of roman and italic type]'; p. 208: act-scene synopsis; pp. 209–288: text, headed 'ACT ONE | SCENE ONE'.

Typography and paper: $3\frac{1}{2}''$ × $5\frac{3}{16}''$ ($5\frac{5}{8}''$); twenty-seven to thirty-one lines per page. Running heads: rectos, individual play titles in full caps; versos, 'MOURNING BECOMES ELECTRA'. White wove paper.

Binding: Blue V cloth (fine linen-like grain). Front: '[goldstamped EO signature]'. Spine: '[goldstamped] [line of decorations] | EUGENE | O'NEILL | [decoration] | MOURNING | BECOMES | ELECTRA | JONATHAN | CAPE | [line of decorations]'. Back: blindstamped publisher's device. White endpapers of heavier stock than text paper. All edges trimmed.

Dust jacket: Off-white background. Front: '[green border of sea motif with porpoises riding crest of waves] | [black, illustration of EO in profile by SLH] | EUGENE O'NEILL | [green star] | [black] MOURNING BECOMES | ELECTRA | A Trilogy | *Homecoming* [star] *The Hunted* [star] *The Haunted* | [green star] | [green border of wave motif]'. Spine: '[green border of sea motif with porpoises riding crest of waves] | [black] EUGENE | O'NEILL | [green star] | [black] MOURNING | BECOMES | ELECTRA | [green star] | [green publisher's device] | [black] JONATHAN CAPE | [green border of wave motif]'. Back: list of nine EO volumes (beginning with *TEJ* and ending with *LL*) published by Cape. Front flap: blurb for *MBE*, reference to list on back, and at bottom: '*7s. 6d. net*'. Back flap blank.

Publication: Unknown number of copies published in 1932. 7s. 6d.

Locations: BM (deposit-stamp 3 March 1932); ScU (dj); Yale.

REPRINTING

A 32-EI-1.b
London: Jonathan Cape, [1937]. Nobel Prize Edition. (Not a new edition.)

A 32 MOURNING BECOMES ELECTRA
American special publication (n.d.)

A 32-S-1
MOURNING BECOMES ELECTRA BROADSIDE

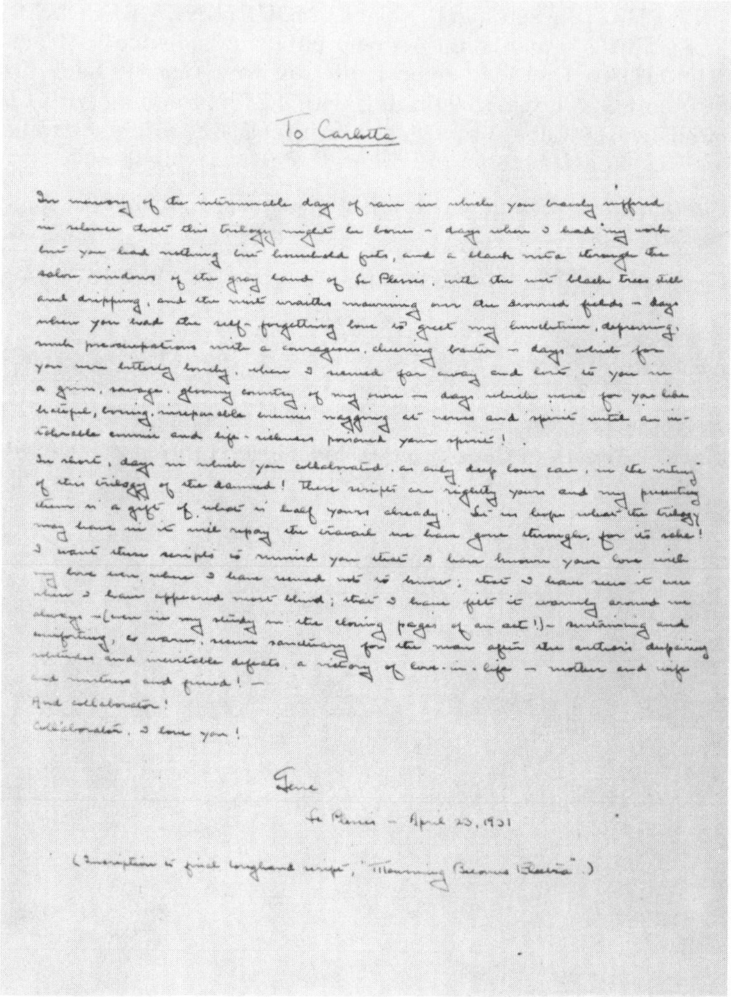

To Carlotta

In memory of the interminable days of rain in which you bravely suffered in silence that this trilogy might be born - days when I had my work but you had nothing but household fits, and a black vista through the salon windows of the gray band of Le Plessis, with the wet black trees still and dripping, and the mist wraiths mourning over the drowned fields - days when you had the self-forgetting love to greet my lunchtime, depressing, mute preoccupations with a courageous, cheering banter - days which for you were bitterly lonely, when I seemed far away and lost to you in a grim, savage, gloomy country of my own - days which were for you like hateful, boring, inseparable enemies nagging at nerves and spirit until an intolerable ennui and life-sickness poisoned your spirit!

In short, days in which you collaborated, as only deep love can, in the writing of this trilogy of the damned! These scripts are rightly yours and my presenting them is a gift of what is half yours already. But we hope what the trilogy may have in it will repay the travail we have gone through for its sake! I want these scripts to remind you that I have known your love with my love even when I have seemed not to know; that I have seen it even when I have appeared most blind; that I have felt it warmly around me always - (even in my study in the closing pages of an act!) - sustaining and comforting, a warm, secure sanctuary for the man after the author's despairing solitudes and inevitable defeats, a victory of love-in-life - mother and wife and mistress and friend! -

And collaborator!

Collaborator, I love you!

Gene

Le Plessis - April 23, 1931

(Inscription in first longhand script, "Mourning Becomes Electra.")

A 32-S-1: 11″ × 7″

Broadside facsimile of EO's inscription to CMO on the final holograph manuscript of *MBE*. Printed on one side only.

Statement of limitation is printed on separate sheet (4″ × 4″) of white, laid paper with vertical chain marks 1¾″ apart. The statement reads: '*Fifty copies of Eugene O'Neill's in-|scription to the final longhand manu-|script of* MOURNING BECOMES ELECTRA | *have been reproduced in facsimile.* | THE ACCOMPANYING REPRODUCTION | IS NUMBER | [four rules]'.

Location: Yale (#17, presentation copy to Prof. G. P. Baker from CMO, and #47, presentation copy to Dr. Horwitz from CMO).

A 33 AH, WILDERNESS!
American first book publication (1933)

A 33-I-1.a
AH, WILDERNESS!
American first edition, trade printing

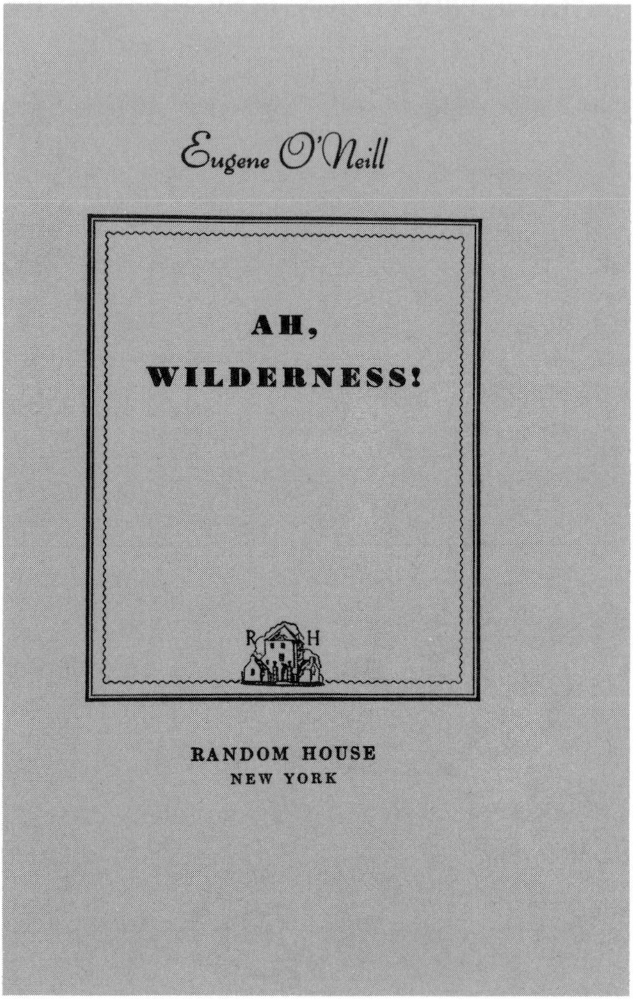

Eugene O'Neill

AH, WILDERNESS!

RANDOM HOUSE
NEW YORK

A 33-I-1.a: frame and publisher's device in blue; $8\frac{1}{16}'' \times 5\frac{3}{8}''$

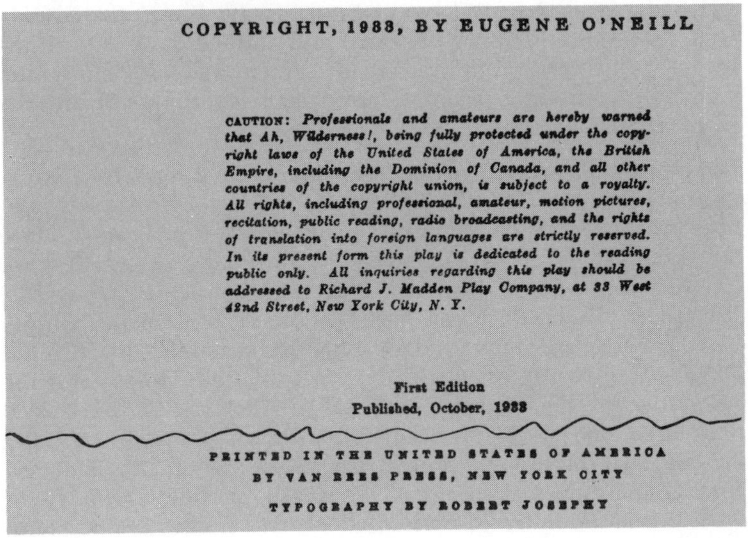
COPYRIGHT, 1933, BY EUGENE O'NEILL

CAUTION: *Professionals and amateurs are hereby warned that Ah, Wilderness!, being fully protected under the copyright laws of the United States of America, the British Empire, including the Dominion of Canada, and all other countries of the copyright union, is subject to a royalty. All rights, including professional, amateur, motion pictures, recitation, public reading, radio broadcasting, and the rights of translation into foreign languages are strictly reserved. In its present form this play is dedicated to the reading public only. All inquiries regarding this play should be addressed to Richard J. Madden Play Company, at 33 West 42nd Street, New York City, N. Y.*

First Edition
Published, October, 1933

PRINTED IN THE UNITED STATES OF AMERICA
BY VAN REES PRESS, NEW YORK CITY
TYPOGRAPHY BY ROBERT JOSEPHY

[1–14] 15–44 [45–46] 47–77 [78–80] 81–112 [113–114] 115–159 [160]

$[1–10]^8$

Contents: p. 1: half title; p. 2: blank; p. 3: title; p. 4: copyright; p. 5: 'TO GEORGE JEAN NATHAN | *who also, once upon a time, in peg-top trousers* | *went the pace that kills along the road to ruin*'; p. 6: blank; p. 7: second half title; p. 8: blank; p. 9: '*CHARACTERS* | [fifteen lines of roman and italic type]'; p. 10: blank; p. 11: act-scene synopsis; p. 12: blank; p. 13: '*ACT ONE*'; p. 14: blank; pp. 15–44: text, headed 'AH, WILDERNESS! | *ACT ONE*'; p. 45: '*ACT TWO*'; p. 46: blank; pp. 47–77: text, headed '*ACT TWO*'; p. 78: blank; p. 79: '*ACT THREE*'; p. 80: blank; pp. 81–112: text, headed '*ACT THREE—SCENE ONE*'; p. 113: '*ACT FOUR*'; p. 114: blank; pp. 115–159: text, headed '*ACT FOUR—SCENE ONE*'; p. 160: blank.

Typography and paper: 10 point on 14, Scotch. $3^{13}/_{16}'' \times 5^{13}/_{16}''$ ($6^{1}/_{16}''$); twenty-nine or thirty lines per page. Running heads: rectos and versos, 'AH, WILDERNESS!'. White laid paper with vertical chain marks $1^{11}/_{16}''$ apart, with the publisher's device as watermark.

Binding: Dark blue S cloth (fine, uniform, diagonal grain) with beveled edges. Front: '[goldstamped EO signature]'. Spine: '[goldstamped wavy line] | *EUGENE* | *O'NEILL* | [wavy line] |

AH, | WILDER-|NESS! | [wavy line] | [wavy line] | *RANDOM* | *HOUSE*'. Top edge only trimmed and stained dark blue. Illustrated endpapers front and rear: (green and grayish white) steamship on rolling sea silhouetted against setting sun with the word 'O'NEILL' above.

Dust jacket: Front: '[white lettering against dark blue background] *Eugene O'Neill* | [illustration of two figures near rowboat against black background] | [black lettering against white background] AH, | WILDERNESS! | *A Comedy of Recollection* | [white lettering against dark blue background] *Published by* RANDOM HOUSE, *New York* [publisher's device]'. Spine: '[white lettering against dark blue background] *EUGENE* | *O'NEILL* | [two lines vertically, top to bottom, black lettering against white background] AH, | WILDERNESS! | [horizontal dark blue rule] | [black publisher's device] | [white lettering against dark blue background] *RANDOM* | *HOUSE*'. Back: ad for EO and eleven volumes of his works, including *Nine Plays* with introduction by Joseph Wood Krutch. Front flap: blurb for *AW;* back flap: ad for Random House.

Publication: Unknown number of copies published 2 October 1933. $2.50.

Locations: JM^{c}A (dj); LC (deposit-stamp 5 October 1933); Lilly (three, djs); Yale.

A 33 AH, WILDERNESS!
American limited publication (1933)

A 33-I-1.b
AH, WILDERNESS!
American first edition, limited printing

Eugene O'Neill

AH,
WILDERNESS!

RANDOM HOUSE
NEW YORK

A 33-I-1.b: frame and publisher's device in blue; $9\frac{9}{16}'' \times 6\frac{5}{8}''$

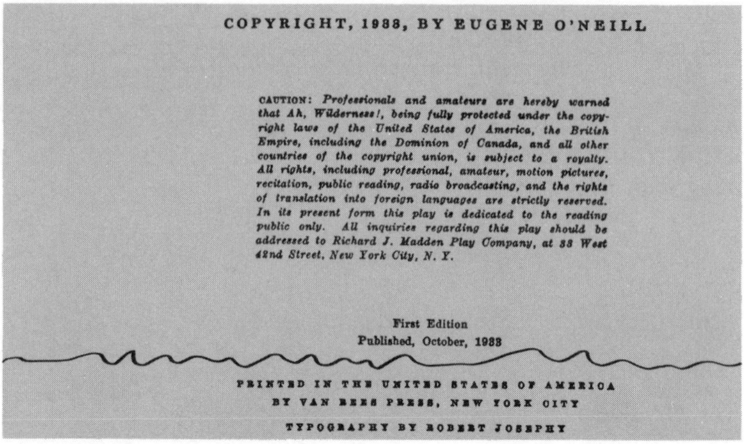
COPYRIGHT, 1933, BY EUGENE O'NEILL

CAUTION: *Professionals and amateurs are hereby warned that Ah, Wilderness!, being fully protected under the copyright laws of the United States of America, the British Empire, including the Dominion of Canada, and all other countries of the copyright union, is subject to a royalty. All rights, including professional, amateur, motion pictures, recitation, public reading, radio broadcasting, and the rights of translation into foreign languages are strictly reserved. In its present form this play is dedicated to the reading public only. All inquiries regarding this play should be addressed to Richard J. Madden Play Company, at 33 West 42nd Street, New York City, N. Y.*

First Edition
Published, October, 1933

PRINTED IN THE UNITED STATES OF AMERICA
BY VAN REES PRESS, NEW YORK CITY
TYPOGRAPHY BY ROBERT JOSEPHY

[1–14] 15–44 [45–46] 47–77 [78–80] 81–112 [113–114] 115–159 [160]

Contents: p. 1: half title; p. 2: statement of limitation: 'THIS EDITION OF *Ah, Wilderness!* | IS LIMITED TO THREE HUNDRED AND TWENTY-FIVE COPIES | PRINTED ON ALL-RAG PAPER AND SIGNED BY THE AUTHOR, | OF WHICH THIS IS NUMBER'; p. 3: title; p. 4: copyright; p. 5: 'TO GEORGE JEAN NATHAN | *who also, once upon a time, in peg-top trousers* | *went the pace that kills along the road to ruin*'; p. 6: blank; p. 7: second half title; p. 8: blank; p. 9: list of characters; p. 10: blank; p. 11: act-scene synopsis; p. 12: blank; p. 13: '*ACT ONE*'; p. 14: blank; pp. 15–44: text, headed 'AH, WILDERNESS! | *ACT ONE*'; p. 45: *'ACT TWO';* p. 46: blank; pp. 47–77: text, headed *'ACT TWO';* p. 78: blank; p. 79: *'ACT THREE';* p. 80: blank; pp. 81–112: text, headed *'ACT THREE—SCENE ONE';* p. 113: *'ACT FOUR';* p. 114: blank; pp. 115–159: text, headed *'ACT FOUR—SCENE ONE';* p. 160: blank.

Typography and paper: 10 point on 14, Scotch. $3^{13}/_{16}'' \times 5^{13}/_{16}''$ ($6^{1}/_{16}''$); twenty-nine or thirty lines per page. Running heads: rectos and versos, 'AH, WILDERNESS!'. White laid paper with vertical chain marks $1^{1}/_{8}''$ apart with '[gothic] Vidalon' and heraldic crest as watermarks.

Binding: Navy blue leather. Spine: pasted-on leather label ($2^{1}/_{8}'' \times {}^{7}/_{8}''$), '[gold rule] | [gold lettering against light blue background] *EUGENE* | *O'NEILL* | [gold rule] | [gold lettering against red background] AH, | WILDER-|NESS! | [gold rule]'. Endpapers same as text paper. Top edge only trimmed and gilded.

Dust jacket: Not seen.

Slipcase: Silvery gray paper-covered boards in batik pattern. No labels.

Publication: 325 copies published 2 October 1933.

Locations: JM^{c}A (#264); Lilly (#115 boxed); PSt (#182 boxed) ScU (#301 boxed); Yale (#11 boxed, #12 boxed, #19 boxed, and #21).

REPRINTINGS

First edition, trade printing

A 33-I-1.c
New York: Random House, [October 1933]. Second printing before publication.

A 33-I-1.d
New York: Random House, [October 1933].

A 33 AH, WILDERNESS!
American second book publication (1934)

A 33-II-1
The Plays of Eugene O'Neill. New York: Scribners, [1934–35]. Twelve volumes. Wilderness Edition.

Limited to 770 numbered copies.

AW appears in volume three, pp. 55–268. See A 15-IX-1, *TEJ*.

On pp. xi and xii, in a note written by EO's Random House editor, the following statement is made about *AW*: '*Written in my home at Sea Island, Georgia, in the fall of 1932, this | Comedy of Recollection was produced in New York by the Theatre | Guild, with George M. Cohan in the rôle of Nat Miller, on October 2, | 1933. My purpose was to write a play true to the spirit of the American | large small-town at the turn of the century. Its quality depended upon | atmosphere, sentiment, an exact evocation of the mood of the dead past. | To me, the America which was (and is) the real America found its | unique expression in such middle-class families as the Millers, among | whom so many of my own generation passed from adolescence into man-|hood. | In May of 1934 Will Rogers made his début in*

San Francisco in the | part of Nat Miller. The tour of the company which he headed has been immensely successful on the Pacific Coast.'

Publication: 770 copies published 28 December 1934.

A 33 AH, WILDERNESS!
American third book publication (1936?)

A 33-III-1
Ah, Wilderness! and Two Other Plays. New York: Modern Library, [1936?]. ML #342.

Includes *AGCGW* and *BTH*. *AW* appears on pp. 1–141.

A 33 AH, WILDERNESS!
American fourth book publication (1941)

A 33-IV-1.a
The Plays of Eugene O'Neill. New York: Random House, [1941]. Three volumes.

On copyright page: 'FIRST PRINTING'.

AW appears in volume two, pp. 181–298. See A 16-V-1.a, *Gold*.

REPRINTINGS

A 33-IV-1.b
New York: Random House, [1941].

On copyright page: 'SECOND PRINTING'.

A 33-IV-1.c
New York: Random House, [1951].

A 33-IV-1.d
New York: Random House, [1954–55].

A 33 AH, WILDERNESS!
English first book publication (1934)

A 33-EI-1.a
AH, WILDERNESS! AND DAYS WITHOUT END
English first edition, first printing

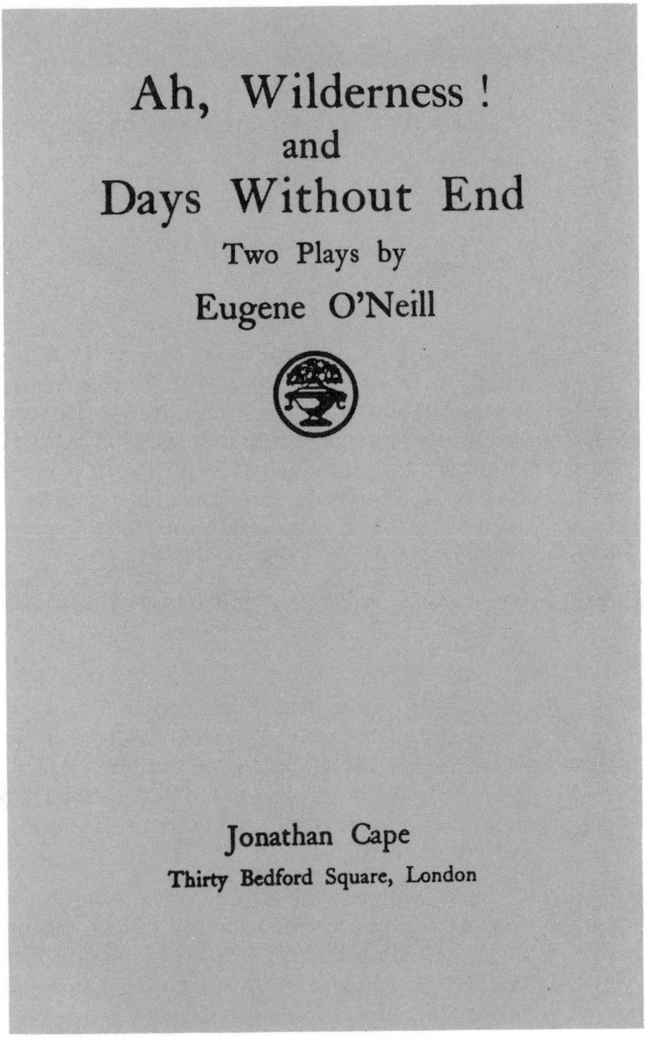
Ah, Wilderness!
and
Days Without End
Two Plays by
Eugene O'Neill

Jonathan Cape
Thirty Bedford Square, London

A 33-EI-1.a: $7\frac{7}{16}'' \times 4\frac{11}{16}''$

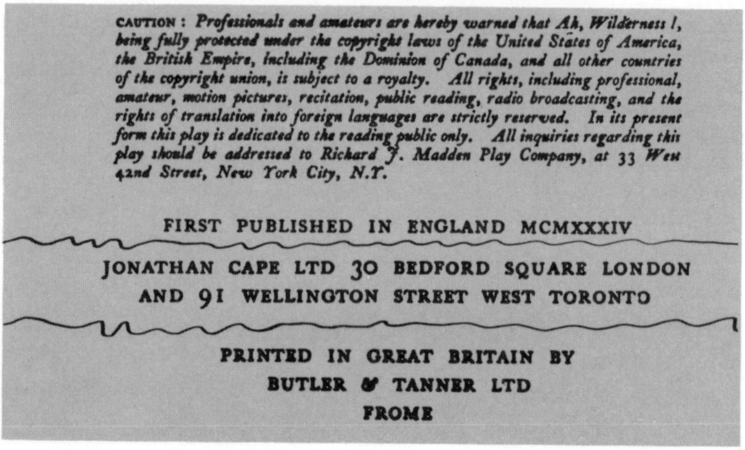

CAUTION: *Professionals and amateurs are hereby warned that Ah, Wilderness!, being fully protected under the copyright laws of the United States of America, the British Empire, including the Dominion of Canada, and all other countries of the copyright union, is subject to a royalty. All rights, including professional, amateur, motion pictures, recitation, public reading, radio broadcasting, and the rights of translation into foreign languages are strictly reserved. In its present form this play is dedicated to the reading public only. All inquiries regarding this play should be addressed to Richard J. Madden Play Company, at 33 West 42nd Street, New York City, N.Y.*

FIRST PUBLISHED IN ENGLAND MCMXXXIV

JONATHAN CAPE LTD 30 BEDFORD SQUARE LONDON
AND 91 WELLINGTON STREET WEST TORONTO

PRINTED IN GREAT BRITAIN BY
BUTLER & TANNER LTD
FROME

[1–8] 9–164 [1–4] 5–108

[A]^{8} B–I^{8} K–R^{8}

Contents: p. 1: half title; p. 2: card page; p. 3: title; p. 4: copyright; p. 5: dedication; p. 6: blank; p. 7: 'Ah, Wilderness!'; p. 8: blank; p. 9: act-scene synopsis; p. 10: 'Characters | [fifteen lines of roman and italic type]'; pp. 11–164: text, headed 'ACT ONE'; p. 1: 'Days Without End | A Modern Miracle Play'; p. 2: blank; p. 3: dedication; p. 4: blank; p. 5: act-scene synopsis; p. 6: 'Characters | [ten lines of roman and italic type]'; pp. 7–108: text, headed 'ACT ONE | PLOT FOR A NOVEL'.

Type and paper: $3\frac{13}{16}'' \times 5\frac{5}{8}''$ ($5\frac{13}{16}''$); thirty-one lines per page. Running heads: rectos and versos, individual play titles. Wove paper.

Binding: Blue V cloth (fine linen-like grain). Front: '[goldstamped EO signature]'. Spine: '[goldstamped border of decorations] | EUGENE | O'NEILL | [decoration] | AH, | WILDERNESS! | JONATHAN CAPE | [border of decorations]'. Back: '[blindstamped publisher's device]'. Endpapers of same stock as text paper. All edges trimmed.

Dust jacket: Yellow background. Front: '[green border of sea motif with porpoises riding crest of waves] | [black woodcut of EO profile by SLH] | EUGENE O'NEILL | [green star] | [black] AH, WILDERNESS! | *and Days Without End* | [green star] | [border of sea motif]'. Spine: '[green border of sea motif with porpoises riding the crest of waves] | [black] EUGENE |

O'NEILL | [green star] | [black] AH, | WILDERNESS! | [green star] | [publisher's device] | [black] JONATHAN CAPE | [green border of sea motif]'. Back lists ten EO titles published by Cape, beginning with *TEJ* and ending with *MBE*. Front flap has blurb for *AW* and *DWE;* back flap blank.

Note: A later dust jacket has on the front: '[within red horizontal oval] NOBEL PRIZE EDITION | 5s. net'; and on the spine: '[within red vertical oval] NOBEL | PRIZE | EDITION | 5s. | net'.

Publication: Unknown number of copies published in 1934.

Locations: BM (deposit-stamp 14 August 1934); JM^{c}A (Nobel Prize dj); LC (deposit-stamp 22 November 1935); Yale (both djs).

REPRINTINGS

A 33-EI-1.b
London: Jonathan Cape, [1937]. Nobel Prize Edition. [Not a new edition.]

A 33-EI-1.c
London: Jonathan Cape, [1955].

A 34 DAYS WITHOUT END
American first book publication (1934)

A 34–I-1.a
DAYS WITHOUT END
American first edition, trade printing

Eugene O'Neill

DAYS WITHOUT END

RANDOM HOUSE
NEW YORK

A 34-I-1.a: frame and publisher's device in blue; $8\frac{1}{16}'' \times 5\frac{7}{16}''$

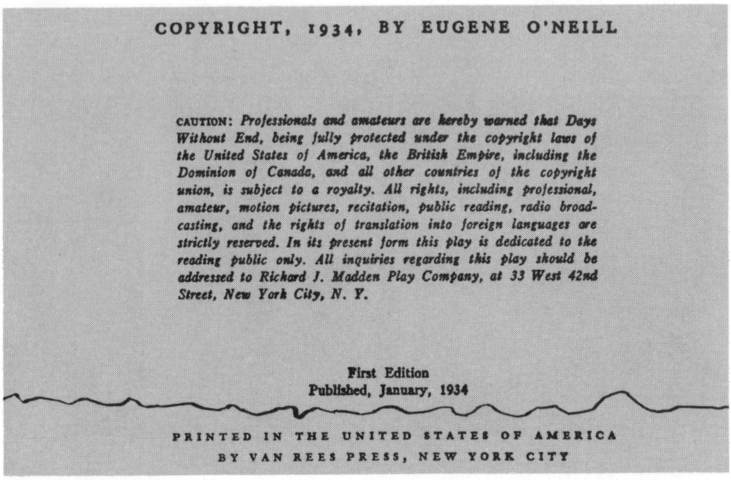

COPYRIGHT, 1934, BY EUGENE O'NEILL

CAUTION: *Professionals and amateurs are hereby warned that Days Without End, being fully protected under the copyright laws of the United States of America, the British Empire, including the Dominion of Canada, and all other countries of the copyright union, is subject to a royalty. All rights, including professional, amateur, motion pictures, recitation, public reading, radio broadcasting, and the rights of translation into foreign languages are strictly reserved. In its present form this play is dedicated to the reading public only. All inquiries regarding this play should be addressed to Richard J. Madden Play Company, at 33 West 42nd Street, New York City, N. Y.*

First Edition
Published, January, 1934

PRINTED IN THE UNITED STATES OF AMERICA
BY VAN REES PRESS, NEW YORK CITY

[1–14] 15–53 [54–56] 57–87 [88–90] 91–127 [128–130] 131–157 [158–160]

[1–10]^{8}

Contents: p. 1: half title; p. 2: blank; p. 3: title; p. 4: copyright; p. 5: '*To* | CARLOTTA'; p. 6: blank; p. 7: second half title; p. 8: blank; p. 9: 'CHARACTERS | [ten lines of roman and italic type]'; p. 10: blank; p. 11: act-scene synopsis; p. 12: blank; p. 13: 'ACT ONE | PLOT FOR A NOVEL'; p. 14: blank; pp. 15–53: text, headed 'DAYS WITHOUT END | ACT ONE'; p. 54: blank; p. 55: 'ACT TWO | PLOT FOR A NOVEL | *(Continued)*'; p. 56: blank; pp. 57–87: text, headed 'ACT TWO'; p. 88: blank; p. 89: 'ACT THREE | PLOT FOR A NOVEL | *(Continued)*'; p. 90: blank; pp. 91–127: text, headed 'ACT THREE | SCENE I'; p. 128: blank; p. 129: 'ACT FOUR | THE END OF THE END'; p. 130: blank; pp. 131–157: text, headed 'ACT FOUR | SCENE I; pp. 158–160: blank.

Typography and paper: 11 point on 13, Granjon. $3\frac{5}{8}'' \times 5\frac{7}{16}''$ ($5\frac{7}{8}''$); twenty-six to twenty-nine lines per page. Running heads: rectos and versos, 'DAYS WITHOUT END'. Laid paper with vertical chains $1\frac{11}{16}''$ apart, with the publisher's device as watermark.

Binding: Dark blue S cloth (fine, uniform, diagonal grain) with beveled edges. Front: '[goldstamped EO signature]'. Spine: '[goldstamped wavy line] | *EUGENE* | *O'NEILL* | [wavy line] | DAYS | WITHOUT | END | [wavy line] | [wavy line] | *RANDOM*

Dust jackets for A 34-I-1.a and A 33-I-1.a

HOUSE'. Illustrated endpapers front and rear: (green and grayish white) steamship on rolling sea silhouetted against setting sun with the word 'O'NEILL' above. Top edge only trimmed and stained dark blue.

Dust jacket: (designed by Lee Simonson) Front: '[white lettering against red background] *Eugene O'Neill* | [illustration of figures kneeling before crucifix from original drawing by Lee Simonson] | [black lettering against white background] DAYS | WITHOUT END | *A Modern Miracle Play* | [white lettering against red background] *Published by* RANDOM HOUSE, *New York* [publisher's device]'. Spine: '[white lettering against red background] *EUGENE* | *O'NEILL* | [two lines, vertically, top to bottom, black lettering against white background] DAYS | WITHOUT END | [horizontal red line] | [black publisher's device against white background] | [white lettering against red background] *RANDOM* | *HOUSE*'. Back: blurb on EO and twelve volumes of his plays, including *Nine Plays* with an introduction by Joseph Wood Krutch. Front flap: blurb for *DWE;* back flap: ad for Random House.

Publication: Unknown number of copies published 17 January 1934.

Locations: JM^c^A (dj); LC (deposit-stamp 27 January 1934); Lilly (three, djs); PSt; Yale.

A 34 DAYS WITHOUT END
American limited publication (1934)

A 34-I-1.b
DAYS WITHOUT END
American first edition, limited printing

Eugene O'Neill

DAYS
WITHOUT
END

RH

RANDOM HOUSE
NEW YORK

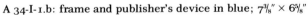

A 34-I-1.b: frame and publisher's device in blue; $7\frac{3}{8}'' \times 6\frac{5}{8}''$

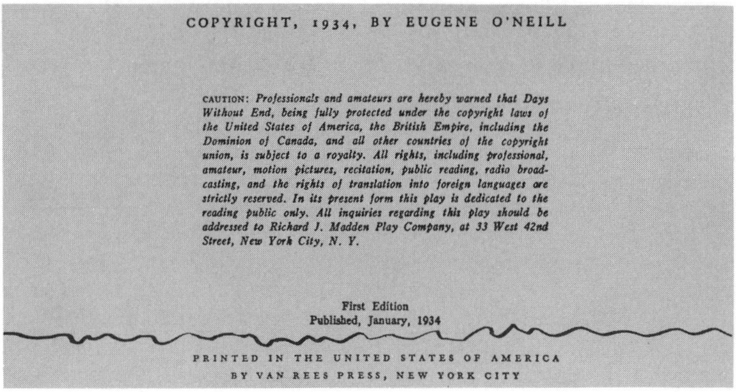

COPYRIGHT, 1934, BY EUGENE O'NEILL

CAUTION: *Professionals and amateurs are hereby warned that Days Without End, being fully protected under the copyright laws of the United States of America, the British Empire, including the Dominion of Canada, and all other countries of the copyright union, is subject to a royalty. All rights, including professional, amateur, motion pictures, recitation, public reading, radio broadcasting, and the rights of translation into foreign languages are strictly reserved. In its present form this play is dedicated to the reading public only. All inquiries regarding this play should be addressed to Richard J. Madden Play Company, at 33 West 42nd Street, New York City, N. Y.*

First Edition
Published, January, 1934

PRINTED IN THE UNITED STATES OF AMERICA
BY VAN REES PRESS, NEW YORK CITY

[1–14] 15–53 [54–56] 57–87 [88–90] 91–127 [128–130] 131–157 [158–160]

[1–20]^{4}

Contents: p. 1: half title; p. 2: statement of limitation: 'THIS EDITION OF *Days Without End.* | IS LIMITED TO THREE HUNDRED AND TWENTY-FIVE | COPIES PRINTED ON ALL-RAG PAPER AND SIGNED BY | THE AUTHOR, OF WHICH THIS IS NUMBER'; p. 3: title; p. 4: copyright; p. 5: dedication; p. 6: blank; p. 7: second half title; p. 8: blank; p. 9: 'CHARACTERS | [ten lines of roman and italic type]'; p. 10: blank; p. 11: act-scene synopsis; p. 12: blank; p. 13: 'ACT ONE | PLOT FOR A NOVEL'; p. 14: blank; pp. 15–53: text, headed 'DAYS WITHOUT END | ACT ONE'; p. 54: blank; 55: 'ACT TWO | PLOT FOR A NOVEL | *(Continued)*'; p. 56: blank; pp. 57–87: text, headed 'ACT TWO'; p. 88: blank; p. 89: 'ACT THREE | PLOT FOR A NOVEL | *(Continued)*'; p. 90: blank; pp. 91–127: text, headed 'ACT THREE | SCENE I'; p. 128: blank; p. 129: 'ACT FOUR | THE END OF THE END'; p. 130: blank; pp. 131–157: text, headed 'ACT FOUR | SCENE I'; pp. 158–160: blank.

Typography and paper: 11 point on 13, Granjon. $3\frac{5}{8}'' \times 5\frac{7}{16}''$ ($5\frac{7}{8}''$); twenty-six to twenty-nine lines per page. Running heads: rectos and versos, 'DAYS WITHOUT END'. Laid paper with vertical chain marks $1\frac{1}{16}''$ apart with '[gothic] Vidalon' and heraldic crest as watermark.

Binding: Dark blue leather. Spine: pasted-on light blue and red label [$2\frac{1}{16}'' \times \frac{7}{8}''$), '[goldstamped rule] | [two lines goldstamped against light blue] *EUGENE* | *O'NEILL* | [goldstamped rule] | [three lines goldstamped against red] DAYS | WITHOUT | END | [goldstamped rule]'. White laid endpapers of same stock as text paper. Top edge only trimmed and gilded.

Dust jacket: Not seen.

Slipcase: Batik, gray, paper-covered boards. No labels, no printing.

Publication: 325 copies published 17 January 1934.

Locations: Lilly (#277); PSt (#271); ScU (#177); Yale (#239 boxed, #252 boxed, and #257).

REPRINTING
First edition, trade printing

A 34-I-1.c
New York: Random House, [March 1934].

A 34 DAYS WITHOUT END
American second book publication (1935)

A 34-II-1
The Plays of Eugene O'Neill. New York: Scribners, [1934–35]. Twelve volumes. Wilderness Edition.

Limited to 770 numbered copies.

DWE appears in volume nine, pp. 1–138. See A 16-IV-1, *Gold.*

On p. xi, in a note written by EO's Random House editor, the following statement is made about *DWE:* '[display P]RIMARILY *a psychological study, this modern miracle play, | written at my home in Sea Island, Georgia, in 1932 and 1933, | reveals a man's search for truth amid the conflicting doctrines of | the modern world and his return to his old religious faith. "Days With-|out End" was produced by the Theatre Guild, under the direction of | Philip Moeller, on January 8, 1934, at the Henry Miller Theatre, | with Earle Larimore, Stanley Ridges, Robert Lorraine, Selena Royle | and Ilka Chase in the leading parts. The Abbey Theatre in Dublin, | directed by Lennox Robinson, has recently produced "Days Without | End" with great success. It is soon to be produced in the Scandinavian | countries and in Holland and Czechoslovakia.*'

Publication: 770 copies published 22 March 1935.

A 34 DAYS WITHOUT END
American third book publication (1941)

A 34-III-1.a
The Plays of Eugene O'Neill. New York: Random House, [1941]. Three volumes.

On copyright page: 'FIRST PRINTING'.

DWE appears in volume three, pp. 491–567. See A 14-VI-1.a, *BTH.*

REPRINTINGS

A 34-III-1.b
New York: Random House, [1941].

On copyright page: 'SECOND PRINTING'.

A 34-III-1.c
New York: Random House, [1951].

A 34-III-1.d
New York: Random House, [1954–55].

A 34 DAYS WITHOUT END
English first book publication (1934)

A 34-EI-1.a
Ah, Wilderness! and Days Without End. London: Jonathan Cape, 1934.

DWE appears on pp. 1–108. See A 33-EI-1.a, *AW.*

REPRINTINGS

A 34-EI-1.b
London: Jonathan Cape, [1937]. Nobel Prize Edition. (Not a new edition.)

A 34-EI-1.c
London: Jonathan Cape, [1955].

A 35 THE ICEMAN COMETH
American first book publication (1946)

A 35-I-1.a
THE ICEMAN COMETH
American first edition, first printing

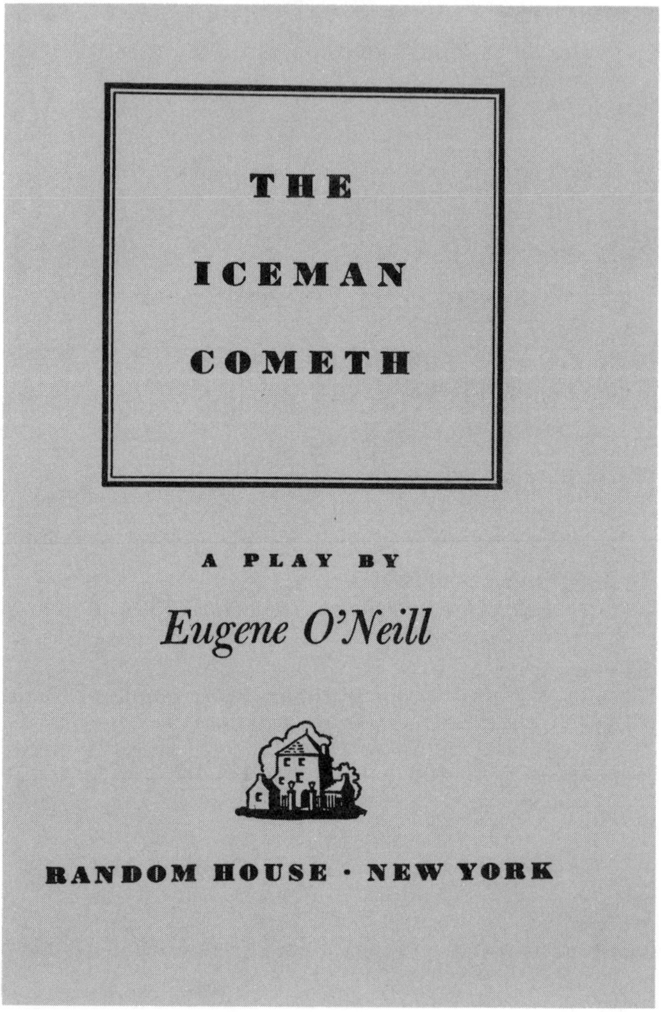
THE
ICEMAN
COMETH

A PLAY BY
Eugene O'Neill

RANDOM HOUSE · NEW YORK

A 35-I-1.a: frame and publisher's device in blue; $7\frac{15}{16}'' \times 5\frac{5}{16}''$

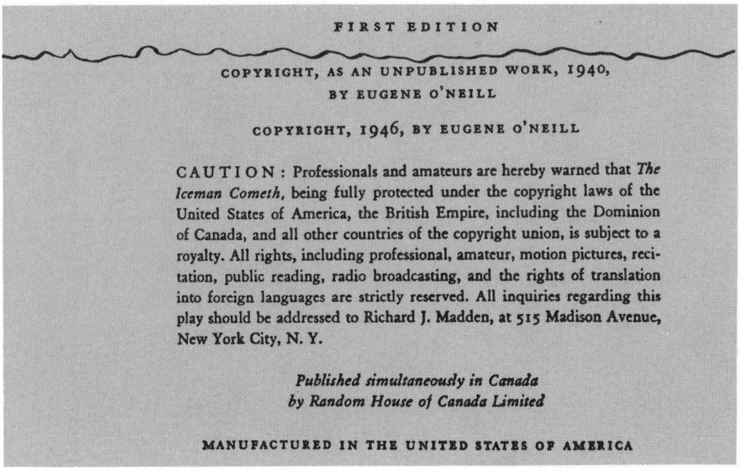

FIRST EDITION

COPYRIGHT, AS AN UNPUBLISHED WORK, 1940,
BY EUGENE O'NEILL

COPYRIGHT, 1946, BY EUGENE O'NEILL

CAUTION: Professionals and amateurs are hereby warned that *The Iceman Cometh*, being fully protected under the copyright laws of the United States of America, the British Empire, including the Dominion of Canada, and all other countries of the copyright union, is subject to a royalty. All rights, including professional, amateur, motion pictures, recitation, public reading, radio broadcasting, and the rights of translation into foreign languages are strictly reserved. All inquiries regarding this play should be addressed to Richard J. Madden, at 515 Madison Avenue, New York City, N. Y.

Published simultaneously in Canada
by Random House of Canada Limited

MANUFACTURED IN THE UNITED STATES OF AMERICA

[A–B] [i–vi] vii–viii [1–2] 3–90 [91–92] 93–151 [152–154] 155–207 [208–210] 211–260 [261–262]

[1–17]^{8}

Contents: pp. A–B: blank; p. i: half title; p. ii: blank; p. iii: title; p. iv: copyright; p. v: 'CHARACTERS | [twenty-three lines of type]'; p. vi: blank; pp. vii–viii: act-scene synopsis; p. 1: 'ACT ONE'; p. 2: blank; pp. 3–90: text, headed 'THE ICEMAN COMETH | ACT ONE'; p. 91: 'ACT TWO'; p. 92: blank; pp. 93–151: text, headed 'ACT TWO'; p. 152: blank; p. 153: 'ACT THREE'; p. 154: blank; pp. 155–207: text, headed 'ACT THREE'; p. 208: blank; p. 209: 'ACT FOUR'; p. 210: blank; pp. 211–260: text, headed 'ACT FOUR'; pp. 261–262: blank.

Typography and paper: 11 point on 13, Granjon. $3\frac{5}{8}'' \times 5\frac{13}{16}''$ ($6\frac{1}{4}''$); twenty-six to thirty-two lines per page. Running heads: rectos and versos, 'THE ICEMAN COMETH'. Laid paper with vertical chains $1\frac{11}{16}''$ apart, with the Random House publisher's device as watermark.

Binding: Blue B cloth (linen-like grain). Front: '[goldstamped EO signature]'. Spine: '[all vertically top to bottom, goldstamped] EUGENE O'NEILL [goldstamped in red box with gold border] The Iceman Cometh [goldstamped] RANDOM HOUSE'. White wove endpapers. All edges trimmed; top edge stained red.

Dust jacket: Gray background. Front: '[white] THE | ICEMAN | COMETH | [wide red rule] | [white] *A New Play by* | EUGENE | O'NEILL | [publisher's device] | A RANDOM HOUSE BOOK'.

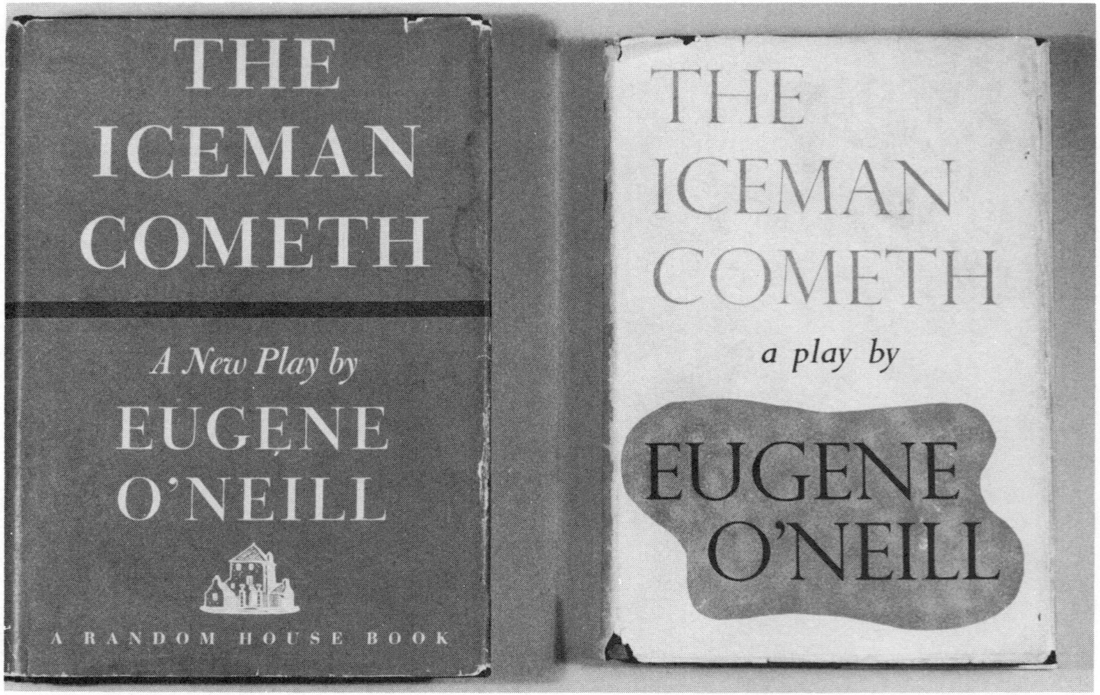

Dust jackets for A 35-I-1.a and A 35-EI-1

Spine: '[vertically top to bottom, white] The Iceman Cometh | [horizontal wide red rule] | [vertically, white] BY EUGENE O'NEILL | [horizontal publisher's device] | RANDOM | HOUSE'. Back has drawing of EO by Mai-mai Sze and blurb for Random House three-volume set of his plays. Front flap: blurb for *TIC*. Back flap: blurb for EO volumes published by Random House in the Modern Library.

Publication: Unknown number of copies published 10 October 1946. $2.75.

Locations: JM^c^A (dj); LC (deposit-stamp 4 October 1946); Lilly (two, djs and a set of page proofs); Yale.

REPRINTINGS

A 35-I-1.b
New York: Vintage Books, [1946]. V-18.

A 35-I-1.c
New York: Random House. [1957]. Modern Library paperback P 28.

A 35 THE ICEMAN COMETH
American second book publication (1951)

A 35-II-1.a
The Plays of Eugene O'Neill. New York: Random House, [1951]. Three volumes.

TIC appears in volume three, pp. 569–728. Five gatherings of sixteen leaves each were added at the end of volume three to include *TIC*, thus making an augmented printing. See A 14-VI-1.a, *BTH*.

REPRINTING

A 35-II-1.b
New York: Random House, [1954–55].

A 35 THE ICEMAN COMETH
American third book publication (1967)

A 35-III-1
Selected Plays of Eugene O'Neill. New York: Random House, [1967].

On copyright page: 'First Printing'.

TIC appears on pp. 613–758. See A 15-XIII-1, *TEJ*.

A 35 THE ICEMAN COMETH
English first book publication (1947)

A 35-EI-1
THE ICEMAN COMETH
English first edition

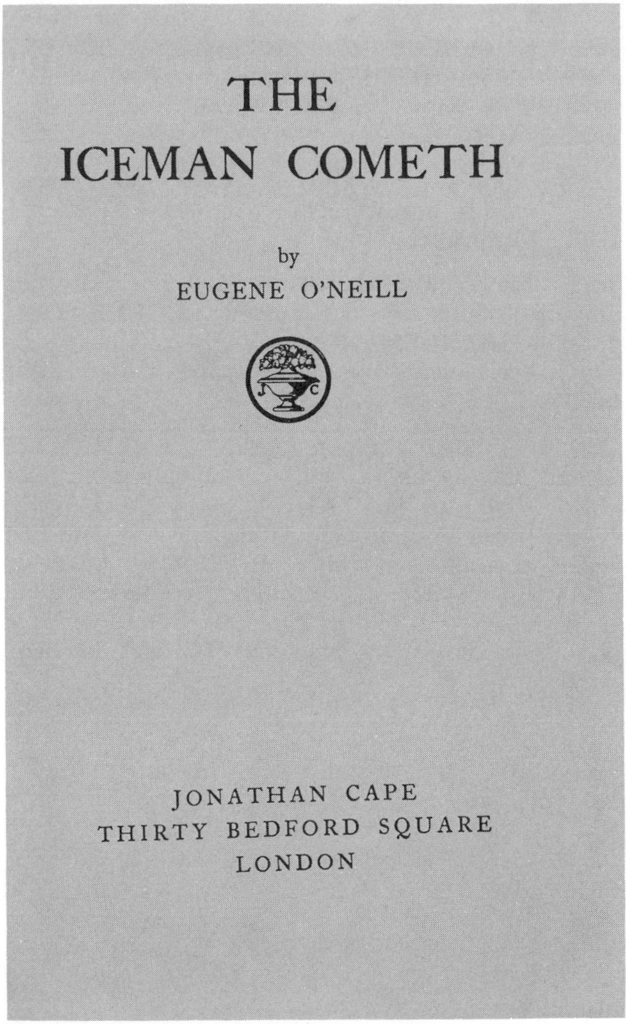
THE
ICEMAN COMETH

by
EUGENE O'NEILL

JONATHAN CAPE
THIRTY BEDFORD SQUARE
LONDON

A 35-EI-1: 7$^{7}/_{16}$" × 5"

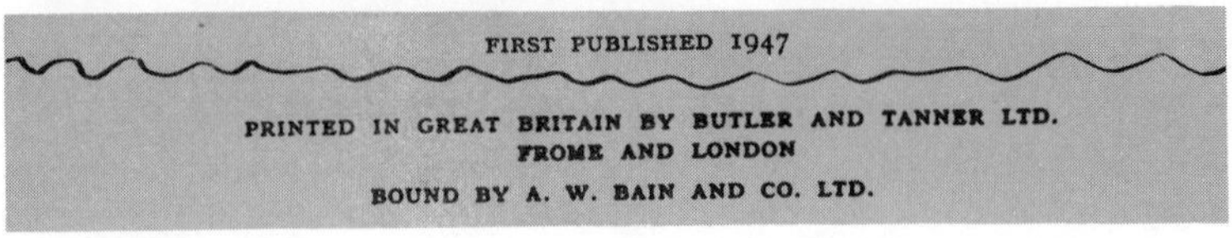
FIRST PUBLISHED 1947

PRINTED IN GREAT BRITAIN BY BUTLER AND TANNER LTD.
FROME AND LONDON

BOUND BY A. W. BAIN AND CO. LTD.

[1–4] 5 [6] 7–224

$[A]^8$ $B\text{–}I^8$ $K\text{–}O^8$

Contents: p. 1: half title; p. 2: card page; p. 3: title; p. 4: copyright; p. 5: 'CHARACTERS | [twenty-three lines of roman and italic type]'; p. 6: blank; pp. 7–8: act-scene synopsis; pp. 9–224; text, headed 'ACT ONE'.

Typography and paper: $3\frac{13}{16}'' \times 5\frac{5}{8}''$ (6″); thirty-three lines per page. Running heads: rectos and versos, 'THE ICEMAN COMETH'. Wove paper.

Binding: Blue B cloth (linen-like grain). Front: '[silverstamped EO signature]'. Spine: '[silverstamped] EUGENE | O'NEILL | [decoration | THE | ICEMAN | COMETH | [publisher's device]'. Wove endpapers of same stock as text paper. Top and right edges trimmed.

Dust jacket: White background. Front: '[blue] THE | ICEMAN | COMETH | [black] *a play by* | [black on blue patch] EUGENE | O'NEILL'. Spine: '[black] THE | [blue] ICEMAN | [black] COMETH | [three lines on blue patch] *a* | *play* | *by* | EUGENE | O'NEILL | *author of* | [blue] MOURNING | BECOMES | ELECTRA | [black] *etc.* | [blue publisher's device]'. Back lists eleven EO plays published by Cape, beginning with *TEJ* and ending with *AW*. Front flap: blurb for *TIC;* back flap blank.

Publication: Unknown number of copies published in 1947. 8s. 6d.

Locations: BM (deposit-stamp 20 November 1947); JM^{c}A (dj); Yale (dj).

A 36 "ABORTION"
American first book publication (1950)

A 36-I-1.a
LOST PLAYS OF EUGENE O'NEILL
American first edition, first printing

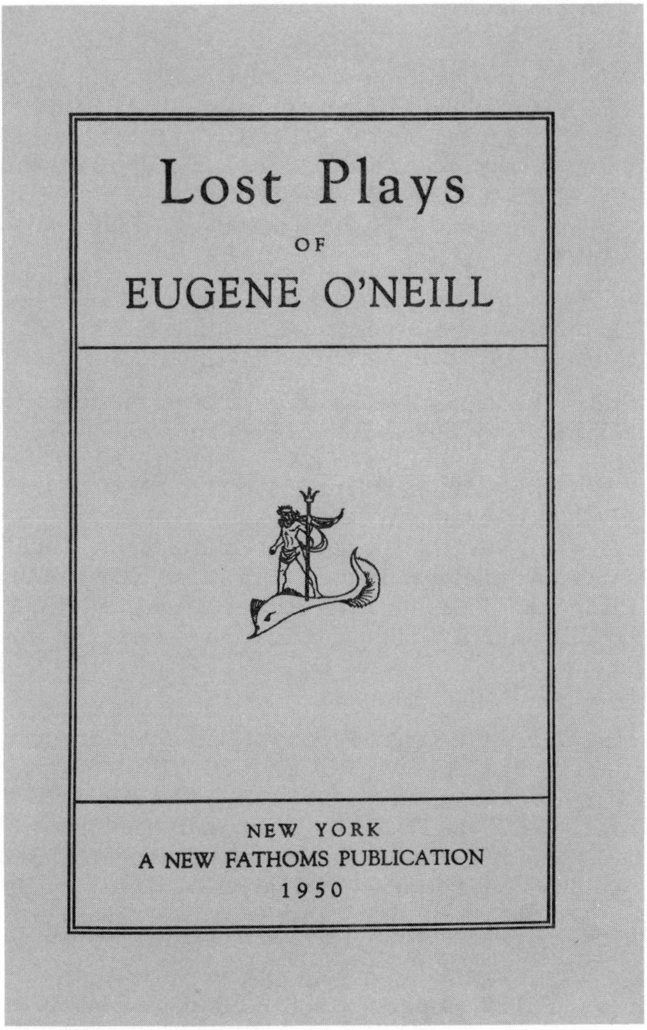
Lost Plays
OF
EUGENE O'NEILL

NEW YORK
A NEW FATHOMS PUBLICATION
1950

A 36-I-1.a: $8\frac{1}{4}'' \times 5\frac{1}{2}''$

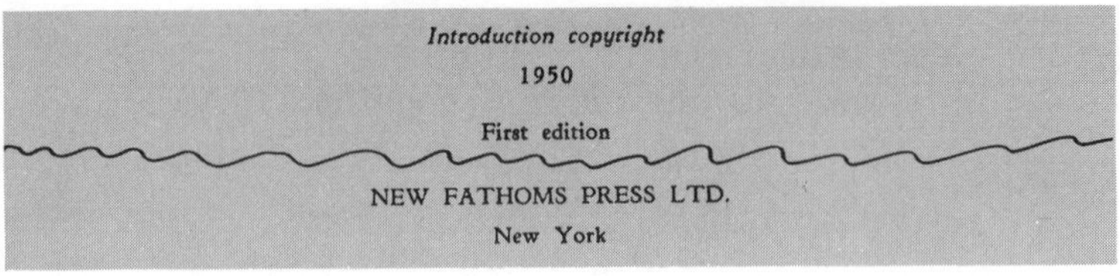
Introduction copyright
1950
First edition
NEW FATHOMS PRESS LTD.
New York

[1–10] 11–156 [157–160]

[1–10]^{8}

Contents: p. 1: half title; p. 2: blank; p. 3: title; p. 4: copyright; p. 5: 'CONTENTS'; p. 6: blank; pp. 7–10: 'INTRODUCTION'; pp. 11–156: text, headed '"ABORTION" (1914) | A PLAY IN ONE ACT'; p. 157: publisher's device; pp. 158–160: blank. Includes: "Abortion," "The Movie Man" (pp. 35–50), "The Sniper" (pp. 51–69), *Servitude* (pp. 70–144), and "A Wife For a Life" (pp. 145–156).

Typography and paper: type face undetermined. 4″ × $6\frac{3}{8}$″ ($6\frac{13}{16}$″); thirty-one lines per page. Running heads: rectos and versos, play titles. Wove paper.

Binding: There are two binding variants for this volume:
Binding A: Gray B cloth (linen-like grain). Spine: '[vertically, top to bottom, black] LOST PLAYS OF EUGENE O'NEILL–NEW FATHOMS'. White endpapers of different stock from text paper. All edges trimmed.
Binding B: Navy blue cloth (buckram). Front: '[light blue within double-rule box frame] Lost Plays | OF | EUGENE O'NEILL | [rule] | [publisher's device] | [rule] | A NEW FATHOMS PUBLICATION'. Spine: '[light blue, vertically from top to bottom] LOST PLAYS OF EUGENE O'NEILL–NEW FATHOMS'. All edges trimmed.

Dust jacket: Dark beige. Front: '[beige letters in navy blue box] LOST | PLAYS | OF | EUGENE | O'NEILL'. Spine: '[vertically top to bottom, navy blue] LOST PLAYS OF EUGENE O'NEILL–NEW FATHOMS'. Front and back flaps: blurb for *Lost Plays* and biographical note on Lawrence Gellert. Dj on copy at Lilly is beige printed in blue gray.

Publication: Unknown number of copies published 15 May 1950.

Locations: JM^{c}A (Binding A in dj); LC (deposit-stamp 29 May 1950); Lilly (Binding B, dj); PSt (Binding B); ScU (Binding B); Yale.

Note: This volume was an unauthorized collection. EO gave no approval for it.

REPRINTING

A 36-I-1.b
New York: Citadel Press, [1958].

A 36 "ABORTION"
American second book publication (1964)

A 36-II-1.a
Ten "Lost" Plays. New York: Random House, [1964].

On copyright page: 'FIRST PRINTING'.

"Abortion appears on pp. 139–165. See A 1-II-1.a, "Thirst."

A 36 "ABORTION"
English first book publication (1965)

A 36-EI-1.b
Ten "Lost" Plays. London: Random House, [1965].

Abortion appears on pp. 139–165. See A 1-EI-1.b, "Thirst."

A 37 "THE MOVIE MAN"
American first book publication (1950)

A 37-I-1.a
Lost Plays of Eugene O'Neill. New York: New Fathoms Press, Ltd., 1950.

On copyright page: 'FIRST PRINTING'.

"The Movie Man" appears on pp. 35–50. See A 36-I-1.a, "Abortion."

REPRINTING

A 37-I-1.b
New York: Citadel Press, [1958].

A 37 "THE MOVIE MAN"
American second book publication (1964)

A 37-II-1.a
Ten "Lost" Plays. New York: Random House, [1964].

"The Movie Man" appears on pp. 167–185. See A 1-II-1.a, "Thirst."

A 37 "THE MOVIE MAN"
English first book publication (1965)

A 37-EI-1.b
Ten "Lost" Plays. London: Random House, [1965].

"The Movie Man" appears on pp. 167–185. See A 1-EI-1.b, "Thirst."

A 38 "THE SNIPER"
American first book publication (1950)

A 38-I-1.a
Lost Plays of Eugene O'Neill. New York: New Fathoms Press, Ltd., 1950.

"The Sniper" appears on pp. 51–69. See A 36-I-1.a, "Abortion."

REPRINTING

A 38-I-1.b
New York: Citadel Press,[1958].

A 38 "THE SNIPER"
American second book publication (1964)

A 38-II-1.a
Ten "Lost" Plays. New York: Random House, [1964].

On copyright page: 'FIRST PRINTING'.

"The Sniper" appears on pp. 187–207. See A 1-II-1.a, "Thirst."

A 38 "THE SNIPER"
English first book publication (1965)

A 38-EI-1.b
Ten "Lost" Plays. London: Random House, 1965.

"The Sniper" appears on pp. 187–207. See A 1-EI-1.b, "Thirst."

A 39 SERVITUDE
American first book publication (1950)

A 39-I-1.a
Lost Plays of Eugene O'Neill. New York: New Fathoms Press, Ltd., 1950.

Servitude appears on pp. 70–144. See A 36-I-1.a, "Abortion."

REPRINTING

A 39-I-1.b
New York: Citadel Press, [1958].

A 39 SERVITUDE
American second book publication (1964)

A 39-II-1.a
Ten "Lost" Plays. New York: Random House, [1964].

On copyright page: 'FIRST PRINTING'.

Servitude appears on pp. 225–303. See A 1-II-1.a, "Thirst."

A 39 SERVITUDE
English first book publication (1965)

A 39-EI-1.b
Ten "Lost" Plays. London: Random House, [1965].

Servitude appears on pp. 225–303. See A 1-EI-1.b, "Thirst."

A 40 "A WIFE FOR A LIFE"
American first book publication (1950)

A 40-I-1.a
Lost Plays of Eugene O'Neill. New York: New Fathoms Press, Ltd., 1950.

"A Wife for a Life" appears on pp. 145–156. See A 36-I-1.a, "Abortion."

REPRINTING

A 40-I-1.b
New York: Citadel Press, [1958].

A 40 "A WIFE FOR A LIFE"
American second book publication (1964)

A 40-II-1.a
Ten "Lost" Plays. New York: Random House, [1964].

On copyright page: 'FIRST PRINTING'.

"A Wife for a Life" appears on pp. 209–223. See A 1-II-1.a, "Thirst."

A 40 "A WIFE FOR A LIFE"
English first book publication (1965)

A 40-EI-1.b
Ten "Lost" Plays. London: Random House, [1965].

"A Wife for a Life" appears on pp. 209–223. See A 1-EI-1.b, "Thirst."

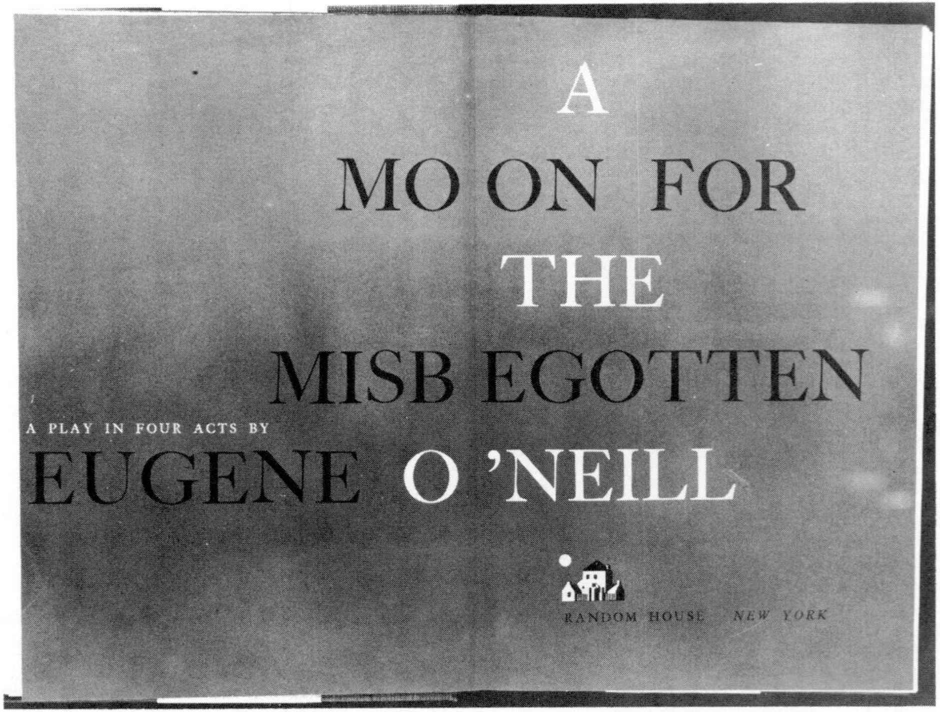

A 41-I-1: two-page title, white and black against charcoal gray background; 8″ × $5\frac{3}{8}$″

A 41 A MOON FOR THE MISBEGOTTEN
American first book publication (1952)

A 41-I-1
A MOON FOR THE MISBEGOTTEN
American first edition

> *First Edition*
>
> *Copyright, as an Unpublished Work, 1945,*
> *by Eugene O'Neill*
>
> *Copyright, 1952, by Eugene O'Neill*
>
> All rights reserved under International and Pan-American Copyright Conventions. Published in New York by Random House, Inc., and simultaneously in Toronto, Canada, by Random House of Canada, Limited.
> *Library of Congress Catalog Card Number: 52-6668.*
>
> CAUTION: Professionals and amateurs are hereby warned that *A Moon for the Misbegotten,* being fully protected under the copyright laws of the United States of America, the British Empire, including the Dominion of Canada, and all other countries of the copyright union, is subject to a royalty. All rights, including professional, amateur, motion picture, recitation, public reading, radio broadcasting, and the rights of translation into foreign languages are strictly reserved. All inquiries regarding this play should be addressed to the Richard J. Madden Play Co., Inc., at 522 Madison Avenue, New York City, N. Y.
>
> *Manufactured in the United States of America*
> *by H. Wolff, New York*
> *Designed by Jerome Kuhl*

[i–xiv] [1–4] 5–68 [69–71] 72–107 [108–111] 112–153 [154–157] 158–177 [178–182]

$[1_{+3,4}]^{16}$ $[2\text{–}6]^{16}$

Contents: pp. i–ii: blank; p. iii: half title; pp. iv–v: blank; pp. vi–vii: title; p. viii: copyright; p. ix: prefatory note by EO; p. x: blank; p. xi: 'CHARACTERS | [five lines of roman and italic type]'; pp. xii–xiii: act-scene synopsis and set description; p. xiv: blank; p. 1: 'ACT | ONE'; p. 2: blank; pp. 3–68: text, no heading; p. 69: 'ACT | TWO'; p. 70: blank; pp. 71–107: text, no heading; p. 108: blank; p. 109: 'ACT | THREE'; p. 110: blank; pp. 111–153: text, no heading; p. 154: blank; p. 155: 'ACT | FOUR'; p. 156: blank; pp. 157–177: text, no heading; pp. 178–182: blank.

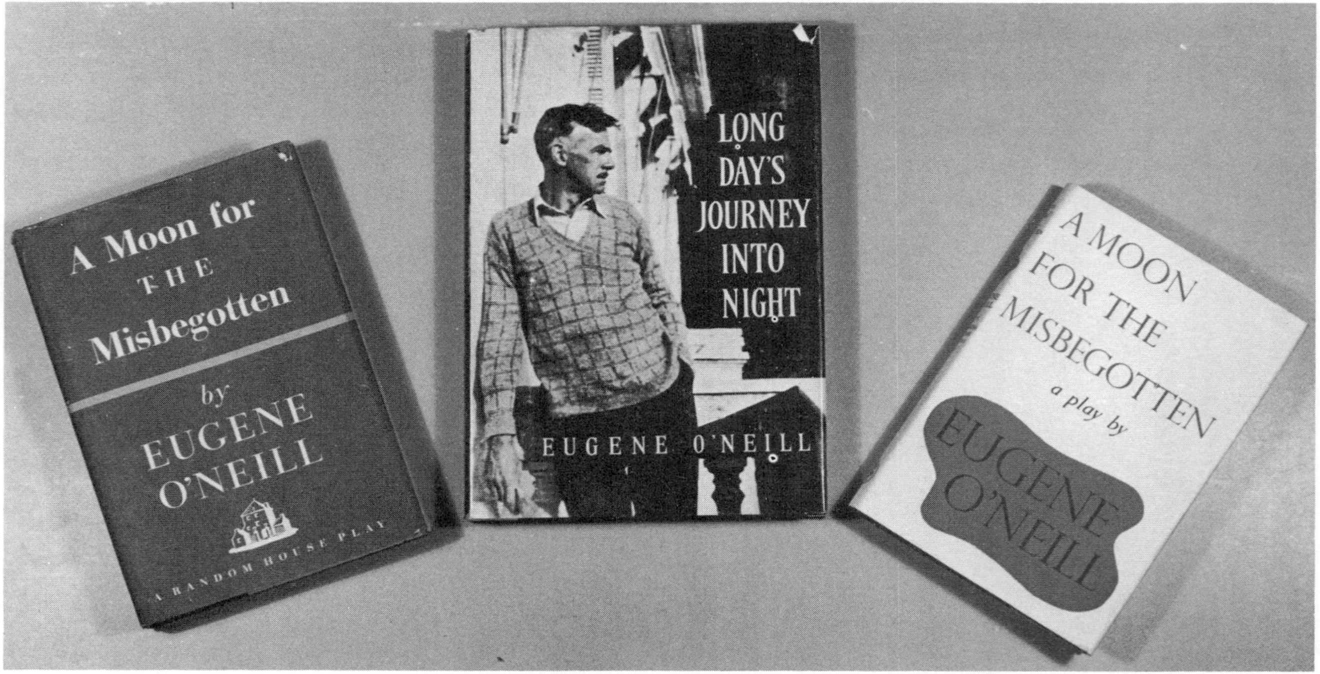

Dust jackets for A 41-I-1, A 42-I-1.a, and A 41-EI-1

Typography and paper: 11 point on 13, Granjon. $3\frac{5}{8}'' \times 5\frac{3}{4}''$ ($6\frac{1}{16}''$); twenty-seven to thirty-one lines per page. Running heads: rectos, 'EUGENE O'NEILL'; versos, 'A MOON FOR THE MISBEGOTTEN'. Laid paper with vertical chains $\frac{15}{16}''$ apart.

Binding: Black and gray paper-covered boards with strip of brown B cloth (linen-like grain) on spine. Spine: '[vertically top to bottom, white on black background] A MOON FOR THE MISBEGOTTEN [gray] O'NEILL | [horizontally, brown publisher's device]'. Off-white endpapers of different stock from text paper. All edges trimmed; top edge stained charcoal gray.

Dust jacket: Charcoal gray background. Front: '[white] A Moon for | T H E | Misbegotten | [wide gold rule] | [white] *by* | EUGENE | O'NEILL | [publisher's device] | A RANDOM HOUSE PLAY'. Spine: [two lines vertically top to bottom, white] A MOON FOR | THE MISBEGOTTEN | [horizontally, wide, gold rule] | [vertically top to bottom, white] BY EUGENE O'NEILL | [horizontally] [publisher's device] | RANDOM | HOUSE'. Back: illustration of EO 'FROM A DRAWING BY MAI-MAI SZE'; blurb on EO and list of titles in three-volume boxed set published by Random House. Front flap: Blurb for *AMFTM*. Back flap: blurb for The Modern Library collections of EO plays.

Publication: Unknown number of copies published 30 June 1952.

Locations: JM^c^A (dj); Lilly (dj); PSt; Yale.

A 41 A MOON FOR THE MISBEGOTTEN
English first book publication (1953)

A 41-EI-1
A MOON FOR THE MISBEGOTTEN
English first edition

A Moon
for the Misbegotten
A Play in Four Acts
by
Eugene O'Neill

Jonathan Cape
Thirty Bedford Square London

A 41-EI-1: $7\frac{7}{16}'' \times 4\frac{13}{16}''$

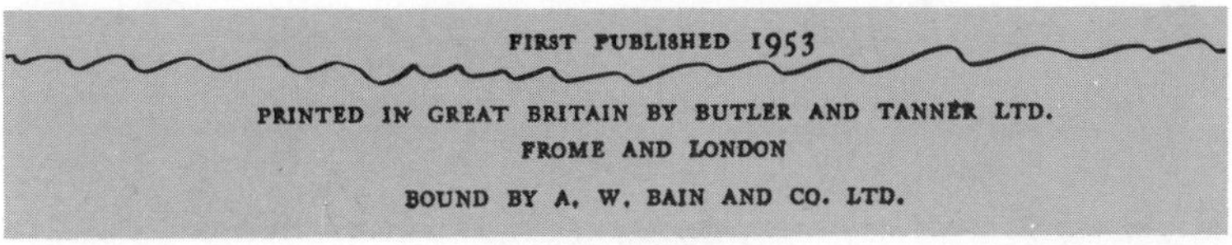
FIRST PUBLISHED 1953

PRINTED IN GREAT BRITAIN BY BUTLER AND TANNER LTD.
FROME AND LONDON

BOUND BY A. W. BAIN AND CO. LTD.

[1–4] 5 [6] 7 [8] 9 [10] 11–156 [157–160]

$[A]^8$ B–I^8 K^8

Contents: p. 1: half title; p. 2: card page; p. 3: title; p. 4: copyright; p. 5: prefatory note by EO; p. 6: blank; p. 7: 'CHARACTERS | [five lines of roman and italic type]'; p. 8: blank; p. 9: act-scene synopsis; p. 10: blank; pp. 11–12: 'SCENE OF THE PLAY'; pp. 13–156: text, headed 'ACT ONE'; pp. 157–160: blank.

Typography and paper: $3^{13}/_{16}''$ × $5^{3}/_{4}''$ ($5^{13}/_{16}''$); twenty-seven to twenty-nine lines per page. Running heads: rectos and versos, 'A MOON FOR THE MISBEGOTTEN'. Wove paper.

Binding: Blue paper-covered boards of imitation BF cloth. Front: '[silverstamped EO signature]'. Spine: '[silverstamped line of decoration] | EUGENE | O'NEILL | [decoration] | A | MOON | FOR THE | MIS-|BEGOTTEN | [publisher's device] | [line of decorations]'. White endpapers of different stock from text paper. All edges trimmed.

Dust jacket: White background. Front: '[green] A MOON | FOR THE | MISBEGOTTEN | [black] *a play by* | [black on green patch] EUGENE | O'NEILL'. Spine: '[black] A | [green] MOON | [black] for the | [green] MIS-|BEGOTTEN | [three lines in black on green patch] *a* | *play* | *by* | [black against white] EUGENE | O'NEILL | *author of* | [green] MOURNING | BECOMES | ELECTRA | [black] *etc.* | [green publisher's device]'. Back lists EO's plays published by Cape, beginning with *TEJ* and ending with *TIC*. Front flap: blurb for *AMFTM;* back flap blank.

Publication: Unknown number of copies published in 1953. 12s. 6d.

Locations: BM (deposit-stamp 17 April 1953); JM^{c}A (dj); Yale.

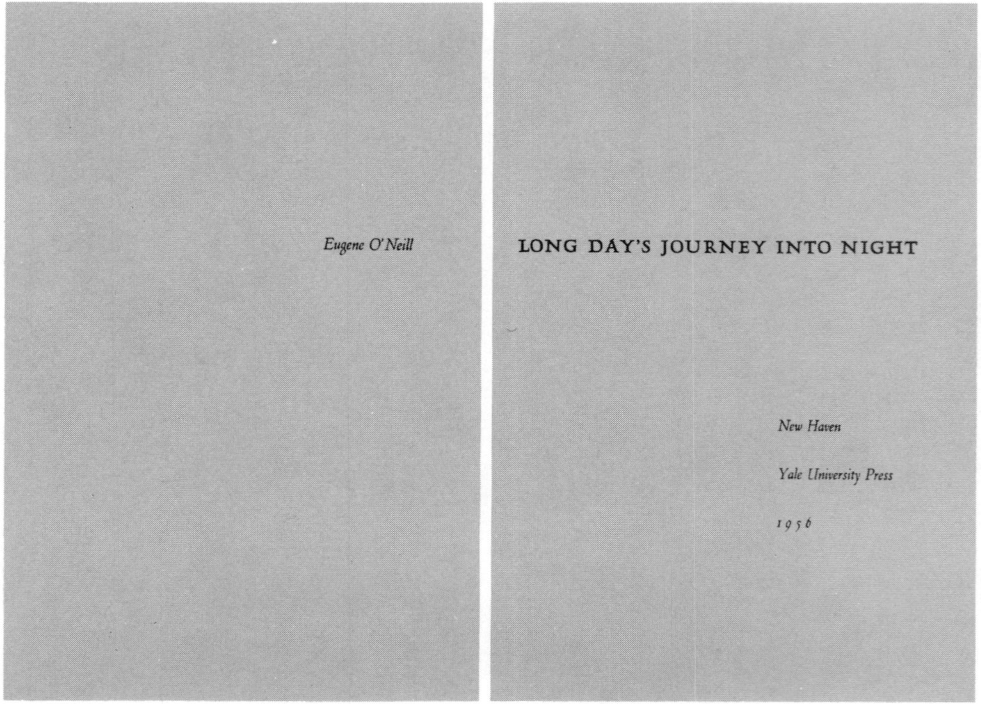

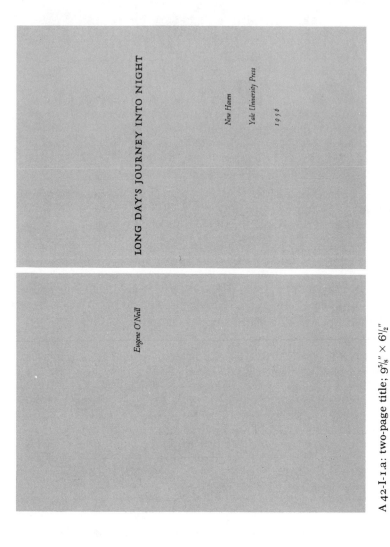

Eugene O'Neill

LONG DAY'S JOURNEY INTO NIGHT

New Haven

Yale University Press

1956

A 42-I-1.a: two-page title; $9^{5}/_{8}'' \times 6^{1}/_{2}''$

A 42 LONG DAY'S JOURNEY INTO NIGHT
American first book publication (1956)

A 42-I-1.a
LONG DAY'S JOURNEY INTO NIGHT
American first edition, first printing

> FIRST EDITION
>
> © As an unpublished work, 1955, by Carlotta Monterey O'Neill
>
> © 1955, by Carlotta Monterey O'Neill
>
> All rights reserved under International and Pan-American Copyright Conventions.
>
> Library of Congress catalog card number: 56-5944
>
> CAUTION: Professionals and amateurs are hereby warned that *Long Day's Journey into Night*, being fully protected under the copyright laws of the United States of America, the British Empire, including the Dominion of Canada, and all other countries of the copyright union, is subject to a royalty. All rights, including professional, amateur, motion picture, recitation, public reading, radio broadcasting, and the rights of translation into foreign languages, are strictly reserved. All inquiries regarding this play should be addressed to the Richard J. Madden Play Co., Inc., at 522 Fifth Avenue, New York City, N.Y.

[1–10] 11–49 [50] 51–95 [96] 97–123 [124] 125–176 [177–180]

$[1\text{–}10]^{8}$ $[11]^{10}$

Contents: pp. 1–2: blank; p. 3: half title; pp. 4–5: title; p. 6: copyright; p. 7: '*For Carlotta, on our 12th Wedding Anniversary* | [nine lines of italic type] | *These twelve years, Beloved One, have been a* | *Journey into Light—into love. You know my gratitude.* | *And my love!* | GENE | *Tao House* | *July 22, 1941.*'; p. 8: '*Characters* | [five lines of roman and italic type]'; p. 9: act-scene synopsis; p. 10: blank; pp. 11–49: text, headed '*Act One*'; p. 50: blank; pp. 51–95: text, headed '*Act Two, Scene One*'; p. 96: blank; pp. 97–123: text, headed '*Act Three*'; p. 124: blank; pp. 125–176: text, headed '*Act Four*'; p. 177: blank; p. 178: 'AT THE PRINTING-OFFICE OF THE YALE UNIVERSITY PRESS'; pp. 179–180: blank.

Typography and paper: 13 point on 14, Aldine Bembo. $4\frac{1}{2} \times 7\frac{5}{16}''$ ($7\frac{9}{16}''$); thirty-six lines per page. No running heads. Wove paper with 'WARREN'S OLDE STYLE' watermark.

Binding: Black V cloth (fine linen-like grain) with gray burlap cloth shelf back. Spine: '[vertically top to bottom, goldstamped in black box] O'NEILL: LONG DAY'S JOURNEY INTO NIGHT | [horizontally, in black below box] Yale'. White wove endpapers of different stock from text paper. All edges trimmed.

Dust jacket: Front: 'photo of O'Neill taken by Carlotta Monterey O'Neill, [superimposed on photo in white] LONG | DAY'S | JOURNEY | INTO | NIGHT | E U G E N E | O' N E I L L'. Spine: '[vertically top to bottom, white lettering against black background] O'NEILL LONG DAY'S JOURNEY INTO NIGHT | [horizontally] *Yale*'. Back has list of EO's plays. Front flap: blurb for *LDJ* and photo credit for CMO; back flap blank.

Publication: 5,000 copies published 20 February 1956. $3.75.

Locations: JM^cA (dj); LC (deposit-stamp 5 March 1956); Lilly (dj and a set of page proofs); Yale.

Note: Excerpts from the play appeared in *Life*, XXI (14 October 1946), preceding book publication. See C 87.

REPRINTING

A 42-I-1.b
New Haven: Yale University Press, [February 1956]. 5,000 copies.

A 42-I-1.c
New Haven: Yale University Press, [April 1956]. 5,000 copies.

A 42-I-1.d
New Haven: Yale University Press, [October 1956]. 5,000 copies.

A 42-I-1.e
New Haven: Yale University Press, [February 1957]. 5,000 copies.

Note one: The following textual emendation was made in the fifth printing: 167.10–11 God bless you, K.O. | *He falls* [God bless you, Kid. | *His eyes close. He mumbles.* | That last drink—the old K. O. | *He falls*

A 42-I-1.f
New Haven: Yale University Press, [August 1957]. 5,000 copies.

A 42-I-1.g
New Haven: Yale University Press, [June 1958]. 5,000 copies.

A 42-I-1.h
New Haven: Yale University Press, [November 1959]. 2,500 copies.

A 42-I-1.i
New Haven: Yale University Press, [February 1964]. 2,500 copies.

A 42-I-1.j
New Haven: Yale University Press, [April 1967]. 2,500 copies.

A 42-I-1.k
New Haven: Yale University Press, [November 1969]. 2,500 copies.

Note two: Dates for reprintings were supplied by Yale University Press and do not always coincide with dates on the copyright pages.

PAPERBACK REPRINTINGS

Between October 1962 and February 1972 there have been twenty-four paperback printings, totaling 470,000 copies.

A 42 LONG DAY'S JOURNEY INTO NIGHT
English first book publication (1956)

A 42-EI-1
LONG DAY'S JOURNEY INTO NIGHT
English first edition

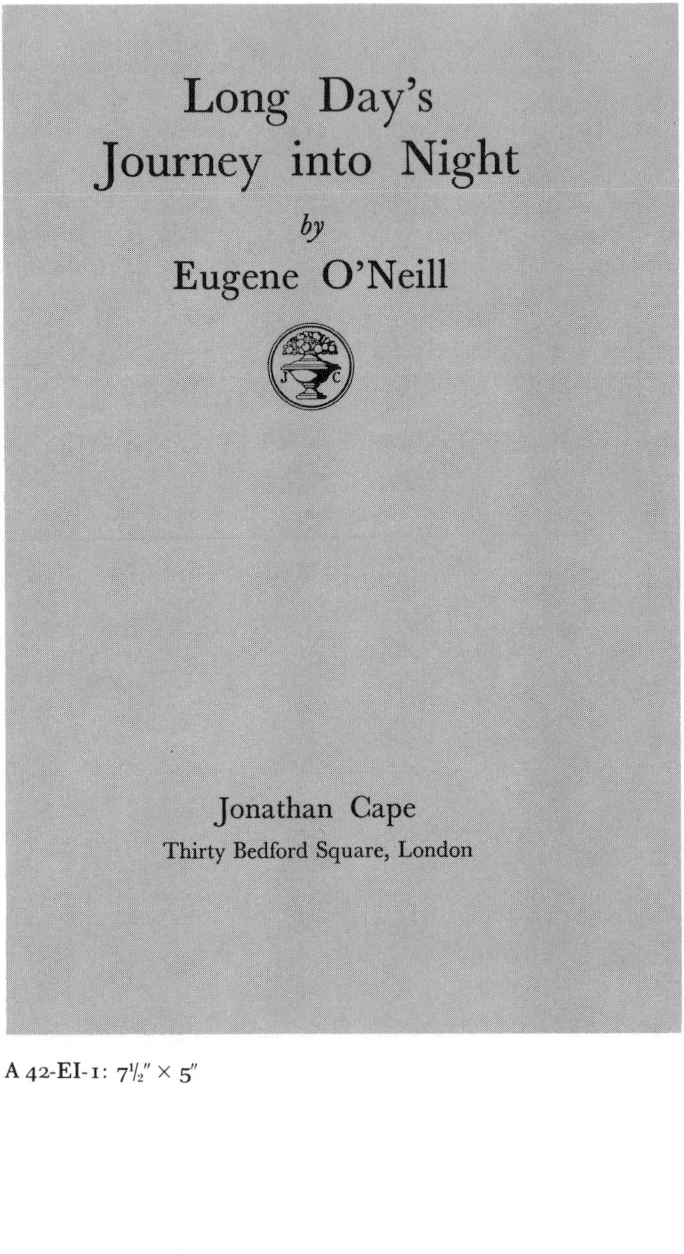

Long Day's
Journey into Night
by
Eugene O'Neill

Jonathan Cape
Thirty Bedford Square, London

A 42-EI-1: 7½″ × 5″

FIRST PUBLISHED IN GREAT BRITAIN 1956

PRINTED IN GREAT BRITAIN BY BUTLER AND TANNER LTD.
FROME AND LONDON
BOUND BY A. W. BAIN AND CO. LTD.

[1–8] 9–156 [157–160]

[A]^8 B–I^8 K^8

Contents: p. 1: half title; p. 2: card page; p. 3: title; p. 4: copyright; p. 5: dedication; p. 6: blank; p. 7: act-scene synopsis and list of characters; p. 8: blank; pp. 9–156: text, headed 'ACT ONE'; pp. 157–160: ad for nine volumes of EO plays published by Cape, beginning with *TEJ* and ending with *AMFTM*.

Typography and paper: $3\frac{5}{8}'' \times 5\frac{15}{16}''$ ($6\frac{1}{8}''$); thirty-three lines per page. No running heads. Wove paper.

Binding: Blue paper-covered boards of imitation BF cloth. Front: '[silverstamped EO signature]'. Spine: '[silverstamped line of decorations] | EUGENE | O'NEILL | [single decoration] | LONG | DAY'S | JOURNEY | INTO | NIGHT | [publisher's device] | [line of decorations]'. White wove endpapers of different stock from text paper. All edges trimmed.

Dust jacket: White background. Front: '[blue] LONG DAY'S | JOURNEY | INTO NIGHT | [black] *a play by* | [black on blue patch] EUGENE | O'NEILL'. Spine: '[black] LONG | DAY'S | JOURNEY | INTO | NIGHT | [black on blue patch] *a* | *play* | *by* | [black on white] EUGENE | O'NEILL | *author of* | [blue] MOURNING | BECOMES | *ELECTRA* | [black] etc. | [blue publisher's device]'. Back lists nine EO plays published by Cape, beginning with *TEJ* and ending with *AMFTM*. Front flap has blurb for *LDJ;* back flap has the following lines printed diagonally in lower left-hand corner: 'LONG DAY'S JOURNEY INTO NIGHT | O'NEILL | CAPE | 12s. 6d. net'.

Publication: Unknown number of copies published in 1956.

Locations: BM (deposit-stamp 28 May 1956); Yale (dj).

A 43 THE LAST WILL AND TESTAMENT OF SILVERDENE EMBLEM O'NEILL
American first book publication (1956)

A 43-I-1.a
THE LAST WILL AND TESTAMENT OF SILVERDENE EMBLEM O'NEILL
American first edition, first printing

[1–4]

Quarto (one page folded twice) stapled in center and tied.

On copyright page: '© 1956 BY CARLOTTA MONTEREY O'NEILL'.

The colophon on p. 4 reads: 'PRINTED FOR CARLOTTA MONTEREY O'NEILL | BY HER FRIENDS | AT THE YALE UNIVERSITY PRESS'.

Typography and paper: $5^{5}/_{16}$" × 3"; thirty lines per page. 5" × $7^{5}/_{8}$" heavy, white paper cover. $7^{1}/_{2}$" × $4^{15}/_{16}$" white laid text paper with vertical chain marks 1" apart.

Binding: Blue wrapper with silver high fiber content.

Publication: Unknown number of copies published 20 February 1956.

Location: Yale (two copies).

REPRINTING

A 43-I-1.b
New Haven, Connecticut: Yale University Press, [1959].

The colophon on p. 4 reads: 'FIRST PRINTED IN 1956, AND | REPRINTED IN 1959 BY | THE YALE UNIVERSITY PRESS'.

A 43 THE LAST WILL AND TESTAMENT OF SILVERDENE EMBLEM O'NEILL
American second book publication (1972)

A 43-II-1
THE LAST WILL AND TESTAMENT OF AN EXTREMELY DISTINGUISHED DOG
American first edition

Title page: 'THE LAST WILL | AND TESTAMENT OF | AN EXTREMELY | DISTINGUISHED | DOG | *by Eugene O'Neill* | ACHILLE J. ST. ONGE | WORCESTER | 1972'

Note: This book is a miniature. Title page measures: 2¾″ × 2″.

Copyright page: '*The Last Will and Testament of* | *Silverdene Emblem O'Neill* | by Eugene O'Neill, © 1956 by | Carlotta Monterey O'Neill, | and Published by permission of | the Trustees under the will of | Carlotta Monterey O'Neill.'

[1–6] 7–9 [10–12] 13–15 [16] 17–19 [20] 21–26 [27–28]

$[1\text{–}2]^4$ $[3]^6$

The colophon on p. 28 reads: '*Thousand copies of this book* | *have been printed from* | *Lutetia type* | *by Joh. Enschedé en Zonen* | *Haarlem, Holland* | *and bound by* | *Reliure du Centre S.A.,* | *Limoges, France* | [publisher's device]'.

Binding: Tan leather. Front: '[goldstamped] THE LAST WILL | AND TESTAMENT OF | AN EXTREMELY | DISTINGUISHED DOG | [image of Dalmatian stamped in brown] | [goldstamped] EUGENE O'NEILL'. Marbled endpapers; all edges gilded.

Locations: JMcA; Yale.

A 44 A TOUCH OF THE POET
American first book publication (1957)

A 44-I-1.a
A TOUCH OF THE POET
American first edition, first printing

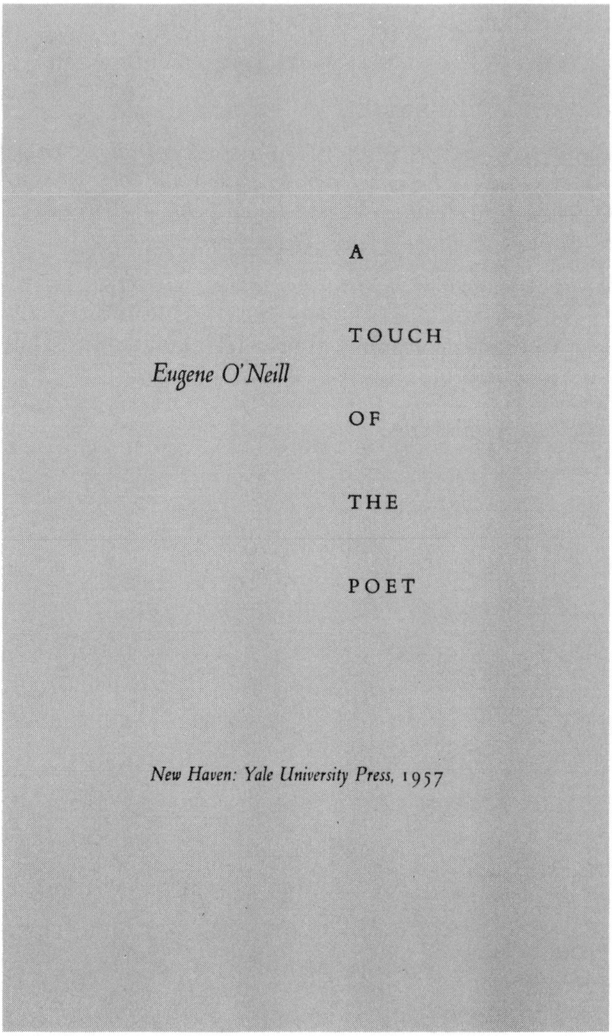
A

TOUCH

Eugene O'Neill

OF

THE

POET

New Haven: Yale University Press, 1957

A 44-I-1.a: $8\frac{7}{16}'' \times 5\frac{1}{2}''$

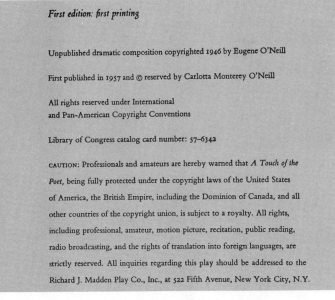

> *First edition: first printing*
>
> Unpublished dramatic composition copyrighted 1946 by Eugene O'Neill
>
> First published in 1957 and © reserved by Carlotta Monterey O'Neill
>
> All rights reserved under International
> and Pan-American Copyright Conventions
>
> Library of Congress catalog card number: 57-6342
>
> CAUTION: Professionals and amateurs are hereby warned that *A Touch of the Poet,* being fully protected under the copyright laws of the United States of America, the British Empire, including the Dominion of Canada, and all other countries of the copyright union, is subject to a royalty. All rights, including professional, amateur, motion picture, recitation, public reading, radio broadcasting, and the rights of translation into foreign languages, are strictly reserved. All inquiries regarding this play should be addressed to the Richard J. Madden Play Co., Inc., at 522 Fifth Avenue, New York City, N.Y.

[i–ii] [1–6] 7–182

Glued

Contents: pp. i–ii: blank; p. 1: title; p. 2: copyright; p. 3: act-scene synopsis; p. 4: blank; p. 5: '*Characters* | [ten lines of roman and italic type]'; p. 6: blank; pp. 7–182: text, headed '*Act One*'.

Typography and paper: 12 point on 13, Aldine Bembo. $3\frac{5}{8}'' \times 5\frac{7}{8}''$ ($6\frac{1}{8}''$); thirty-two lines per page. No running heads. Wove paper with 'WARREN'S OLDE STYLE' watermark.

Binding: There are two binding variants for this volume:

Binding A: Green B cloth (linen-like grain). Spine: '[goldstamped] *O'Neill* | A | TOUCH | OF | THE | POET | YALE'. White wove endpapers of different stock from text paper. All edges trimmed.

Binding B: Green B cloth. Front: '[goldstamped circle] [green clover leaf within the circle]'. Spine: same as Binding A. All edges trimmed.

Priority of bindings undetermined.

Dust jacket: by Burt Jackson. Front: '[against a white background, charcoal stylistic drawing of man in orange military jacket viewing himself in a black mirror; above drawing in

Dust jackets for A 44-I-1.a and A 44-EI-1

white against black background] *Eugene O'Neill* | *A Touch of the Poet*'. Spine: '[vertically, top to bottom, white against black] *O'Neill* [black against white above a strip of orange and white] *A Touch of the Poet Yale*'. Back: blurb for *LDJ*, quoting Lewis Gannett, Sterling North, Walter F. Kerr, Paul Pickerel, and George F. Reedley. Front flap: blurb for *Poet;* back flap: blurb for EO and his published work.

Publication: 10,000 copies published 18 September 1957. $3.75.

Locations: JM^c^A (dj); LC (deposit-stamp 12 November 1957); Lilly (dj); ScU (dj); Yale (and page proofs).

REPRINTING

A 44-I-1.b
New Haven: Yale University Press, [November 1957]. 15,000 copies.

PAPERBACK REPRINTINGS

Between February 1959 and March 1972 there were eight paperback printings, totaling 45,000 copies.

A 44 A TOUCH OF THE POET
English first book publication (1957)

A 44-EI-1
A TOUCH OF THE POET
English first edition

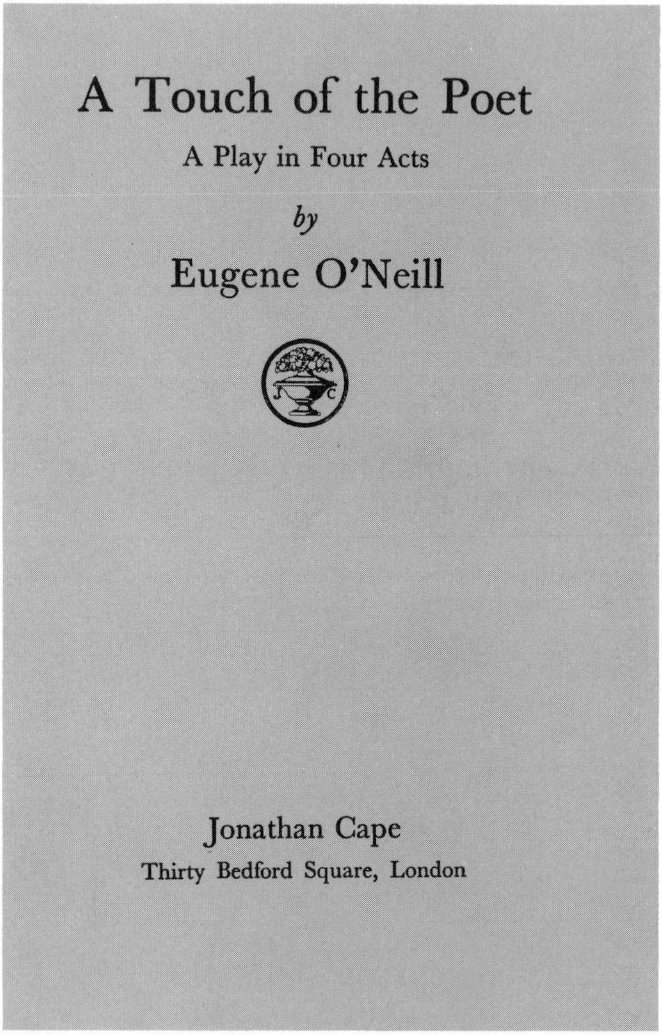
A Touch of the Poet
A Play in Four Acts
by
Eugene O'Neill
Jonathan Cape
Thirty Bedford Square, London

A 44-EI-1: $7\frac{3}{8}'' \times 4\frac{7}{8}''$

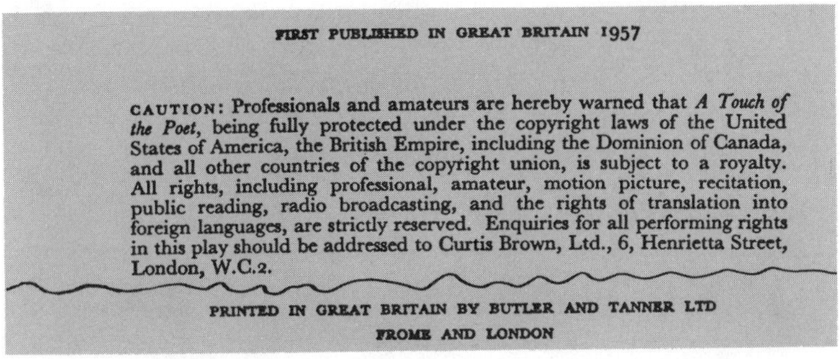

FIRST PUBLISHED IN GREAT BRITAIN 1957

CAUTION: Professionals and amateurs are hereby warned that *A Touch of the Poet*, being fully protected under the copyright laws of the United States of America, the British Empire, including the Dominion of Canada, and all other countries of the copyright union, is subject to a royalty. All rights, including professional, amateur, motion picture, recitation, public reading, radio broadcasting, and the rights of translation into foreign languages, are strictly reserved. Enquiries for all performing rights in this play should be addressed to Curtis Brown, Ltd., 6, Henrietta Street, London, W.C.2.

PRINTED IN GREAT BRITAIN BY BUTLER AND TANNER LTD
FROME AND LONDON

[1–6] 7–138 [139–144]

$[A]^8$ B–I^8

Contents: p. 1: half title; p. 2: card page; p. 3: title; p. 4: copyright; p. 5: act-scene synopsis and character list; p. 6: blank; pp. 7–138: text, headed 'ACT ONE'; pp. 139–142: ads for a 'Uniform Edition' of EO's plays (including ten volumes in the series); pp. 143–144: blank.

Typography and paper: $3\frac{5}{8}'' \times 5\frac{15}{16}''$ ($6\frac{1}{8}''$); thirty-one to thirty-four lines per page. No running heads. Wove paper.

Binding: Blue paper-covered boards of imitation BF cloth. Front: '[silverstamped EO signature]'. Spine: [silverstamped line of decorations] | EUGENE | O'NEILL | [decoration] | A | TOUCH | OF THE | POET | [publisher's device] | [line of decorations]'. White endpapers of different stock from text paper. All edges trimmed.

Dust jacket: White background. Front: '[green] A TOUCH | OF | THE POET | [black] *a play by* | [black in green patch] EUGENE | O'NEILL'. Spine: '[black] A | TOUCH | OF | THE | POET | [black in green patch] *a* | *play* | *by* | [black against white] EUGENE | O'NEILL | *author of* | [green] MOURNING | BECOMES | ELECTRA | [black] *etc.* | [green publisher's device]'. Back: list of EO's plays published by Cape, beginning with *TEJ* and ending with *LDJ*. Front flap: blurb for *Poet;* back flap blank.

Publication: Unknown number of copies published in 1957. 13s. 6d.

Locations: BM (deposit-stamp 4 September 1957); JM^{c}A (dj).

A 45 "HUGHIE"
American first book publication (1959)

A 45-I-1.a
HUGHIE
American first edition, first printing

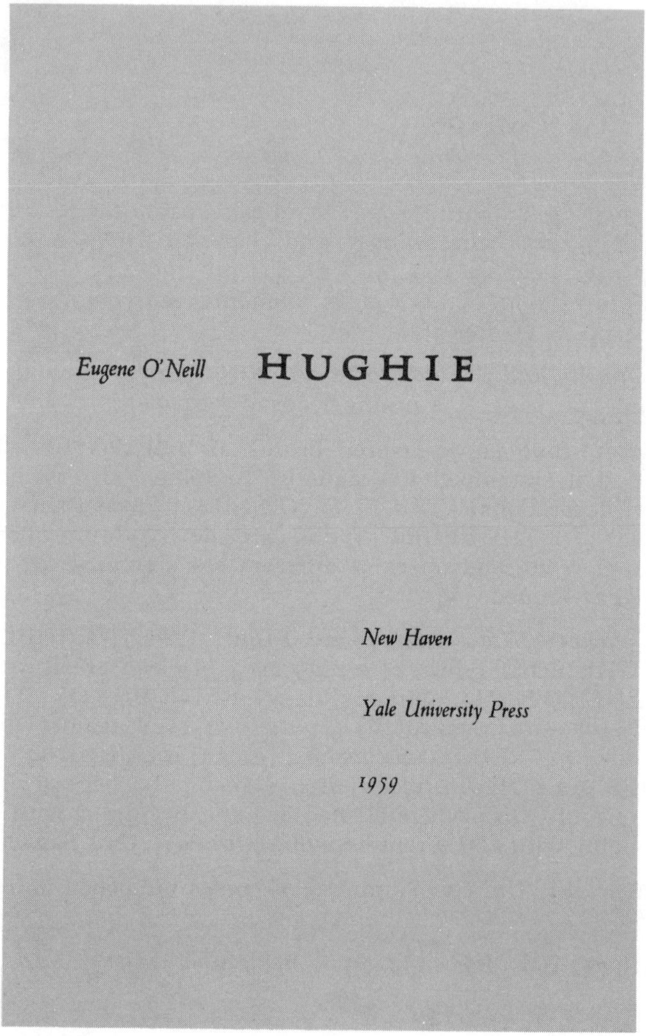

Eugene O'Neill HUGHIE

New Haven

Yale University Press

1959

A 45-I-1.a: $9\frac{5}{8}'' \times 6\frac{1}{8}''$

FIRST EDITION: FIRST PRINTING

© as an unpublished work 1959 by Carlotta Monterey O'Neill.

© 1959 by Carlotta Monterey O'Neill.

All rights reserved under International and Pan-American Copyright Conventions.

Library of Congress catalog card number: 58–11259.

Caution: Professionals and amateurs are hereby warned that *Hughie*, being fully protected under the copyright laws of the United States of America, the British Empire, including the Dominion of Canada, and all other countries of the copyright union, is subject to a royalty. All rights, including professional, amateur, motion picture, recitation, public reading, radio broadcasting, and the rights of translation into foreign languages, are strictly reserved. All inquiries regarding this play should be addressed to the Richard J. Madden Play Co., Inc., at 522 Fifth Avenue, New York City, N.Y.

[i–ii] [1–6] 7–37 [38]

$[1\text{–}5]^{4}$

Contents: p. i: blank; p. ii: blank; p. 1: half title; p. 2: blank; p. 3: title; p. 4: copyright; p. 5: '*Characters* | [two lines of type]'; p. 6: blank; pp. 7–38: text, headed: '*Scene*'.

Typography and paper: 13 point on 16, Aldine Bembo. $4\frac{5}{16}'' \times 7\frac{1}{16}''$ ($7\frac{7}{16}''$); thirty-one lines per page. Wove paper. No running heads.

Binding: Black V cloth (fine linen-like grain). Front has horizontal rule blindstamped $3\frac{3}{4}''$ down from top edge. Spine: '[vertically top to bottom, silver] *Eugene O'Neill* | [horizontally, blindstamped rule] | [vertically, gold] HUGHIE | [silver] *Yale*'. White endpapers of different stock from text paper. All edges trimmed.

Dust jacket: Front: '[black background with photo of lighted hotel windows in lower right-hand corner] [in center in simulated telegraph tapes] Hughie | a new one act play | by Eugene O'Neill'. Spine: '[vertically top to bottom, in simulated telegraph tape] HUGHIE A ONE ACT PLAY BY EUGENE O'NEILL [white against black background] YALE'. Back has blurbs for *LDJ* and *Poet.* Front flap: blurb for *Hughie;* back flap: biographical statement on EO and list of his works.

Publication: 3,000 copies published 25 March 1959.

Locations: JM^{c}A (dj); LC (deposit-stamp 3 April 1959); Yale.

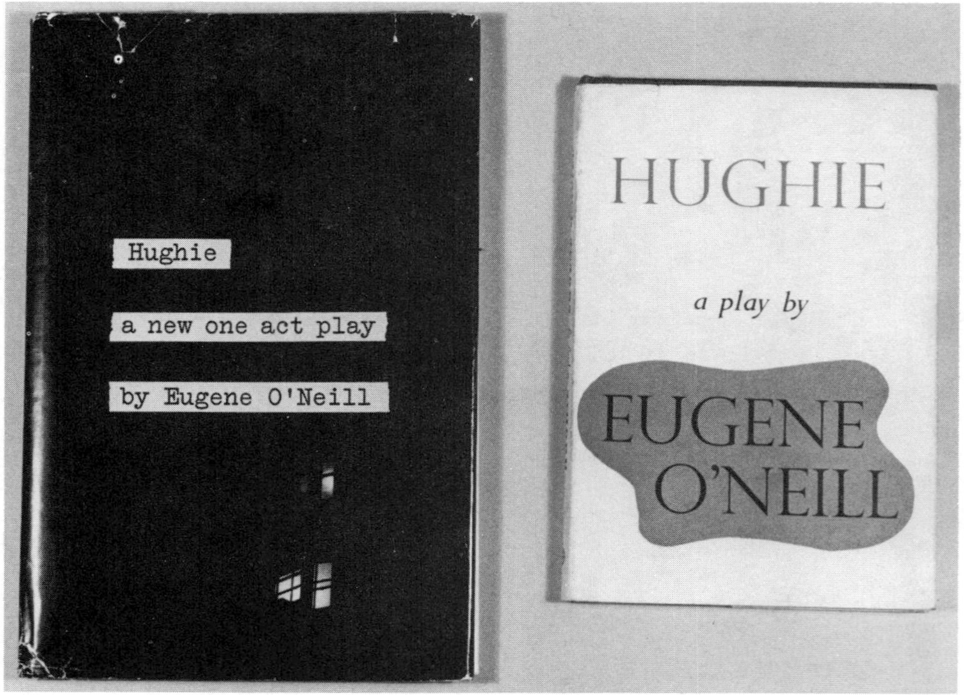

Dust jackets for A 45-I-1.a and A 45-EI-1

REPRINTINGS

A 45-I-1.b
New Haven: Yale University Press, [October 1959]. 2,000 copies.

A 45-I-1.c
New Haven: Yale University Press, [March 1968]. 1,000 copies.

Note: This information was provided by the publisher from his records. The copyright page of the second printing reads: 'FIRST EDITION: *First printing February, 1959*: | *second printing August, 1959.*'

A 45 "HUGHIE"
English first book publication (1962)

A 45-EI-1
HUGHIE
English first edition

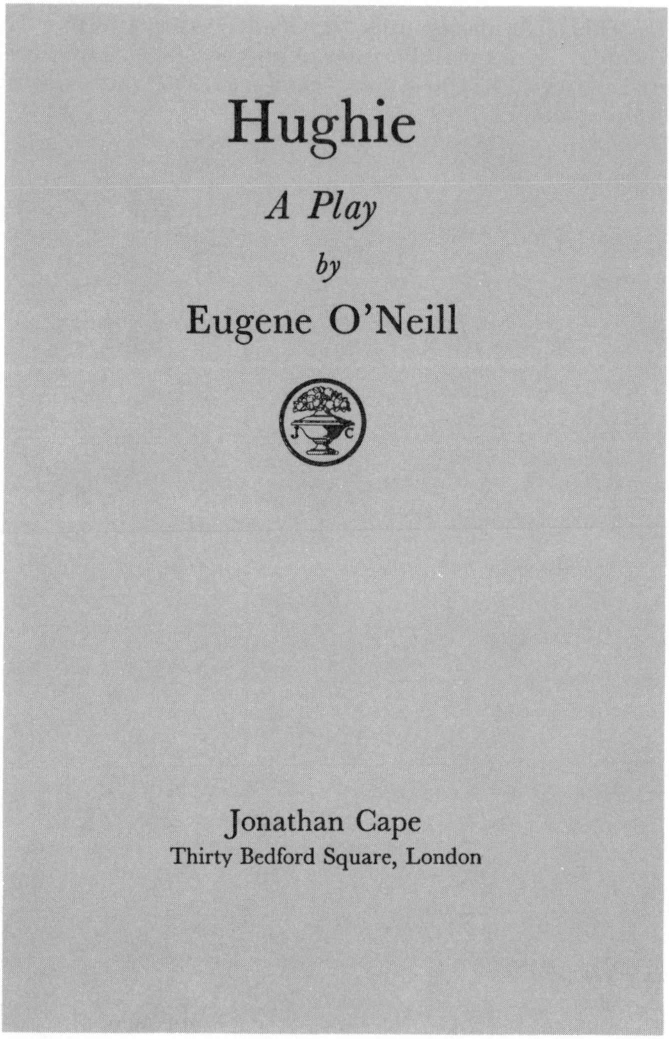
Hughie

A Play

by

Eugene O'Neill

Jonathan Cape
Thirty Bedford Square, London

A 45-EI-1: $7\frac{3}{8}'' \times 4\frac{7}{8}''$

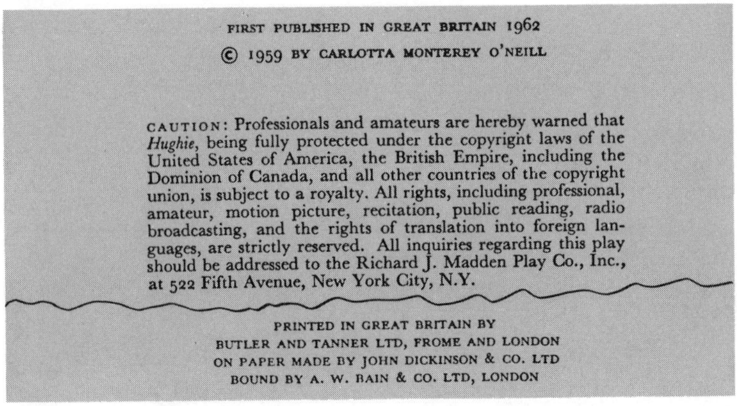

FIRST PUBLISHED IN GREAT BRITAIN 1962

© 1959 BY CARLOTTA MONTEREY O'NEILL

CAUTION: Professionals and amateurs are hereby warned that *Hughie*, being fully protected under the copyright laws of the United States of America, the British Empire, including the Dominion of Canada, and all other countries of the copyright union, is subject to a royalty. All rights, including professional, amateur, motion picture, recitation, public reading, radio broadcasting, and the rights of translation into foreign languages, are strictly reserved. All inquiries regarding this play should be addressed to the Richard J. Madden Play Co., Inc., at 522 Fifth Avenue, New York City, N.Y.

PRINTED IN GREAT BRITAIN BY
BUTLER AND TANNER LTD, FROME AND LONDON
ON PAPER MADE BY JOHN DICKINSON & CO. LTD
BOUND BY A. W. BAIN & CO. LTD, LONDON

[1–6] 7–41 [42–48]

[A]^8 B–C^8. C$_8$ is pastedown endpaper.

Contents: p. 1: half title; p. 2: card page; p. 3: title; p. 4: copyright; p. 5: '*Characters* | [two lines of type]'; p. 6: blank; pp. 7–41: text, no heading; pp. 42–48: blank (pp. 47 and 48 are the pastedown, rear endpaper).

Typography and paper: $3\frac{5}{16}'' \times 5\frac{1}{2}''$ ($5\frac{11}{16}''$); thirty-one lines per page. No running heads. Wove paper.

Binding: Blue paper-covered boards of imitation BF cloth. Front: '[silverstamped EO signature]'. Spine: (reading from bottom to top) '[horizontally, silverstamped line of decorations] | [publisher's device] | [line of decorations] | [vertically] HUGHIE | [horizontal line of decorations] | [vertically] EUGENE O'NEILL | [horizontal line of decorations]'. White endpapers of different stock from text paper. All edges trimmed.

Dust jacket: White background. Front: '[green] HUGHIE | [black] *a play by* | [black in green patch] EUGENE | O'NEILL'. Spine: '[black, from bottom to top] [horizontal publisher's device] | [vertically] HUGHIE *a play by* EUGENE O'NEILL'. Back: list of EO's plays published by Cape, beginning with *TEJ* and ending with *Poet*. Front flap: blurb for *Hughie;* back flap blank.

Publication: Unknown number of copies published in 1962. 10s.6d.

Locations: BM (deposit-stamp 12 October 1962); JM^{c}A (dj).

A 46 INSCRIPTIONS
American first book publication (1960)

A 46-I-1
INSCRIPTIONS
American first edition, only printing

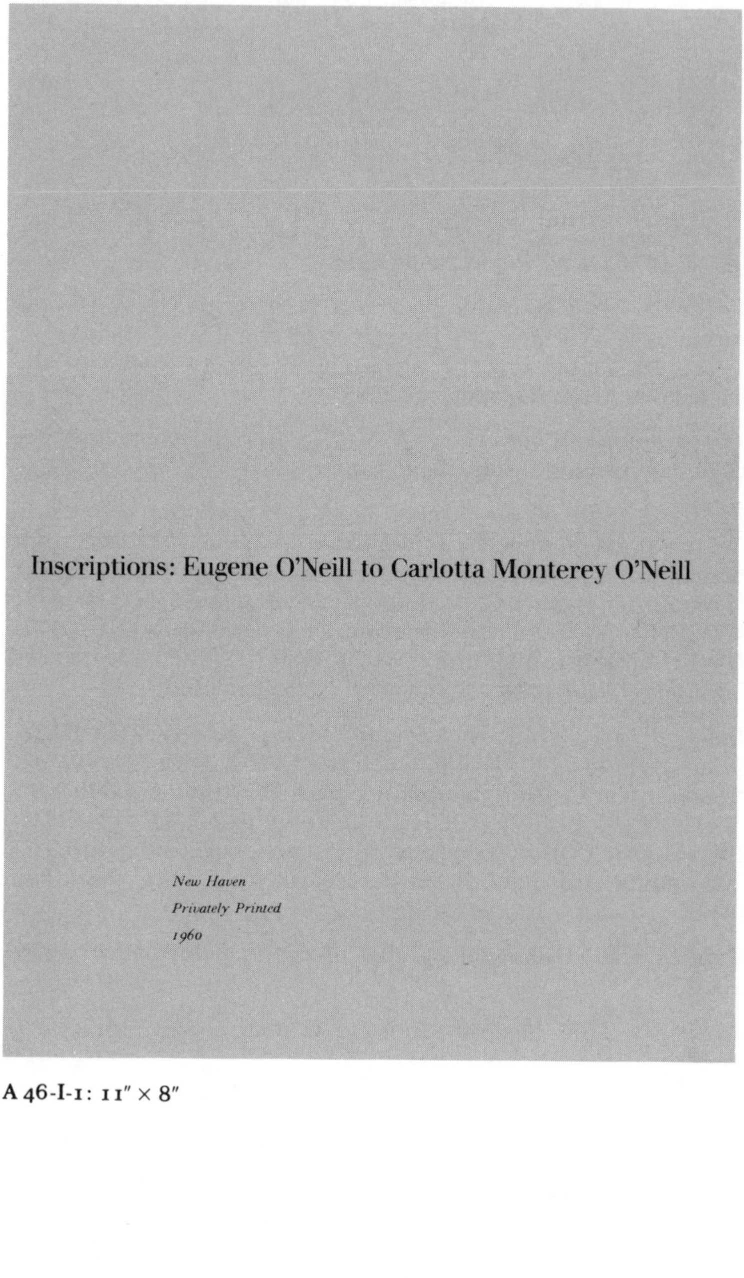
Inscriptions: Eugene O'Neill to Carlotta Monterey O'Neill

New Haven
Privately Printed
1960

A 46-I-1: 11″ × 8″

> NOTE: The originals of these inscriptions have been given by Carlotta Monterey O'Neill to the Yale University Library for the Eugene O'Neill Collection, from which copies of this volume may be secured and for which all proceeds from the sale of this book will be used. The Library is indebted to Fania Marinoff, Edward Steichen, and Carl Van Vechten for permission to reproduce photographs made by them.
>
> Copyright 1960 by the Yale University Library
>
> Edited by Donald Gallup.
> Designed by Alvin Eisenman and George S. Chappell 3rd.
>
> FRONTISPIECE: In New York, September 5, 1933
> Photograph by Carl Van Vechten

[1–160]

[1–10]^{8}

Contents: p. 1: blank; p. 2: frontispiece; p. 3: title; p. 4: copyright; p. 5: blank; pp. 6–159: facsimiles and text; p. 160: colophon: 'Five hundred copies printed by | the Meriden Gravure Company. | Set in Walbaum types by Clarke & Way'.

Paper: Off-white laid paper with vertical chain marks 1″ apart. Laid endpapers of heavier stock than text paper.

Binding: Black V cloth (fine, linen-like grain). Front: '[goldstamped facsimile of scrap of paper with goldstamped holograph] To Carlotta | from | Gene'. Spine: '[goldstamped vertically from bottom to top] Inscriptions: Eugene O'Neill to Carlotta Monterey O'Neill'. All edges trimmed.

Dust jacket: Plain, glassine dust jacket.

Slipcase: Black paper-covered box of imitation V cloth.

Publication: 550 copies published in 1960.

Location: JM^{c}A (#364 boxed).

A 47 MORE STATELY MANSIONS
American first book publication (1964)

A 47-I-1.a
MORE STATELY MANSIONS
American first edition, first printing

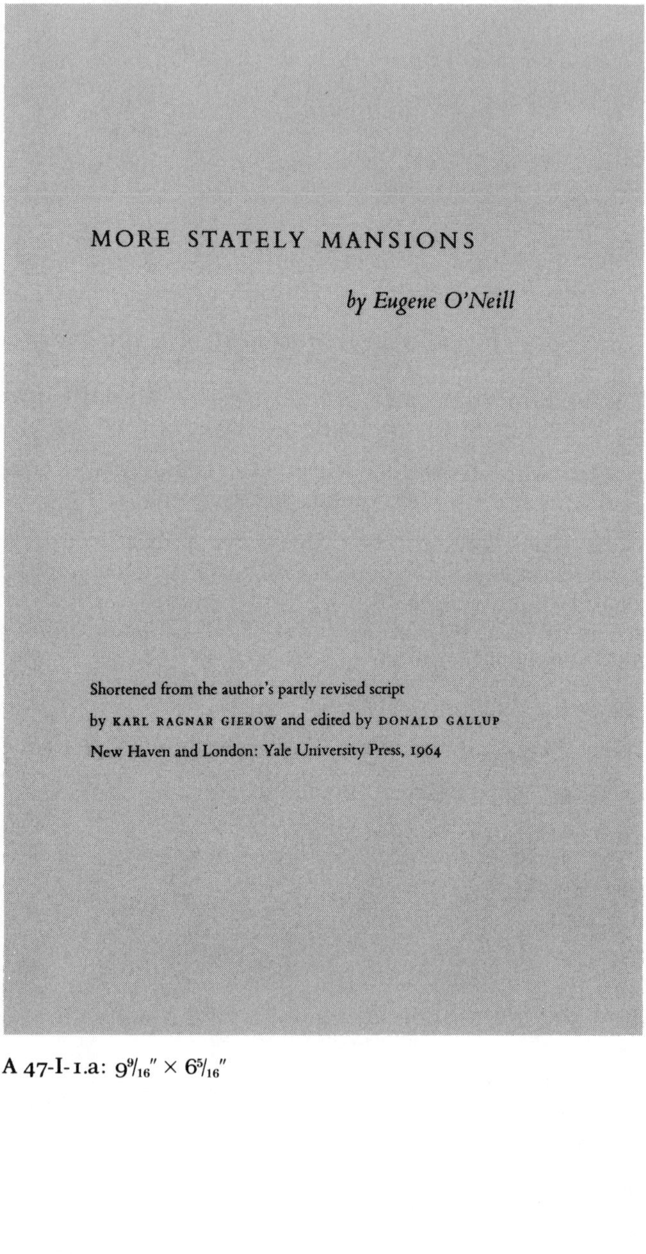
MORE STATELY MANSIONS

by Eugene O'Neill

Shortened from the author's partly revised script
by KARL RAGNAR GIEROW and edited by DONALD GALLUP
New Haven and London: Yale University Press, 1964

A 47-I-1.a: $9\frac{9}{16}'' \times 6\frac{5}{16}''$

FIRST EDITION

Copyright © 1964 by Carlotta Monterey O'Neill

Set in Aldine Bembo
and printed in the United States of America by
The Carl Purington Rollins Printing-Office of
the Yale University Press, New Haven, Connecticut.
All rights reserved. This book may not be
reproduced, in whole or in part, in any form
(except by reviewers for the public press),
without written permission from the publishers.

Library of Congress catalog card number: 64-12655

CAUTION: All rights, including professional, amateur,
motion picture, television, recitation, public reading,
radio broadcasting, and the rights of translation
into foreign languages, are strictly reserved.

THE EUGENE O'NEILL COLLECTION was founded at the Yale
University Library in 1931 by Carlotta Monterey O'Neill.
It includes books, photographs, manuscripts, and typescripts,
among them *More Stately Mansions.* All royalties
from the sale of editions and translations of this book go to
Yale University for the benefit of the Eugene O'Neill
Collection, for the purchase of books in the field of
the drama, and for the possible establishment of Eugene
O'Neill Scholarships in the Yale School of Drama.

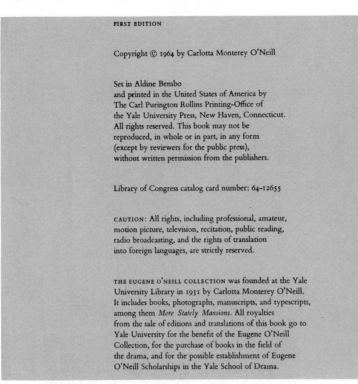

[i–vi] vii [viii–ix] x–xi [xii–xvi] 1–21 [22–24] 25–41 [42] 43–67 [68] 69–115 [116] 117–137 [138] 139–194

$[1\text{–}13]^{8}$

Contents: p. i: half title; p. ii: frontispiece; p. iii: title; p. iv: copyright; p. v: *'List of Illustrations'*; p. vi: blank; p. vii: beginning of prefatory note; pp. viii–ix: facsimile of page from the original typescript; pp. x–xii: remainder of prefatory note; p. xiii: second half title; p. xiv: *'Characters* | [six lines of roman and italic type]'; p. xv: act-scene synopsis; p. xvi: illustration; pp. 1–22: text, headed *'Act One, Scene One'*; p. 23: blank; p. 24: illustration; pp. 25–41: text, headed *'Act One, Scene Two'*; p. 42: illustration; pp. 43–67: text, headed *'Act One, Scene Three'*; p. 68: illustration; pp. 69–115: text, headed *'Act Two, Scene One'*; p. 116: illustration; pp. 117–137: text, headed *'Act Two, Scene Three'*; p. 138: blank; pp. 139–194: text, headed *'Act Three, Scene One'*.

Dust jackets for A 47-I-1.a and A 47-EI-1

Typography and paper: 13 point on 14, Aldine Bembo. 4⁵⁄₁₆″ × 7⁷⁄₁₆″ (7¹¹⁄₁₆″); thirty-three to thirty-seven lines per page. No running heads. Wove paper.

Binding: Black V cloth (fine linen-like grain). Front: '[goldstamped EO signature]'. Spine: '[vertically top to bottom, goldstamped] EUGENE O'NEILL: MORE STATELY MANSIONS [four squares] Yale'. Wove endpapers of different stock from text paper. All edges trimmed.

Dust jacket: White background. Front: '[black] *More Stately Mansions* | [gray] *a new play by* [black] *Eugene O'Neill* | [photograph of EO by Carl Van Vechten inside green and blue frame]'. Spine: [vertically top to bottom, black] *Eugene O'Neill: More Stately Mansions* | [horizontally] Yale'. Back has ad for *LDJ*. Front flap: blurb for *MSM*, at bottom, 'FIRST EDITION'. Back flap: ad for *Poet* and *Hughie*.

Publication: 5,000 copies published 12 March 1964. $7.50.

Locations: JM^{c}A (dj); LC (deposit-stamp 1 May 1964); Lilly (dj); Yale.

Note one: Karl-Ragnar Gierow, manager of the Royal Dramatic Theatre, Stockholm, has a special relationship with EO's work. The Royal Dramatic Theatre was the first European theatre to produce an EO play (*Anna Christie*, 1923) and thereafter was the first European theatre to produce several of EO's plays.

When EO died in 1953, the manuscript for *More Stately Mansions* was unfinished. "O'Neill himself drew up a detailed plan for the revision and condensation of the play, and the copy is at present at the Royal Dramatic Theatre." * The version we have today is one edited according to EO's plan by Messrs. Gierow and Donald Gallup, curator of the American Literature Collection, Beinecke Library, Yale.

REPRINTINGS

A 47-I-1.b
New Haven: Yale University Press, [March 1964]. 10,000 copies. Paperback.

---

* Karl-Ragnar Gierow, "Eugene O'Neill's Posthumous Plays," *World Theatre*, VII (Spring 1958), 46–52.

A 47-I-1.c
New Haven: Yale University Press, [October 1967]. 2,500 copies. Paperback.

A 47-I-1.d
New Haven: Yale University Press, [October 1968]. 2,500 copies. Paperback.

A 47 MORE STATELY MANSIONS
English first book publication (1965)

A 47-EI-1
MORE STATELY MANSIONS
English first edition

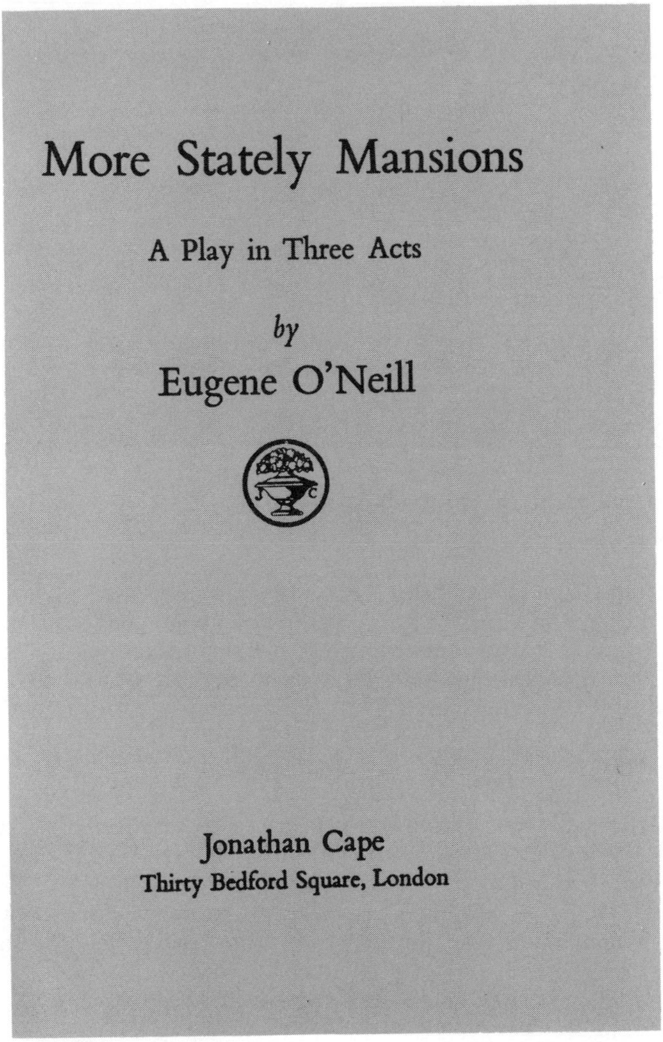
More Stately Mansions

A Play in Three Acts

by

Eugene O'Neill

Jonathan Cape
Thirty Bedford Square, London

A 47-EI-1: $7\frac{3}{8}'' \times 4\frac{15}{16}''$

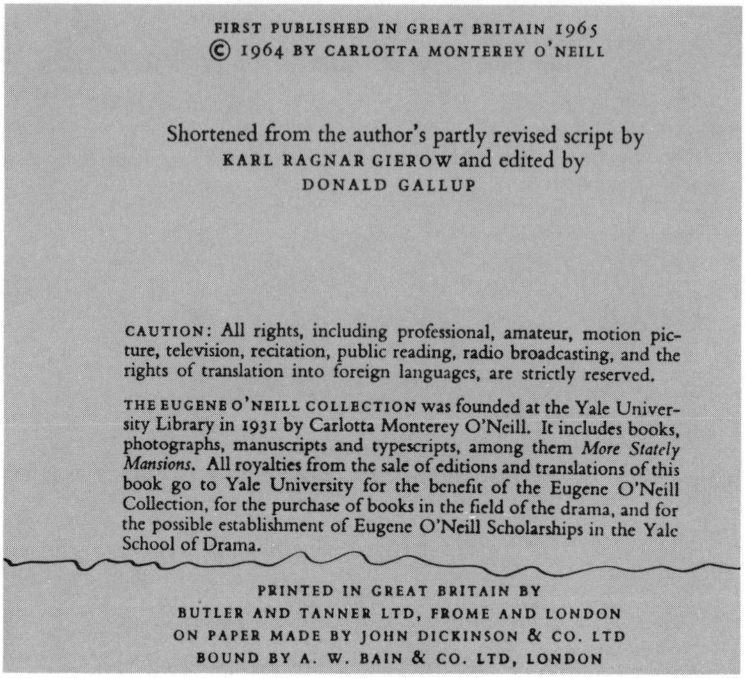

FIRST PUBLISHED IN GREAT BRITAIN 1965
© 1964 BY CARLOTTA MONTEREY O'NEILL

Shortened from the author's partly revised script by
KARL RAGNAR GIEROW and edited by
DONALD GALLUP

CAUTION: All rights, including professional, amateur, motion picture, television, recitation, public reading, radio broadcasting, and the rights of translation into foreign languages, are strictly reserved.

THE EUGENE O'NEILL COLLECTION was founded at the Yale University Library in 1931 by Carlotta Monterey O'Neill. It includes books, photographs, manuscripts and typescripts, among them *More Stately Mansions*. All royalties from the sale of editions and translations of this book go to Yale University for the benefit of the Eugene O'Neill Collection, for the purchase of books in the field of the drama, and for the possible establishment of Eugene O'Neill Scholarships in the Yale School of Drama.

PRINTED IN GREAT BRITAIN BY
BUTLER AND TANNER LTD, FROME AND LONDON
ON PAPER MADE BY JOHN DICKINSON & CO. LTD
BOUND BY A. W. BAIN & CO. LTD, LONDON

[1–8] 9–13 [14] 15–188 [189–192]

$[A]^{16}$ $B\text{–}F^{16}$

Contents: p. 1: half title; p. 2: card page; p. 3: title; p. 4: copyright; p. 5: 'CHARACTERS | [six lines of roman and italic type]'; p. 6: blank; p. 7: act-scene synopsis; p. 8: blank; pp. 9–13: 'PREFACE'; p. 14: blank; pp. 15–188: text, headed 'ACT ONE, SCENE ONE'; pp. 189–192: blank.

Typography and paper: 3½" × 5⁷⁄₁₆" (5⅝"); twenty-six to thirty-three lines per page. No running heads. Wove paper.

Binding: Blue imitation V cloth, paper-covered boards. Front: '[silverstamped EO signature]'. Spine: '[silver border of decorations] | EUGENE | O'NEILL | [decoration] | MORE | STATELY | MANSIONS | [publisher's device] | [border of decorations]'. White endpapers of different stock from text paper. All edges trimmed.

Dust jacket: White background. Front: '[green] MORE | STATELY | MANSIONS | [black] *a play by* | [black in green patch] EUGENE | O'NEILL'. Spine: '[black] MORE | STATELY | MANSIONS | [black in green patch] *a* | *play* | *by* | [black against white] EUGENE | O'NEILL | author of | [green] MOURNING | BECOMES | ELECTRA | etc. | [publisher's device]'. Back lists EO's plays, beginning with *TEJ* and ending with *Hughie*. Front flap: blurb for *More Stately Mansions;* back flap blank.

Publication: Unknown number of copies published in 1965. 21s.

Locations: BM (deposit-stamp 29 December 1964); JM^c^A (dj); Yale.

A 48 BREAD AND BUTTER
American first book publication

A 48-I-1
"Children of the Sea" and Three Other Unpublished Plays by Eugene O'Neill. Washington, D.C.: NCR Microcard Editions, [1972]. Edited by Jennifer McCabe Atkinson.

BB appears on pp. 1–84. See A 49-I-1(T) and A 49-I-1(L), "Children."

Dust jackets for A 1-II-1.a, A 36-I-1.a, and A 49-I-1(T)

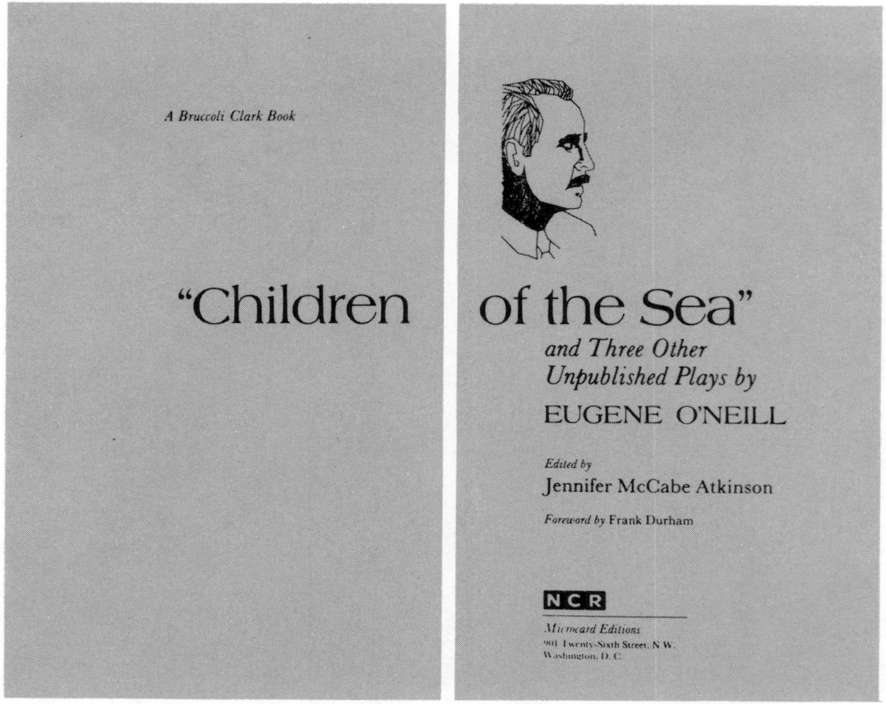

A Bruccoli Clark Book

"Children of the Sea"

and Three Other Unpublished Plays by

EUGENE O'NEILL

Edited by

Jennifer McCabe Atkinson

Foreword by Frank Durham

NCR

Microcard Editions

901 Twenty-Sixth Street, N.W.

Washington, D.C.

A 49-I-1(T): two-page title; $8^{15}/_{16}'' \times 5^{7}/_{16}''$

A 49 "CHILDREN OF THE SEA"
American first book publication (1972)

A 49-I-1(T)
"CHILDREN OF THE SEA" AND THREE OTHER UNPUBLISHED PLAYS BY EUGENE O'NEILL
American first edition, first printing, trade issue

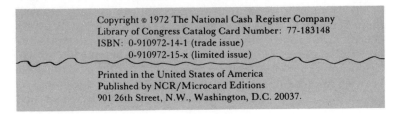

> Copyright © 1972 The National Cash Register Company
> Library of Congress Catalog Card Number: 77-183148
> ISBN: 0-910972-14-1 (trade issue)
> 0-910972-15-x (limited issue)
>
> Printed in the United States of America
> Published by NCR/Microcard Editions
> 901 26th Street, N.W., Washington, D.C. 20037.

[i–viii] ix [x] xi–xv [xvi] xvii–xviii [xix–xx] [1–2] 3 [4] 5–84 [85–86] 87 [88] 89–105 [106–108] 109 [110] 111–187 [188–190] 191 [192] 193–209 [210] 211–214 [215–220]

$[1\text{–}4]^{16}$ $[5]^{8}$ $[6\text{–}8]^{16}$

Contents: p. i: half title; pp. ii–iii: title; p. iv: copyright; p. v: 'For the McCabe sisters: | *Elizabeth* | *Marjorie* | *Jean* | *Ruth* | *Mary Lou';* p. vi: blank; p. vii: 'Contents'; p. viii: blank; pp. ix–x: 'Foreword'; pp. xi–xv: 'Introduction'; p. xvi: blank; pp. xvii–xviii: 'A Note on the Text'; p. xix: second half title; p. xx: blank; p. 1: 'Bread and Butter'; p. 2: blank; p. 3: '"BREAD AND BUTTER" | A Play In Four Acts | by | Eugene Gladstone O'Neill. | (ACT FIRST.)'; p. 4: blank; pp. 5–84: text, headed '"BREAD AND BUTTER"'; p. 85: 'Children of the Sea'; p. 86: blank; p. 87: '"CHILDREN OF THE SEA" | A Play in One Act | By | Eugene G. O'Neill.'; p. 88: blank; pp. 89–105: text, headed '"Children of The Sea"'; p. 106: blank; p. 107: 'Now I Ask You'; p. 108: blank; p. 109: title, character, and act-scene synopsis; p. 110: blank; pp. 111–187: text, headed 'PROLOGUE'; p. 188: blank; p. 189: 'Shell Shock'; p. 190: blank; p. 191: 'SHELL SHOCK | A Play In One Act | by | Eugene G. O'Neill | [three lines of type]'; p. 192: blank; pp. 193–209: text, headed 'Eugene G. O'Neill, | Provincetown, | Mass. | SHELL SHOCK'; p. 210: blank; pp. 211–212: 'Authorial Revisions | and Corrections'; pp. 213–214: 'Editorial Emendations'; pp. 215–220: blank.

Typography and paper: 10 point on 12, Baskerville. $3^{15}/_{16}$″ × $6^{7}/_{8}$″ ($7^{1}/_{8}$″); thirty-seven lines per page. No running heads. Wove paper.

Binding: Tan B cloth (linen-like grain). Front: '[stamped in red] "Children of | the Sea" | [stamped in brown] and Three Other Unpublished Plays | [stamped in red] by EUGENE O'NEILL | [stamped in brown] Edited by | Jennifer | McCabe | Atkinson | [to the left of the title covering the lower two-thirds of the front is a woodcut of EO's profile stamped in brown]'. Spine: '[vertically top to bottom, stamped in brown] EUGENE O'NEILL [stamped in red] "Children of the Sea" [stamped in brown] Atkinson | [horizontally, double rule stamped in brown] | [tan letters in solid brown boxes] [N|C|R] | [stamped in brown] Microcard | Editions'. Endpapers have facsimiles of pages from EO's typescripts of the plays. All edges trimmed.

Dust jacket: White background. Front: '[red] "Children of | the Sea" | [brown] And Three Other Unpublished Plays | [red] by EUGENE O'NEILL | [brown] Edited by | Jennifer | M^c^Cabe | Atkinson | [to the left of the title, covering the lower two-thirds of the front, is a brown woodcut of EO's profile]'. Spine: '[vertically top to bottom] [brown] EUGENE O'NEILL [red] "Children of the Sea" [brown] Atkinson | [horizontally, brown] [double rule] | [white letters against brown background] [N|C|R] | Microcard | Editions'. Back: blank. Front flap contains blurb for *"Children";* back contains ad for other NCR books.

This volume was originally sold without a dust jacket. Six months after publication, the dust jacket was added.

Publication: 2,000 copies published 29 February 1972. $8.95.

Printing: Printed by Science Press, Ephrata, Pa.; bound by the Complete Book Co., Philadelphia.

Locations: JM^c^A (dj); LC (deposit-stamp 20 March 1972); Lilly (dj).

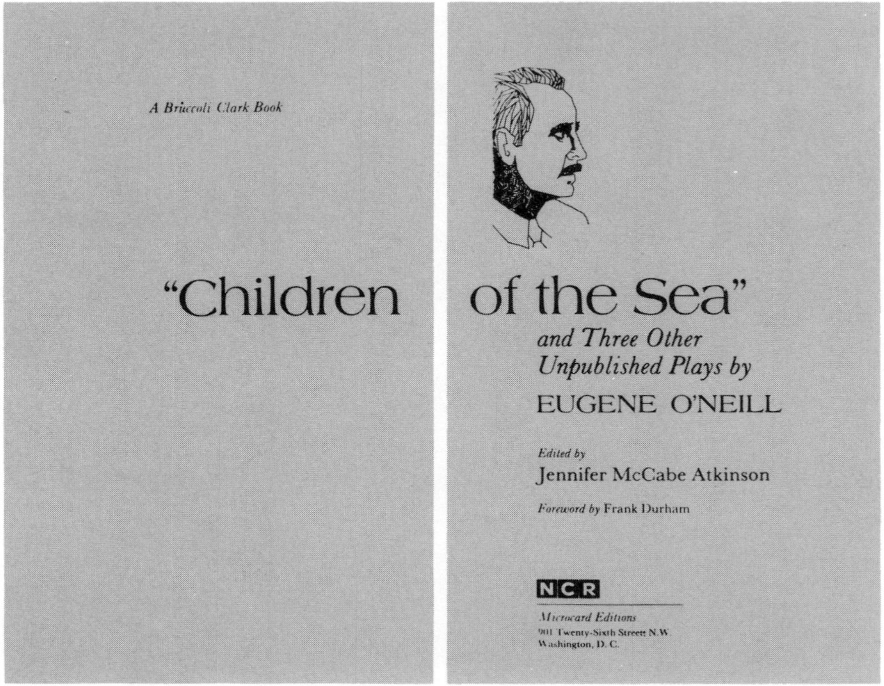

A Bruccoli Clark Book

"Children of the Sea"
and Three Other
Unpublished Plays by
EUGENE O'NEILL

Edited by
Jennifer McCabe Atkinson

Foreword by Frank Durham

NCR
Microcard Editions
901 Twenty-Sixth Street N.W.
Washington, D. C.

A 49-I-1(L): two-page title, line 2 and publisher's logo in brown; 8$^{15}/_{16}$" × 5$^{7}/_{16}$"

A 49 "CHILDREN OF THE SEA"
American limited book publication

A 49-I-1(L)
"CHILDREN OF THE SEA" AND THREE OTHER UNPUBLISHED PLAYS BY EUGENE O'NEILL
American first edition, first printing, limited issue

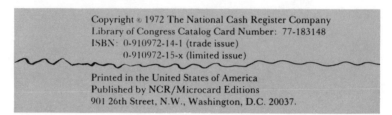

>
> Library of Congress Catalog Card Number: 77-183148
> ISBN: 0-910972-14-1 (trade issue)
> 0-910972-15-x (limited issue)
>
> Printed in the United States of America
> Published by NCR/Microcard Editions
> 901 26th Street, N.W., Washington, D.C. 20037.

[A–D] [i–viii] ix [x] xi–xv [xvi] xvii–xviii [xix–xx] [1–2] 3 [4] 5 [6] 7–84 [85–86] 87 [88] 89–105 [106–108] 109 [110] 111–187 [188–190] 191 [192] 193–209 [210] 211–214 [215–220]

$[1_{+1.2}]^{16}$ $[2\text{–}4]^{16}$ $[5]^{8}$ $[6\text{–}8]^{16}$

Contents: pp. A–D: (tipped in, single leaf, folded once to make four pages) facsimile of EO's *Who's Who in America* form; p. i: half title; pp. ii–iii: title page; p. iv: copyright page; p. v: 'For the McCabe sisters: | *Elizabeth* | *Marjorie* | *Jean* | *Ruth* | *Mary Lou*'; p. vi: blank; p. vii: 'Contents'; p. viii: blank; pp. ix–x: 'Foreword'; pp. xi–xv: 'Introduction'; p. xvi: blank; pp. xvii–xviii: 'A Note on the Text'; p. xix: second half title; p. xx: blank; p. 1: 'Bread and Butter'; p. 2: blank; p. 3: '"BREAD AND BUTTER" | A Play In Four Acts | by | Eugene Gladstone O'Neill. | (ACT FIRST.)'; p. 4: blank; pp. 5–84: text, headed '"BREAD AND BUTTER"'; p. 85: 'Children of the Sea'; p. 86: blank; p. 87: '"CHILDREN OF THE SEA" | A Play In One Act | By | EugeneG.O'Neill.'; p. 88: blank; pp. 89–105: text, headed '"Children Of The Sea"'; p. 106: blank; p. 107: 'Now I Ask You'; p. 108: blank; p. 109: title, character, and act-scene synopsis; p. 110: blank; pp. 111–187: text, headed 'PROLOGUE'; p. 188: blank; p. 189: 'Shell Shock'; p. 190: blank; p. 191: 'SHELL SHOCK | A Play In One Act | by | Eugene G. O'Neill | [three lines of type]; p. 192: blank; pp. 193–209: text, headed 'Eugene G. O'Neill, | Provincetown, | Mass. | SHELL SHOCK'; p. 210: blank; pp. 211–212: 'Authorial Revisions | and Corrections'; pp. 213–214: 'Editorial Emendations'; pp. 215–220: blank; colophon on inside of rear endpaper: '[display T]his limited issue of | "CHILDREN OF THE SEA" AND THREE OTHER | UNPUBLISHED PLAYS BY EUGENE O'NEILL | has been set in the Photon version | of Baskerville. Of the 200 copies of this limited issue, | this is number | signed by the editor,'.

Typography and paper: 10 point on 12, Baskerville. $3^{15}/_{16}''$ × $6^{7}/_{8}''$ ($7^{1}/_{8}''$); thirty-seven lines per page. No running heads. Wove paper.

Binding: Brown B cloth (linen-like grain). Front: goldstamped woodcut of EO's profile in double-rule frame. Spine: '[horizontally, goldstamped] Atkinson | [double rule] | [two lines vertically top to bottom] EUGENE O'NEILL | "Children of the Sea" | [horizontally] [double rule] | [brown in goldstamped squares] N | C | R | Microcard | Editions'. Cordovan endpapers of different stock from text paper. All edges trimmed.

Slipcase: Cordovan-colored paper-covered boards. Front: black woodcut of EO's profile against solid red background within double-rule black frame.

Publication: 200 copies published 29 February 1972. $15.00.

Locations: JM^c^A (#1 boxed); Lilly (#112 boxed); Yale (#140 boxed).

A 50 NOW I ASK YOU
American first book publication (1972)

A 50-I-1
"Children of the Sea" and Three Other Unpublished Plays by Eugene O'Neill. Washington, D.C.: NCR Microcard Editions, [1972]. Edited by Jennifer McCabe Atkinson.

NIAY appears on pp. 107–187. See A 49-I-1(T) and A 49-I-1(L), "Children."

A 51 "SHELL SHOCK"
American first book publication (1972)

A 51-I-1
"Children of the Sea" and Three Other Unpublished Plays by Eugene O'Neill. Washington, D.C.: NCR Microcard Editions, [1972]. Edited by Jennifer McCabe Atkinson.

"SS" appears on pp. 189–209. See A 49-I-1(T) and A 49-I-1(L). "Children."

AA. Supplement
Published Acting Scripts

Published acting scripts present a special bibliographical problem. The playwright revises during rehearsals, tailoring the play to the demands of the production. When the play is published in book form, the playwright can restore deleted material or make additions to aid the reader in better visualizing the characters and setting. Thus, there are sometimes two distinct versions of a play – the acting script and the book version – both available for purchase.

Rather than classifying the published acting scripts as editions of the plays and including them in the major section of this bibliography, I have created a related, but separate, section for acting scripts which have been or are for sale. Sometimes the scripts are printed by the book publisher (e.g., Random House) for another publisher – either a publisher specializing in acting scripts like Samuel French or Dramatists Play Service or a paperback publisher – and the copyright information may be the same as that in the book version. At other times, the scripts are published independently by the specialist publishers, but the number of reprintings is not indicated on the copyright page. Consequently, it is difficult to place the scripts in the proper chronological order with the book editions, and it seemed advisable simply to group the acting scripts together.

I have given a quasi-facsimile of each title page, pertinent information from the copyright page, and a quasi-facsimile of the wrappers. In some instances, I have given publication dates on the basis of external evidence. The scripts described in this section are those I have seen. The plays are presented in alphabetical order.

AA 1 AH, WILDERNESS!
Date undetermined

Title page: 'AH, WILDERNESS! | *A COMEDY OF RECOLLECTION* | *IN THREE ACTS* | BY | EUGENE O'NEILL | COPYRIGHT, 1933, BY EUGENE O'NEILL | [nineteen lines of type giving translation and production rights notice] | SAMUEL

FRENCH | 25 West 45th Street, New York, N.Y. | 811 West 7th Street, Los Angeles, Calif. | SAMUEL FRENCH, Ltd., London | SAMUEL FRENCH (Canada), Ltd., Toronto'

On copyright page: *'Printed in the United States of America by* | THE RICHMOND HILL RECORD, RICHMOND HILL, N.Y.'

Wrappers: Orange background. Front: 'AH, Wilderness! | *By* EUGENE O'NEILL | [illustration of rampant lion against elaborate vine decoration with scroll bearing the following words] FRENCH'S STANDARD LIBRARY EDITION | [below the illustration] SAMUEL FRENCH, 25 West 45th Street., New York | Price 85 cents'. Spine: '[vertically from top to bottom] AH, WILDERNESS! By Eugene O'Neill.' Back is blank.

OTHER PRINTINGS

New York: Samuel French, [1960?]. In blue wrappers.

Location: JM^{c}A (both printings).

AA 2 BEYOND THE HORIZON

AA 2.1
BEYOND THE HORIZON
Date undetermined

Title page: '[seven vertical rules along left side] BEYOND | THE HORIZON | ACTING EDITION | * | [seven horizontal rules; the second and fourth are interrupted by the following two lines] PLAY IN THREE ACTS | BY EUGENE O'NEILL | [seven vertical rules along right side] * | DRAMATISTS | PLAY | SERVICE | INC.'

On copyright page: 'Copyright, 1921, by Eugene O'Neill'.

Wrappers: Gold background. Front: '[eight vertical rules along left side] BEYOND | THE HORIZON | BY EUGENE O'NEILL | ACTING EDITION | * | [eight horizontal rules; the second is interrupted by the following line] PLAY IN THREE ACTS | [eight vertical rules along the right side] * | DRAMATISTS | PLAY SERVICE | INC.' Spine: '[vertically from top to bottom] BEYOND THE HORIZON – O'NEILL'. Back lists thirteen new plays beginning with *Tall Story* and ending with *Comes a Day*.

Location: JM^{c}A.

AA 2.2
BEYOND THE HORIZON
1936/37

Title page: '[within wavy double-rule frame] BEYOND THE | HORIZON | By | EUGENE O'NEILL | PUBLISHED FOR | THE DRAMATISTS PLAY SERVICE | *by* | RANDOM HOUSE · NEW YORK'

On copyright page: 'Copyright, 1921, by Eugene O'Neill'.

Wrappers: Brown ink against tan background. Front: '[within wavy double-rule frame] BEYOND THE | HORIZON | By | EUGENE O'NEILL | PUBLISHED FOR | THE DRAMATISTS PLAY SERVICE | *by* | RANDOM HOUSE · NEW YORK | PRICE 75 CENTS'.

Location: Yale.

Note: The dates of this script have been arrived at on the basis of an advertisement on the back cover of the acting-script wrappers for Random House's Nobel Prize printing of EO's *Nine Plays*. See A 15-VII-1.b, *TEJ*.

AA 3 THE EMPEROR JONES

AA 3.1
THE EMPEROR JONES
1936/37

Title page: '[within wavy double-rule frame] THE | EMPEROR JONES | By | EUGENE O'NEILL | PUBLISHED FOR | THE DRAMATISTS PLAY SERVICE | *by* | RANDOM HOUSE · NEW YORK'

On copyright page: 'Copyright, 1920, by Eugene O'Neill'.

Wrappers: Brown ink against tan background. Front: '[within wavy double-rule frame] THE | EMPEROR JONES | By | EUGENE O'NEILL | PUBLISHED FOR | THE DRAMATISTS PLAY SERVICE | *by* | RANDOM HOUSE · NEW YORK | PRICE 75 CENTS'.

Location: Yale.

Note: The dates for this script have been arrived at on the basis of an advertisement on the back cover of the acting-script wrappers for Random House's Nobel Prize printing of EO's *Nine Plays*. See A 15-VII-1.b, *TEJ*.

AA 3.2
THE EMPEROR JONES
1949

Title page: 'EUGENE O'NEILL | [double rule] | THE EMPEROR JONES | WITH A STUDY GUIDE FOR THE | SCREEN VERSION OF THE PLAY | BY | WILLIAM LEWIN | MAX J. HERZBERG | *STUDENTS'* EDITION | [publisher's device] | APPLETON-CENTURY-CROFTS, INC. | NEW YORK'

Copyright page: 'COPYRIGHT, 1921, BY | D. APPLETON AND COMPANY | STUDY GUIDE AND KEY, COPYRIGHT, 1934, BY | WILLIAM LEWIN AND MAX J. HERZBERG | [ten lines of type] | Copyright, 1949, by Eugene O'Neill | Printed in the United States of America'

Wrappers: Gray green background. Front: '[white] EUGENE | O'NEILL | [white against black illustration of Jones in the forest] THE | EMPEROR | JONES'. Spine is blank. Back: '[white] APPLETON-CENTURY-CROFTS, INC.'.

Location: JM^c^A.

AA 4 "ILE"
1936/37

Title page: '[within wavy double-rule frame] ILE | By | EUGENE O'NEILL | PUBLISHED FOR | THE DRAMATISTS PLAY SERVICE | *by* | RANDOM HOUSE · NEW YORK'

On copyright page: 'Copyright, 1923, by Eugene O'Neill'.

Wrappers: Brown ink against tan background. Front: '[within wavy double-rule frame] ILE | By | EUGENE O'NEILL | PUBLISHED FOR | THE DRAMATISTS PLAY SERVICE | *by* | RANDOM HOUSE · NEW YORK | PRICE 35 CENTS'.

Location: Yale.

Note: The dates for this script have been arrived at on the basis of an advertisement on the back cover of the acting-script wrappers for Random House's Nobel Prize printing of EO's *Nine Plays*. See A 15-VII-1.b, *TEJ*.

AA 5 "IN THE ZONE"
[1936/37]

Title page: '[within wavy double-rule frame] IN THE ZONE | By | EUGENE O'NEILL | PUBLISHED FOR | THE DRAMATISTS PLAY SERVICE | *by* | RANDOM HOUSE · NEW YORK'

On copyright page: *'Copyright, 1923, by Eugene O'Neill'.*

Wrappers: Brown ink against tan background. Front: '[within wavy double-rule frame] IN THE ZONE | By | EUGENE O'NEILL | PUBLISHED FOR | THE DRAMATISTS PLAY SERVICE | *by* RANDOM HOUSE · NEW YORK | PRICE 35 CENTS'.

Location: Yale.

Note: The dates for this script have been arrived at on the basis of an advertisement on the back cover of the acting-script wrappers for Random House's Nobel Prize printing of EO's *Nine Plays*. See A 15-VII-1.b, *TEJ*.

AA 6 A MOON FOR THE MISBEGOTTEN
1958

Title page: *'A Moon for the* | *Misbegotten* | A PLAY IN FOUR ACTS | *By Eugeue O'Neill* | [publisher's device] | SAMUEL FRENCH, INC. | 25 WEST 45TH STREET NEW YORK 36 | 7623 SUNSET BOULEVARD HOLLYWOOD 46 | *LONDON TORONTO'*

On copyright page: 'A MOON FOR THE MISBEGOTTEN | COPYRIGHT, 1945, BY EUGENE O'NEILL | COPYRIGHT, 1952, BY EUGENE O'NEILL | COPYRIGHT ©, 1958, ACTING EDITION, | BY SAMUEL FRENCH, INC.'.

Wrappers: Yellow background. Front: '[all within three vertical rules on the right and left and three horizontal rules below] *A Moon for the* | *Misbegotten* | A PLAY IN FOUR ACTS | *by Eugene O'Neill* | [publisher's device] | Samuel French Inc.' Spine: '[vertically from top to bottom] A MOON FOR THE MISBEGOTTEN'. Back: ads for *Poor Bitos* and *In White America* and '#39'.

Location: JM^c^A.

AA 7 "WHERE THE CROSS IS MADE" *1936/37*

Title page: '[Within wavy double-rule frame] WHERE THE CROSS | IS MADE | By | EUGENE O'NEILL | PUBLISHED FOR | THE DRAMATISTS PLAY SERVICE | *by* | RANDOM HOUSE · NEW YORK'

On copyright page: *'Copyright, 1923, by Eugene O'Neill'.*

Wrappers: Brown ink against tan background. '[within wavy double-rule frame] WHERE THE CROSS | IS MADE | By | EUGENE O'NEILL | PUBLISHED FOR | THE DRAMATISTS PLAY SERVICE | *by* | RANDOM HOUSE · NEW YORK | PRICE 35 CENTS'.

Location: Yale.

Note: The dates for this script have been arrived at on the basis of an advertisement on the back cover of the acting-script wrappers for Random House's Nobel Prize printing of EO's *Nine Plays*. See A 15-VII-1.b, *TEJ*.

B. Contributions to Books and Pamphlets

Material by EO appearing for the first time in a book or pamphlet, arranged chronologically. Title pages of American first printings are given in quasi-facsimile. Items which EO contributed to a volume are designated; material making its appearance for the first time anywhere in print is so stipulated. Locations are provided only for scarce items.

B 1 PLEIADES CLUB YEAR BOOK
1912

[all within red line frame and black line frame] [gothic, red]P[black]leiades | [red]C[black]lub | Year | [white in black square]B[black]ook | [red] AM [ornament] ENT

"Free," p. 120. Poem contributed by EO.

Note: The publication of this poem marked the first EO appearance in a book. The poem is also collected in Sanborn and Clark. See B 12.

Location: Yale.

B 2 OUR AMERICAN THEATRE
1923

Our American Theatre | *By* | OLIVER M. SAYLER | *Author of "The Russian Theatre," etc.* | WITH TWENTY-FIVE ILLUSTRATIONS | FROM DRAWINGS | BY | LUCIE R. SAYLER | [publisher's device] | NEW YORK | [swash] BRENTANO'S | [roman] PUBLISHERS

Chapter III on EO quotes his credo, pp. 42–43. See C 45.

B 3 PEOPLE YOU KNOW
1923

PEOPLE YOU KNOW | BY | YOUNG BOSWELL | *WITH A PREFACE BY* | HAROLD STARK | [two lines of type] | [publisher's device] | BONI AND LIVERIGHT | PUBLISHERS :: :: NEW YORK

Contains an interview with EO, pp. 244–247. See C 49.

B 4 W. E. B. DUBOIS DINNER
1924

Program for dinner honoring W. E. B. DuBois – 13 April 1924 at Cafe Savarin, New York City.

A thirty-four-line appreciation of W. E. B. DuBois by EO appears on p. 4. EO's appreciation was read at the dinner by Jessie Fauset. Contributed by EO. First appearance in print.

Location: Yale.

B 5 EUGENE O'NEILL
1926

EUGENE O'NEILL | *By* | BARRETT H. CLARK | ROBERT M. McBRIDE & COMPANY | NEW YORK :: :: :: :: :: :: 1926

Quotes from letters, conversations, an autobiographical sketch from EO (pp. 4–5), the poem "It's Great When You Get In" (pp. 31–33), and lines from the poem "The Call" (p. 33). "The Call" is collected in Sanborn and Clark. See B 12 and C 24.

B 6 THE THEATRE OF GEORGE JEAN NATHAN
1926

[within triple-rule frame] THE THEATRE OF | GEORGE JEAN NATHAN | [red rule] | [black] CHAPTERS AND DOCUMENTS TOWARD A | HISTORY OF THE NEW AMERICAN DRAMA | [red rule] | [black] *by Isaac Goldberg* | [red rule] | [publisher's device] | [rule] | [black] *New York* SIMON AND SCHUSTER *MCMXXVI*.

Contains fourteen letters by EO to Nathan, pp. 143–165, and an EO letter to Goldberg, p. 77. The first eleven letters appeared in the *Boston Evening Transcript*. See C 62.

B 7 THE AMERICAN CARAVAN
1927

[decorated rule] | [all decorated type] THE AMERICAN | CARAVAN | [decorated rule] | A YEARBOOK | OF AMERICAN

LITERATURE | Edited by | VAN WYCK BROOKS LEWIS MUMFORD | ALFRED KREYMBORG PAUL ROSENFELD | □ □ | NEW YORK | THE MACAULAY COMPANY

Act One of *Lazarus Laughed,* pp. 807–833. This publication of Act One precedes book publication of the entire play. EO considerably revised Act One for book publication of the play. Contributed by EO. First appearance in print. See A 29-I-1.a.

B 8 A HISTORY OF THE AMERICAN DRAMA FROM THE CIVIL WAR TO THE PRESENT DAY, VOLUME II
1927

A HISTORY OF | THE AMERICAN DRAMA | *From the Civil War to the Present Day* | BY | ARTHUR HOBSON QUINN | [followed by three lines of type] | [rule] | VOLUME II | FROM WILLIAM VAUGHAN MOODY TO THE PRESENT DAY | [rule] | [publisher's device] | HARPER & BROTHERS PUBLISHERS | NEW YORK AND LONDON | 1927

On copyright page: 'FIRST EDITION'.

Reprinted in 1936 and 1945 by F. S. Crofts (now Appleton-Century-Crofts).

Contains EO letter to Quinn, p. 199. In 1936 reprint, the holograph letter is facsimiled between pp. 198 and 199. Also, the frontispiece for the 1945 printing is a photo of a sculptured bust of EO with a facsimile of EO's holograph inscription to Quinn. First appearance in print.

B 9 ANATHEMA!
1928

[within decorated frame] ANATHEMA! | [gothic] Litanies of Negation | [roman] BY | BENJAMIN DECASSERES | WITH A FOREWORD BY | EUGENE O'NEILL | [publisher's device] | [swash *N*]*ew* [swash *Y*]*ork* | GOTHAM BOOK MART | *1928*

Foreword by EO appears on pp. vii–xi. Contributed by EO. First appearance in print.

Note: There are 1,250 numbered, signed copies and an unknown number of unnumbered, unsigned copies of this edition.

Errata slips are pasted in on pp. xi and 32. In an unsigned copy seen, the erratum slip is incorrectly pasted to p. ix.

Locations: JM[c]A (#1205 boxed and unnumbered boxed); Yale.

B 10 SIXTEEN AUTHORS TO ONE
1928

[within double-rule frame] SIXTEEN | AUTHORS | TO ONE | DAVID KARSNER | *Intimate Sketches of* | *Leading American* | *Story Tellers* | *Illustrations by* | ESTHER M. MATTSSON | LEWIS COPELAND | COMPANY : : NEW YORK | *M C M X X V I I I*

On copyright page: 'First Printing—November, 1928'.

Chapter VI on EO, pp. 101–122, quotes from conversations.

B 11 EUGENE O'NEILL: THE MAN AND HIS PLAYS
1929

EUGENE O'NEILL | *The Man and His Plays* | *BY* | BARRETT H. CLARK | [publisher's device] | NEW YORK | ROBERT M. McBRIDE & COMPANY | 1929

On copyright page: 'First published, April, 1929'.

Adds conversations to the material quoted in Clark's 1926 volume. See B 5.

B 12 A BIBLIOGRAPHY OF THE WORKS OF EUGENE O'NEILL
1931

[within red decorated frame] [black] A BIBLIOGRAPHY | OF THE WORKS OF | EUGENE O'NEILL | BY | RALPH SANBORN | AND | BARRETT H. CLARK | [publisher's device] | NEW YORK · RANDOM HOUSE, INC · 1931

First book appearance of the following poems (pp. 113–161): "Fratricide," "Speaking, to the Shade of Dante, of Beatrices," "Submarine," "The Waterways Convention," "Villanelle of Ye Young Poet's First Villanelle to His Ladye and Ye Difficulties

Thereof," "Ballard of Old Girls," (Untitled)–"(With apologies to J. W. Riley)," (Untitled)–"All night I lingered at the Beach," "To a Bull Moose," (Untitled)–"I might forget the subway guard," (Untitled)–"I used to ponder deeply o'er," "Nocturne," "Ballard of the Modern Music Lover," (Untitled)–"As I scan the pages of history's scroll," "Only You," "The Shut-Eye Candidate," "Love's Lament," "The Quest of the Golden Girl," "The Glints of Them," "Hitting the Pipe," "Sentimental Stuff," "A Regular Sort of a Guy," "The Long Tale," "The Call," "The Haymarket," "Noon," "Ballard of the Seamy Side," "The Lay of the Singer's Fall," and "To Winter." "Free" is reprinted on pp. 111–112 (see B 1). EO agreed to the collection of these poems. See C 3–C 14 and C 16–C 31.

Note: 500 numbered copies published May 1931.

Locations: JM^c^A (#372); MJB (#117); Yale.

B 13 OUR CHANGING THEATRE
1931

[within decorated frame] OUR CHANGING THEATRE | *by* | R. DANA SKINNER | [publisher's device] | LINCOLN MAC VEAGH | [rule] | DIAL PRESS INC. | NEW YORK · MCMXXXI | LONGMANS, GREEN & CO., TORONTO

Quotes EO letter to George Jean Nathan, p. 86. This publication of this letter precedes its publication in *The Intimate Notebooks of George Jean Nathan*. See B 15 and C 70.

B 14 THE PROVINCETOWN
1931

The Provincetown | A STORY OF THE THEATRE | *by* | Helen Deutsch and Stella Hanau | [publisher's device] | FARRAR & RINEHART, Inc. | On Murray Hill New York

First book appearance for the following EO essays:

"Strindberg and Our Theater," pp. 191–193. See C 52.
"Are the Actors to Blame?" pp. 197–198. See C 64.

B 15 THE INTIMATE NOTEBOOKS OF GEORGE JEAN NATHAN
1932

THE INTIMATE NOTEBOOKS | *of* | *GEORGE JEAN NATHAN* | [six rules] | 19 [publisher's device] 32 | ALFRED · A · KNOPF · NEW YORK

On copyright page: 'FIRST EDITION'.

Quotes EO letter about completion of *MBE*, pp. 26–27 (see B 13 and C 70), and conversations, pp. 21–38.

B 16 EUGENE O'NEILL: A POET'S QUEST
1935

EUGENE O'NEILL | [swash *A*] [swash *P*]*oet's* [swash *Q*]*uest* | BY | RICHARD DANA SKINNER | AUTHOR OF "OUR CHANGING THEATRE" | *With a correct chronology* | *of the O'Neill plays* | *as furnished by* | *Eugene O'Neill* | [illustration] | LONGMANS, GREEN AND CO. | NEW YORK · TORONTO | 1935

On copyright page: 'FIRST EDITION'.

EO's letter is quoted on pp. vii–viii; the chronological list of his plays contributed by him appears on pp. viii–x. First appearance in print.

B 17 PASSING JUDGMENTS
1935

[within single-rule frame] [three-rule frame broken at each corner by an asterisk] PASSING | [script] Judgments | · | *by* [roman] GEORGE JEAN NATHAN | [publisher's device] | ALFRED · A · KNOPF | NEW YORK · 1935

Quotes EO conversation, pp. 119–120.

B 18 THE THEATRE OF THE MOMENT
1936

[within four-rule frame with a star at each corner] THE THEATRE | *OF THE* | MOMENT | A JOURNALISTIC COMMEN-

TARY | · | GEORGE JEAN NATHAN | [publisher's device] *NEW YORK · ALFRED · A · KNOPF · LONDON* | 1936

Reprints "The Recluse of Sea Island" (pp. 196–207), which quotes EO conversations. See C 82.

B 19 GEORGE PIERCE BAKER: A MEMORIAL *1939*

[all within double-rule frame] George Pierce Baker | *A Memorial* | NEW YORK CITY | DRAMATISTS PLAY SERVICE | 1939

Contains EO's tribute, "Prof. George Pierce Baker," pp. 20–23, which includes two complete letters and a portion of a third letter from EO. The tribute is reprinted from the *New York Times*. See C 81. The letters are printed here for the first time. Contributed by EO.

Note: There exist an unknown number of copies signed by the contributors. A note on the copyright page reads: 'This is one of a few copies of this booklet | printed on large paper, and signed by the authors.' Although I have not seen any, there may be unsigned copies of the book. Also, I have not seen any small paper printings.

Locations: JM^cA (signed): Yale (signed).

B 20 THIS IS MY BEST *1942*

America's 93 Greatest Living Authors Present | *This Is My Best* | [leaf decoration] OVER 150 SELF-CHOSEN AND | COMPLETE MASTERPIECES, TOGETHER WITH | THEIR REASONS FOR THEIR SELECTIONS | [publisher's device] *Edited by Whit Burnett* | Burton C. Hoffman THE DIAL PRESS New York, 1942

Quotes 24 May 1942 letter from EO on p. 738. The selection made by EO was *GGB*.

B 21 EUROPEAN THEORIES OF THE DRAMA *1947*

[All within single-rule frame] *European Theories* | *of The Drama* | WITH A SUPPLEMENT ON THE | AMERICAN

DRAMA | [followed by five lines of type] | BY | *Barrett H. Clark* | CROWN PUBLISHERS NEW YORK

On copyright page: '*Revised Edition* | COPYRIGHT, 1947, BY BARRETT H. CLARK'

Quotes letter from EO, p. 530; reprints EO's working notes for *MBE*, pp. 530–536. See A 32-I-1.b and C 75.

B 22 THESE THINGS ARE MINE
1947

GEORGE MIDDLETON | These Things Are Mine | THE AUTOBIOGRAPHY OF A | JOURNEYMAN PLAYWRIGHT | THESE THINGS ARE MINE AS THEY WERE, AND | ALWAYS WILL BE AS LONG AS I REMEMBER. | 1947 | THE MACMILLAN COMPANY · NEW YORK

On copyright page: 'First Printing'.

Includes a reproduction of an EO photograph with holograph inscription to GM, facing p. 113; quotes letters, pp. 118–119, 160, 229, 232; quotes conversations, pp. 250 and 317.

B 23 THE MAGIC CURTAIN
1951

[script] The | [roman] MAGIC CURTAIN | [theatre curtain] | THE STORY OF A LIFE IN TWO | FIELDS, THEATRE AND INVENTION | BY THE FOUNDER OF THE THEATRE GUILD | *Lawrence Langer* | E. P. DUTTON & COMPANY, INC., NEW YORK · 1951 | A STORY PRESS BOOK

Quotes letters from EO: pp. 275–278, 282–285, 397–399, and one inscription, p. 406.

B 24 GEORGE PIERCE BAKER AND THE AMERICAN THEATRE
1954

[Illustration of pince-nez] [display type] George Pierce Baker | [roman] AND THE AMERICAN THEATRE | *Wisner Payne*

Kinne | 1954 | HARVARD UNIVERSITY PRESS | CAMBRIDGE

Quotes letters from EO, pp. 193–194, 205–206, 287–288, and facsimiles an EO holograph inscription to GPB between pp. 208 and 209. See C 93.

B 25 THE LIVING STAGE
1955

[two-page title] [left page] THE | LIVING | [illustration] | *including 50 illustrations* | *by* Gerda Becker With | [right page] STAGE | [swash *A*] [swash *H*]*istory of the* [swash *W*]*orld* [swash *T*]*heatre* | Kenneth Macgowan | *Professor of Theatre Arts* | *University of California, Los Angeles* | William Melnitz | *Professor of Theatre Arts* | *University of California, Los Angeles* | PRENTICE-HALL, INC. *Englewood Cliffs, N.J.*

Reprints EO's original sketches of the setting for *DUTE*, p. 491. See C 60.

B 26 AUTHORS AT WORK
1957

Authors at Work | AN ADDRESS DELIVERED BY | Robert H. Taylor | AT THE OPENING OF AN EXHIBITION | OF LITERARY MANUSCRIPTS | AT THE GROLIER CLUB | TOGETHER WITH A | CATALOGUE OF THE EXHIBITION BY | Herman W. Liebert | AND FACSIMILES OF MANY | OF THE EXHIBITS | [line of squares] | New York · The Grolier Club · 1957

Contains a facsimile of a page of the holograph first draft of *MBE* (catalogue number 68).

B 27 PART OF A LONG STORY
1958

Part of | a Long Story | [decorated rule] | *Agnes Boulton* | Doubleday & Company, Inc. | Garden City, New York | 1958

On copyright page: 'First Edition'.

Quotes conversations with EO extensively throughout.

B 28 EUGENE O'NEILL AND THE TRAGIC TENSION *1958*

EUGENE O'NEILL | AND THE TRAGIC TENSION | *an interpretive study of the plays* | DORIS V. FALK | RUTGERS UNIVERSITY PRESS | NEW BRUNSWICK, NEW JERSEY, 1958

Quotes throughout from manuscript material.

B 29 A WAYWARD QUEST *1960*

'A | Wayward | Quest | [row of five diamond-shaped decorations] | *THE AUTOBIOGRAPHY OF* | Theresa Helburn | [publisher's device] | WITH ILLUSTRATIONS | Little, Brown and Company | BOSTON TORONTO'

On copyright page: 'FIRST EDITION'.

Quotes from fifteen EO letters and one wire, pp. 258–264, 266–279.

B 30 O'NEILL AND HIS PLAYS *1961*

O'NEILL | AND HIS PLAYS | *FOUR DECADES OF CRITICISM* | EDITED BY | Oscar Cargill | N. Bryllion Fagin | William J. Fisher | *NEW YORK UNIVERSITY PRESS 1961* | [publisher's device]

The following items by EO have first book appearance in this volume (some titles supplied by the volume editors):

"Damn the Optimists," pp. 104–106. Article. See C 41.
"O'Neill Talks About His Plays," pp. 110–112. Interview. See C 58.
"Memoranda on Masks," pp. 116–118. Essay. See C 78.
"Second Thoughts," pp. 118–120. Essay. See C 79.
"A Dramatist's Notebook," pp. 120–122. Essay. See C 80.
"O'Neill's Ideal of a Theatre," pp. 123–124. Letter. See C 77.

B 31 EUGENE O'NEILL AND THE SENATOR FROM TEXAS *1961*

EUGENE O'NEILL AND THE SENATOR FROM TEXAS | BY JOHN S. MAYFIELD | *With a Note by* EARLE B. MAYFIELD | THE YALE UNIVERSITY LIBRARY GAZETTE | NEW HAVEN 1961

Quotes four letters from EO to John S. Mayfield and one letter to Sen. Earle B. Mayfield (pp. 2–7); facsimiles on inside front cover an EO inscription to John Mayfield in Mayfield's copy of *All God's Chillun Got Wings and Welded.*

Note: There are 100 numbered copies, signed by Senator Mayfield.

Locations: JM^c^A (#12); Yale.

B 32 O'NEILL *1962*

[white lettering on black rectangle] O'NEILL | [black against white background] ARTHUR & BARBARA GELB | HARPER & BROTHERS · NEW YORK

Quotes EO extensively throughout.

B 33 O'NEILL: SON AND PLAYWRIGHT *1968*

O'NEILL | SON AND PLAYWRIGHT | [decoration] | by LOUIS SHEAFFER | *With photographs* | [publisher's device] | LITTLE, BROWN AND COMPANY · BOSTON · TORONTO

Sheaffer attributes two poems to EO which do not appear in Sanborn and Clark: "Shut In," p. 193, and "Not Understood," p. 201. See C 1, C 2. Facsimile of page of manuscript for the short story "Tomorrow" appears on pp. 212–213. Quotes extensively in passing from previously unpublished EO letters and conversations.

B 34 A DRAMA OF SOULS
1969

EGIL TORNQVIST | A Drama of Souls | *Studies in* | *O'Neill's Super-naturalistic* | *Technique* | YALE UNIVERSITY PRESS | NEW HAVEN AND LONDON, 1969

Quotes throughout from manuscript material and previously unpublished letters.

B 35 CONTOUR IN TIME
1972

Two-page title. '[left page] C O N T O U R I N | NEW YORK [publisher's device]'; '[right page] TRAVIS BOGARD | TIME | *The Plays of Eugene O'Neill* | OXFORD UNIVERSITY PRESS 1972'

Quotes from seven previously unpublished letters and one telegram from EO to Kenneth Macgowan (pp. 178–181, 261–262), two letters from EO to Joseph Wood Krutch (pp. 299, 316–317), two letters from EO to Benjamin de Casseres (pp. 319, 321), two letters from EO to Eleanor Fitzgerald (pp. 322, 335), and one letter from EO to Theresa Helburn (p. 383).

B 36 THE NEW PHOENIX PAMPHLET
1972

Two-page cover title: '[left page or back cover] [white against black] [phoenix decoration] | THE NEW | PHOENIX | REPERTORY | COMPANY | 149 West 45th St., New York, N.Y. 10036 | [signature of designer] | [spread across the two pages is a white caricature of EO outlined in red]'; '[right page or front cover] [photo of statue of Dionysus against black background]'.

Page one facsimiles in gray green a page of the EO holograph fair copy for *GGB* as background for the section title: '[white] THE GREAT | GOD BROWN | by | EUGENE O'NEILL'. The pamphlet was edited by Daniel N. Freudenberger and designed by Karl Leabo.

B 37 O'NEILL: SON AND ARTIST
1973

O'NEILL | SON AND ARTIST | [decoration] | by LOUIS SHEAFFER | *with photographs* | [publisher's device] | LITTLE, BROWN AND COMPANY · BOSTON · TORONTO

Quotes extensively throughout from previously unpublished letters as well as EO's personal diaries and working notes for plays.

C. First Appearances in Newspapers, Periodicals, or Occasional Publications

Works by EO published in newspapers, periodicals, or occasional publications (theatre playbills), arranged chronologically. The material includes plays, poems, essays, one short story, letters, and interviews which quote EO.

C 1
"Shut In," *New London Telegraph* (1 September 1911), p. 4.

Poem appeared in "Laconics" column, which ran daily with a variety of material ranging from topical comments to poetry. Attributed to EO by Louis Sheaffer, not in Sanborn and Clark. See B 33.

C 2
"Not Understood," *New London Telegraph* (27 November 1911), p. 4.

Poem appeared in "Laconics" column. Attributed to EO by Louis Sheaffer, not in Sanborn and Clark. See B 33.

C 3
"The Waterways Convention," *New London Telegraph* (26 August 1912), p. 4.

Poem appeared in "Laconics" column. Collected in Sanborn and Clark. See B 12.

C 4
"Villanelle of Ye Young Poet's First Villanelle to His Ladye and Ye Difficulties Thereof," *New London Telegraph* (27 August 1912), p. 4.

Poem appeared in "Laconics" column. Collected in Sanborn and Clark. See B 12.

C 5
"Ballard of Old Girls," *New London Telegraph* (28 August 1912), p. 4.

Poem appeared in "Laconics" column. Collected in Sanborn and Clark. See B 12.

C 6
Untitled—"'(With apologies to J. W. Riley)'," *New London Telegraph* (2 September 1912), p. 4.

Poem appeared in "Laconics" column. Collected in Sanborn and Clark. See B 12.

C 7
Untitled—"All night I lingered at the Beach," *New London Telegraph* (6 September 1912), p. 4.

Poem appeared in "Laconics" column. Collected in Sanborn and Clark. See B 12.

C 8
"To a Bull Moose," *New London Telegraph* (11 September 1912), p. 4.

Poem appeared in "Laconics" column. Collected in Sanborn and Clark. See B 12.

C 9
Untitled—"I might forget the subway guard," *New London Telegraph* (11 September 1912), p. 4.

Poem appeared in "Laconics" column. Collected in Sanborn and Clark. See B 12.

C 10
Untitled—"I used to ponder deeply o'er," *New London Telegraph* (13 September 1912), p. 4.

Poem appeared in "Laconics" column. Collected in Sanborn and Clark. See B 12.

C 11
"Nocturne," *New London Telegraph* (13 September 1912), p. 4.

Poem appeared in "Laconics" column. Collected in Sanborn and Clark. See B 12.

C 12
"Ballard of the Modern Music Lover," *New London Telegraph* (17 September 1912), p. 4.

Poem appeared in "Laconics" column. Collected in Sanborn and Clark. See B 12.

C 13
Untitled—"As I scan the pages of history's scroll," *New London Telegraph* (23 September 1912), p. 4.

Poem appeared in "Laconics" column. Collected in Sanborn and Clark. See B 12.

C 14
"Only You," *New London Telegraph* (27 September 1912), p. 4.

Poem appeared in "Laconics" column. Collected in Sanborn and Clark. See B 12.

C 15
"'It's Great When You Get In'," *New London Telegraph* (28 September 1912), p. 4.

Poem appeared in "Laconics" column. Reprinted in Barrett H. Clark's *Eugene O'Neill*. See B 5.

C 16
"The Shut-Eye Candidate," *New London Telegraph* (3 October 1912), p. 4.

Poem appeared in "Laconics" column. Collected in Sanborn and Clark. See B 12.

C 17
"Love's Lament," *New London Telegraph* (16 October 1912), p. 4.

Poem appeared in "Laconics" column. Collected in Sanborn and Clark. See B 12.

C 18
"The Quest of the Golden Girl," *New London Telegraph* (17 October 1912), p. 4.

Poem appeared in "Laconics" column. Collected in Sanborn and Clark. See B 12.

C 19
"The Glints of Them," *New London Telegraph* (19 October 1912), p. 4.

Poem appeared in "Laconics" column. Collected in Sanborn and Clark. See B 12.

C 20
"Hitting the Pipe," *New London Telegraph* (22 October 1912), p. 4.

Poem appeared in "Laconics" column. Collected in Sanborn and Clark. See B 12.

C 21
"Sentimental Stuff," *New London Telegraph* (28 October 1912), p. 4.

Poem appeared in "Laconics" column. Collected in Sanborn and Clark. See B 12.

C 22
"A Regular Sort of a Guy," *New London Telegraph* (4 November 1912), p. 4.

Poem appeared in "Laconics" column. Collected in Sanborn and Clark. See B 12.

C 23
"The Long Tale," *New London Telegraph* (5 November 1912), p. 4.

Poem appeared in "Laconics" column. Collected in Sanborn and Clark. See B 12.

C 24
"The Call," *New London Telegraph* (19 November 1912), p. 4.

Poem appeared in "Laconics" column. Collected in Sanborn and Clark. See B 5 and B 12.

C 25
"The Haymarket" and "Noon," *New London Telegraph* (21 November 1912), p. 4.

Poems appeared in "Laconics" column. Collected in Sanborn and Clark. See B 12.

C 26
"Ballard of the Seamy Side," *New London Telegraph* (22 November 1912), p. 4.

Poem appeared in "Laconics" column. Collected in Sanborn and Clark. See B 12.

C 27
"The Lay of the Singer's Fall," *New London Telegraph* (27 November 1912), p. 4.

Poem appeared in "Laconics" column. Collected in Sanborn and Clark. See B 12.

C 28
"To Winter," *New London Telegraph* (9 December 1912), p. 4.

Poem appeared in "Laconics" column. Collected in Sanborn and Clark. See B 12.

C 29
"Fratricide," *New York Call* (17 May 1914), p. 10.

Poem. Collected in Sanborn and Clark. See B 12.

C 30
"Speaking, to the Shade of Dante, of Beatrices," *New York Tribune* (5 July 1915), p. 7.

Poem appeared in F.P.A.'s "The Conning Tower" column. Collected in Sanborn and Clark. See B 12.

C 31
"Submarine," *The Masses* (February 1917), p. 43.

Poem. Collected in Sanborn and Clark. See B 12.

C 32
"Tomorrow," *The Seven Arts* (June 1917), 147–170.

Short Story. EO's only published story.

C 33
"The Long Voyage Home," *The Smart Set*, LIII, 2 (October 1917), 83–94.

One-act play. Preceded book publication. See A 9-I-1.a.

C 34
"Ile," *The Smart Set*, LV, 1 (May 1918), 89–100.

One-act play. Preceded book publication. Reprinted in *New York Times* (11 May 1919), IV, p. 2. See A 11-I-1.a.

C 35
"The Moon of the Caribbees," *The Smart Set*, LV, 4 (August 1918), 73–86.

One-act play. Preceded book publication. See A 8-I-1.a.

C 36
Clark, Barrett H. "The Plays of Eugene O'Neill," *New York Sun* (18 May 1919), VI, p. 11.

Includes autobiographical sketch sent him by EO.

C 37
"The Dreamy Kid," *Theatre Arts*, IV, 1 (January 1920), 41–56.

One-act play. Preceded book publication. See A 19-I-1.

C 38
Coleman, Alta May. "Personality Portraits No. 3. Eugene O'Neill," *Theatre*, XXXI (April 1920), 264, 302.

Article quotes EO.

C 39
"A Letter from O'Neill," *New York Times* (11 April 1920), VI, p. 2.

About *BTH*.

C 40
The Emperor Jones, *Theatre Arts*, V, 1 (January 1921), 29–59.

One-act play. Preceded book publication. See A 15-I-1.a.

C 41
"Eugene O'Neill's Credo and His Reasons for His Faith," *New York Tribune* (13 February 1921), pp. 1, 6.

Article defending *Diff'rent*. See B 30.

C 42
Loving, Pierre. "Eugene O'Neill," *Bookman*, LIII (August 1921), pp. 511–520.

Article quotes an EO letter to the author.

C 43
Letter to the Drama Editor, *New York Times* (18 December 1921), VI, p. 1.

About *AC*.

C 44
Mollan, Malcolm. "Making Plays With a Tragic End," *Philadelphia Public Ledger* (22 January 1922), Magazine Sec., p. 3.

Interview quotes EO.

C 45
Sayler, Oliver M. "The Real Eugene O'Neill," *Century*, CIII (January 1922), 341–359.

Interview quotes EO. See B 2.

C 46
Sayler, Oliver M. "The Artist in the Theatre," *Shadowland* (April 1922), 49, 66, 77.

Interview quotes EO.

C 47
"The Hairy Ape," *Theatre*, XXXVI (August 1922), 80, 82, 84, 122.

Excerpts from the play. Followed book publication. See A 20-I-1.

C 48
Mullett, Mary B. "The Extraordinary Story of Eugene O'Neill," *American Magazine*, XCIV (November 1922), 34, 112, 114, 116, 118, 120.

Interview quotes EO.

C 49
"Young Boswell Interviews Eugene O'Neill," *New York Tribune* (24 May 1923), p. 13.

Interview quotes EO. See B 3.

C 50
O'Neill, J. F. "What a Sanatorium Did for Eugene O'Neill," *Journal of the Outdoor Life*, XX (June 1923), 191–192, 221.

Article quotes EO.

C 51
Merrill, Charles A. "Eugene O'Neill, World-Famed Dramatist, and Family Live in Abandoned Coast Guard Station at Cape Cod," *Boston Globe* (8 July 1923), Editorial and News Feature Sec., p. 1.

Interview quotes EO.

o

C 52
"Strindberg and Our Theatre," *Provincetown Playbill,* No. 1 (1923–24), pp. 1, 3. Reprinted in *New York Times* (6 January 1924), VII, p. 1.

Essay. See B 14.

C 53
All God's Chillun Got Wings, The American Mercury, V, 2 (February 1924), 129–148.

Three-act play. Preceded book publication. See A 23-I-1.

C 54
"'All God's Chillun' Defended by O'Neill," *New York Times* (19 March 1924), p. 19.

Statement by EO.

C 55
"The Play That Is Talked About," *Theatre,* XXXIX (June 1924), 26, 28, 54.

Excerpts from *DUTE*. Preceded book publication. See A 25-I-1.

C 56
Bird, Carol. "Eugene O'Neill–The Inner Man," *Theatre,* XXXIX (June 1924), 8, 60.

Interview quotes EO.

C 57
Sweeney, Charles P. "Back to the Source of Plays Written by Eugene O'Neill," *New York World* (9 November 1924).

C 58
"Eugene O'Neill Talks of His Own Plays," *New York Herald Tribune* (16 November 1924), VII-VIII, p. 14.

Article quotes EO. See B 30.

C 59
Kalonyme, Louis. "O'Neill Lifts Curtain on His Early Days," *New York Times* (21 December 1924), IV, p. 7.

Interview quotes EO.

C 60
Illustration, *Theatre Arts*, IX (April 1925), 224.

EO's sketches of the Cabot farmhouse for *DUTE*.

C 61
Merrill, Flora. "Fierce Oaths and Blushing Complexes Find No Place in Eugene O'Neill's Talk," *New York World* (19 July 1925).

Article quotes EO. See B 37.

C 62
"Playwright and Critic: The Record of a Stimulating Correspondence," *Boston Transcript* (31 October 1925), III, p. 8.

Correspondence with George Jean Nathan, includes facsimile of EO holograph letter. See B 6.

C 63
"The Fountain," *Greenwich Playbill*, No. 3 (1925–26), p. 1.

Essay.

C 64
"Are the Actors to Blame?" *Provincetown Playbill*, No. 1 (1925–26). Reprinted in *New York Times* (8 November 1925), VIII, p. 2.

Essay. See B 14.

C 65
"The Playwright Explains," *New York Times* (14 February 1926), VIII, p. 2.

Essay by EO on *GGB*.

C 66
Letter to the Drama Editor, *New York Times* (7 March 1926), VIII, p. 2.

About Franz Werfel's *Goat Song*.

C 67
Clark, Barrett H. "Eugene O'Neill, A Chapter in Biography," *Theatre Arts*, X (May 1926), 325–326.

Quotes letters and conversations by EO. See B 5.

C 68
Karsner, David. "Eugene O'Neill at Close Range in Maine," *New York Herald Tribune* (8 August 1926), VIII, pp. 4–6.

Interview quotes EO.

C 69
"A Eugene O'Neill Miscellany," *New York Sun* (12 January 1928), p. 31.

Interview quotes EO.

C 70
Letter to George Jean Nathan, *The American Mercury*, XVI (January 1929), 119.
See B 13 and B 15.

C 71
Kemp, Harry. "Out of Provincetown: A Memoir of Eugene O'Neill," *Theatre*, LI (April 1930), 22–23, 66.

Article quotes EO.

C 72
"Producers, Players and Pictures," *New York Times* (15 February 1931), VIII, p. 6.

Article quotes EO.

C 73
Lindley, Ernest K. "Exile Made Him Appreciate U.S. O'Neill Admits," *New York Herald Tribune* (22 May 1931), p. 19.

News item quotes EO.

C 74
Woolf, S. J. "O'Neill Plots A Course for the Drama," *New York Times* (4 October 1931), V, p. 6.

Interview quotes EO.

C 75
"O'Neill's Own Story of Electra in the Making," *New York Herald Tribune* (8 November 1931), VII, p. 2.

Excerpts from EO's working diary for *MBE*. See A 32-I-1.b and B 21.

C 76
Anderson, John. "Eugene O'Neill I," *Theatre Arts*, XV (November 1931), 938–942.

Article quotes EO.

C 77
"O'Neill Says Soviet Stage Has Realized His Dream," *New York Herald Tribune* (19 June 1932), VII, p. 2.

News story quotes 2 June 1930 EO letter to Kamerny Theatre about *DUTE* and *AGCGW* productions. See B 30.

C 78
"Memoranda on Masks," *American Spectator* (November 1932), p. 3.

Essay. See B 30.

C 79
"Second Thoughts," *American Spectator* (December 1932), p. 2.

Essay. See B 30.

C 80
"A Dramatist's Notebook," *American Spectator* (January 1933), p. 2.

Essay. See B 30.

C 81
"Prof. George Pierce Baker," *New York Times* (13 January 1935), IX, p. 1.

Tribute to Prof. G. P. Baker. See B 19.

C 82
Nathan, George Jean. "The Recluse of Sea Island," *Redbook*, LXV (August 1935), 34.

Article quotes EO. See B 18.

C 83
Brown, John Mason. "Eugene O'Neill Salutes Mr. Anderson's Winterset," *New York Post* (6 April 1936), Theatre Sec., p. 11.

Quotes EO letter to Drama Critics' Circle.

C 84
"Gustav Presents Nobel Prize to 3," *New York Times* (11 December 1936), p. 34.

News story prints EO's Nobel acceptance speech.

C 85
Woolf, S. J. "Eugene O'Neill Returns After Twelve Years," *New York Times* (15 September 1946), VI, pp. 11, 61–62.

Interview quotes EO.

C 86
" 'The Iceman Cometh,' " *New York Times* (6 October 1946), II, p. 1.

Interview quotes EO.

C 87
Prideaux, Tom. "Eugene O'Neill," *Life,* XXI (14 October 1946), 102–104, 106, 108, 110, 113–114, 116.

Interview quotes EO and excerpts for the first time in print a speech by Edmund from *LDJ*. See A 42-I-1.a.

C 88
Crichton, Kyle. "Mr. O'Neill and the Iceman," *Collier's,* CXVIII (26 October 1946), 18, 39–40, 42.

Interview quotes EO.

C 89
Bowen, Croswell. "The Black Irishman," *PM* (3 November 1946).

Interview quotes EO. Collected in Cargill, B 30.

C 90
Basso, Hamilton. "The Tragic Sense–I," *The New Yorker,* XXIV (28 February 1948), 34–38, 40, 42, 44–45.

Profile quotes EO.

C 91
Basso, Hamilton. "The Tragic Sense–II," *The New Yorker,* XXIV (6 March 1948), 34–38, 40, 43–44, 46, 48–49.

Profile quotes EO. Reprints his Nobel prize speech.

C 92
Basso, Hamilton. "The Tragic Sense—III," *The New Yorker,* XXIV (13 March 1948), 37–40, 42, 44, 46–47.

Profile quotes EO.

C 93
Kinne, Wisner Payne. "George Pierce Baker and Eugene O'Neill," *Chrysalis,* VII, 9–10 (1954), 3–14.

Quotes EO letters. Followed book publication. See B 24.

C 94
Hamilton, Gladys. "Untold Tales of Eugene O'Neill," *Theatre Arts,* XL (August 1956), 31–32, 88.

Quotes letters from EO.

C 95
Welsh, Mary. "Softer Tones for Mr. O'Neill's Portrait," *Theatre Arts,* XLI (May 1957), 67–68, 82–83.

Article quotes conversation with EO and card he sent her on opening of 1947 production of *MFTM* in Columbus, Ohio. Collected in Cargill, B 30.

C 96
Cowley, Malcolm. "A Weekend with Eugene O'Neill," *Reporter,* XVII (5 September 1957), 33–36.

Quotes EO conversation.

C 97
Gelb, Arthur. "An Epitaph for the O'Neills," *New York Times* (4 October 1959), II, pp. 1, 3.

Quotes EO letters on *GGB.*

C 98
Gallup, Donald. "Eugene O'Neill's 'The Ancient Mariner'," *The Yale University Library Gazette,* XXXV (October 1960), 61–86.

Text of EO's "manuscript," i.e., holograph notes he made in his personal copy of Coleridge's "The Ancient Mariner," appears on pp. 63–86. The play was performed at Provincetown Theatre, New York, in April 1924. It was never published during EO's lifetime.

C 99
Gelb, Arthur. "Onstage He Played the Novelist," *The New York Times Book Review* (30 August 1964), pp. 1, 23.

Review of *MSM* and *Ten "Lost" Plays* which includes a facsimile of a portion of the *MSM* original manuscript on p. 23.

C 100
Flory, Claude R. "Notes on the Antecedents of *Anna Christie*," *PMLA*, LXXXVI, 1 (January 1971), 77–83.

Contains two letters from EO to John Rodgers.

C 101
Frazer, Winifred L. "O'Neill's Iceman – Not Ice Man," *American Literature*, XLIV, 4 (January 1973), pp. 677–678.

Quotes from three EO letters to George Jean Nathan written during February and August 1940.

D. Blurbs

Promotional blurbs by EO for works by other authors, arranged chronologically.

D 1
THE THEATRE OF TOMORROW

An ad for Kenneth Macgowan's *The Theatre of Tomorrow* (New York: Boni & Liveright, 1922) on the verso of leaf one of four leaves of advertisements between pp. 176 and 177 in *Theatre Arts*, VI, 2 (April 1922) contains an EO blurb.

The statement reads: 'I have just finished reading your book. Now that I have "got" | it as a whole for the first time, I have the same feeling I had | after I read Well's "Outline"—that of having seen a thing in | its entire significance which before was scattered about and | had meaning only in its own episodes. I think you have done | a remarkable and inspiring thing for the future of the theatre. | Speaking as a playwright, I feel your book *can not help but* | encourage and sustain anyone worth his or her salt in our craft to shoot at new stars. | —EUGENE O'NEILL.'

D 2
THE REHABILITATION OF EVE (1924)

Title page: 'The | REHABILITATION OF EVE | *by* SALLIE HOVEY | *"The weariest and most loathed worldly life that* | *age, ache, penury and imprisonment* | *Can lay on nature is a paradise* | *To what we fear of death."* | SHAKESPEARE: *Measure for Measure—Act III* | CHICAGO | HYMAN-McGEE Co. | 1924'

Copyright page: 'Copyright, 1924 | HYMAN-McGEE Co. | CHICAGO'.

A facsimile of a holograph letter from EO appears on the front of the dust jacket. On Brook Farm, Ridgefield, Connecticut, stationery, it reads:

June 11, 1924.

Dear Miss Hovey

I finished reading your script a few days ago. My sincerest congratulations! It seems to me a most extraordinary and stimulating piece of writing. It interested me immensely from the first to the last chapter.

With best wishes,
Eugene O'Neill

Location: JM^c^A (dj).

D 3
WHITE BUILDINGS (1926)

Title page: 'White Buildings: | Poems by Hart Crane | With a *Foreword by* | ALLEN TATE | [publisher's device] | BONI & LIVERIGHT, 1926'

On copyright page: 'COPYRIGHT 1926 : : BY | BONI & LIVERIGHT, INC.'.

EO blurb appears on front cover of dust jacket: 'EUGENE O'NEILL *writes*: | "Hart Crane's poems are profound | and deep-seeking. In them he re-|veals, with a new insight, and unique | power, the mystic undertones of | beauty which move words to express | vision."'

Note: EO had been asked to write a foreword for the volume and apparently agreed, but he did not do it. The publishers settled for an advertising blurb from him. See Joseph Schwartz and Robert C. Schweik, *Hart Crane: A Descriptive Bibliography* (Pittsburgh: University of Pittsburgh Press, 1972).

Locations: ICU (dj); NBuU (dj); NNC (dj).

D 4
NAVIGATOR (1927)

Title page: '[within double-rule frame] NAVIGATOR | [illustration of ship on high seas] [swash *T*]*he* [swash *S*]*tory* of [swash *N*]*athaniel* [swash *B*]*owditch* | *By* ALFRED STANDORD | [star] | 1927 | WILLIAM MORROW & COMPANY NEW YORK'.

Copyright page: '*Copyright, 1927,* | BY WILLIAM MORROW & COMPANY, INC. | FIRST PRINTING, SEPTEMBER, 1927 | PRINTED IN THE U.S.A. BY | QUINN & BODEN COMPANY, INC. | RAHWAY, N.J.'.

There are two EO blurbs. The first appears on the front cover of the dust jacket: '"A fine piece of work . . . glamorous days . . . all the fascination | of true romance."—EUGENE O'NEILL.'

The second blurb appears on the inside front flap of the dust jacket: '[italic] EUGENE O'NEILL | *writes*: | "NAVIGATOR caught my interest | in the first chapters and held it to | the end. A fine piece of work! | After reading it one feels as if one | had known Bowditch personally | and lived in Old Salem in the | glamorous days of 'iron men and | wooden ships.' And the story of | Bowditch's strange intense love for | Elizabeth Boardman has all the | deep fascination of true romance."'

Location: Yale (dj).

E. Material Quoted in Catalogues

Material by EO (manuscript or typescript material) in auction or book dealer catalogues. Books are listed only if they are inscribed. Items are listed chronologically with undated catalogues at the end.

E 1

STANDARD SETS | DRAMA [decoration] MUSIC | . . . | THE FINE LIBRARY OF THE LATE | PHILIP MOELLER | . . . | . . . SEPTEMBER 10th, 1958, . . . | . . . September 11th, 1958 . . . | SALE NO. 504 | . . . | SWANN GALLERIES, INC. | . . .

#441. ALS, 1¼ pp., 25 February 1933, from Sea Island, Georgia, to Philip Moeller: 'Explains a delay in his expected "presentable draft of the opus . . . . . still butting my brains out on a fourth draft of it and far from satisfied . . . . I've also written the first draft of another, but of course, that hardly counts as a play yet. . . . A little inspiration is needed to see me out . . . . ."'

#442. ALS, 2 pp. 19 August 1933, from Wurzburg Camp, Faust, New York, to Philip Moeller. About casting *AW:* '"I have a very great affection for it because for me it is a true evocation of a mood of the past, of an American life that is dead. . . . Don't think of this play as a New England play! ! ! . . . . should be easy to cast with fresh faces that will help remove it from the routine theatre. Aren't all these Summer theatres bringing out any new talent! . . . ."'

#443. ALS, 2 pp., 30 October 1933, from Sea Island, Georgia, 30 October 1933, to Philip Moeller. About *AW:* '"From what I heard of Wilderness over the radio last night, I gather Essie and Nat still don't know their lines! A most disgraceful, slovenly exhibition . . . . I think it's up to you, to protect the Guild and my play . . . . I hope this radio last scene was no indication of the way it's given nightly in the theatre, or believe me, Ah, W! won't continue a big hit for long! . . . . make them leave MY lines!"'

#444. *Marco Millions*. First Edition inscribed: 'To Phil, with all best. Gene.'

#445. *Lazarus Laughed*. Inscribed: 'To Phil, with all friendship. Gene.'

#446. *Dynamo*. First Edition, with autograph postcard to Philip Moeller: '"Here's luck to Dynamo from its author (at present

steaming through the Suez and feeling pretty darned hot!) . . . . I find I'm able to work in the a.m.s. on shipboard—so all in jake! Gene."'

#447. Mourning Becomes Electra. First edition inscribed: 'To Phil, with all grateful friendship. Gene, Nov. 1931'.

#449. Ah, Wilderness! Limited printing inscribed: 'To Phil, here's the one we put over, all dressed up in Sunday best! Gene, Nov. 1933'.

#450. Days Without End. Limited printing inscribed: 'To Phil . . . grateful friendship! Gene, Feb. 1934'.

E 2
AUTOGRAPH LETTERS MANUSCRIPTS & DOCUMENTS . . . Catalogue No. 47 KENNETH W. RENDELL, INC. [Somerville, Mass., 1970]

#155. TLS, 1 p., 3 April 1921, from Provincetown, Mass. 'To Joseph D. Little, explaining that it will be impossible for him to accept an invitation to a dedication. "But I am nonetheless grateful to you for having remembered me. . . ."'

#156. Inscribed photo: 'to "Gaga," "with my love, as always".'

E 3
SALE NUMBER 3151 . . . AUTOGRAPHS . . . *February* 2 . . . *February* 3 . . . PARKE-BERNET GALLERIES · INC . . . *New York* · 1971

#256. ALS, 1½ pages, from EO in New York to John Barrymore, n.d. [February 1925]: '. . . Your Hamlet was the finest thing I have known in the theatre—an inspiring experience for me! Discouragement with our stage becomes a rotten pose when one faces such an achievement . . . When one is trying to create oneself, in however humble a way, there is nothing so wonderfully stimulating as seeing Art really live and breathe. It leaves no alibi to a playwright. Everything becomes possible—if he is . . .'

E 4
AUTOGRAPHS & . . . FIRST EDITIONS PAUL C. RICHARDS —Autographs . . . Brookline, Mass. . . . [Catalogue 69, August / September 1971]

#164. ALS, 1½ pages, from EO in France to "Joe," n.d.: '. . . damned sorry to learn the breaks are not coming your way. I sure hope the luck will soon change for you and you'll get on your feet again . . . I am your friend and will always do anything I can to help you. I haven't forgotten the old days and your loyal friendship for me. I'm enclosing a check to give you a boost over this rough spot you've run into . . .' . . . 'I'm fine in every way. Don't pay any attention to the newspaper crap about my dying or this or that . . . I never felt more in the pink . . . Buck up, Joe! You're not going to confess the game has you licked, are you? That isn't like you! Get a new grip on yourself and you can knock it dead yet! . . .'

E 5

Rare Books AND Autographs AT PUBLIC AUCTION THURSDAY, MAY 4TH, 1972 AT 2 P.M. . . . Sale 880 . . . SWANN GALLERIES, INC. . . . NEW YORK . . .

#226. *TIC*, inscribed: 'To Teresa, with all good wishes. Eugene O'Neill. Jan. 27, 1947.'

E 6

SALE NUMBER 3476 . . . PUBLIC AUCTION *Tuesday: February* 20 *at* 2:00 *p.m.* EXHIBITION AND SALE AT SOTHEBY PARKE BERNET INC . . . NEW YORK 10021 . . . 1973

Photo of three covers of typescript of *MBE*—item #226, typescript (carbon) of *MBE* with ink and pencil changes by EO. Each cover has ink holograph title and EO's signature. On page facing #226.

E 7

First Editions | & | Rare Books | DAVID L. O'NEAL | Fall 1973 [New Ipswich, New Hampshire]

#214. *Days Without End*, first edition with an EO letter laid in. TLS, 1 p., 5 March 1934, to W. E. Brooks. About Brooks' review of *DWE* which appeared in the *Presbyterian Banner*. '. . . says in part "especially gratifying [the review] . . . in view of the narrow-minded hostility and anti-religious prejudice which recently greeted this play . . . All my past plays, even when most materialistic are, in their spiritual implications a search and cry in the wilderness. . . ."'

E 8
M.A.C. CO-OPERATIVE CATALOGUE XIV ARGOSY Book STORES, INC. . . . *New York* . . . [n.d.]

#435. *LL,* presentation copy to Mrs. Tuwa Drew, CMO's maid, inscribed: 'To Tuwa with all friendship and grateful memories of your many kindnesses to me. Eugene O'Neill, Feb. 11, '29.'

E 9
AUTOGRAPHS, BOOKS BROADSIDES, EPHEMERA . . . Catalogue 127 ROBERT K. BLACK . . . Upper Montclair, N.J. . . . [n.d.]

#128. TLS with ink corrections, 1 p., from EO in Bermuda to Ruth Mason, May 5, 1927: '--- I have just looked through the notices you sent, and I am very pleased that your husband has made such a fine production of 'The Field God'. I am a sincere admirer of Mr. Green's work, and I hope the play will keep on for a good run. I have no copy of my latest play 'Strange Interlude' here, except my private one, and that I dare not send away. As the play is practically under contract already --- I do not believe there is anything to be done on that score. But as soon as there is a copy free I should like very much to have you both read it.'

F. Plays in Collections and Anthologies

A listing of both complete texts and abridged versions appearing in collections and anthologies which have been edited by someone other than EO. The collections are grouped chronologically under each play title; the play titles are arranged alphabetically.

F 1 AH, WILDERNESS!
1933

Best Plays of 1894/1899–1969/70; and The Yearbook of the Drama in America. Ed. R. B. Mantle et al. New York: Dodd, Mead, 1920–70. 53 vols. 1933, vol. 33.

Five Contemporary American Plays. Ed. William Henry Hildreth and Wilson Randle Dumble. New York: Harper, 1939.

Contemporary Drama: American, English and Irish, European Plays. Ed. Ernest Bradlee Watson and Benfield Pressey. New York: Scribners, 1941.

Sixteen Famous American Plays. Ed. Bennett Cerf and Van H. Cartmell. New York: Garden City Publishing Co., 1941.

A Complete College Reader. Ed. John Albert Holmes and Carroll S. Towle. Boston: Houghton Mifflin, 1950.

The Laureate Fraternity. Ed. Adrian H. Jaffe and Herbert Wisinger. Evanston, Illinois: Row, Peterson, 1950.

A Modern Repertory. Ed. Harlan Henthorne Hatcher. New York: Harcourt, Brace, 1953.

Readings for Enjoyment. Ed. Earle R. David and William C. Hummel. Englewood Cliffs, New Jersey: Prentice-Hall, 1959.

Ah, Wilderness!, The Hairy Ape, All God's Chillun Got Wings. Ed. E. Martin Browne. Harmondsworth, Middlesex: Penguin, 1960. PL18.

Ah, Wilderness! and Other Plays by Eugene O'Neill. Ed. E. Martin Browne, Harmondsworth, Middlesex: Penguin, 1966. PL67.

The Later Plays of Eugene O'Neill. Ed. Travis Bogard. New York: Modern Library, 1967.

F 2 ANNA CHRISTIE
1921

Best Plays of 1894/1899–1969/70; and The Yearbook of the Drama in America. Ed. R. B. Mantle et al. New York: Dodd, Mead, 1920–70. 53 vols. 1921, vol. 21.

The Pulitzer Prize Plays, 1918–1934. Ed Kathryn (Coe) and William Howard Cordell. New York: Random House, 1935.

A Treasury of the Theatre . . . from Aeschylus to Eugene O'Neill. Ed. Burns Mantle and John Gassner. New York: Simon and Schuster, 1935.

The Pulitzer Prize Plays . . . New Edition. Ed. Kathryn (Coe) and William Howard Cordell. New York: Random House, 1938.

Twentieth Century Plays, American. Ed. Frank Wadleigh Chandler and Richard Albert Cordell. Revised edition. New York: Nelson, 1939.

A New Edition of the Pulitzer Prize Plays. Ed. Kathryn (Coe) and William Howard Cordell. New York: Random House, 1940.

A Treasury of the Theatre. Ed. Burns Mantle and John Gassner. Revised and adapted for colleges by Philo M. Buck, Jr., John Gassner, and H. S. Alberson. New York: Simon and Schuster, 1940. 2 vols. *AC* appears in vol. 1.

Types of English Drama. Ed. John William Ashton. New York: Macmillan, 1940.

Twentieth Century Plays, British, American Continental . . . Third Edition. Ed. Richard Albert Cordell. New York: Ronald Press, 1947.

Better Reading, Vol. 2. Ed. Walter Blair and John C. Gerber. Chicago: Scott, Foresman, 1949. Also published in one volume under the title, *The College Anthology.*

Modern American Plays. Ed. Frederic G. Cassidy. New York: Longmans, Green, 1949.

A Treasury of the Theatre. Ed. John Gassner. Revised edition for colleges. New York: Simon and Schuster, 1950–51. 2 vols. *AC* appears in vol. 2.

The Heritage of American Literature. Ed. Lyon Norman Richardson, George H. Orians, and Herbert T. Brown. Boston: Ginn, 1951. 2 vols. *AC* appears in vol. 2.

A Treasury of the Theatre. Ed. John Gassner. Revised edition. New York: Simon and Schuster, 1951. 3 vols. *AC* appears in vol. 3.

Modern Drama for Analysis. Ed. Paul M. Cubeta. Revised edition. New York: Dryden, 1955.

Anna Christie, The Emperor Jones, Desire Under the Elms. Ed. E. Martin Browne. Harmondsworth, Middlesex: Penguin, 1960. PL17.

A Treasury of the Theatre: from Henrik Ibsen to Eugene Ionesco. Ed. John Gassner. Third college edition. New York: Simon and Schuster, 1960.

A Treasury of the Theatre. Ed. John Gassner. Revised edition. New York: Simon and Schuster, 1963. 3 vols. *AC* appears in vol. 3.

F 3 "BEFORE BREAKFAST"
1916

A Treasury of Plays for Women. Ed. by Frank Shay. Boston: Little, Brown, 1922.

Six Short Plays. New York: Vintage, 1965.

F 4 BEYOND THE HORIZON
1920

Best Plays of 1894/1899–1969/70; and The Yearbook of the Drama in America. Ed. R. B. Mantle et al. New York: Dodd, Mead, 1920–70. 53 vols. 1919, vol. 19.

Representative American Plays, 1767–1923. Ed. Arthur Hobson Quinn. Third edition revised and enlarged. New York: Century, 1925.

Representative American Plays from 1880 to the Present Day. Ed. Arthur Hobson Quinn. Modern Drama Edition. New York: Century, 1928.

Representative American Plays from 1767 to the Present Day. Ed. Arthur Hobson Quinn. Fifth edition revised and enlarged. New York: Century, 1930.

Seven Contemporary Plays. Ed. Charles Huntington Whitman. Boston: Houghton Mifflin, 1931.

The Pulitzer Prize Plays, 1918–1934. Ed. Kathryn (Coe) and William Howard Cordell. New York: Random House, 1935.

Modern English Readings. Ed. Roger Sherman Loomis and Donald Leman Clark. Revised edition. New York: Farrar and Rinehart, 1936.

The Pulitzer Prize Plays. Ed. Kathryn (Coe) and William Howard Cordell. New edition. New York: Random House, 1938?

Representative Plays from 1767 to the Present Day. Ed. Arthur Hobson Quinn. Sixth edition revised and enlarged. New York: Appleton-Century, 1938.

Western World Literature. Ed. Harry Wolcott Robbins and William Harold Coleman. New York: Macmillan, 1938.

Modern English Readings. Ed. Roger Sherman Loomis and Donald Leman Clark. Third edition. New York: Farrar and Rinehart, 1939.

Tragedies Old and New. Ed. Helen Elizabeth Harding. New York: Noble and Noble, 1939. Also published under the title, *Hamlet and Other Tragedies.*

A New Edition of the Pulitzer Prize Plays. Ed. Kathryn (Coe) and William Howard Cordell. New York: Random House, 1940.

Modern American Dramas. Ed. Harlan Henthorne Hatcher. New York: Harcourt, Brace, 1941.

Modern English Readings. Ed. Roger Sherman Loomis and Donald Leman Clark. Fourth edition. New York: Farrar and Rinehart, 1942.

Modern Dramas. Ed. Harlan Henthorne Hatcher. Shorter edition. New York: Harcourt, Brace, © 1944.

Drama and Theatre, Illustrated by Seven Modern Plays. Ed. Albert Rondthaler Fulton. New York: Holt, 1946.

Modern Dramas. Ed. Harlan Henthorne Hatcher. New shorter edition. New York: Harcourt, Brace, 1948.

Reading Drama: A Method of Analysis with Selections for Study. Fred Benjamin Millett. New York: Harper, 1950.

Modern English Readings. Ed. Roger Sherman Loomis and Donald Leman Clark. Fifth edition. New York: Rinehart, 1946. Also in sixth edition, 1950 and seventh edition, 1953.

Representative American Plays from 1767 to the Present Day. Ed. Arthur Hobson Quinn. Seventh edition, revised and enlarged. New York: Appleton-Century-Crofts, 1953.

Twelve American Plays, 1920–1960. Ed. Richard K. Corbin and Miriam Balf. New York: Scribners, 1969.

F 5 "BOUND EAST FOR CARDIFF" *1916*

American Scene. Ed. Barrett H. Clark and K. Nicholson. New York: Appleton, 1930.

Contemporary Trends: American Literature Since 1900. Ed. John Herbert Nelson and Oscar Cargill. Revised edition. New York: Macmillan, 1941. (*American Literature: A Period Anthology* [vol. 4], Oscar Cargill, General Editor.)

College Reading. Ed. George Sanderlin. Boston: Heath, 1953.

The Types of Literature. Ed. Francis X. Connolly. New York: Harcourt, Brace. 1955.

Freshman English Program. Ed. Cary B. Graham. Chicago: Scott, Foresman, 1960.

Repertory. Ed. Walter Blair and John Gerber. Chicago: Scott, Foresman, 1960.

S. S. Glencairn Four Plays of the Sea. Minneapolis: Cornelius Publishers, 1966.

F 6 DESIRE UNDER THE ELMS
1924

Best Plays of 1894/1899–1969/70; and The Yearbook of the Drama in America. Ed. R. B. Mantle et al. New York: Dodd, Mead, 1920–70. 53 vols. 1924, vol. 24.

Dramas of Modernism and Their Forerunners. Ed. Montrose J. Moses. Boston: Little, Brown, 1931.

Dramas of Modernism and Their Forerunners. Ed. Montrose J. Moses and Oscar James Campbell. Boston: Little, Brown, 1941.

The Nobel Prize Treasury. Ed. Marshall McClintock. Garden City, New York: Doubleday, 1948.

Twenty-five Best Plays of the Modern American Theatre: Early Series. Ed. John Gassner. New York: Crown, 1949.

The Book of the Play. Ed. Harold R. Walley. New York: Scribners, 1950.

Eight Great Tragedies. Ed. Sylvan Barnet, Morton Berman, and William Burto. New York: New American Library, 1957.

Masters of American Literature. Ed. Gordon Ray et al. Boston: Houghton, 1959. 2 vols.

Anna Christie, The Emperor Jones, Desire Under the Elms. Ed. E. Martin Browne. Harmondsworth: Penguin, 1960. PL 17.

American Dramatic Literature. Ed. Jordan Y. Miller. New York: McGraw-Hill, 1961.

Modern Drama for Analysis. Ed. Paul M. Cubeta. Third edition. New York: Holt, Rinehart and Winston, 1962.

Introduction to Literature: Plays. Ed. Lynn Altenbernd and Leslie L. Lewis. New York: Macmillan, 1963.

Studies in Drama. Ed. B. O. Bonazza and Emil Roy. New York: Harper and Row, 1963–64.

Drama in the Modern World. Ed. Samuel A. Weiss. Boston: Heath, 1964.

The Modern Theatre. Ed. Robert W. Corrigan. New York: Macmillan, 1964.

Representative Modern Plays: Ibsen to Tennessee Williams, Comp. Robert Warnock. Chicago: Scott, Foresman, 1964.

Twentieth Century American Writing. Ed. William T. Stafford. New York: Odyssey Press, 1965.

Modern Drama: Authoritative Texts . . . Backgrounds and Criticism. Ed. Anthony F. Caputi. New York: Norton, 1966.

Phaedra and Hippolytus: Myth and Dramatic Form. Ed. James L. Sanderson and Irwin Gopnik. Boston: Houghton Mifflin, 1966.

An Introduction to Literature: Drama. Comp. Edward L. Volpe and Marvin Magalaner. New York: Random House, 1967.

Drama: Principles and Plays. Comp. Theodore W. Hatlen. New York: Appleton-Century-Crofts, 1967.

Poetry, Drama, Fiction. Ed. Edward L. Volpe et al. New York: Random House, 1967.

Drama in the Western World: 15 Plays with Essays. Comp. Samuel A. Weiss. Boston: Heath, 1968.

Studies in Drama. Eds. B. O. Bonazza and Emil Roy. Second edition. New York: Harper and Row, 1968.

50 Best Plays of the American Theatre. Comp. John Gassner and Clive Barnes. New York: Crown, 1969. 4 vols.

Introduction to Literature: Plays. Ed. Lynn Altenbernd and L. L. Lewis. Second edition. New York: Macmillan, 1969.

Tragedy: Texts and Commentary. Ed. Morris Freedman. New York: Scribners, 1969.

F 7 DIFF'RENT
1920

Representative Modern Plays. Ed. Richard A. Cordell. New York: Nelson, 1929.

Six Short Plays. New York: Vintage, 1965.

F 8 "THE DREAMY KID"
1919

Plays of Negro Life. Ed. Alain L. Locke and Gregory Montgomery. New York: Harper, 1927.

Five Modern Plays. Boston: International Pocket Library, 1936.

Six Short Plays. New York: Vintage, 1965.

F 9 THE EMPEROR JONES
1920

Best Plays of 1894/1899–1969/70; and The Yearbook of the Drama in America. Ed. R. B. Mantle et al. New York: Dodd, Mead, 1920–70. 53 vols. 1920, vol. 20.

Contemporary American Plays. Ed. Arthur Hobson Quinn. New York: Scribners, 1923.

Representative American Dramas, National and Local. Ed. Montrose J. Moses. Boston: Little, Brown, 1925.

An Introduction to Drama. Ed. Jay B. Hubbell and John Owen Beatty. New York: Macmillan, 1927.

Plays of Negro Life. Ed. Alain L. Locke and Gregory Montgomery. New York: Harper, 1927.

Chief Contemporary Dramatists, Third Series. Ed. T. H. Dickinson. Boston: Houghton Mifflin, 1930.

Curtain! A Book of Modern Plays. Ed. Mrs. Virginia Woodson (Frome) Church. New York: Harper, 1932.

Modern Plays. Ed. John F. McDermott. New York: Harcourt, Brace, 1932.

Modern Plays. Ed. Samuel M. Tucker. New York: Macmillan, 1932.

Representative American Dramas, National and Local. Ed. Montrose J. Moses. Boston: Little, Brown, 1933.

The College Omnibus. Ed. James D. McCallum. New York: Harcourt, Brace, 1934.

Adventures in American Literature. Ed. Harry C. Schweikert, R. B. Inglis, John Gehlmann, and Norman Foerster. Revised edition. New York: Harcourt Brace, 1936.

The 1936 College Omnibus. Ed. James D. McCallum. New York: Harcourt, Brace, 1936.

The American Mind. Ed. Harry R. Warfel, Ralph H. Gabriel, and Stanley T. Williams. New York: American Book Company, 1937.

Contemporary Drama: American Plays. Comp. Ernest B. Watson and Benfield Pressey. New York: Scribners, 1937–38. 2 vols.

Explorations in Literature. Ed. Edwin Lillie Miller. Revised edition. Chicago: Lippincott, 1937–38. 2 vols.

The Revised College Omnibus. Ed. James D. McCallum. New York: Harcourt, Brace, 1939.

The Voices of England and America. Ed. David L. Clark, William B. Gates, and Ernest E. Leisy. New York: Nelson, 1939. 2 vols.

Milestones of the Drama. Ed. Helen Louise Cohen. New York: Harcourt, Brace, 1940.

Contemporary Drama: American, English and Irish, European Plays. Comp. Ernest B. Watson and Benfield Pressey. New York: Scribners, 1941.

Representative American Dramas, National and Local. Ed. Montrose J. Moses and Joseph Wood Krutch. Revised edition. Boston: Little, Brown, 1941.

World's Great Plays. Cleveland: World Publishing, 1944.

The College Omnibus. Ed. James D. McCallum. Sixth edition. New York: Harcourt, Brace, 1947.

Introduction to Literature. Ed. Louis G. Locke, William M. Gibson, and George Arms. New York: Rinehart, 1948.

Patterns in Modern Drama. Ed. L. C. Hartley and Arthur I. Ladu. New York: Prentice-Hall, 1948.

A College Book of American Literature. Ed. Harold M. Ellis, Louise Pound, George W. Spohn, and Frederick Hoffman, Jr. Second edition. New York: American Book Co., 1949.

American Life in Literature. Ed. Jay B. Hubbell. New York: Harper, 1949. 2 vols.

Modern American Dramas. Ed. Harlan H. Hatcher. New edition. New York: Harcourt, Brace, 1949.

A Quarto of Modern Literature. Ed. Leonard S. Brown and Porter G. Perrin. Third edition. New York: Scribners, 1950.

Modern Drama for Analysis. Ed. Paul M. Cubeta. New York: William Sloane Associates, 1950.

Nine Great Plays from Aeschylus to Eliot. Ed. Leonard F. Dean. New York: Harcourt, Brace, 1950.

Six Modern American Plays. New York: Modern Library, 1951.

The American Twenties. Ed. John K. Hutchens. Philadelphia: Lippincott, 1952.

The Art of the Play. Ed. Alan S. Downer. New York: Henry Holt, 1955.

Four Modern Verse Plays. Ed. Henry Popkin. New York: Holt, Rinehart and Winston, 1957, 1961. 2 vols. First and second series.

The Britannica Library of Great American Writing. Ed. Louis Untermeyer. Chicago: Lippincott, 1960. 2 vols.

Anna Christie, The Emperor Jones, Desire Under the Elms. Ed. E. Martin Browne. Harmondsworth: Penguin, 1960. PL 17.

Masters of Modern Drama. Ed. Haskell M. Block and Robert G. Shedd. New York: Random House, 1962.

Four Modern Plays: First Series. Revised edition. New York: Holt, Rinehart and Winston, 1963.

Classic Through Modern Drama. Ed. Otto Reinert. Boston: Little, Brown, 1970.

F 10 GOLD
1920

Six Short Plays. New York: Vintage, 1965.

F 11 THE GREAT GOD BROWN
1926

Best Plays of 1894/1899–1969/70; and The Yearbook of the Drama in America. Ed. R. B. Mantle et al. New York: Dodd, Mead, 1920–70. 53 vols. 1925, vol. 25.

Modern American and British Plays. Ed. Samuel M. Tucker. New York: Harper, 1931.

Plays from the Modern Theatre. Ed. Harrison R. Steeves. Boston: Heath, 1931.

Twenty-five Modern Plays. Ed. Samuel M. Tucker. New York: Harper, 1931.

American Plays. Ed. Allan G. Halline. New York: American Book Company, 1935.

British and American Plays, 1830–1945. Ed. W. H. Durham and John W. Doods. New York: Oxford University Press, 1947.

Twenty-five Modern Plays. Ed. Samuel M. Tucker and Alan S. Downer. Revised edition by Alan S. Downer. New York: Harper, 1948.

Masters of American Literature. Ed. Henry A. Pochmann and Gay Wilson Allen. New York: Macmillan, 1949. 2 vols.

Twenty-five Modern Plays. Ed. Samuel M. Tucker and Alan S. Downer. Third edition. New York: Harper, 1953.

Aspects of Modern Drama. Ed. M. W. Steinberg. New York: Henry Holt, 1960.

F 12 THE HAIRY APE
1922

Contemporary American Plays. Ed. Arthur Hobson Quinn. New York: Scribners, 1923.

Contemporary Plays. Ed. Thomas H. Dickinson and Jack R. Crawford. Boston: Houghton Mifflin, 1925.

American Literature. Ed. Robert Shafer. New York: Doubleday, Doran, 1926. 2 vols.

The Play's the Thing. Ed. Fred B. Millett and Gerald E. Bentley. New York: Appleton-Century, 1936.

Representative Modern Dramas. Ed. Charles H. Whitman. New York: Macmillan, 1936.

The New College Omnibus. Ed. James Fitz-James Fullington, Harry B. Reed, and Julia Norton McCorkle. New York: Harcourt, Brace, 1938.

This Generation. Ed. George K. Anderson and Edna Lou Walton. Chicago: Scott, Foresman, 1939.

Contemporary Drama: American, English and Irish, European Plays. Comp. Ernest B. Watson and Benfield Pressey. New York: Scribners, 1941.

Chief Patterns of World Drama. Ed. William S. Clark II. Boston: Houghton Mifflin, 1946.

Writers of the Western World. Ed. Clarence A. Hibbard. Revised edition. (United States Naval Academy Edition edited by Cyril B. Judge.) Boston: Houghton Mifflin, 1946.

The Literature of the United States. Ed. Walter Blair, Theodore Hornberger, and Randall Stewart. Chicago: Scott, Foresman, 1946–47. 2 vols.

Literature for Our Time. Ed. Leonard S. Brown, Harlow O. Waite, and Benjamin P. Atkinson. New York: Holt, 1947.

Dominant Types in British and American Literature. Ed. William H. Davenport, Lowry C. Wimberley, and Harry Shaw. New York: Harper, 1949. 2 vols.

The Literature of the United States. Ed. Walter Blair, Theodore Hornberger, and Randall Stewart. Single-volume edition. Chicago: Scott, Foresman, 1949.

This Generation. Ed. George K. Anderson and Edna Lou Walton. Revised edition. Chicago: Scott, Foresman, 1949.

Twenty-five Best Plays of the Modern American Theatre: Early Series. Ed. John Gassner. New York: Crown, 1949.

Seven Plays of the Modern Theater. Ed. Vincent Wall and James Patton McCormick. New York: American Book Company, 1950.

A Treasury of the Theatre. Ed. John Gassner. Revised edition for colleges. New York: Simon and Schuster, 1950–51. 2 vols.

Nine Modern Plays. Ed. Barrett H. Clark and William H. Davenport. New York: Appleton-Century-Crofts, 1951.

Ten Plays. Ed. Morton W. Bloomfield and Robert C. Elliot. New York: Rinehart, 1951.

A Treasury of the Theatre. Ed. John Gassner. Revised edition. New York: Simon and Schuster, 1951. 3 vols.

Literature for Our Time. Ed. Harlow O. Waite and Benjamin P. Atkinson. New York: Henry Holt, 1953.

Writers of the Western World. Ed. Clarence A. Hibbard and Horst Frenz. Second edition. Boston: Houghton Mifflin, 1954.

America's Literature. Ed. James D. Hart and Clarence Gohdes. New York: Dryden, 1955.

The American Tradition in Literature. Ed. Scully Bradley, Richard Beatty, and E. Hudson Long. New York: W. W. Norton, 1956.

The American Tradition in Literature. Ed. Sculley Bradley, Richmond Beatty, and E. Hudson Long. Shorter edition. New York: W. W. Norton, 1956.

Literature For Our Time. Ed. Harlow O. Waite and Benjamin P. Atkinson. New York: Henry Holt, 1958.

American Drama. Ed. Alan S. Downer. New York: Thomas Y. Crowell, 1960.

Ah, Wilderness!, The Hairy Ape, All God's Chillun Got Wings. Ed. E. Martin Browne. Harmondsworth: Penguin, 1960. PL 18.

Tragedy: Plays, Theory, Criticism. Ed. Richard L. Levin. New York: Harcourt Brace and World, 1960.

A Treasury of the Theatre: From Henrik Ibsen to Eugene Ionesco. Ed. John Gassner. Third college edition. New York: Simon and Schuster, 1960.

American Literature Survey. Ed. Milton R. Stern and Seymour L. Cross. New York: Viking, 1962. 4 vols.

A Treasury of the Theatre. Ed. John Gassner. Revised edition. New York: Simon and Schuster, 1963. 3 vols.

Great Plays, Sophocles to Brecht. Ed. Morton W. Bloomfield and Robert C. Elliott. New York: Holt, Rinehart and Winston, 1965.

50 Best Plays of the American Theatre. Comp. John Gassner and Clive Barnes. New York: Crown, 1969. 4 vols.

F 13 "HUGHIE"
1958

The Later Plays of Eugene O'Neill. Ed. Travis Bogard. New York: Modern Library, 1967.

What is the Play? Ed. Richard A. Cassell and Henry Knepler. Glenview, Illinois: Scott, Foresman, 1967.

Contexts of the Drama. Comp. Richard H. Goldstone. New York: McGraw-Hill, 1968.

F 14 THE ICEMAN COMETH
1946

Best Plays of 1894/1899–1969/70; and The Yearbook of the Drama in America. Ed. R. B. Mantle et al. New York: Dodd, Mead, 1920–70. 53 vols. 1946, vol. 46.

Best American Plays: Third Series—1945–51. Ed. John Gassner. New York: Crown, 1952.

Major Writers of America. Ed. Haskell M. Block and Robert G. Shedd. New York: Random House, 1962.

Masters of Modern Drama. Ed. Haskell M. Block and Robert G. Shedd. New York: Random House, 1962.

Twentieth Century Drama: England, Ireland and The United States. Ed. Ruby Cohn, Bernard F. Dukore, and Haskell M. Block. New York: Random House, 1966.

Plays of Our Time. Comp. Bennett Cerf. New York: Random House, 1967.

F 15 "ILE"
1916

Atlantic Book of Modern Plays. Ed. S. A. Leonard. Boston: Atlantic Monthly Press, 1921.

Twenty Contemporary One-Act Plays (American). Ed. Frank Shay. Cincinnati: Kidd, 1922.

One-Act Plays. Ed. G. A. Goldstone. Boston: Allyn, 1926.

Dramas by Present-Day Writers. Ed. Raymond Woodbury Pence. New York: Scribners, 1927.

One-Act Plays by Modern Authors. Ed. H. L. Cohen. New York: Harcourt, 1934.

Beacon Lights of Literature. Ed. Marquis E. Shattuck, Rudolph W. Chamberlain, and Edwin B. Richards. Syracuse, New York: Iroquois, 1940. 7 vols.

Twenty-five Best Plays of the Modern American Theatre: Early Series. Ed. John Gassner. New York: Crown, 1949.

Interpreting Literature. Ed. Kenneth L. Knickerbocker. New York: Henry Holt, 1955.

Interpreting Literature. Ed. Kenneth L. Knickerbocker and H. Willard Reninger. Revised edition. New York: Holt, Rinehart and Winston, 1960.

Interpreting Literature. Ed. Kenneth L. Knickerbocker and H. Willard Reninger. Third edition. New York: Holt, Rinehart and Winston, 1969.

F 16 "IN THE ZONE"
1917

Representative One-Act Plays by American Authors. Ed. M. Mayorga. Boston: Little, 1919.

A Quarto of Modern Literature. Ed. Leonard S. Brown and P. G. Penin. New York: Scribners, 1935.

Plays and the Theatre. Ed. Russell B. Thomas. Boston: Little, Brown, 1937.

Harbrace Omnibus. Ed. H. B. Reed, J. N. McCorkle, W. H. Hildreth, and J. D. McCallum. New York: Harcourt, Brace, 1942.

Our Reading Heritage. Ed. Harold H. Wagenheim, Elizabeth Voris Brattig, and Matthew Dolkey. New York: Henry Holt, © 1956. 4 vols.

Introduction to Imaginative Literature. Ed. Bernard D. Grebanier and Seymour Reiter. New York: Thomas Y. Crowell Company, 1960.

S. S. Glencairn Four Plays of the Sea. Minneapolis: Cornelius Publishers, 1966.

American Literature: Themes and Writers. Ed. George R. Carlsen. St. Louis, Missouri: Webster, 1967.

The Dimensions of Literature. Comp. James E. Miller and Bernice Slate. New York: Random House, 1967.

Drama: Literature on Stage. Ed. Charles O. Burgess. Philadelphia: Lippincott, 1969.

F 17 LAZARUS LAUGHED
1928

The Literature of America. Ed. Arthur Hobson Quinn, A. C. Baugh, and W. D. Howe. New York: Scribners, 1929.

Oxford Anthology of American Literature. William Rose Benét and Norman Holmes Pearson. New York: Oxford University Press, 1938.

Contemporary Trends: American Literature Since 1900. Ed. J. H. Nelson and Oscar Cargill. New York: Macmillan, 1949. Revised edition. (*American Literature: A Period Anthology* [vol. 4], Oscar Cargill, General Editor.)

F 18 LONG DAY'S JOURNEY INTO NIGHT
1956

Best Plays of 1894/1899–1969/70; and The Yearbook of the Drama in America. Ed. R. B. Mantle et al. New York: Dodd, Mead, 1920–70. 53 vols. 1956, vol. 56.

F 19 "THE LONG VOYAGE HOME"
1919

A Book of Dramas. Ed. Bruce Carpenter. Revised edition. New York: Prentice-Hall, 1949.

Introduction to Literature. Ed. L. G. Locke, William M. Gibson, and George Arms. Revised edition. New York: Rinehart, 1952. (Readings for Liberal Education, vol. 2.)

Preface to Drama. Ed. Charles W. Cooper. New York: Ronald Press, 1955.

Introduction to Literature. Ed. L. G. Locke, William M. Gibson, and George Arms. Third edition. New York: Rinehart, 1957. (Readings for Liberal Education, vol. 2.)

Masters of American Literature. Ed. Gordon Ray, Leon Edel, Thomas H. Johnson, Sherman Paul, and Claude Simpson. Boston: Houghton, 1959. 2 vols.

Makers of the Modern Theatre. Ed. Barry Ulanov. New York: McGraw-Hill, 1961.

Introduction to Literature. Ed. L. G. Locke, William Gibson, and George Arms. Fourth edition. New York: Holt, Rinehart and Winston, 1962. (Readings for Liberal Education, vol. 2.)

S. S. Glencairn Four Plays of the Sea. Minneapolis: Cornelius Publishers, 1966.

F 20 MARCO MILLIONS
1928

Twentieth Century Plays. Ed. Frank W. Chandler and Richard A. Cordell. New York: Nelson, 1934.

American Life in Literature. Ed. Jay B. Hubbell. New York: Harper, 1936.

Nelson's College Caravan. Ed. Arthur P. Hudson, Leonard B. Hurley, and Joseph D. Clark. New York: Nelson, 1936.

Nelson's College Caravan. Ed. Arthur P. Hudson, Leonard B. Hurley, and Joseph D. Clark. Third edition. New York: Nelson, 1942.

F 21 A MOON FOR THE MISBEGOTTEN
1957

Best Plays of 1894/1899–1969/70; and The Yearbook of the Drama in America. Ed. R. B. Mantle et al. New York: Dodd, Mead, 1920–70. 53 vols. 1956, vol. 56.

Best American Plays. Ed. John Gassner. New York: Crown, 1958. Fourth series, 1951–57.

Modern Drama: An Anthology of Nine Plays. Ed. Ernest J. Lovell and Willis W. Pratt. Boston: Ginn, 1963.

The Later Plays of Eugene O'Neill. Ed. Travis Bogard. New York: Modern Library, 1967.

F 22 "THE MOON OF THE CARIBBEES" *1918*

Fifty Contemporary One-Act Plays. Ed. Frank Shay. Cincinnati: Kidd, 1922.

Plays for the College Theatre. Ed. G. H. Leverton. New York: French, 1932.

Plays for the College Theatre. Ed. Garrett Hasty Leverton. New York: French, 1934.

Modern English Readings. Ed. Roger S. Loomis and Donald Leman Clark. New York: Farrar and Rinehart, 1934.

The Famous American Plays of the 1920's. Ed. Kenneth Macgowan. New York: Dell, 1959. Laurel Drama Series.

S. S. Glencairn Four Plays of the Sea. Minneapolis: Cornelius Publishers, 1966.

F 23 MOURNING BECOMES ELECTRA *1931*

Best Plays of 1894/1899–1969/70; and The Yearbook of the Drama in America. Ed. R. B. Mantle et al. New York: Dodd, Mead, 1920–70. 53 vols. 1931, vol. 31.

Representative Modern Plays—American. Ed. Robert Warnock. Chicago: Scott, Foresman, 1952.

Barron's Simplified Approach to Eugene O'Neill: Mourning Becomes Electra. Ed. John M. Callahan. Woodbury, New York: Barron's Educational Series, 1970.

F 24 "THE ROPE"
1919

A College Book of American Literature. Ed. Harold M. Ellis, Louise Pound, George W. Spohn. New York: American Book Co., 1939. 2 vols.

Themes in the One-Act Play. Ed. R. David Cox and Shirley S. Cox. New York: McGraw-Hill, 1971.

F 25 STRANGE INTERLUDE
1928

Best Plays of 1894/1899–1969/70; and The Yearbook of the Drama in America. Ed. R. B. Mantle et al. New York: Dodd, Mead, 1920–70. 53 vols. 1927, vol. 27.

The Pulitzer Prize Plays, 1918–1934. Ed. Kathryn (Coe) Cordell and William Howard Cordell. New York: Random House, 1935.

The Theatre Guild Anthology. Theatre Guild. New York: Random House, 1936.

The Pulitzer Prize Plays. Ed. Kathryn (Coe) Cordell and William Howard Cordell. New edition. New York: Random House, 1938?

A New Edition of the Pulitzer Prize Plays. Ed. Kathryn (Coe) Cordell and William Howard Cordell. New York: Random House, 1940.

F 26 THE STRAW
1921

Six Short Plays. New York: Vintage, 1965.

F 27 A TOUCH OF THE POET
1957

Best Plays of 1894/1899–1969/70; and The Yearbook of the Drama in America. Ed. R. B. Mantle et al. New York: Dodd, Mead, 1920–70. 53 vols. 1958, vol. 58.

Best American Plays: Fifth Series, 1957–1963. Ed. John Gassner. New York: Crown, 1963.

Image and Value: an Invitation to Literature. Ed. Martha Heasley Cox. New York: Harcourt Brace and World, 1966.

The Later Plays of Eugene O'Neill. Ed. Travis Bogard. New York: Modern Library, 1967.

F 28 WELDED
1924

Six Short Plays. New York: Vintage, 1965.

F 29 "WHERE THE CROSS IS MADE"
1918

More One-Act Plays by Modern Authors. Ed. H. L. Cohen. New York: Harcourt, 1921.

A Book of Modern Plays. Ed. George R. Coffman. Chicago: Scott, Foresman, 1925.

Adventures in American Literature. Ed. Harry C. Schweikert, R. B. Inglis, and John Gehlmann. New York: Harcourt, Brace, 1930.

On the High Road. Ed. Henry G. Bennett. New York: American Book Company, 1935.

Today's Literature. Ed. Dudley C. Gordon, Vernon R. King, and William W. Lyman. New York: American Book Company, 1935.

Adventures in American Literature. Ed. R. B. Inglis, John Gehlmann, Mary Rives Bowman, and Norman Foerster. Third edition. New York: Harcourt, Brace, 1941.

Prose and Poetry of the World. Ed. John R. Barnes et al. Syracuse, New York: Singer, 1941. The Prose and Poetry Series.

Adventures in American Literature. Ed. R. B. Inglis, Mary Rives Bowman, John Gehlmann, and Wilbur Schramm. Fourth edition. New York: Harcourt, Brace, 1947.

F 30 ALL GOD'S CHILLUN GOT WINGS
1924

Ah, Wilderness!, The Hairy Ape, All God's Chillun Got Wings. Ed. E. Martin Browne. Harmondsworth, Middlesex: Penguin, 1960. PL 18.

Note: This entry was added in proof and belongs alphabetically after F 1.

Appendix / Index

Appendix
Adaptations of Works by Eugene O'Neill

Adaptations of EO's plays for the film, radio, musical comedy, and opera.

FILM ADAPTATIONS

Anna Christie. Thomas H. Ince, producer, 1923. Directed by John Griffith Wray. Silent film.

Anna Christie. MGM, 1930. Screenplay by Frances Marion. Greta Garbo's first talking film.

Strange Interlude. MGM, 1932. Screenplay credit unlocated.

The Emperor Jones. United Artists, 1933. Screenplay by Dubose Heyward.

Ah, Wilderness! MGM, 1936. Screenplay by Albert Hackett and Frances Goodrich.

The Long Voyage Home. United Artists, 1940. Screenplay by Dudley Nichols. Based on "Moon of the Caribbees," "The Long Voyage Home," "Bound East for Cardiff," and "In the Zone."

The Hairy Ape. Jules Levey Productions, 1944. Screenplay by Robert D. Andrews and Decla Dunning.

Mourning Becomes Electra. RKO Pictures, Inc. 1947. Screenplay by Dudley Nichols.

Summer Holiday. MGM, 1948. Based on the 1936 Hackett and Goodrich adaptations of *Ah, Wilderness!*

Desire Under the Elms. Paramount, 1958. Screenplay by Irwin Shaw.

Long Day's Journey Into Night. Ely Landau, producer. Embassy Pictures, distributor. 1962. No screenplay credit; based directly on the play.

RADIO ADAPTATIONS

Beyond the Horizon. 2 August 1937. WJZ, New York. 9:30–10:30 P.M.

The Fountain. 9 August 1937. WJZ, New York. 9:30–10:30 P.M.

"Where the Cross Is Made". 16 August 1937. WJZ, New York. 9:30–10:30 P.M.

The Straw. 23 August 1937. WJZ, New York. 9:30–10:30 P.M.

MUSICAL ADAPTATIONS

The Emperor Jones. Metropolitan Opera Company. Adapted by the composer Louis Gruenberg. Premiered at the Met 7 January 1933. Opera based on *The Emperor Jones.*

New Girl In Town. Produced by Frederick Brisson, Robert E. Griffith, and Harold S. Prince. Book by George Abbott. Music and lyrics by Bob Merrill. Opened on Broadway 14 May 1957. Musical comedy based on *Anna Christie.*

Take Me Along. Produced by David Merrick. Book by Joseph Stein and Robert Russell. Music and lyrics by Bob Merrill. Opened on Broadway 22 October 1959. Musical comedy based on *Ah, Wilderness!*

Index

Full book entries are italicized. When a book appears in both full and brief entries, the index gives only the full entries. App. indicates that the material will be found in the Appendix; and T indicates a trade edition; L, a limited edition; and LP, a later printing.

Abbey Theatre, A 34-II-1
"Abortion," A 36
Adventures in American Literature, F 9, F 29
Ah, Wilderness!:
—as book: *A 33-I-1.a, A 33-I-1.b*, A 33-I-1.c–d, *A 33-EI-1.a*, A 33-EI-1.b–c
—as play: A 33, AA 1, E 1, F 1, App.
Ah, Wilderness! and Days Without End, A 34-EI-1.a–c
Ah, Wilderness! and Other Plays by Eugene O'Neill, F 1
Ah, Wilderness! and Two Other Plays, A 14-V-1, A 23-VI-1, A 33-III-1
Ah, Wilderness!, The Hairy Ape, All God's Chillun Got Wings, F 1, F 12, F 30
Allen, Gay Wilson, F 11
All God's Chillun Got Wings, A 23, C 53
All God's Chillun Got Wings and Welded, A 23-I-1
All God's Chillun Got Wings, Desire Under the Elms, and Welded, A 23-EI-1.a, A 23-EI-1.b
"All night I lingered at the Beach" (untitled poem), B 12, C 7
Altenbernd, Lynn, F 6
The American Caravan, A 29-I-1.a, B 7
American Drama, F 12
American Dramatic Literature, F 6
American Dramatists Series, A 1-I-1
American Life in Literature, F 9, F 20
American Literature, C 101, F 12
American Literature: A Period Anthology, F 5, F 17
American Literature Survey, F 12
American Literature: Themes and Writers, F 16
American Magazine, C 48
The American Mercury, C 53, C 70
The American Mind, F 9
American Play Company, A 15-I-1.A, A 15-II-1, A 20-I-1
American Plays, F 11
American Scene, F 5
American Spectator, C 78–80
The American Tradition in Literature, F 12
The American Twenties, F 9
America's Literature, F 12
Anathema!, B 9
Anderson, George K., F 12
Anderson, John, C 76
Anna Christie:
—as book: *A 21-IV-1, A 21-EII-1.a*, A 21-EII-1.b
—as play: A 21, F 2, App.
Anna Christie, The Emperor Jones, Desire Under the Elms, F 2, F 6, F 9

Appleton-Century-Crofts, Inc., AA 3.2
"Are the Actors to Blame?" B 14, C 64
Argosy Book Stores, Inc., E 8
Arms, George, F 9, F 19
The Art of the Play, F 9
Ashton, John William, F 2
"As I scan the pages of history's scroll" (untitled poem), B 12, C 13
Aspects of Modern Drama, F 11
Atkinson, Benjamin P., F 12
Atkinson, Jennifer McCabe, A 48-I-1, A 49-I-1(T), A 49-I-1(L), A 50-I-1, A 51-I-1
Atlantic Book of Modern Plays, F 15
Authors at Work, B 26

Balf, Miriam, F 4
"Ballard of Old Girls," B 12, C 5
"Ballard of the Modern Music Lover," B 12, C 12
"Ballard of the Seamy Side," B 12, C 26
Barnes, Clive, F 6, F 12
Barnes, John R., F 29
Barnet, Sylvan, F 6
Barron's Simplified Approach to Eugene O'Neill: Mourning Becomes Electra, F 23
Basso, Hamilton, C 90–92
Baugh, A. C., F 17
Beacon Lights of Literature, F 15
Beatty, John Owen, F 9
Beatty, Richard, F 12
Bechhofer, C. E., A 15-EI-1.a
"Before Breakfast":
—as book: *A 7-II-1*
—as play: A 7, F 3
Belasco, David, A 28-IV-1
Benét, William Rose, F 17
Bennet, Henry G., F 29
Bentley, Gerald E., F 12
Berman, Morton, F 6
Best American Plays, F 21
Best American Plays: Fifth Series, 1957–1963, F 27
Best American Plays: Third Series—1945–51, F 14
Best Plays of 1894/1899–1969/70; and The Yearbook of the Drama in America, F 1, F 2, F 4, F 6, F 9, F 11, F 14, F 18, F 21, F 23, F 25, F 27
Better Reading, F 2
Beyond the Horizon:
—as book: *A 14-I-1.a,* A 14-I-1.b–c
—as play: A 14, AA 2, F 4, App.
Beyond the Horizon and Gold, *A 14-EI-1.a,* A 14-EI-1.b
Beyond the Horizon and Marco Millions, A 14-EI(LP), A 28-EI(LP)
A Bibliography of the Works of Eugene O'Neill, B 12
Bird, Carol, C 56
Blair, Walter, F 2, F 5, F 12
Block, Haskell M., F 9, F 14
Bloomfield, Morton W., F 12
Bogard, Travis, F 1, F 13, F 21, F 27
Bonazza, B. O., F 6
Boni & Liveright, Inc., A 6-II-1.a–b, A 6-III-1, A 6-IV-1, A 6-V-1.a–c, A 7-III-1, A 7-IV-1.a–g, A 8-I-1.a–b, A 8-II-1, A 8-III-1.a–c, A 9-I-1.a–b, A 9-II-1, A 9-III-1.a–c, A 10-I-1.a–b, A 10-II-1, A 10-III-1.a–c, A 11-I-1.a–b, A 11-II-1, A 11-III-1.a–c, A 12-I-1.a–b, A 12-II-1, A 12-III-1.a–c, A 13-I-1.a–b, A 13-II-1, A 13-III-1.a–c, A 14-I-1.a–e, A 14-II-1, A 14-III-1.a–g, A 15-I-1.a–f, A 15-III-1, A 15-IV-1.a–f, A 15-V-1, A 15-VII-1.a, A 16-I-1, A 16-II-1, A 16-III-1.a–f, A 17-I-1.a–f, A 17-II-1, A 17-III-1.a–g, A 18-I-1.a–f, A 18-II-1, A 18-III-1.a–g, A 19-II-1, A 19-III-1.a–f, A 20-I-1, A 20-II-1, A 20-III-1.a–f, A 21-I-1, A 21-II-1, A 21-III-1.a–g, A 22-I-1, A 22-II-1, A 22-III-1.a–f, A 23-I-1, A 23-II-1, A 23-III-1.a–g, A 24-I-1, A 24-II-1, A 24-III-1.a–f, A 25-I-1, A 25-II-1, A 25-III-1.a–f,

A 26-I-1.a–c, A 27-I-1.a–c, A 28-I-1.a–f, A 29-I-1.a–b, A 30-I-1.a, A 30-II-1, B 3. *See also* Horace Liveright, Inc.; Liveright, Inc.
Bookman, C 42
A Book of Dramas, F 19
A Book of Modern Plays, F 29
The Book of the Play, F 6
Book Press, Inc., A 15-XIII-1
Boston Globe, C 51
Boston Transcript, C 62
"Bound East for Cardiff," A 6, F 5, App.
Bowen, Croswell, C 89
Bowman, Mary Rives, F 29
Bradley, Scully, F 12
Brattig, Elizabeth Voris, F 16
Bread and Butter, A 48
The Britannica Library of Great American Writing, F 9
British and American Plays, 1830–1945, F 11
Brown, Gilmore, A 29-III-1
Brown, Herbert T., F 2
Brown, John Mason, C 83
Brown, Leonard S., F 9, F 12, F 16
Browne, E. Martin, F 1, F 2, F 6, F 9, F 12, F 30
Bruccoli Clark, A 49-I-1(T), A 49-I-1(L)
Burto, William, F 6

"The Call," B 5, B 12, C 24
Callahan, John M., F 23
Campbell, Oscar James, F 6
Caputi, Anthony F., F 6
Cargill, Oscar, F 5, F 17
Carlsen, George R., F 16
Carpenter, Bruce, F 19
Cartmell, Van H., F 1
Cassell, Richard A., F 13
Cassidy, Frederic G., F 2
Century, C 45
Cerf, Bennett, A 1-II-1.a, A 1-EI-1.b, A 33-I-1.b, A 34-I-1.b, F 1, F 14
Chamberlain, Rudolph W., F 15
Chandler, Frank Wadleigh, F 2, F 20
Charles Scribner's Sons, A 6-IV-1, A 6-VI-1, A 7-V-1, A 8-V-1, A 9-V-1, A 10-IV-1, A 11-IV-1, A 12-V-1, A 13-IV-1, A 14-IV-1, A 15-IX-1, A 16-IV-1, A 17-IV-1, A 18-V-1, A 19-IV-1, A 20-VI-1, A 21-VI-1, A 22-IV-1, A 23-V-1, A 24-IV-1, A 25-V-1, A 26-III-1, A 27-II-1, A 28-IV-1, A 29-III-1, A 30-IV-1, A 31-III-1, A 32-III-1, A 33-II-1, A 34-II-1
Chief Contemporary Dramatists, Third Series, F 9
Chief Patterns of World Drama, F 12
"Children of the Sea," A 49
"Children of the Sea" and Three Other Unpublished Plays by Eugene O'Neill, A 49-I-1(T), A 49-I-1(L)
"Chris Christopherson," A 21-I-1
Chrysalis, C 93
Church, Mrs. Virginia Woodson (Frome), F 9
Citadel Press, A 36-I-1.b, A 37-I-1.b, A 38-I-1.b, A 39-I-1.b, A 40-I-1.b
Clark, Barrett H., C 36, C 67, F 5, F 12
Clark, David L., F 9
Clark, Donald Leman, F 4, F 22
Clark, Joseph D., F 20
Clark, William S., II, F 12
Classic Through Modern Drama, F 9
Coe, Kathryn, F 2, F 4, F 25
Coffman, George R., F 29
Cohen, Helen Louise, F 9, F 15, F 29
Cohn, Ruby, F 14
Coleman, Alta May, C 38
Coleman, William Harold, F 4
The College Anthology, F 2
A College Book of American Literature, F 9, F 24
The College Omnibus, F 9
College Reading, F 5
Collier's, C 88
Comedy Theatre, A 10-IV-1
Commins, Saxe, A 6-IV-1
A Complete College Reader, F 1
The Complete Works of Eugene O'Neill, A 6-IV-1, A 8-II-1,

A 9-II-1, A 10-II-1, A 11-II-1, A 16-II-1, A 17-II-1, A 21-II-1, A 22-II-1, *A 25-I-1*
Connolly, Francis X., F 5
Contemporary American Plays, F 9, F 12
Contemporary Drama: American, English and Irish, European Plays, F 1, F 9, F 12
Contemporary Drama: American Plays, F 9
Contemporary One-Act Plays of 1921, A 19-I-1
Contemporary Plays, F 12
Contemporary Trends: American Literature Since 1900, F 5, F 17
Contexts of the Drama, F 13
Contour in Time, B 35
Cook, George Cram, A 6-III-1
Cooper, Charles W., F 19
Corbin, Richard K., F 4
Cordell, Kathryn (Coe), F 2, F 4, F 25
Cordell, Richard Albert, F 2, F 7, F 20
Cordell, William Howard, F 2, F 4, F 25
Corrigan, Robert W., F 6
Cowley, Malcolm, C 96
Cox, Martha Heasley, F 27
Crane, Hart, D 3
Crawford, Jack R., F 12
Crichton, Kyle, C 88
Cross, Seymour L., F 12
Cubeta, Paul M., F 2, F 6, F 9
Curtain! A Book of Modern Plays, F 9
Curtis Brown, Ltd., A 42-EI-1, A 44-EI-1

"Damn the Optimists," B 30
Davenport, William H., F 12
David, Earle R., F 1
David L. O'Neal, E 7
Days Without End:
–as book; *A 34-I-1.a, A 34-I-1.b,* A 34-I-1.c
–as play: A 34, E 1, E 7
Dean, Leonard F., F 9
Desire Under the Elms:
–as book: *A 25-II-1,* A 25-VII-1
–as play: A 25, F 6, App.
Dickinson, Thomas H., F 9, F 12
Diff'rent, A 17, F 7
The Dimensions of Literature, F 16
Dolkey, Matthew, F 16
Dominant Types in British and American Literature, F 12
Doods, John W., F 11
Downer, Alan S., F 9, F 11, F 12
Drama and Theatre, Illustrated by Seven Modern Plays, F 4
Drama in the Modern World, F 6
Drama in the Western World: 15 Plays with Essays, F 6
Drama: Literature on Stage, F 16
A Drama of Souls, B 34
Drama: Principles and Plays, F 6
Dramas by Present-Day Writers, F 15
Dramas of Modernism and Their Forerunners, F 6
"A Dramatist's Notebook," B 30, C 80
Dramatists Play Service, Inc., AA 2.1, B 19
"The Dreamy Kid," A 19, C 37, F 8
Dukore, Bernard F., F 14
Dumble, Wilson Randle, F 1
Durham, Frank, A 49-I-1(T), A 49-I-1(L)
Durham, W. H., F 11
Dynamo:
–as book: *A 31-I-1.a,* A 31-I-1.b–d, *A 31-II-1*
–as play: A 31, E 1

Earl Carroll Theatre, A 25-V-1
Edel, Leon, F 19
Eight Great Tragedies, F 6
Elliot, Robert C., F 12
Ellis, Harold M., F 9, F 24
The Emperor Jones:
–as book: *A 15-II-1, A 15-V-1, A 15-EII-1*
–as play: A 15, AA 3.1, AA 3.2, C 40, F 9, App.
The Emperor Jones, Anna Christie, The Hairy Ape

(Random House), *A 15-X-1*, A 20-VII-1, A 21-VII-1
The Emperor Jones, Anna Christie, The Hairy Ape (Vintage Books), A 15-XIV-1, A 20-X-1, A 21-XI-1
The Emperor Jones, Diff'rent, The Straw, A 15-I-1.a, A 15-I-1.b–f
The Emperor Jones, The Straw, A 15-VI-1, A 18-IV-1
The Emperor Jones, The Straw, and Diff'rent, A 15-EI(LP), A 17-EI(LP), A 18-EI(LP)
Ervine, St. John, A 8-EI-1.a
Eugene O'Neill, B 5
Eugene O'Neill and the Senator from Texas, B 31
Eugene O'Neill and the Tragic Tension, B 28
Eugene O'Neill: A Poet's Quest, B 16
Eugene O'Neill: The Man and His Plays, B 11
European Theories of the Drama, B 21
Explorations in Literature, F 9
Extracts from "Strange Interlude," A 30-S-1

The Famous American Plays of the 1920's, F 22
50 Best Plays of the American Theatre, F 6, F 12
Fifty Contemporary One-Act Plays, F 22
The First Man, A 22
Five Contemporary American Plays, F 1
Five Modern Plays, F 8
Flory, Claude R., A 21-I-1, C 100
Foerster, Norman, F 9, F 29
"Fog," A 4
The Fountain, A 27, App.
"The Fountain," C 63
Four Modern Plays: First Series, F 9
Four Modern Verse Plays, F 9
Frank Shay, A 6-I-1, A 7-I-1, A 7-II-1
"Fratricide," B 12, C 29
Frazee Theatre, A 16-IV-1
Frazer, Winifred L., C 101
"Free," B 1, B 12
Freedman, Morris, F 6
Frenz, Horst, F 12
Freshman English Program, F 5
Frome, Virginia Woodson, F 9
Fullington, James Fitz-James, F 12
Fulton, Albert Rondthaler, F 4

Gabriel, Ralph H., F 9
Gallup, Donald, A 46-I-1, A 47-I-1.a, A 47-EI-1, C 98
Garrick Theatre, A 26-III-1
Gassner, John, F 2, F 6, F 12, F 14, F 15, F 21, F 27
Gates, William B., F 9
Gehlmann, John, F 9, F 29
Gelb, Arthur, C 97, C 99
George Pierce Baker: A Memorial, B 19
George Pierce Baker and the American Theatre, B 24
Gerber, John C., F 2, F 5
Gibson, William M., F 9, F 19
Gierow, Karl-Ragnar, A 47-I-1.a, A 47-EI-1
"The Glints of Them," B 12, C 19
Gohdes, Clarence, F 12
Gold:
–as book: *A 16-I-1*
–as play: A 16, F 10
Goldstone, G. A., F 15
Goldstone, Richard H., F 13
Gopnik, Irwin, F 6
Gordon, Dudley C., F 29
Gorham Press, A 2-I-1, A 3-I-1, A 4-I-1, A 5-I-1
Graham, Cary B., F 5
The Great God Brown, A 26, F 11
The Great God Brown and Lazarus Laughed, A 26-EI(LP), A 29-EI(LP)
The Great God Brown, Including The Fountain, The Dreamy Kid and Before Breakfast, *A 26-EI-1.a*, A 26-EI-1.b
The Great God Brown, The Fountain, The Moon of the

Caribbees, and Other Plays, *A 26-I-1.a,* A 26-I-1.b–c
Great Plays, Sophocles to Brecht, F 12
Grebanier, Bernard D., F 16
Greenwich Playbill, C 63
Greenwich Village Theatre, A 18-V-1, A 25-V-1, A 26-III-1, A 27-II-1
Guild Theatre, A 28-IV-1

The Hairy Ape:
–as book: *A 20-IV-1*
–as play: A 20, F 12, App.
"The Hairy Ape," C 47
The Hairy Ape and Other Plays, *A 20-EI-1.a,* A 20-EI-1.b
The Hairy Ape, Anna Christie, The First Man, A 20-I-1
Halline, Allan G., F 11
Hamilton, Gladys, C 94
Hamlet and Other Tragedies, F 4
Harbrace Omnibus, F 16
Harding, Helen Elizabeth, F 4
Hart, James D., F 12
Hartley, L. C., F 9
Hatcher, Harlan Henthorne, F 1, F 4, F 9
Hatlen, Theodore W., F 6
"The Haymarket," B 12, C 25
Henry Miller Theatre, A 34-II-1
The Heritage of American Literature, F 2
Hibbard, Clarence A., F 12
Hildreth, William Henry, F 1, F 16
A History of American Drama From the Civil War to the Present Day, B 8
"Hitting the Pipe," B 12, C 20
Hoffman, Frederick, Jr., F 9
Holmes, John Albert, F 1
Hopkins, Arthur, A 20-I-1, A 20-VI-1, A 21-VI-1
Horace Liveright, Inc., A 15-VII-1.a, A 20-IV-1, A 21-IV-1, A 29-I-1.c–f, A 30-I-1.b–o, A 31-I-1.a–d, A 31-II-1, A 32-I-1.b. *See also* Boni & Liveright, Inc.; Liveright, Inc.
Hornberger, Theodore, F 12
Hovey, Sallie, D 2
Howe, W. D., F 17
Hubbell, Jay B., F 9, F 20
Hudson, Arthur P., F 20
Hughie, A 45-I-1.a, A 45-I-1.b–c, *A 45-EI-1*
"Hughie," A 45, F 13
Hummel, William C., F 1
Hurley, Leonard B., F 20
Hutchens, John K., F 9

The Iceman Cometh:
–as book: *A 35-I-1.a,* A 35-I-1.b–c, *A 35-EI-1*
–as play: A 35, E 5, F 14
"The Iceman Cometh," C 86
"Ile," A 11, AA 4, C 34, F 15
Image and Value: An Invitation to Literature, F 27
"I might forget the subway guard" (untitled poem), B 12, C 9
Inglis, R. B., F 9, F 29
Inscriptions, A 46
Interpreting Literature, F 15
Interviews, C 44–46, C 48, C 49, C 51, C 56, C 59, C 67–69, C 74, C 85, C 87–89
"In the Zone," A 10, AA 5, F 16, App.
The Intimate Notebooks of George Jean Nathan, B 15
An Introduction to Drama, F 9
Introduction to Imaginative Literature, F 16
Introduction to Literature, F 9, F 19
An Introduction to Literature: Drama, F 6
Introduction to Literature: Plays, F 6
"It's Great When You Get In," B 5, C 15
"I used to ponder deeply o'er" (untitled poem), B 12, C 10

Jaffe, Adrian H., F 1
John Golden Theatre, A 30-IV-1

Johnson, Thomas H., F 19
Jonathan Cape, A 1-EI-1.b, A 6-EI-1.a–h, A 7-EI-1.a–b, A 8-EI-1.a–h, A 9-EI-1.a–h, A 10-EI-1.a–h, A 11-EI-1.a–h, A 12-EI-1.a–h, A 13-EI-1.a–h, A 14-EI-1.a–b, A 14-EI(LP), A 15-EI-1.a, A 15-EI(LP), A 15-EII-1, A 16-EI-1.a–b, A 17-EI-1.a–b, A 17-EI(LP), A 18-EI-1.a–b, A 18-EI(LP), A 19-EI-1.a–b, A 20-EI-1.a–b, A 21-EI-1.a–b, A 21-EII-1.a–b, A 22-EI-1.a–b, A 23-EI-1.a–b, A 24-EI-1.a–b, A 25-EI-1.a–b, A 26-EI-1.a–b, A 26-EI(LP), A 27-EI-1.a–b, A 28-EI-1, A 28-EI(LP), A 29-EI-1.a, A 29-EI(LP), A 30-EI-1.a–c, A 32-EI-1.a–b, A 33-EI-1.a–c, A 34-EI-1.a–c, A 35-EI-1, A 41-EI-1, A 42-EI-1, A 44-EI-1, A 45-EI-1, A 47-EI-1
Jones, Robert Edmund, A 24-IV-1, A 25-V-1, A 26-III-1, A 27-II-1
Journal of the Outdoor Life, C 50
Judge, Cyril B., F 12

Kalonyme, Louis, C 59
Kamerny Theatre, A 23-V-1
Karsner, David, C 68
Kemp, Harry, C 71
Kenneth W. Rendell, Inc., E 2
King, Vernon R., F 29
Kinne, Wisner Payne, C 93
Klopfer, Donald, A 6-IV-1
Knepler, Henry, F 13
Knickerbocker, Kenneth L., F 15
Krutch, Joseph Wood, F 9

Ladu, Arthur I., F 9
The Last Will and Testament of an Extremely Distinguished Dog, A 43-II-1
The Last Will and Testament of Silverdene Emblem O'Neill, *A 43-I-1.a,* A 43-I-1.b
The Later Plays of Eugene O'Neill, F 1, F 13, F 21, F 27
The Laureate Fraternity, F 1
"The Lay of the Singer's Fall," B 12, C 27
Lazarus Laughed:
–as book: *A 29-I-1.a, A 29-I-1.b,* A 29-I-1.c–f, *A 29-EI-1.a*
–as play: A 29, B 7, E 1, E 8, F 17
Leisy, Ernest E., F 9
Leonard, S. A., F 15
"A Letter from O'Neill," C 39
Letters, C 43, C 66, C 70, E 1–4, E 7, E 9
Leverton, Garrett Hasty, F 22
Levin, Richard L., F 12
Lewis, Leslie L., F 6
Life, C 87
Lindley, Ernest K., C 73
Literature for Our Time, F 12
The Literature of America, F 17
The Literature of the United States, F 12
Liveright, Inc., A 7-IV-1.h–i, A 8-IV-1, A 12-IV-1, A 14-III-1.h–i, A 15-IV-1.g, A 15-VII-1.a, A 15-VIII-1, A 16-III-1.g, A 18-III-1.h–i, A 19-III-1.g, A 20-V-1.a, A 21-V-1, A 22-III-1.g, A 25-IV-1.a, A 26-II-1.a, A 28-II-1, A 28-III-1.a, A 29-II-1.a, A 30-III-1.a, A 32-I-1.a–j, A 32-II-1.a. *See also* Boni & Liveright, Inc.; Horace Liveright, Inc.
The Living Stage, B 25
Locke, Alain L., F 8, F 9
Locke, Louis G., F 9, F 19
Long, E. Hudson, F 12
Long Day's Journey Into Night:
–as book: *A 42-I-1.a,* A 42-I-1.b–k, *A 42-EI-1*
–as play: A 42, F 18, App.
"The Long Tale," B 12, C 23
The Long Voyage Home, A 6-II-1.c, A 8-I-1.c, A 9-I-1.c, A 10-I-1.c, A 12-I-1.c, A 13-I-1.c, App.

"The Long Voyage Home," A 9, C 33, F 19, App.
Loomis, Roger Sherman, F 4, F 22
Lovell, Ernest J., F 21
"Love's Lament," B 12, C 17
Loving, Pierre, C 42
Lyman, William W., F 29

McCallum, James D., F 9, F 16
McClintock, Marshall, F 6
McCorkle, Julia Norton, F 12, F 16
McCormick, James Patton, F 12
McDermott, John F., F 9
Macgowan, Kenneth, A 24-IV-1, A 25-V-1, A 26-III-1, A 27-II-1, B 25, D 1, F 22
Madden, Richard J., A 1-II-1.a, A 1-EI-1.b
Magalaner, Marvin, F 6
The Magic Curtain, B 23
Major Writers of America, F 14
Makers of the Modern Theatre, F 19
Mantle, R. B., F 1, F 2, F 4, F 6, F 9, F 11, F 14, F 18, F 21, F 23, F 25, F 27
Marco Millions:
–as book: *A 28-I-1.a, A 28-I-1.b,* A 28-I-1.c–f, *A 28-EI-1*
–as play: A 28, E 1, F 20
Martin Beck Theatre, A 31-III-1
The Masses, C 31
Masters of American Literature, F 6, F 11, F 19
Masters of Modern Drama, F 9
Mayorga, M., F 16
"Memoranda on Masks," B 30, C 78
Merrill, Charles A., C 51
Merrill, Flora, C 61
Milestones of the Drama, F 9
Miller, Edwin Lillie, F 9
Miller, James E., F 16
Miller, Jordan Y., F 6
Millett, Fred Benjamin, F 4, F 12
Modern American and British Plays, F 11
Modern American Dramas, F 4, F 9
Modern American Plays, F 2
Modern Drama: An Anthology of Nine Plays, F 21
Modern Drama: Authoritative Texts . . . Backgrounds and Criticism, F 6
Modern Drama for Analysis, F 2, F 6, F 9
Modern Dramas, F 4
Modern English Readings, F 4, F 22
Modern Library, A 6-II-1.b–c, A 8-I-1.b–c, A 9-I-1.b–c, A 10-I-1.b–c, A 11-I-1.b–c, A 12-I-1.b–c, A 13-I-1.b–c, A 14-V-1, A 15-VI-1, A 18-IV-1, A 20-VII-1, A 21-VII-1, A 23-VI-1, A 33-III-1, A 35-I-1.c
Modern Plays, F 9
A Modern Repertory, F 1
The Modern Theatre, F 6
Moeller, Philip, A 34-II-1
Mollan, Malcolm, C 44
Montgomery, Gregory, F 8, F 9
A Moon for the Misbegotten:
–as book: *A 41-I-1, A 41-EI-1*
–as play: A 41, AA 6, F 21
"The Moon of the Caribbees," A 8, C 35, F 22, App.
The Moon of the Caribbees and Six Other Plays of the Sea, *A 8-I-1.a*, A 8-I-1.b, *A 8-EI-1.a*, A 8-EI-1.b–h
More One-Act Plays by Modern Authors, F 29
More Stately Mansions:
–as book: *A 47-I-1.a*, A 47-I-1.b–d, *A 47-EI-1*
–as play: A 47
Morosco Theatre, A 14-IV-1
Moses, Montrose J., F 6, F 9
Mourning Becomes Electra:
–as book: *A 32-I-1.a, A 32-I-1.b,* A 32-I-1.c–j, *A 32-EI-1.a,* A 32-EI-1.b

– broadside of manuscript page of: *A 32-S-1*
– as play: A 32, E 1, E 6, F 23, App.
"The Movie Man," A 37
Mullett, Mary B., C 48
Music Box, A 29-III-1

Nathan, George Jean, C 82
Navigator, D 4
NCR Microcard Editions, A 48-I-1, A 49-I-1(T), A 49-I-1(L), A 50-I-1, A 51-I-1
Neighborhood Playhouse, A 20-I-1, A 22-IV-1
Nelson, John Herbert, F 5, F 17
Nelson's College Caravan, F 20
The New American Library, A 25-VII-1
The New College Omnibus, F 12
A New Edition of the Pulitzer Prize Plays, F 2, F 4, F 25
New Fathoms Press, Ltd., A 36-I-1.a, A 37-I-1.a, A 38-I-1.a, A 39-I-1.a, A 40-I-1.a
New Girl In Town, App.
New London Telegraph, C 1–28
The New Phoenix Pamphlet, B 36
New York Call, C 29
The New Yorker, C 90–92
New York Herald Tribune, C 58, C 68, C 73, C 75, C 77
New York Post, C 83
New York Sun, C 36, C 69
New York Times, C 34, C 39, C 43, C 52, C 54, C 59, C 64–66, C 72, C 74, C 81, C 84–86, C 97
The New York Times Book Review, C 99
New York Tribune, C 30, C 41, C 49
New York World, C 57, C 61
Nicholson, K., F 5
Nine Great Plays from Aeschylus to Eliot, F 9
Nine Modern Plays, F 12
Nine Plays by Eugene O'Neill, *A 15-VII-1.a*, A 15-VII-1.b–d, A 20-V-1.a–d, A 23-IV-1.a–d, A 25-IV-1.a–d, A 26-II-1.a–d, A 28-III-1.a–d, A 29-II-1.a–d, A 30-III-1.a–d, A 32-II-1.a–d
The 1936 College Omnibus, F 9
The Nobel Prize Treasury, F 6
"Nocturne," B 12, C 11
"Noon," B 12, C 25
"Notes on the Antecedents of *Anna Christie*," A 21-I-1
"Not Understood," B 33, C 2
Now I Ask You, A 50

"The Ole Davil," A 21-I-1
One-Act Plays, F 15
One-Act Plays by Modern Authors, F 15
O'Neill, B 32
O'Neill, J. F., C 50
O'Neill and His Plays, B 30
"O'Neill's Ideal of a Theatre," B 30
O'Neill: Son and Artist, B 37
O'Neill: Son and Playwright, B 33
"O'Neill's Own Story of Electra in the Making," C 75
"O'Neill Talks About His Plays," B 30
"Only You," B 12, C 14
On the High Road, F 29
Orians, George H., F 2
Our American Theatre, B 2
Our Changing Theatre, B 13
Our Reading Heritage, F 16
Oxford Anthology of American Literature, F 17

Parke-Bernet Galleries, Inc., E 3, E 6
Part of a Long Story, B 27
Pasadena Community Players, A 29-III-1
Pasadena Theatre, A 29-III-1
Passing Judgments, B 17
Patterns in Modern Drama, F 9
Paul, Sherman, F 19

Paul C. Richards, E 4
Pearson, Norman Holmes, F 17
Pence, Raymond Woodbury, F 15
Penin, P. G., F 16
People You Know, B 3
Perkins, Maxwell, A 6-IV-1
Perrin, Porter G., F 9
Phaedra and Hippolytus: Myth and Dramatic Form, F 6
Philadelphia Public Ledger, C 44
Plays and the Theatre, F 16
Plays, Anna Christie, All God's Chillun Got Wings, Diff'rent, A 17-III-1.a–g, A 21-III-1.a–g, A 23-III-1.a–g
Plays, Beyond the Horizon, The Straw, Before Breakfast, A 7-IV-1.a–i, A 14-III-1.a–i, A 18-III-1.a–i
Plays, Desire Under the Elms, The Hairy Ape, Welded, A 20-III-1.a–f, A 24-III-1.a–f, A 25-III-1.a–f
Plays: First Series, The Straw, The Emperor Jones, and Diff'rent, A 15-EI-1.a
Plays for the College Theatre, F 22
Plays from the Modern Theatre, F 11
The Plays of Eugene O'Neill (Random House), *A 6-VII-1.a*, A 6-VII-1.b–d, A 7-VI-1.a–d, A 8-VI-1.a–d, A 9-V-1.a–d, A 10-V-1.a–d, A 11-V-1.a–d, A 12-VI-1.a–d, A 13-V-1.a–d, *A 14-VI-1.a*, A 14-VI-1.b–d, A 15-XI-1.a–d, *A 16-V-1.a*, A 16-V-1.b–d, A 17-V-1.a–d, A 18-VI-1.a–d, A 19-V-1.a–d, A 20-VIII-1.a–d, A 21-VIII-1.a–d, A 22-V-1.a–d, A 23-VII-1.a–d, A 24-V-1.a–d, A 25-VI-1.a–d, A 26-IV-1.a–d, A 27-III-1.a–d, A 28-V-1.a–d, A 29-IV-1.a–d, A 30-V-1.a–d, A 31-IV-1.a–d, A 32-IV-1.a–d, A 33-IV-1.a–d, A 34-III-1.a–d
The Plays of Eugene O'Neill (Wilderness Edition), *A 6-VI-1*, A 7-V-1, A 8-V-1, A 9-IV-1, A 10-IV-1, A 11-IV-1, A 12-V-1, A 13-IV-1, *A 14-IV-1*, *A 15-IX-1*, *A 16-IV-1*, *A 17-IV-1*, *A 18-V-1*, A 19-IV-1, *A 20-VI-1*, *A 21-VI-1*, A 22-IV-1, *A 23-V-1*, A 24-IV-1, *A 25-V-1*, A 26-III-1, A 27-II-1, A 28-IV-1, A 29-III-1, *A 30-IV-1*, A 31-III-1, *A 32-III-1*, A 33-II-1, A 34-II-1
Plays of Negro Life, F 8, F 9
Plays of Our Time, F 14
Plays, The Emperor Jones, Gold, The First Man, The Dreamy Kid, A 15-IV-1.a–g, A 16-III-1.a–g, A 19-III-1.a–g, A 22-III-1.a–g
The Play's the Thing, F 12
"The Play That Is Talked About," C 55
"The Playwright Explains," C 65
Pleiades Club Year Book, B 1
Plymouth Theatre, A 20-VI-1
PM, C 89
PMLA, A 21-I-1, C 100
Pochmann, Henry A., F 11
Poetry, Drama, Fiction, F 6
Popkin, Henry, F 9
Pound, Louise, F 9, F 24
Pratt, Willis W., F 21
Preface to Drama, F 19
Pressey, Benfield, F 1, F 9, F 12
Prideaux, Tom, C 87
Princess Theatre, A 17-IV-1
"Prof. George Pierce Baker," B 19, C 81
Prose and Poetry of the World, F 29
The Provincetown, B 14
Provincetown-Greenwich Plays, A 25-II-1
Provincetown Playbill, C 52, C 64
Provincetown Players, A 6-I-1, A 6-VI-1, A 7-I-1, A 7-II-1, A 15-I-1.a, A 15-II-1, A 20-I-1, A 20-VI-1

The Provincetown Plays, A 6-III-1
The Provincetown Plays: First Series, A 6-I-1
The Provincetown Plays: Third Series, A 7-I-1
Provincetown Theatre, A 7-V-1, A 8-V-1, A 9-IV-1, A 11-IV-1, A 12-V-1, A 13-IV-1, A 15-IX-1, A 17-IV-1, A 19-IV-1, A 23-V-1
The Pulitzer Prize Plays, F 4, F 25
The Pulitzer Prize Plays . . . New Edition, F 2
The Pulitzer Prize Plays, 1918–1934, F 2

A Quarto of Modern Literature, F 9, F 16
"The Quest of the Golden Girl," B 12, C 18
Quinn, Arthur Hobson, F 4, F 9, F 12, F 17

Random House, A 1-II-1.a, A 2-II-1.a, A 2-EI-1.b, A 3-II-1.a, A 3-EI-1.b, A 4-II-1.a, A 4-EI-1.b, A 5-II-1.a, A 5-EI-1.b, A 6-IV-1, A 6-VII-1.a–d, A 6-VIII-1, A 7-VI-1.a–d, A 8-VI-1.a–d, A 8-VII-1, A 9-V-1.a–d, A 9-VI-1, A 10-V-1.a–d, A 10-VI-1, A 11-V-1.a–d, A 11-VI-1, A 12-VI-1.a–d, A 12-VII-1, A 13-V-1.a–d, A 13-VI-1, A 14-VI-1.a–d, A 15-VII-1.b–d, A 15-X-1, A 15-XI-1.a–d, A 15-XII-1, A 15-XIII-1, A 16-V-1.a–d, A 17-V-1.a–d, A 18-VI-1.a–d, A 19-V-1.a–d, A 20-V-1.b–d, A 20-VII-1, A 20-VIII-1.a–d, A 20-IX-1, A 21-VII-1, A 21-VIII-1.a–d, A 21-IX-1, A 21-X-1, A 22-V-1.a–d, A 23-IV-1.a–d, A 23-VII-1.a–d, A 24-V-1.a–d, A 25-IV-1.b–d, A 25-VI-1.a–d, A 25-VIII-1, A 26-II-1.b–d, A 26-IV-1.a–d, A 26-V-1, A 27-III-1.a–d, A 28-III-1.b–d, A 28-V-1.a–d, A 29-II-1.b–d, A 29-IV-1.a–d, A 30-III-1.b–d, A 30-V-1.a–d, A 30-VI-1, A 31-IV-1.a–d, A 32-II-1.b–d, A 32-IV-1.a–d, A 32-V-1, A 33-I-1.a–d, A 33-IV-1.a–d, A 34-I-1.a–c, A 34-III-1.a–d, A 35-I-1.a–c, A 35-II-1.a–b, A 35-III-1, A 36-II-1.a, A 36-EI-1.b, A 37-II-1.a, A 37-EI-1.b, A 38-II-1.a, A 38-EI-1.b, A 39-II-1.a, A 39-EI-1.b, A 40-II-1.a, A 40-EI-1.b, A 41-I-1, AA 2.2, AA 3.1, AA 4, AA 5, AA 7, B 12
Ray, Gordon, F 6, F 19
Reading Drama: A Method of Analysis with Selections for Study, F 4
Readings for Enjoyment, F 1
"Recklessness," A 5
"The Recluse of Sea Island," B 18
Redbook, C 82
Reed, Harry B., F 12, F 16
"A Regular Sort of a Guy," B 12, C 22
The Rehabilitation of Eve, D 2
Reinert, Otto, F 9
Reiter, Seymour, F 16
Reninger, H. Willard, F 15
Repertory, F 5
Reporter, C 96
Representative American Dramas, National and Local, F 9
Representative American Plays from 1880 to the Present Day, F 4
Representative American Plays from 1767 to the Present Day, F 4
Representative American Plays, 1767–1923, F 4
Representative Modern Dramas, F 12
Representative Modern Plays, F 7

Representative Modern Plays—American, F 23
Representative Modern Plays: Ibsen to Tennessee Williams, F 6
Representative One-Act Plays by American Authors, F 16
Representative Plays from 1767 to the Present Day, F 4
Representative Plays of Eugene O'Neill, *A 8-IV-1*, A 12-IV-1, A 15-VIII-1, A 21-V-1, A 28-II-1
The Revised College Omnibus, F 9
Richard G. Badger, A 1-I-1
Richard J. Madden Play Co., A 33-I-1.a–b, A 33-EI-1.a, A 34-I-1.a–b, A 35-I-1.a, A 41-I-1, A 42-I-1.a, A 44-I-1.a, A 45-I-1.a, A 45-EI-1
Richards, Edwin B., F 15
Richardson, Lyon Norman, F 2
Robbins, Harry Wolcott, F 4
Robert K. Black, E 9
Robinson, Lennox, A 34-II-1
"The Rope," A 13, F 24
Roy, Emil, F 6
Royal Dramatic Theatre, A 47-I-1.a

Samuel French, AA 1, AA 6
Sanderlin, George, F 5
Sanderson, James L., F 6
Sayler, Oliver M., C 45, C 46
Schramm, Wilbur, F 29
Schweikert, Harry C., F 9, F 29
"Second Thoughts," B 30, C 79
Selected Plays of Eugene O'Neill (Random House), *A 15-XIII-1*, A 20-IX-1, A 25-VIII-1, A 26-V-1, A 30-VI-1, A 32-V-1, A 35-III-1
Selected Plays of Eugene O'Neill (Editions for the Armed Services), A 6-VIII-1, A 8-VII-1, A 9-VI-1, A 10-VI-1, A 11-VI-1, A 12-VII-1, A 13-VI-1, A 15-XII-1, A 21-IX-1
Selwyn, Archibald and Edgar, A 24-IV-1
"Sentimental Stuff," B 12, C 21
Servitude, A 39
The Seven Arts, C 32
Seven Contemporary Plays, F 4
Seven Plays of the Modern Theater, F 12
Seven Plays of the Sea, A 6-IX-1, A 8-VIII-1, A 9-VII-1, A 10-VII-1, A 11-VII-1, A 12-VIII-1, A 13-VII-1
Shadowland, C 46
Shafer, Robert, F 12
Shattuck, Marquis E., F 15
Shaw, Harry, F 12
Shay, Frank, A 6-III-1, A 15-II-1, A 19-I-1, F 3, F 15, F 22
Sheaffer, Louis, B 33, B 37
Shedd, Robert G., F 9, F 14
"Shell Shock," A 51
"The Shut-Eye Candidate," B 12, C 16
"Shut In," B 33, C 1
Simpson, Claude, F 19
Six Modern American Plays, F 9
Six Short Plays, F 3, F 7, F 8, F 10, F 26, F 28
Sixteen Authors to One, B 10
Sixteen Famous American Plays, F 1
Slate, Bernice, F 16
The Smart Set, C 34, C 35
"The Sniper," A 38
Sotheby Parke Bernet Inc., E 3, E 6
"Speaking, to the Shade of Dante, of Beatrices," B 12, C 30
Spohn, George W., F 9, F 24
S.S. Glencairn Four Plays of the Sea, F 5, F 16, F 19, F 22
Stafford, William T., F 6
Standord, Alfred, D 4
Steeves, Harrison R., F 11
Steinberg, M. W., F 11
Stern, Milton R., F 12
Stewart, Randall, F 12

Stewart Kidd Company, A 6-III-1, A 15-II-1, A 19-I-1
Strange Interlude:
–as book: *A 30-I-1.a,* A 30-I-1.b–o, *A 30-II-1, A 30-EI-1.a,* A 30-EI-1.b–c
–as play: A 30, F 25, App.
The Straw, A 18, F 26, App.
"Strindberg and Our Theater," B 14, C 52
Studies in Drama, F 6
"Submarine," B 12, C 31
Summer Holiday, App.
Swann Galleries, Inc., E 1, E 5
Sweeney, Charles P., C 57

Tairov, Alexander, A 23-V-1
Take Me Along, App.
Ten "Lost" Plays, A 1-II-1.a, A 1-EI-1.b
Ten Plays, F 12
Theatre, C 38, C 47, C 55, C 56, C 71
Theatre Arts, C 37, C 40, C 60, C 67, C 76, C 94, C 95
Theatre Guild, A 28-IV-1, A 30-IV-1, A 31-III-1, A 32-III-1, A 33-II-1, A 34-II-1
The Theatre Guild Anthology, F 25
The Theatre of George Jean Nathan, B 6
The Theatre of the Moment, B 18
The Theatre of Tomorrow, D 1
Themes in the One-Act Play, F 24
These Things Are Mine, B 22
"Thirst," A 1
Thirst and Other One-Act Plays, A 1-I-1
Thirty-ninth Street Theatre, A 24-IV-1
This Generation, F 12
This Is My Best, B 20
Thomas, Russell B., F 16
"To a Bull Moose," B 12, C 8
Today's Literature, F 29
"Tomorrow," C 32
A Touch of the Poet:
–as book: *A 44-I-1.a,* A 44-I-1.b, *A 44-EI-1*
–as play: A 44, F 27
"To Winter," B 12, C 28
Towle, Carroll S., F 1
Tragedies Old and New, F 4
Tragedy: Plays, Theory, Criticism, F 12
Tragedy: Texts and Commentary, F 6
The Traveller's Library, A 6-EI-1.c, A 8-EI-1.c, A 9-EI-1.c, A 10-EI-1.c, A 11-EI-1.c, A 12-EI-1.c, A 13-EI-1.c
A Treasury of Plays for Women, F 3
A Treasury of the Theatre, F 2, F 12
A Treasury of the Theatre . . . from Aeschylus to Eugene O'Neill, F 2
A Treasury of the Theatre: from Henrik Ibsen to Eugene Ionesco, F 2, F 12
Tucker, Samuel M., F 9, F 11
Twelve American Plays, 1920–1960, F 4
Twentieth Century American Writing, F 6
Twentieth Century Drama: England, Ireland and the United States, F 14
Twentieth Century Plays, F 20
Twentieth Century Plays, American, F 2
Twentieth Century Plays, British, American Continental . . . Third Edition, F 2
Twenty Contemporary One-Act Plays (American), F 15
Twenty-five Best Plays of the Modern American Theatre: Early Series, F 6, F 12, F 15
Twenty-five Modern Plays, F 11
Tyler, George C., A 18-V-1
Types of English Drama, F 2
The Types of Literature, F 5

Ulanov, Barry, F 19
Untermeyer, Louis, F 9

Vanderbilt Theatre, A 20-I-1, A 21-VI-1
"Villanelle of Ye Young Poet's First Villanelle to His Ladye and Ye Difficulties Thereof," B 12, C 4
Vintage Books, A 6-IX-1, A 8-VIII-1, A 9-VII-1, A 10-VII-1, A 11-VII-1, A 12-VIII-1, A 13-VII-1, A 15-XIV-1, A 20-X-1, A 21-XI-1, A 35-I-1.b
The Voices of England and America, F 9
Volpe, Edward L., F 6

Wagenheim, Harold H., F 16
Waite, Harlow O., F 12
Wall, Vincent, F 12
Walley, Harold R., F 6
Walton, Edna Lou, F 12
Warfel, Harry R., F 9
"Warnings," A 3
Warnock, Robert, F 6, F 23
Washington Square Players, A 10-IV-1
"The Waterways Convention," B 12, C 3
Watson, Ernest Bradlee, F 1, F 9, F 12
A Wayward Quest, B 29
"The Web," A 2
W. E. B. DuBois Dinner program, B 4
Weiss, Samuel A., F 6
Welded, A 24, F 28
Welsh, Mary, C 95
Western World Literature, F 4
Wharf Theatre, A 6-VI-1
What is the Play?, F 13
"Where the Cross Is Made," A 12, AA 7, F 29, App.
White Buildings, D 3
Whitman, Charles Huntington, F 4, F 12
"A Wife for a Life," A 40
Williams, John D., A 14-IV-1, A 16-IV-1
Williams, Stanley T., F 9
Wimberley, Lowry C., F 12
Wisinger, Herbert, F 1
"With apologies to J. W. Riley" (untitled poem), B 12, C 6
Woolf, S. J., C 74, C 85
World's Great Plays, F 9
Writers of the Western World, F 12

The Yale University Library Gazette, C 98
Yale University Press, A 42-I-1.a–k, A 43-I-1.a–b, A 43-II-1, A 44-I-1.a–b, A 45-I-1.a–c, A 47-I-1.a–d, B 34